EXPLORING THE ⋆ SKY

Projects for Beginning Astronomers

EXPLORING THE * SKY

Revised Edition

Richard Moeschl

CHICAGO REVIEW PRESS

Library of Congress Cataloging-in-Publication Data

Moeschl, Richard.
   Exploring the sky : projects for beginning astronomers / Richard Moeschl. — Rev. ed.
      p.   cm.
   Includes bibliographical references and index.
   Summary: Presents 100 astronomy projects, with information on related mythology and
pertinent history, cultures, and people.
   ISBN 1-55652-160-X : $14.95
   1. Astronomy projects—Juvenile literature.   2. Astronomy—Observers' manuals—Juvenile
literature. [1. Astronomy projects.   2. Astronomy.   3. Science projects.]   I. Title.
   QB64.M6   1993
   520′.78—dc20
                                                                            92-18863
                                                                                CIP
                                                                                 AC

Since it is not possible for the publisher to control the circumstances under which the projects in
Exploring the Sky are to be performed, Chicago Review Press cannot assume any liability for injury
to persons or property occuring as a result of any of these projects.

Published by Chicago Review Press, Incorporated, 814 N. Franklin Street,
   Chicago, Illinois 60610
ISBN: 1-55652-160-X
Printed in the United States of America

1   2   3   4   5   6   7   8   9   10

CONTENTS

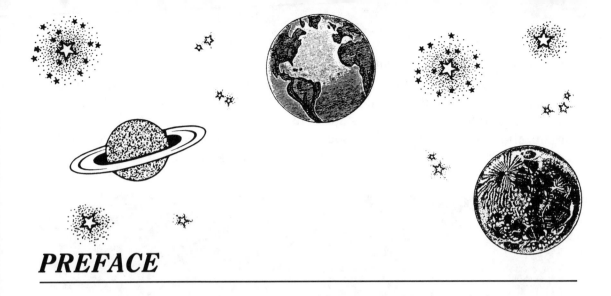

PREFACE

Exploring the Sky will help you understand the wonders of the night sky by taking you on a journey of exploration. It begins where our ancestors did, with little or no understanding of what they saw in the skies each night. This is where most of us find ourselves today. The journey takes you through history, mythology, science, and various other ways in which people have looked at the stars and planets over the centuries—with and without telescopes. Many of the projects are the same experiments used in making discoveries in astronomy. You will meet some of the men and women who invented these projects and who added to our growing understanding of the universe. You will also learn about how other cultures looked at the same things that you do and came up with different names and explanations for them. I have made a special effort to include the point of view from the Southern Hemisphere whenever possible. People who live south of the equator enjoy some spectacular views that can't be seen from the Northern Hemisphere.

Some of the projects in this book are fairly simple, others are more complicated, but they are all fun and will help you to enjoy the world of the stars. At the back of this book is a section called Sky Files. In this section are charts, lists, a glossary, and an index to help you find whatever information you need quickly. There is also a list of where to find some of the less common materials for the projects.

I send very special thanks to Ted Brattstrom, Greeley Wells, Joanne Moeschl, and my editor, Amy Teschner. All of these people helped me revise this book by generously sharing their knowledge, talent, time, and understanding. *Exploring the Sky* is a much better book thanks to their corrections and suggestions. Thank you.

The sky really does belong to everyone, it's there for you to enjoy. If you want to continue to learn more about the wonders of the universe, contact your local astronomy club, or visit a science museum or planetarium. Ask your librarian to help you find different books and magazines about astronomy. There are astronomy radio and television shows, videos, cassettes, computer software, and even a Space Camp. Several organizations also can provide you with books, slides, posters, charts, classes, etc. NightStar Products, Inc., located at 695 Mistletoe Road, Suite D, Ashland, Oregon, 97520, makes and sells astronomy education tools. The oldest organization is the Astronomical Society of the Pacific, 390 Ashton Avenue, San Francisco, California, 94112. The best teacher is the sky itself. Go out and look up.

Chapter 1 CELEBRATING THE SKY

Section 1 THE CHANGING FACE OF THE HEAVENS

The Dome of the Sky   How do you feel when you're out camping or just going for a walk alone and you find yourself under the night sky surrounded by darkness and thousands of points of light overhead? You probably can't hear anything except the sounds of nature and the whisperings of your own inner thoughts. You might wonder how many people in how many ages have stood under the stars just as you are standing now, looking up, asking questions and thinking.

Your ancient ancestors learned a great deal about the sky without telescopes and space probes, simply by looking. You can too. You don't have to be an astronomer to understand the world of the stars. The sky and its treasures belong to everyone.

Imagine yourself like your ancestors, without any information about the sky except what you find out yourself, with your own eyes, your imagination, and your ability to figure things out. When you look up, you can imagine that the sky wraps around you like a great blanket of stars. Being under this blanket feels like being inside a tent, shaped like an upside-down bowl. The stars are on the inside of this bowl, so are the Sun, the Moon, and the planets. In the daytime, the bowl becomes a blue dome, filled with light, clouds, and birds. Each person is in the center of this dome. No matter where you walk, the dome is around you. In this next project, you can stand under the dome of the sky and begin to get to know it.

★ ★ ★ ★ ★ ★ ★ ★ ★ ★ **Project 1: Observing the Night Sky** ★ ★ ★ ★ ★ ★ ★ ★ ★ ★

MATERIALS
a clear night

PROCEDURE
1. Go outside to the same spot for a few minutes several times a night for a week or more.
2. Select a group of stars that you can easily recognize.
3. Find something near the stars that you can use as a landmark, such as the branch of a tree, a telephone pole, the roof of your house, a distant mountain, etc.
4. Look for your landmark when you come out every night to check on your stars. Stand in the exact same place each time.

| Facing west | Facing north | Facing south | Facing east |

OBSERVATIONS
Did your group of stars stay where you left them the night before? Did all the stars in your group remain more or less in the same group? **Leonardo da Vinci** used to look at the stars through a sheet of glass and draw a tree or building on the glass as a landmark. He would then draw the changing positions of the stars on different nights.

Your observations have given you enough information to begin to see what is happening in the sky. The stars are moving. They move together and they all move in the same direction, making curves across the sky.

The curve the stars make in the sky depends on which direction you face when you look at them. You can combine all four views in the drawing above and see what trails stars leave by doing the next project.

★ ★ ★ ★ ★ ★ ★ ★ ★ ★ **Project 2: Drawing Star Trails** ★ ★ ★ ★ ★ ★ ★ ★ ★ ★

MATERIALS
Polestars illustration from Project 3   cardboard or stiff paper
sheet of plastic   paper fastener
grease pencil or crayon   pencil
straight pin

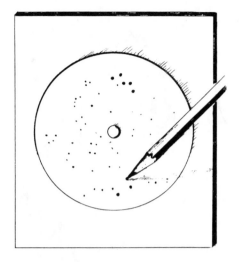

PROCEDURE

1. Cut out a 2-inch (5 cm) circle for the Northern or Southern Hemisphere from the plastic sheet.

2. Place the circle on the polestar illustration so that the + is in the center. This is the pole position.

3. Mark the star positions onto the circle using the grease pencil.

4. Remove the plastic circle and make holes through the plastic for each star using the straight pin.

5. Attach the plastic circle to a piece of cardboard or stiff paper by pushing the paper fastener through the +. Be sure the plastic circle can rotate freely.

6. Starting with the innermost star, put the point of a pencil through the pole and move the plastic circle counterclockwise (Northern Hemisphere) or clockwise (Southern Hemisphere) so you end up drawing a circular "star trail."

7. Draw trails for each star.

OBSERVATIONS

What do these star trails tell you about the movement of the stars? What did the polestar do?

Looking at star trails can give you a sense that the sky is moving. In this next project you can see how the sky moves by making a model of it.

★ ★ ★ ★ ★ ★ ★ ★ Project 3: Making a Tennis Ball Sky Dome ★ ★ ★ ★ ★ ★ ★ ★

MATERIALS

an old tennis ball
felt-tip pen
scissors

dowel, chopstick, or pencil
two pushpins

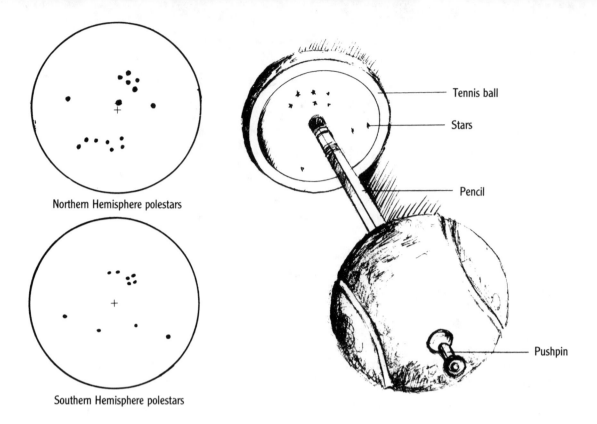

Northern Hemisphere polestars

Southern Hemisphere polestars

Tennis ball

Stars

Pencil

Pushpin

PROCEDURE

1. Cut the tennis ball exactly in half with the scissors.

2. Draw the stars inside each half just as they appear in the polestars illustration using the felt-tip pen.

3. Attach the dowel to the inside center of each half using pushpins. The center is marked by a +.

USING THE TENNIS BALL SKY DOME

1. Hold the dowel in one hand with your fingers and thumb.

2. Choose which half you are going to look at—north or south. Move your fingers and thumb as close as you can toward the half you are not looking at.

3. Hold the dowel in front of you so that one half of the sky dome blocks the other half.

4. Move the half nearest your eye down until you can see the stars on the other half just like they look where you live. The half nearest you is the Earth and your horizon.

5. Turn the dowel slowly so that the tennis ball halves move from right to left (counterclockwise) for viewing the Northern Hemisphere and left to right (clockwise) for the Southern Hemisphere.

OBSERVATIONS

Do any of the stars set below the horizon level so that you can't see them for awhile until they rise? What paths do the stars follow as they move? What does the star in the middle do?

The Planets   If you were a regular skywatcher, as your ancestors were, you would get to know what the stars look like and which ones belong where. You would also notice some "stars" that do not stay fixed to the sky dome. After awhile, you would be able to easily spot these five mavericks who stray from the rest of the herd. The ancient Greeks called them wanderers. So do we, using the same word the Greeks did: *planet.*

The planets move with the sky dome while inching along on curves of their own in the opposite direction. Some of them move quite fast. If you know where to look, you can see them traveling a little each night. Chapter 6 will tell you about the planets and how to find them.

Planet comes from the Greek word πλανητης (*planetes*) = wanderer.

The Moon   The Moon has its own path across the sky that it follows in the opposite direction from the way the sky dome is turning. As part of the heavenly family, it also moves with the stars and planets as the sky dome turns. The Moon is easy to spot and, unlike the stars and the planets, can be seen clearly in the daylight or at night. Looking at the Moon, you notice it can be found in various places in the sky and with varying degrees of brightness. See chapter 6, section 2 for more about the Moon.

The Movement of the Sun   From our point of view, the Sun appears to rise every morning, travel across the sky during the day, and set in the evening replacing daylight with night. You can mark this movement in the next project.

★ ★ ★ ★ ★ ★ ★ ★Project 4: Marking Sunrise and Sunset ★ ★ ★ ★ ★ ★ ★ ★ ★

MATERIALS
hammer

nine sticks the size and strength of tent pegs

pen or pencil

newspaper, almanac, or radio

PROCEDURE
1. Mark the sticks as follows: R1, S1, R2, S2, R3, S3, R4, S4. Leave the last stick unmarked.

2. Find a place where nothing blocks your view of the sunrise in the east. This should also be a place no one will disturb for a month.

3. Drive the unmarked stick in the ground to mark where you will stand to observe.

4. Each day for a month find out from the newspaper, almanac, or radio when the Sun will rise.

5. Stand at your premarked observing place with your hammer and the stick labeled R1. (*R* stands for *Rising*.) As soon as the complete ball of the Sun has risen, drive stick R1 in the ground about 10 feet (3 m) in front of you, right in the middle of your view of the Sun. You might want a friend along to help. One of you can sight the Sun and tell the other person the exact positioning for the stick.

6. Return to your observing spot that same night and mark the sunset with S1 in the same way.

7. Repeat this process with the remaining sets of sticks three times—one set each week for four weeks (one month).

OBSERVATIONS
Where are sticks 2–4 compared to the first set of sticks? On which side of the first sticks did you have to place the others? Are the rising and setting sticks in the same order and on the same side as the first ones? What do you notice is happening? How do you think your sticks would look if you did this project for 12 months?

Since the sunrise and sunset positions keep moving, you can find out where they will be. By marking shadows, just as you did, your ancestors knew *exactly* where the Sun would rise and set throughout the year and how high it would be in the sky. You can see how the sun moves across the sky in one day by doing the next project. Putting the information from the sunrise and sunset project with the information from this next project will give you a clearer picture of how the Sun moves.

★ ★ ★ ★ ★ Project 5: Keeping Track of the Sun During the Day ★ ★ ★ ★ ★

MATERIALS

a clear glass or plastic bowl (or the
bottom of a 1- or 2-liter plastic
soda bottle)

sheet of stiff paper (larger than the
diameter of the bowl)

grease pencil or crayon
regular pen or pencil
scissors

PROCEDURE

1. Place the bowl on the paper and trace a circle around the bowl. Remove the bowl and mark the center of the circle on the paper. Draw a little person (½ in. or about 1 cm) standing at the center mark. This person is you, and the bowl is the sky dome that you are under.

2. Cut around the top and sides of the drawing of yourself. Bend it so you are standing straight up.

3. Take the bowl and paper outside to a place where they will be free of shadows and disturbances for 6 hours. Put the paper on the ground so the little drawing of you faces the Sun. Put the bowl on top of the paper so it lines up with the circle outline.

4. Place the point of the grease pencil on the bowl so the tip of its shadow touches the little drawing of you underneath. Put a dot on the bowl using the grease pencil to show where it was. Write the time of your observation next to the dot.

5. Repeat step 4 every hour for the next 6 hours.

6. Draw a line through all seven dots on the bowl to see how the Sun moved across the sky this day.

OBSERVATIONS

How much did the Sun move? Imagine that the line on the bowl is an arrow. What is the arrow pointing to? Where did it come from? It's tempting to answer "west" and "east," but you have no way of knowing that with the information you have. You can say, however, that it's likely that the arrow is pointing in the direction the Sun is traveling. It indicates the place where the Sun rose and the place where it will set. If you can, see if the arrow helps you find the sunrise and sunset points for the Sun tomorrow.

About what angle does the Sun make with east when it rises? About what is the highest angle of the Sun from the south at noon? Try this project in each of the four seasons. See chapter 6, section 1 for more about the Sun.

To notice the changing positions of the Sun and the planets, you would need to keep records for several months, preferably for a whole year. That seems like a long time for us, but serious students of the sky make many observations over long periods of time. This was easy to do in early civilizations that lasted for thousands of years. One generation of observers would hand their list of sky watches to the next. You would end up with long, uninterrupted lists of observations that you could study.

The ancients could see that the sky was constantly changing. They learned that if they watched carefully, they could see patterns in these changes. These patterns occurred at regular intervals or cycles. The Sun rose and set once a day. The Moon changed its brightness from dark to light every month. The planets moved across the night sky at different times during the year. It wasn't long before people figured out how to measure all of these rhythms and predict them. It soon became possible to plan ahead for the seasons by relying on detailed permanent records of continuous observation. Astronomy, the first science, had begun.

READING MORE
Jobb, Jamie. *The Night Sky Book: An Everyday Guide to Every Night.* Boston: Little, Brown, 1977.
Simon, Seymour. *Look to the Night Sky: An Introduction to Star Watching.* New York: Penguin Books, 1977.

Section 2   SEASONS AND FESTIVALS
The Four Directions   The sky dome is a hemisphere, half of a sphere or globe. Since the sky dome is located in the heavens and not on the Earth, we call it the celestial hemisphere. It spins around carrying the stars with it.

North and south tend to be directions up and down, while east and west are directions going across. People in the United States talk about their relatives "up" north, "down" south, "out" west, and "back" east. When you start thinking globally, "up" and "down," "above" and "below" don't apply. It is more accurate to speak of a place as lying *north* or *south* or *east* or *west* of your particular location. You need the Earth and the sky together to find the four directions. The four basic directions, north, south, east, and west—are called the **cardinal points.**

Celestial comes from the Latin word *caelestis* = of the heavens, heavenly.
Hemisphere comes from the Greek words ήμι (*hemi*) = half and σφαιρα (*sphaira*) = ball.
Cardinal comes from the Latin word *cardinalis* = basic.
Imagine that there are no calendars, no months, no days of the week. How could you predict the coming of important events like the seasons?

Write down the four directions as you would find them on a map, north on top, south on the bottom, east to the right, and west to the left. Now draw two lines, one connecting the north to the south and one connecting the east to the west. You now have a cross, which, when you place a circle around it, is the astronomical symbol for the Earth. This symbol often appears in paintings and sculptures of kings and queens holding in their hands a round globe marked with a cross. Each point of the cross represented the "four corners of the Earth" (N, S, E, W), symbolizing the power of the king or queen.

If you take the first letter of each word *north*, *east*, *west*, and *south*, you'll find that you have the name for the information that the reporters gather from the four corners of the Earth: *news*.

The four directions were especially important to our ancient ancestors. It was crucial to have the places where people worshipped lined up along these directions. The ancients were able to orient their buildings with great precision without using a compass. You can find directions without a compass in the next project.

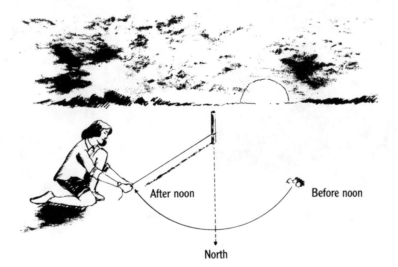

After noon   Before noon

North

★ ★ ★ ★ ★ Project 6: Finding Directions from a Shadow Stick ★ ★ ★ ★ ★

MATERIALS

a stick   rocks
a piece of string with a nail tied to
    one end

PROCEDURE

1. Find a spot where the ground is level and free from disturbances.

2. Drive the stick into the ground. Make sure it is straight up and down by checking it all around using the weighted string as a guide.

3. Use rocks to mark the tip of the stick's shadow a few hours before noon (standard time). Tie the end of the string to the bottom of the shadow stick. Use the string and the nail to draw a long arc on the ground from the stick to the tip of the shadow.

4. Use rocks to mark the tip of the stick's shadow a few hours *after* noon when it again touches the arc. Halfway between the two marks on the arc facing *away* from the stick is north in the Northern Hemisphere (south in the Southern Hemisphere).

OBSERVATIONS

What does this project tell you about the directions in which sunrise and sunset occur? When the shadow is at its shortest, around noon, it also points north in the Northern Hemisphere (south in the Southern Hemisphere). Why?

Using a shadow stick

Looking down the hall in the Temple of Karnak

10

A straight stick used in this way is one of the earliest astronomical instruments. The sundial is a relative of this instrument. You can build sundials and tell time with straight sticks in section 3 of this chapter (Project 10, Making a Sundial).

The Great Pyramid in Egypt, built around 2600 B.C., displays a tremendous understanding of engineering and astronomy. Its sides line up precisely along the north-south and east-west lines. One of the shafts inside the pyramid pointed to the star Thuban, which was the polestar at that time. Another shaft pointed to the star Sirius.

The ancient Chinese were able to figure out the four directions very precisely. Which direction a house or temple faced was very significant. Therefore, the Chinese carefully arranged their buildings to line up with the four directions and included their knowledge of the directions in yearly rituals.

Cathedral builders in the Middle Ages built their churches along an east-west line. The entrance was from the west. The people and the priest faced the east, the place from which the Sun rises and the direction from which Christ, as the Sun-Being, having risen, would return.

Throughout the world, builders often used the east-west, sunrise-sunset equinox line to set up their buildings. The most dramatic example of this plan was in the temple of Amon-Ra in Karnak, Egypt, built around 2000 B.C. Its main hallway was about 600 yards (500 m) long and built so that the farther you went inside the temple, the narrower the passageway became. The line through the middle of the building (axis) passed through 17 or 18 stages, each with the floor, ceiling, and columned walls closing in. This made the space smaller and smaller until you reached the darkened sanctuary. Here, where only the priests were allowed to go, was an opening to the sky. Through this opening you could behold the rising midwinter Sun for only a few moments on the day of the solstice. Such an alignment made it possible for the Egyptians to determine the length of the solar year. Their calculations were only about one minute off.

The Egyptian temple builders arranged other temples along lines pointing to stars such as Sirius, which traveled around the polestar. Because of the pharaoh's responsibility to maintain the calendar, people expected each of the early kings to build a new temple. When the position of the star changed over many years and the temple no longer pointed to it exactly, the pharaoh added on a new temple with its axis changed.

The Temple of Luxor plan shows how builders altered its axis to keep it aligned with the changing rising position of the star toward which the temple faced.

The Four Seasons, Equinoxes, and Solstices   People who study ancient history mainly by examining the ruins and remains left behind by earlier cultures are called **archaeologists**. Those who combine this study with a particular interest in the astronomical significance of these early structures are called **archaeoastronomers**. One of the pioneers in archaeoastronomy was **J. Norman Lockyer (1836–1920)**.

Archaeologists and archaeoastronomers have found many examples of buildings, including major temples, built along the east-west lines of the equinoxes.

Archaeology comes from the Greek words ἀρχη (*arche*) = beginning and λογος (*logos*) = that which is spoken or thought of.
Astronomy comes from the Greek word ἀστηρ (*aster*) = star and ὀνομα (*onoma*) or the Latin word *nomen* = a way of knowing or a name.

In section 1 you discovered that the Sun's rising and setting positions move during the year. With what you know now, you can make a north-south, east-west line on the ground to see exactly where the Sun rises during the year.

You'll find that only twice does the Sun rise exactly in the east and set exactly in the west: on March 21 and September 23. On these two dates, the Sun rises at about 6:00 in the morning and sets at about 6:00 at night (local Sun time or apparent time). Because day and night are equal (12 hours each) on these two dates, we call each date the **equinox**. In the Northern Hemisphere, March 21 is the spring equinox and September 23 is the autumn equinox. In the Southern Hemisphere, March 21 is the autumn equinox and September 23 is the spring equinox. At the poles, the Sun is half over the horizon for 24 hours on the equinoxes.

Double the Sun's *rising* gives the approximate length of the *night*. For example, if the Sun rises at 8:00, 2 × 8 = 16; the time from sunset to sunrise = 16 hours. Double the time of the Sun's *setting* gives the approximate length of the *day*. For example, if the Sun sets at 7, 2 × 7 = 14; the time from sunrise to sunset = 14 hours.

On the two equinox dates, the line joining the tips of the hourly shadows of the shadow stick is a straight line.

As you can see from the following table, there are many moments to celebrate in the four seasons that have some connection with the rhythms of the Sun and Moon.

People needed to know in advance when these events were going to occur. How did they find out? One way was to figure out how long it would be between the same two events, from one equinox to the next or from Halloween to Halloween, etc. To do this you would use the shadow stick. Over the course of the year you would notice that the lengths of the shadows at noon weren't the same size every day. At one date the shadow was so short that it was hardly there. Six months later, the shadow was quite long. In the tropics, the shadow appears twice, once on each side of the stick. In the polar regions, the sun tends to cast long shadows for most of the year. Watching the size of the shadow from one event until it became the same length again would tell you when that date would be.

The higher the Sun is on the celestial hemisphere, the shorter the shadows it casts on the Earth. "Higher" doesn't mean farther away, it just means the angle at which its rays strike the Earth—the higher the Sun, the greater the angle. This affects the amount of heat and light you receive each season. The next project shows why.

★ ★ ★ ★ ★ ★ ★Project 7: Comparing the Intensity of the Sun★ ★ ★ ★ ★ ★ ★
from Different Angles

MATERIALS
    a ball
    paper tube

PROCEDURE
    1. Go outside. Hold the ball in one hand and the paper tube in the other hand so that the Sun shines through it casting a beam of light straight onto the ball. Notice the size and brightness of the circle of light on the ball.
    2. Tilt the ball so that the beam of sunlight hits the ball at an angle. Be sure to keep the tube at the same height from the ball as in step 1. Observe the lighted area.

OBSERVATIONS
    As the tilt of the ball increases, what happens to the size and brightness of the light on the ball? When the same amount of light gets spread farther this way, what happens to its heat?

In the northern part of the world, summer is 4.5 days longer than winter. Spring is 3.8 days longer than winter and autumn is 0.9 days longer than winter. The time differences are the opposite for those in the southern part of the world (e.g., winter is 4.5 days longer than summer, etc.).

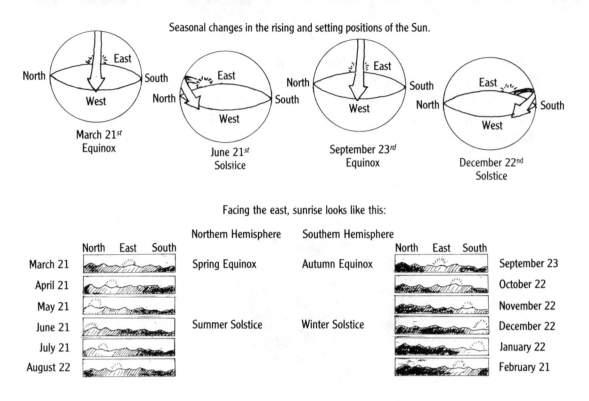

Seasonal changes in the rising and setting positions of the Sun.

March 21st Equinox

June 21st Solstice

September 23rd Equinox

December 22nd Solstice

Facing the east, sunrise looks like this:

	North East South	Northern Hemisphere	Southern Hemisphere	North East South	
March 21		Spring Equinox	Autumn Equinox		September 23
April 21					October 22
May 21					November 22
June 21		Summer Solstice	Winter Solstice		December 22
July 21					January 22
August 22					February 21

In the winter, on December 22, the Sun rises much later than it does in the summer. You get up before it does. The Sun rises at about 8:00 in the morning in the southeast, climbing at only a slight angle to slip quickly out of sight again as it sets in the southwest at around 4:00 in the afternoon after shining on the Earth for only eight hours. The night will last 16 hours—just perfect for an astronomer. On the same date at the North Pole, there is no sunrise; night lasts six months. At the Equator, the Sun rises from the east, and the night lasts about 12 hours. At the South Pole, there is no sunrise and no night for six months.

Ancient Observatories   At the two points in the Sun's journey through the seasons (June 21 and December 22), when sunrise is farthest away from the east and the Sun is at its highest (or lowest) point from the horizon, the Sun seems to stop. Having climbed as high or descended as low in the sky as it could, the Sun now begins to change direction and make its way back toward a middle position in the sky. The name for the two dates when this happens is the **solstice**.

Solstice comes from the Latin words *sol* = Sun and *stare* = to stand. In the Northern Hemisphere, on June 21 the Sun seems to "stand still" at its highest point in the summer sky (summer solstice). On December 22 the Sun seems to "stand still" at its lowest point in the winter sky (winter solstice). In the Southern Hemisphere, the winter solstice occurs on June 21 and the summer solstice on December 22.

If you draw a line in between each section of the cross, you now have eight marks or points on the outside of your circle. Each of these points represents a date starting with March 21 and proceeding counterclockwise. Because you make these four dates by drawing lines across the four quarters of your circle, we call them **cross-quarter days**. The season of spring is an ongoing process, like a wave, which begins gradually, grows in intensity, and then fades. The cross-quarter days mark the gradual beginning and fading periods of the seasons. The equinox dates mark the peak intensity of spring and autumn, or the middles of the two seasons.

Nature's year begins with spring. Light and darkness are in balance. Growth and renewed life are everywhere. Our calendars used to begin the year at this time, at the green or vernal equinox, the morning of the year. In section 4 of this chapter you can find out why the new year now begins in January.

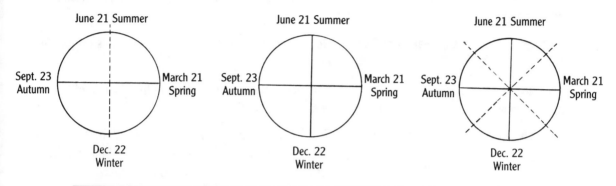

Equinox comes from the Latin words *aequi* = equal and *nox* = night.
Season comes from the French word *saison*, which comes from the Latin word *satio* = sowing.
The word for spring in French is *printemps*, which comes from the Latin words *primus* = the first or best and *tempus* = time.
The word for spring in Latin is *ver* or *vernus*. *Vert* in French means green.
Spring means to shoot forth.
Summer comes from the Middle English word *sumer* = half year.
Autumn comes from the Latin word *autumnus* = changeable.
Fall means to drop to the ground.
Winter comes from the Old English word *wintar* = water.

Here is a glance at the year as it unfolds in the Northern Hemisphere.

Spring — "Comes in like a lion, goes out like a lamb."

February 2	First cross-quarter day Candlemas	Beginning of spring — night wanes. Celebrated by the blessing of candles for sacred use
	Purification or Presentation	Feast of the Purification of the Virgin Mary or Presentation of the child Jesus in the temple
	Groundhog Day	The groundhog (woodchuck) comes out of its burrow. If it sees its shadow, it goes back inside and back to sleep for the 6 weeks remaining until the equinox.

"If Candlemas be bright and clear
we'll have two winters in the year.
If Candlemas be fair and bright,
Come, Winter, have another flight.
If Candlemas bring clouds and rain,
Go, Winter, and come not again."

"Don't use up more than half your provisions by
Candlemas"

February 5 (approximately)	Chinese New Year	Celebrated on first new Moon when the Sun is in Aquarius.
February 29	Leap Year Extra Day	Occurs every four years. See section 4 of this chapter for details.
March 14 (approximately)	Purim	Commemorates the deliverance of the children of Israel with the help of Queen Esther
March 15	The Ides of March	The time of the full Moon in the first month of the Roman calendar. The date when Julius Caesar, the one mostly responsible for our calendar, was assassinated.
March 17	St. Patrick's Day	Feast of St. Patrick, missionary to Ireland and patron saint of that nation. The garden season starts today in Great Britain with the sowing of peas, the earliest of vegetables.
40 Days before Easter	Ash Wednesday	Beginning of Lent. People recognize Lent by having the sign of the cross marked on their foreheads with ashes remaining from the burned palms of last year's Palm Sunday.
	Lent	Days of preparation before Easter
March 21	Vernal Equinox	Middle of spring. Day and night are equal. The Sun is at midheight angle from the Earth at noon, making the days not too warm, not too cool.
Sunday before Easter	Palm Sunday	Commemorates Christ's entry into Jerusalem when the crowds placed palm branches in his pathway
March 22 to April 25	Easter	The festival of Christ's resurrection. Celebrated on the first Sunday following the full Moon after the Vernal Equinox. People often celebrate with sunrise services outside. Our word *Easter* comes from the time when missionaries introduced Christianity among the Saxons, who celebrated a spring festival to their goddess *Eoster*. People celebrate Easter by coloring eggs, a symbol of rebirth and joy.

16

	Passover	Pesach or the Passover is a Jewish holiday in memory of the Jews' deliverance from the bondage of Egypt. The name comes from the "passing over" of the houses of the children of Israel by the angel of death, after the people had marked the door posts and lintels of their houses with the blood of the Paschal lamb. People celebrate with a festive meal commemorating the meal held on the first passover night.
March 25	The Annunciation	The feast commemorating the announcement of the archangel Gabriel to Mary that she was chosen to become the mother of the Messiah. This was the beginning of the year in France and Great Britain until the calendar was changed in 1564 for France and 1752 for Great Britain. (See section 4 of this chapter for details.)
40 Days after Easter	Ascension Day	The festival of Christ's ascending into heaven
50 Days after Easter	Whitsun or Pentecost	Whitsunday commemorates the descent of the Holy Spirit in the form of tongues of fire above the heads of Christ's disciples and the beginning of the Church. *Pentecost* comes from the Greek word πεντε (*pente*) = 50.
50 Days after Passover	Shabuoth or Pentecost	Also called the Festival of Weeks; commemorates the giving of the Law (Ten Commandments) from God to Moses on Mount Sinai
Last Sunday in April	Beginning of Daylight Saving Time	The way to remember which direction to turn the hands of the clock is "spring forward, fall back."

Summer — the noon of the year. For some people, this is their favorite time of the year.

April 30	Second cross-quarter day	Beginning of summer. Days grow longer than nights.
	Walpurgisnacht, May Eve	Fertility festival, celebrating the return of the goddess Flora to the Earth.
May 1	Beltane or May Day	Sacred day to Brigit, the fairy queen. A great Celtic festival with bonfires. Later became May Day, celebrated by young men and maidens dancing around May poles, presided over by the May Queen.
June 21	Summer Solstice	Midsummer's Day. The longest day of the year. Short night. The Sun is at its highest angle from the Earth at noon, making the days hot. Light reigns.

June 23	St. John's Eve	People in Europe celebrate this night when the sun sets late in the evening. They light a huge bonfire to encourage the Sun to shine and ripen the crops. In many parts of the world, bonfires still blaze at this time, while people sing songs around them. Young men leap across the flames to give them strength for the year ahead as people mark the halfway point of the year.
June 24	St. John's Day	The Feast of St. John the Baptist. To have the Sun at its strongest and about to decrease again with the coming of winter reminded people of the words of St. John in reference to Christ, "He must increase, I must decrease." The light grows stronger again after the birth of Christ celebrated at Christmas.
July 3 to August 11	Dog Days	People associate these days of unbearable heat with strange behavior, including dogs going mad with the Dog Star Sirius in the constellation Canis Major (the Great Dog). These days occur 20 days before and 20 days after the time when Sirius is closest to the Sun.
Around July	Ramadan	Month of fasting for followers of Islam
July 15	St. Swithin's Day	Feast of St. Swithin. "St. Swithin's Day, if thou dost rain, for 40 days it will remain. St. Swithin's Day if thou be fair, for 40 days 'twill rain nae mair." Swithin, Bishop of Winchester in England, died in 862. Before he died he asked to be buried outside the church. He was. A hundred years later, however, the monks decided to move the remains inside the church on July 15. The Saint protested by causing a 40-day rain, which persuaded the monks to leave the Saint buried outside.

Autumn — the evening of the year, when the trees are ablaze with color, and the crisp air is sometimes filled with the smell of burning leaves.

August 1	Third cross-quarter day	Beginning of autumn. Daylight wanes.
	Lammas	A wheat harvest festival dating from Saxon times. *Lammas* means loaf-mass from the practice of offering bread at Mass, made from the first fruits of the new wheat.
	Lagnasadh	Gaelic summer games of Lug, the Sungod. Sacred day of the Mother goddesses Kore and Ceres.

Weekend before Labor Day	Labor Day Weekend	Regarded in the U.S. as the end of summer
Around September	Succoth	The Feast of Tabernacles, celebrated for eight days in commemoration of the Israelites who dwelt in booths or tabernacles that they made from branches of trees and covered with leaves, during their 40 years wandering in search of the Promised Land.
In September/ October	Rosh Hashana	The Jewish Festival of the New Year
In September/ October	Yom Kippur	The Jewish Day of Atonement, a day of prayer to obtain forgiveness. "It never rains on the Day of Atonement."
September 11	Harvest Festival	A festive celebration to mark the harvest. Called *Harvest-Home* in England and the *Kern* in Scotland, it's the European Thanksgiving.
September 23	Autumnal Equinox	Middle of autumn. Day and night are equal. The Sun is at midheight at noon, making the days not too warm, not too cool.
September 29	Michaelmas	The festival of the archangel Michael. A call to wake up from the drowsiness of summer. The mood of this day appears in paintings of St. Michael (or St. George) overcoming the forces of darkness (the dragon) while gazing alertly ahead.

Winter — the night of the year

Last Sunday in October	End of Daylight Saving Time	Return to Standard Time.
October 31	Fourth cross-quarter day	Beginning of winter. Nights grow longer than days.
	Halloween	The name *All Hallows E'en* means hallowed or holy evening, the eve before All Saints' Day. Before that it was an old Druid festival that began at midnight and lasted throughout the following day. The festival was in honor of Crone Hecate the destroyer who brought death to all vegetation, returning the seed of life to the unconscious to sleep. To honor Pomona, the goddess of fruits and seed, people shared apples and nuts. Today children dress like souls of the dead and go around asking for food, mostly candy.

November 1	Samhain (pronounced "savin")	Celtic New Year in honor of the departing Sun and beginning of new fires for a new year. At this time dark spirits visit the Earth until the good spirits can send them away. In the U.S. people celebrate a combination of Halloween and Samhain on the night of October 31.
November 1	All Saints' Day	A day to commemorate all the saints and holy ones who do not have a feast especially set for them. A day to reflect on their example.
November 2	All Souls' Day	A day of prayer to remember those who have died
November 11	Martinmas	Feast of St. Martin, patron saint of farmers (at the end of the harvest), outcasts, and beggars (since he divided his cloak with one). On the evening of Martinmas, people in many French homes remember the Saint with a festival of lanterns, carrying the light through the darkened house.
		"If St. Martin's Day be bright and sun-shiny there will be a cold winter, or if the trees and vines shall retain their foliage the same will follow. But if there be frost before Martinmas, the winter will be mild."
		"A la Saint Martin l'hiver en chemin" [with St. Martin on the road is winter]
Last Thursday in November	Thanksgiving	Harvest festival in the U.S. commemorating the help given by the Native Americans to the Pilgrim settlers in New England. People generally celebrate with family gatherings around a sumptuous feast usually featuring turkey. The turkey almost became the national bird of the U.S. instead of the eagle.
4 weeks before Christmas	Advent	Preparation for Christmas. The word advent comes from the Latin word adventus = a coming or approach. People place four candles on the Advent wreath, lighting one for each Sunday until all four are shining to announce the birth of the light at Christmas. People also use Advent calendars with windows to open on each day before Christmas.
December 6	St. Nicholas's Day	The feast day of St. Nicholas, the patron saint of children, Russia, and merchants, and the model for Father Christmas and Santa Claus. This is the day children celebrate Christmas with presents in Holland, Belgium, and parts of Germany. At this time, people in these

countries observe many of the customs we associate with Christmas.

December 13	St. Lucia's Day	The Feast of St. Lucia, formerly thought of as "the year's midnight"
		"Lucy light, shortest day, longest night."
		In Sweden, the festival is celebrated in the home. While the family sings a St. Lucia song, the eldest daughter serves a sweet roll to everyone in the house. She wears a white gown and on her head a wreath with seven lit candles.
December 19	Saturnalia	The Roman midwinter festival in honor of Saturnus. A celebration of light and darkness that the Romans used to mark with wild parties.
in Mid-December	Yule	Germanic celebration of the beginning of the year. *Yule =* wheel.
in December	Hanukkah	The Jewish Festival of Dedication, kept in memory of the purification and rededication of the temple. It is also the Feast of Lights in memory of the relighting of the perpetual lamp in the temple. People celebrate this festival in homes and synagogues by lighting the candles on the eight-branched menorah.
December 22	Winter Solstice	Midwinter Day. The shortest day of the year. Long night. The Sun is at its lowest angle from the Earth at noon, making the days cold. Darkness reigns.
December 24	Christmas Eve	The night before Christmas. Many families in Europe celebrate Christmas on this night. Mass is celebrated at midnight; church bells ring out. Legend has it that the animals speak at midnight as they celebrate the birth of the Christ Child in a stable warmed by an ox, ass, and sheep, many years ago.
December 25	Christmas	The festival celebrating the birth of Jesus, the Christ.
		Christmas = Christes Masse (the Mass of Christ). The Christmas customs used throughout the world are a mixture of local traditions and pre-Christian practices. Thus, Christmas is both a holy day and a holiday. Many decorations include stars made of shiny paper or straw. The celebration of Christmas lasts 12 days (the 12 Days of Christmas or the 12 Holy Nights).

December 26	St. Stephen's Day	The feast of the first Christian to die for his faith.
		"Good King Wenceslas looked out on the feast of Stephen; when the snow lay round about deep and crisp and even."
December 31	New Year's Eve	Called *Hogmanny* in Great Britain, it marks the last day of the year. Many people stay up to welcome in the New Year at midnight. There are a number of old European customs that people practice this night while waiting, including various ways of telling fortunes.
January 1	New Year's Day	The first day of the New Year, formerly celebrated on March 25
January 6	Epiphany	The Twelfth Day of Christmas. *Epiphany* comes from the Greek word ἐπιφανεια (epiphaneia) = coming to light, appearance. This day commemorates the appearance of Christ to all peoples through the visit of the three wise men to Bethlehem. This day also commemorates the baptism of Christ in the Jordan River by John the Baptist when a voice from heaven recognized him publicly.
January 20	St. Agnes's Eve	The night before the Feast of St. Agnes, considered a good time to tell fortunes
January 21	St. Agnes's Day	The Feast of St. Agnes
January 25	St. Paul's Day	The Feast of St. Paul
		"If St. Paul's Day be fair and clear, it doth betide a happy year; but if it chance to snow or rain, there will be dear all kind of grain."

The calendar also includes other celebrations such as birthdates and days to remember a particular idea or group of people.

By watching the changing lengths of the shadows from the shadow stick in Project 6, Finding Directions from a Shadow Stick, you can tell what time of year it is and what season is coming next. You can do the same by noticing where the Sun rises and sets compared to the exact positions of the east and west. Without staring at the Sun you can get a good idea whether its path is at a high or low angle. With what you now know about how to predict the arrival of each season, you can construct your own working version of one of the first astronomical observatories and calendars: Stonehenge.

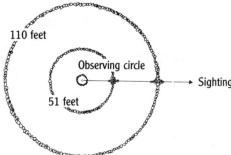

110 feet

Observing circle

Sighting line for sunrise: equinox or solstice

51 feet

★ ★ ★ ★ ★ **Project 8: Building a Stonewheel Observing Circle** ★ ★ ★ ★ ★

MATERIALS

rope (or clothesline) over 60 feet (18 m) long

bag of lime or white powder to mark ground

plenty of rocks

a clear field

at least three people

PROCEDURE

1. Find a site with a clear view of the east and west horizons. Make a mark at the place that will become the center of a circle 110 feet (34 m) in diameter.

2. Stand in the center holding on to one end of the rope. Another person holds the rope and using it as a drawing compass measures out a circle. Use 1½ normal walking steps from the center mark as the radius to make the circle. Knot the rope at this distance. A third person follows behind drawing the circle with lime. Cover the circle with rocks, the larger the better. This is the observing circle.

3. Make two more circles around the first one in the same way always measuring from the center mark. The second circle has a radius of 25½ feet (8 m), the third circle has a radius of 55 feet (17 m). The sizes of these circles come from the "megalithic yard" discovered by the British archaeologist Sir Alexander Thom. You can use any measurement. Instead of using a ruler, count one normal walking step as 2½ feet (1 m).

USING YOUR STONEWHEEL OBSERVING CIRCLE

On the morning of the equinox or solstice, stand in the center of the observing circle and face the direction where the Sun will be rising. Have a companion stand on the outermost circle facing the same direction. When the Sun rises, whoever is standing in the observing circle has the other person stand directly in front of the Sun and mark that spot on the circle with sticks or a pile of stones. Keeping the Sun always in view and lined up with the person in the observing circle, mark the middle circle to help create a straight viewing line from the center. The ancients often included an additional point on the horizon: a tree, a notch in the mountainside, etc. You can too.

You can use the sighting method described above to find and mark other points, such as

    a. north,

    b. sunset on the equinoxes,

    c. sunrise on the solstices, and

    d. sunset on the solstices.

OBSERVATIONS

Your stonewheel is a combination of Stonehenge, built in England around 2000 B.C., and the medicine wheels built by the Native Americans of Wyoming around 1500 A.D. How do you think your stonewheel works? Will it be accurate for the same positions next year? What other activities could you think of for the stonewheel?

Stonehenge, Wiltshire, England. (*photo courtesy of Ministry of Public Buildings & Works, England*)

The ancient Druids did not build Stonehenge, but they used it possibly to celebrate the autumn festival of Samhain and welcome in the seasons of the solstices and equinoxes. Legend has it that Merlin, the wizard friend of King Arthur, built Stonehenge. This becomes more believable when you find that the stones that make up this massive observatory, temple, and calendar are not found locally.

The word *henge* means a circular enclosure, usually earthen with a bank and a ditch.

People made their observations at Stonehenge from inside the horseshoe-shaped group of stones looking through the outer circles, just as in your stonewheel (see illustration). An additional vertical stone stands beyond the outer circle to further mark the summer solstice point. When the Sun rises on June 21, it stands on top of this "heel stone" just as it did for you when you marked the sunrise with a stick in our earlier projects. The observation points at Stonehenge also included the rising and setting positions for the Moon as well as an eclipse calendar. Stonehenge is not the only example of its kind. There are many other standing stones arranged in circles and avenues throughout Great Britain and parts of France.

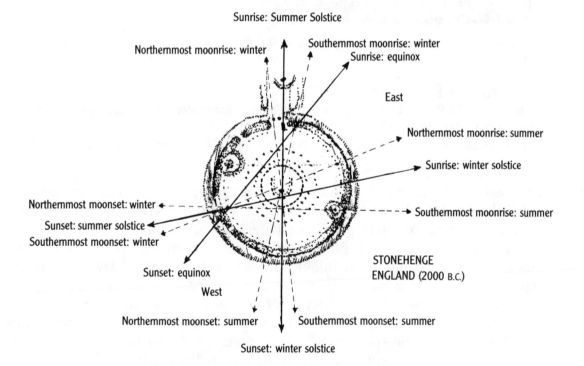

Sunrise: Summer Solstice

Northernmost moonrise: winter

Southernmost moonrise: winter
Sunrise: equinox

East

Northernmost moonrise: summer

Sunrise: winter solstice

Northernmost moonset: winter

Southernmost moonrise: summer

Sunset: summer solstice
Southernmost moonset: winter

Sunset: equinox
West

STONEHENGE
ENGLAND (2000 B.C.)

Northernmost moonset: summer

Southernmost moonset: summer

Sunset: winter solstice

People made their observations at the medicine wheel by standing in one of the circles of stones on the outside of the main circle and sighting along the ground (horizontal) following the lines of stones. The medicine wheel includes the rising positions of stars that observers used in addition to the rising of the Sun to indicate important seasonal points (see illustration).

Medicine wheel, Wyoming, U.S.A. (*photo courtesy of U.S. Forestry Service, Medicine Wheel Ranger District*)

READING MORE

Allison, Linda. *The Reason for Seasons: The Great Cosmic Megagalactic Trip Without Moving from Your Chair.* Boston: Little, Brown, 1975.

Cary, Diana and Judy Large. *Festivals, Family and Food.* Stroud, Gloucestershire: Hawthorn Press, 1982.

Section 3   TIME

The Year   When you stand outside in the dark under the stars or when you watch the sunrise bring in the morning light, you are experiencing the two most basic units of time: *day* and *night*. Two different times, two different worlds. A "day" used to mean the time when the Sun shone, that is, from sunrise to sunset. A day now lasts from midnight to midnight. Thus we have created a "day" that doesn't depend on what we see and begins and ends in the night.

The kind of time most of us keep is for measuring "how long": how long until, how long since, how long from beginning to end. Native Americans counted years by "winters" or "summers," months by "moons," and days by "sleeps." Nature offers us a number of events with which to measure the passing of time.

The Sun and Moon were the first and most widely recognized means of measuring time. Their rhythms divided the year into the four seasons.

The Sun gives us time and direction. During the year, the noon position of the Sun changes. Sometimes it is higher, sometimes lower in the sky. It also moves a number of degrees north or south from a true east-west rising and setting position.

The combination of the change in the Sun's noon positions and the different speeds of the Sun's movement in summer and winter creates a figure-eight pattern in the sky. Like the circle for the sky, there also is a signature for the Sun. We call this figure-eight pattern the **analemma**. It takes the Sun the whole year to etch its signature into the daytime sky.

Our word **year** comes from the Middle English word *yeer* or *yore* and the Avestan word *yara* from the ancient sacred books of the Zoroastrian religion in Babylonia, which is old Iran.
Analemma comes from the Greek word ἀναλημμα (*analemma*) = sundial.

Often modern scientists need to conduct ongoing experiments that may continue over the space of a year or longer. A few years ago, one astronomer aimed his camera toward the south and took a photograph of the Sun in the daytime sky at the same time every 10 days for a whole year. As a reward for his patience he now has an amazing photograph of the analemma, the figure-eight pattern made by the Sun. There are several ways that you too can make the analemma visible. In this next project you can follow the path of the Sun and read its signature.

★ ★ ★ ★ ★ ★ ★ ★ **Project 9: Displaying the Path of the Sun** ★ ★ ★ ★ ★ ★ ★ ★
(Analemma)

MATERIALS

string   thumbtacks
weight (nut, bolt, rock, etc.)   crayon
nail
large sheet of paper

PROCEDURE

1. Find a wall or flat vertical surface outside that is free from disturbances.
2. Attach the large sheet of paper to the wall using the thumbtacks.

3. Tie the weight to the end of the string.

4. Nail the string to the wall so its weighted end hangs in front of the paper.

5. Use the crayon to mark the weight's shadow on the paper at the same time and on the same day of the week every week for a few months. Write the dates next to each mark.

6. Write yourself a reminder on the calendar to mark the shadow. If it's cloudy, rainy, or you miss a day, mark the shadow on the next possible day.

7. Make a drawing or photograph of what you have marked so far and use it to help you map out where the next marks will be and what the final shape will look like. Remember that in the Northern Hemisphere, the summer loop is smaller because the Sun appears to move faster. In the Southern Hemisphere, the winter loop is smaller.

8. Keep marking the weight's shadow and you will be rewarded for your patience, with the Sun's signature.

9. Make a drawing or photograph of your finished analemma.

OBSERVATIONS

Notice the shape your marks are beginning to make. After a year, how close to the actual positions and shape were your predictions?

Mechanical timepieces such as watches do not change how they mark the hours from day to day. The time they give us indicates the time of the average or "mean" position of the Sun. Since the real Sun is neither mechanical nor average, our clocks are always a bit ahead or behind the real Sun in the sky. Only four times a year do our watches and the Sun (as shown on the sundial) agree: December 25, April 14 or 15, June 14 or 15, and September 1 or 2. On February 11, for example, clocks are 14½ minutes faster than the Sun. You would have to subtract 14½ minutes from your clock to make it equal to Sun time. By November 3, clocks are behind the Sun by more than 16 minutes. You would have to add these 16 minutes to make your clock time equal to Sun time. The analemma can help make the necessary adjustments. These adjustments are referred to as the **equation of time**.

The Month   During the year the Moon is busy moving around the celestial hemisphere. The fact that you can see the Moon both in the daylight and night makes it a more convenient timekeeper than the Sun, which you can only see during the day.

Crescent comes from the Latin word *cresco* = to grow, increase, enlarge. Crescent is the name we give to a curved shape like half of the letter *O*.

The time it takes for the Moon to go from one of its phases all the way through the others and back to the first phase again is called a **month**, after the Moon that measures it. In the time it takes the Sun to get from one of its places (solstice or equinox) back to the same place (one year), the Moon has gone through all of its phases 12 times. You can now further divide the year into 12 parts.

EQUATION OF TIME CHART

The number of minutes you have to subtract (−) or add (+) to make your clock time equal to sun time

Day	Jan.	Feb.	March	April	May	June	July	Aug.	Sept.	Oct.	Nov.	Dec.
1	−3.0	−13.5	−12.5	−4.0	+3.0	+2.5	−3.5	−6.5	0.0	+10.0	+16.5	+11.0
2	−3.5	−13.5	−12.5	−3.5	+3.0	+2.5	−4.0	−6.0	0.0	+10.5	+16.5	+11.0
3	−4.0	−14.0	−12.0	−3.5	+3.0	+2.0	−4.0	−6.0	+0.5	+10.5	+16.5	+10.5
4	−4.5	−14.0	−12.0	−3.0	+3.0	+2.0	−4.0	−6.0	+1.0	+11.0	+16.5	+10.0
5	−5.0	−14.0	−12.0	−3.0	+3.5	+2.0	−4.5	−6.0	+1.0	+11.5	+16.5	+9.5
6	−5.5	−14.0	−11.5	−2.5	+3.5	+1.5	−4.5	−6.0	+1.5	+11.5	+16.5	+9.0
7	−6.0	−14.0	−11.5	−2.5	+3.5	+1.5	−4.5	−6.0	+2.0	+12.0	+16.5	+9.0
8	−6.5	−14.0	−11.0	−2.0	+3.5	+1.0	−5.0	−5.5	+2.0	+12.0	+16.5	+8.5
9	−7.0	−14.5	−11.0	−2.0	+3.5	+1.0	−5.0	−5.5	+2.5	+12.5	+16.0	+8.0
10	−7.0	−14.5	−10.5	−1.5	+3.5	+1.0	−5.0	−5.5	+3.0	+13.0	+16.0	+7.5
11	−7.5	−14.5	−10.5	−1.5	+3.5	+0.5	−5.5	−5.0	+3.0	+13.0	+16.0	+7.0
12	−8.0	−14.5	−10.0	−1.0	+3.5	+0.5	−5.5	−5.0	+3.5	+13.5	+16.0	+6.5
13	−8.5	−14.5	−10.0	−0.5	+3.5	+0.5	−5.5	−5.0	+4.0	+13.5	+16.0	+6.0
14	−9.0	−14.5	−9.5	−0.5	+3.5	0.0	−5.5	−4.5	+4.0	+14.0	+15.5	+5.5
15	−9.0	−14.5	−9.0	0.0	+3.5	0.0	−6.0	−4.5	+4.5	+14.0	+15.5	+5.0
16	−9.5	−14.0	−9.0	0.0	+3.5	−0.5	−6.0	−4.5	+5.0	+14.0	+15.5	+4.5
17	−10.0	−14.0	−8.5	+0.5	+3.5	−0.5	−6.0	−4.0	+5.0	+14.5	+15.0	+4.0
18	−10.0	−14.0	−8.5	+0.5	+3.5	−1.0	−6.0	−4.0	+5.5	+14.5	+15.0	+3.5
19	−10.5	−14.0	−8.0	+0.5	+3.5	−1.0	−6.0	−3.5	+6.0	+15.0	+14.5	+3.0
20	−11.0	−14.0	−8.0	+1.0	+3.5	−1.5	−6.0	−3.5	+6.5	+15.0	+14.5	+2.5
21	−11.0	−14.0	−7.5	+1.0	+3.5	−1.5	−6.5	−3.5	+6.5	+15.0	+14.5	+2.0
22	−11.5	−13.5	−7.0	+1.5	+3.5	−1.5	−6.5	−3.0	+7.0	+15.5	+14.0	+1.5
23	−11.5	−13.5	−7.0	+1.5	+3.5	−2.0	−6.5	−3.0	+7.5	+15.5	+14.0	+1.0
24	−12.0	−13.5	−6.5	+2.0	+3.5	−2.0	−6.5	−2.5	+7.5	+15.5	+13.5	+0.5
25	−12.0	−13.5	−6.5	+2.0	+3.5	−2.5	−6.5	−2.0	+8.0	+16.0	+13.0	0.0
26	−12.5	−13.0	−6.0	+2.0	+3.0	−2.5	−6.5	−2.0	+8.5	+16.0	+13.0	−0.5
27	−12.5	−13.0	−5.5	+2.5	+3.0	−3.0	−6.5	−1.5	+9.0	+16.0	+12.5	−1.0
28	−13.0	−13.0	−5.5	+2.5	+3.0	−3.0	−6.5	−1.5	+9.0	+16.0	+12.0	−1.5
29	−13.0	−12.5	−5.0	+2.5	+3.0	−3.0	−6.5	−1.0	+9.5	+16.0	+12.0	−2.0
30	−13.0		−4.5	+2.5	+2.5	−3.5	−6.5	−1.0	+10.0	+16.5	+11.5	−2.0
31	−13.5		−4.5		+2.5		−6.5	−0.5		+16.5		−2.5

The Week   While the shape and brightness of the Moon are constantly changing, four main shapes and brightnesses can be easily recognized: (1) when the Moon is not visible, (2) when the right half of the circle of the Moon is lit, (3) when the full circle of the Moon is lit, and (4) when the left half of the Moon is lit. We call the interval between each of these four shapes or phases a **week.** You can now divide the year into 52 parts. For more about the Moon's phases, see chapter 6, section 2.

Week comes from the Middle English word *weke* or *wike,* which came from the Latin word *vici* = change or turn.
Day comes from the Old English word *doeg* and the Latin word *dies.* Both words mean the time from daylight to night or from night to daylight.

The Day   A day used to be the interval between one sunrise or sunset to the next. There are seven days in one week. Although there are weeks of other lengths throughout the world ranging from 5 to 10 days, the number seven has caught the attention of humankind as the signature or symbol of perfection. There are seven notes in the Western musical scale. Christianity lists seven supreme virtues, seven deadly vices, and seven mansions of heaven. In Japan there are seven gods of happiness. In Rome there were seven hills. There are seven stars in the Pleiades and seven ancient and seven modern wonders of the world.

The Saxon **King Edgar** in 958 A.D. ordered no work to be done from Saturday noon to Monday dawn, thus inventing the "weekend."

The ancient Babylonians, who gave us our word for year, also gave us a convenient way to divide it. They noticed that circles keep showing up when we try to understand what is happening in the sky: the outer rim of the celestial hemisphere, star trails, the shape of the Sun and the Moon, etc.

Other places that have circles are Stonehenge, the medicine wheel and the stonewheel, the spiral of the Anasazi, and the observing station in Caracol.

THE DAYS OF THE WEEK

English	Saxon Usage	Planet/Symbol	Gods & Goddesses Greek/Roman
Sunday	Sun's Day	Sun ☉	Helios/Apollo (Sol)
Monday	Moon's Day	Moon ☽	Artemis/Diana (Luna)
Tuesday	Tiw's Day	Mars ♂	Hermes/Mercurius
Wednesday	Woden's Day	Mercury ☿	Aphrodite/Venus
Thursday	Thor's Day	Jupiter ♃	Ares/Mars
Friday	Frigg's Day	Venus ♀	Zeus/Jupiter
Saturday	Saterne's Day	Saturn ♄	Kronos/Saturnus

German	French	Spanish	Latin
Sontag	Dimanche	Domingo	Dies Solis
Montag	Lundi	Lunes	Dies Lunae
Dienstag	Mardi	Martes	Dies Martis
Mittwoch	Mercredi	Miercoles	Dies Mercurii
Donnerstag	Jeudi	Jueves	Dies Iovis
Freitag	Vendredi	Viernes	Dies Veneris
Samstag	Samedi	Sabado	Dies Saturni

The Babylonians recognized that the circle must be the "signature" of the sky. To be able to read that signature would make it possible for you to better understand the sky. The Babylonian priest-astronomers used the tools of geometry to divide the circle and the year first into 12 equal parts. Then they further divided each section into 30 smaller parts. Each part had an angle of one degree. That meant that each month would have 30 days.

The Hour   The shadow stick can measure time within the day. The shadow stick teams up with the circle to form a sundial. All over the world people have used various kinds of sundials. The Chinese were among the first to use them. The sundial only tells you the day-time intervals, however. People called these intervals **watches** (from the fact that certain people had the task of watching the time pass and, in some cases, watching out for intruders or the enemy). In the earliest Hebrew day there were six watches: three light and three dark. The three dark watches were from sunset to midnight, from midnight to three in the morning, and from three to sunrise. The three light watches were morning, from sunrise till about 10:00 in the morning; "the heat of the day," from 10:00 to about 2:00 in the afternoon; and the "cool of the day," from 2:00 until sunset.

In the New Testament years, people divided the night into four watches: from sunset to 9:00 at night, from 9:00 to midnight, from midnight to 3:00 in the morning, and from 3:00 to sunrise. There were four **hours** of daylight.

Hour comes from the Greek word ὥρα (*hora*) and the Latin word *hora* = time of day.

Morning began with the "third" hour from sunrise to 9 in the morning, then came the "sixth" hour from 9 to noon, then the "ninth" hour from noon to 3 in the afternoon, ending with the "12th" hour from 3 to sunset.

The Chinese day began at 11 at night and had 12 periods of two hours each. Each of these double hours had eight periods equal to 15 minutes each.

The ancient Egyptians in the fourth century B.C. were the first people we know of to divide the complete "day" (daylight and nighttime) into equal parts. They divided the night (from sunset to sunrise) into 12 parts. Astronomer-priests measured the passing of these parts by watching certain stars rise on the eastern horizon. They divided daylight (from sunrise to sunset) into 10 parts. A shadow clock like a sundial kept track of these 10 parts. There were two other parts that were neither day or night. One was dawn, just before sunrise. The other was dusk, just after sunset. These 2 parts, the 10 daytime, and 12 nighttime parts made up their 24-part day.

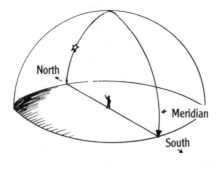

A star crossing the meridian

Meridian comes from the Latin word *meridiem* = midday.

Noon and midnight become the dividing lines when you separate the day into two 12-hour parts. Time occurring after midnight is "morning." Time after midday is "afternoon." Remember that the Sun casts a shadow at noon that points to the north. Imagine a north-south line from this shadow continuing as far behind and as far in front of you as you can see. Imagine that where the line meets the horizon in front of you, it keeps going right up into the sky, arches overhead, and continues down behind you until it reaches the opposite horizon and connects with the line on the ground. Not only does the Sun cross the north-south line on the ground every day, it crosses the same line in the sky, at the same time. When it is right on the line, it is noon. The Sun at noon is in the middle of its daytime journey. For this reason, we call the extended north-south line in the sky the **meridian**.

If the Sun hasn't reached the meridian yet, the hours are called *ante meridiem* = before midday (A.M.). The "morning" hours that occur after midnight and before noon are A.M. hours. 12:00 A.M. = midnight. We call hours after noon *post meridianus* = after midday (P.M.). The "afternoon" hours that occur after midday and before midnight are P.M. hours. For example, 10:00 P.M. = 10 hours after noon, or 10:00 at night. In this next project you can make use of the Sun's movements to tell time by building a sundial.

★ ★ ★ ★ ★ ★ ★ ★ ★ ★ ★ ★**Project 10: Making a Sundial** ★ ★ ★ ★ ★ ★ ★ ★ ★ ★ ★ ★

MATERIALS

piece of cardboard 8½ × 11 inches
or 22 × 28 centimeters
(notebook-paper size)
map showing the latitude for where
you live
protractor

drawing compass
tape
pair of scissors
drinking straw
pen or pencil

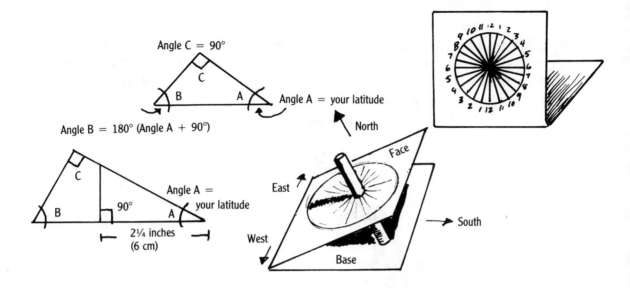

Angle C = 90°

Angle A = your latitude

Angle B = 180° (Angle A + 90°)

Angle A = your latitude

90°

2¼ inches
(6 cm)

North

East

West

South

Face

Base

PROCEDURE

1. Cut a 4 × 8½ inch (10 × 22 cm) piece from the cardboard.

2. Fold the cardboard in half so that it sits up as shown. The part that is standing up is the face. The part underneath is the base.

3. Make a 3-inch (8 cm) diameter circle using the compass in the center of the front of the face.

4. Divide the circle into 24 15° sections using the protractor and label the sections as shown. Be sure that your vertical line (12) is really straight up and down.

5. Poke a hole in the exact center of the circle drawing large enough for the straw to fit through.

6. Cut out one triangle with the dimensions specified and label the angles.

7. Draw a line on the triangle 2¼ inches (6 cm) from Angle A. This line should make a 90° angle.

8. Tape this triangle onto the back of the face next to the hole so that the line drawn on the triangle points to the hole and Angle A fits into the fold between the face and the base and Angle B is on the top.

9. Push the straw through the hole so that it sticks out about 2 inches (5 cm) in the front and about 1½ inches (4 cm) in the back. The straw should match up with the line drawn on the triangle. Tape the straw in place onto the triangle and tape the triangle onto the base making sure it is vertical.

10. Place your finished sundial on a flat, level surface with the straw pointing north if you live in the Northern Hemisphere.

Gnomon comes from the Greek word γνωμων (*gnomon*) = that by which a thing is known.

OBSERVATIONS

The stick in the shadow stick projects and in the sundial "tells the time." For this reason we call it the **gnomon**. Note the position of the gnomon's shadow every hour on the hour. Be careful not to move the sundial. Compare your results with a clock. Why does the gnomon have to point to the north? Will this sundial be accurate in all seasons? What would you need to do to make your sundial accurate in the Southern Hemisphere?

The Romans used sundials. In Elizabethan times, people used pocket sundials.

Egyptian shadow clock, circa 1000 B.C. The gnomon in Egyptian Sun time markers was slightly different from the vertical ones in use elsewhere. At dawn, people set the Sun time marker with its crossbar facing the east. At midday, when the shadow was the shortest, they turned the marker around to face the west.

A.M. — Left hand

P.M. — Right hand

Hand pointing west, pencil pointing north

Hand pointing east, pencil pointing north

Here's a handy timepiece that combines the Egyptian time marker and the sundial. Hold a pencil with your thumb while your hand is pointing horizontally. The angle of the pencil should be as close to that of your latitude as you can manage.

Clock comes from the French word *cloche* = bell. *O'clock* means "of the hour."

One of the first clocks made its appearance around 1550 B.C. It was the creation of the Egyptian astronomer **Amenemhet** for **King Amenophis I** (ca. 1545–1525 B.C.). The clock was a big bucket that was filled with water at nightfall up to a marked line. A small hole near the bottom of the bucket allowed the water to trickle out slowly into another container. On the inside of the big bucket were statuettes of gods and goddesses that appeared at certain times as the water level kept getting lower. At night the pharaoh could tell the time by feeling raised lines inside the bucket. Amenemhet noted that a winter night was 14 hours long and a summer night was 12 hours long. Try making your own version of this water clock. How accurate and useful is a water clock? What problems might exist in very cold or very hot weather?

We call water clocks *clepsydra* from the two Greek words κλεπτης (*cleptes*) = a thief and ὕδορ (*hydor*) = water.

Sand doesn't freeze, doesn't evaporate, and in a sealed glass container no dirt can get in and block the flow. The French monk **Luiprand**, who lived at Chartres in the eighth century, invented the sand-filled hourglass. In 807 **Charlemagne** (742–814) ordered an hourglass so large that he only needed to turn it once every 12 hours.

Archimedes (287–212 B.C.) made the first clock that didn't require water, sand, or Sun. Using a clock like the one **Cleopatra** may have used, Archimedes replaced the water and substituted a weight for the floating piston that dropped as the water level fell. In the 14th century people built large clocks of this type, replacing the piston and shaft with gears. The weights pulled at the gears from long ropes. Since the weights needed plenty of room to pull, these clocks were in tall towers. The big clock at Rouen in Normandy, France, was built in 1389. It was there when **Joan of Arc** was on trial in that city. It is still in use today (its parts have had to be changed over the years). Cuckoo clocks work the same way. Grandfather clocks use a pendulum with the weights making the time more accurate by releasing the weight for a moment with one swing, then holding it up with the next. The device that holds and releases the weight is an **escapement**. The clicking sound of the escapement holding and releasing is the tick-tock we hear.

All clocks until 1687 had only the hour hand and counted only hours and quarter hours.

How old are you in minutes? How old are you in hours?

The Minute   In the Babylonian division of a circle, you can divide each of the 360° into smaller sections called **minutes**. There are 60 minutes (60′) in 1°. While these minutes are meant to measure space and not time, we have borrowed the term and its size. There are 60 minutes of time in an hour. In 1687, clocks started using the minute hand.

The Second   You can divide the degree in a circle even smaller than a minute. Each minute contains 60 **seconds** (60″). Just as there are 60 seconds of space to 1 minute of space, so there are 60 seconds of time to 1 minute of time.

Clock showing only hours. German, 1643.

Minute comes from the Latin word *minuta* = small.
Second comes from the Middle English and French word *second* taken from the Latin word *secundus* = the following, or next in order.

Here on the face of a clock are the 360° of the ancient Babylonians; the hours, minutes, and seconds of several cultures; and on some versions, the calendar. Clocks we wear on our wrists are called **watches** because they tell us the time of the "watches" our ancestors used to observe.

Telling Time at Night   In one day, the celestial hemisphere makes one complete turn carrying the Sun with it bringing day and night. In this next project you can use the circumpolar stars to help you tell time at night.

★ ★ ★ ★ ★ ★ ★ **Project 11: Making a Night Clock (Nocturnal)** ★ ★ ★ ★ ★ ★ ★

MATERIALS

thin, stiff cardboard   glue
metal eyelet   access to a photocopier with enlarger
scissors

PROCEDURE

1. Photocopy and enlarge the four parts of the nocturnal (a–d on the next page), glue them onto the cardboard, and cut them out.

2. Attach the date and time dial, then the pointer, with the metal eyelet. Use the point of the scissors to cut a hole in the center of each part of the nocturnal for the metal eyelet. Be sure the dial and pointer can move freely and that you can see through the sighting hole.

USING YOUR NOCTURNAL

Set the date by lining it up with the marker at the top of the nocturnal. Line up the edge of the Ursa Major tab (or the Ursa Minor tab) with the marker also. Hold the nocturnal so that it is vertical. Look at Polaris through the sighting hole. Line up the pointer with the two pointer stars, Dubhe and Merak in Ursa Major (the Big Dipper) or one of the two guardian stars Kochab and Pherkad in Ursa Minor (the Little Dipper). The top edge of the pointer will line up next to the correct time on the time and date dial. (Adjust for daylight saving time, if necessary.)

Line up stars along this edge.

a. Pointer

Ursa Minor tab

Ursa Major tab

b. Time dial

Date marker

Sighting hole

c. Date dial

d. Handle

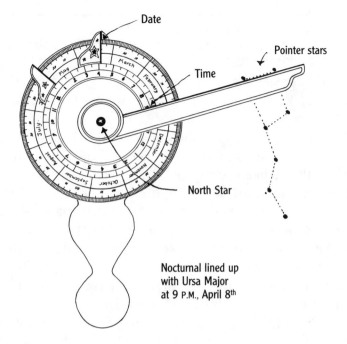

Date

Pointer stars

Time

North Star

Nocturnal lined up
with Ursa Major
at 9 P.M., April 8th

OBSERVATION

With a combination of a sundial and a nocturnal you can keep up with the passing of time by making use of the movements of the heavens. Of course, the nocturnal works only north of the equator and in locations where you can at least see Ursa Minor.

Sidereal Time   Remember the experiment of Leonardo da Vinci in which you watched the stars move past a certain point on the landscape? If you were to do that experiment again, this time marking the first position of the star before it moves and waiting until the next night until it returns to that exact spot, you will have measured the length of one day, according to star time. A star day is 23 hours, 56 minutes, and 4 seconds long. We call this unit of time measurement **sidereal time**.

Synodic Time   If instead you chose to measure the time from sunset to sunset or sunrise to sunrise, you would not need to wait for the Sun to return to its same place in the sky, like the star in sidereal time. You would need for the Sun to return to its same relationship to you—rising, setting, noon, etc. The length of this day, the time between the same relationships, is 24 hours.

If you see the Moon next to a certain star and you wait while it goes through its phases and comes back again to that star, it won't be quite in the phase it was when you first saw it. You will have measured a **sidereal month**, which is 27 days, 7 hours, 43 minutes, and 11.5 seconds (27.32166 days).

A **synodic month** is the time it takes for the Moon to return to the same phase it left a month ago. This takes 29 days, 12 hours, 44 minutes, and 29 seconds, or about 29½ days (29.53059 days).

You use the sidereal times for locating stars on the celestial hemisphere as you can see in chapter 2. You use the synodic amounts in calculating days and in producing calendars.

The father of time is Cronos, the ancient one. He is the son of Ouranos (the Sky) and Gaea (Mother Earth). Cronos is also the god of agriculture; thus time and agriculture have always been connected.

From Cronos and Rhea (the daughter of Gaea) came Zeus (Jupiter). The Romans recognized in their god Saturnus (Saturn) many of the qualities of the Greek god Cronos, although they were two different beings. The Roman feast of Saturnalia held in honor of Saturnus lasted from 5 to 7 days in December. You often see Saturnus with a sickle or curved garden knife as a sign that he was the first to teach the people how to trim the vine and olive. You also see Cronos as the god of the harvest with a sickle. Sometimes he has an hourglass with him and a long beard: "Father Time." From this god's name we get our words **chronological, chronicle, chronometer,** and **chronic.** (From this god's children we get most of our constellation stories and the names of many of the days of the week.)

WHAT IS TIME?

The shadow on the dial
The striking of the clock
The running of the sand
Day and Night, Summer and Winter
Months, Years, Centuries—
These are but arbitrary and
outward signs, the measure
of time, not time itself.
Time is the life of the soul.
                    —*H. W. Longfellow*

Thoth

READING MORE
Burns, Marilyn. *This Book Is About Time.* Boston: Little, Brown, 1978.

Section 4   CALENDARS
Calendars, Ancient and Modern   Our word **calendar** comes from the Roman practice of announcing the new Moon and therefore the new month. A certain official had the task of watching for the first signs of the approaching new Moon in order for the sacrifices in the temple to take place, which officially welcomed in the

new month. To summon the common people to the Capitol, the high priest would cry out, *"Calo,"* which means in Latin, "I call you to assemble." The Romans called the first day of the month the **calends** after this custom.

A true solar year, where the Sun returns to its starting point in the seasons, is 365 days, 5 hours, 48 minutes, and 46 seconds long (or 365.242199 days), which is nearly 365¼ days. A lunar year of 12 synodic months of 29.5 days adds up to only 354 days—11¼ days too short. Since we rely both on the Sun and the Moon to determine our calendar, we have struggled over thousands of years to make the two different measurements work together. The ingredients don't fit. The year ends up being either too long or too short. To avoid this situation, calendar makers have added extra days or taken some away.

Lunar Calendars   The first calendar makers began their work around 3000 B.C. They chose the Moon as the basis for their calendars, since a lunar month of 29½ days was an obvious measurement. But how could you have half a day? One solution was to have 6 months of 29 days each and 6 months of 30 days each. The months would alternate so that one month would have 30 days, the next 29, followed by one with 30, and so on. This is a typical lunar calendar. The early Babylonians used lunar years such as these. Jewish, Islamic, and Chinese calendars still use them.

Solar Calendars   In Egypt, the god Thoth, the divine scribe and father of astronomy, kept watch over the calendar. Agriculture, time, the activity of the heavens, and religion all wove together in the calendar.

The Sun, as source of life and the seasons, became the source of the calendar for the ancient Egyptians. Their earliest calendars contained 12 months of 30 days each. Their calendar was 5 days too short, so they inserted the 5 missing days at the end of the year as holy days. These 5 days honored the birth of the five children of **Geb**, the god of Earth, and **Nut**, the goddess of the sky: **Osiris, Horus the Elder, Set, Isis,** and **Nepthys.**

Osiris was king of Egypt and the Lord of Life. His wife was Isis, who brought crops to the fields and children to the home. Set, the brother of Osiris and husband of Nepthys, was jealous and plotted to murder his brother by having him sealed in a coffin and set adrift on the Nile. Isis set off in search of the casket and when she found it, she restored her husband to life. Again Set attempted to murder his brother by cutting him into 14 pieces and throwing them into the Nile. Horus the Younger, the son of Isis and Osiris, assembled all 14 of the parts of his father that his mother had found in the 14 days from the full moon to the last quarter. Horus then prepared his father to receive the gift of life. This gift would only be possible if the body had been preserved intact. Horus reunited the soul to his father's body. Osiris rose from the dead and ruled the world, crossing it in his Sun boat by day and at night on the Milky Way, the heavenly Nile. Osiris reigned as lord of the dead with his wife and son. There he presided over the judgment of the soul in the journey from death to new life.

The story of Isis and Osiris is one of the oldest and most important among the stories associated with the stars. There are celestial rhythms connected with this story that made it the source of a second Egyptian calendar. The Egyptians used this calendar along with the one containing 360 days and the five divine birthdays.

Practically all cultures, whether in the northern or southern parts of the world, can see the group of stars called **Orion**. In the north, you see this group in the winter night sky; in the south, you see it in the summer night sky. Orion stands on the Milky Way. So does another star group to its south, **Canis Major**. You can find Canis Major very easily because of the exceptionally bright star in it. This sparkling blue gem of a star is **Sirius**, the brightest star in the entire sky.

Orion and Canis Major

To the Egyptians, the Milky Way was the heavenly Nile, and Orion was Osiris sailing on both the heavenly Nile and the earthly one in Egypt. Following close behind on the Nile, as she had done so many times before, was the goddess Isis. Sirius is her star, and its name in Greek is **Sothis** (= Dog Star).

Just as we do, the Egyptians saw Sothis (Sirius) in the evening skies beginning in winter until she vanished from view with Osiris (Orion) in the spring. Just after the beginning of summer in June, Sothis would once again come into view just before sunrise. On that day the priests of ancient Egypt celebrated three risings: first, the rising of Sothis; second, the sunrise; and third, the gradual rise of the Nile River. These three events marked the beginning of the New Year. Sothis had come as the star of Isis to announce that Osiris had returned to his people. He had brought again the life-giving waters of the Nile. Egypt and its people would prosper for another year.

It took 70 days from the passing of Sothis from the night sky in spring to her heliacal rising in the summer. As part of the service for the dead, priests prepared the body for the soul's return, just as it had been when Horus prepared his father's body. It took 70 days for the soul to pass from death to reunion with the body at burial. During those 70 days, priests soaked the body in a brine solution as part of the embalming process.

The heliacal rising of Sothis as well as the flooding of the Nile were major events in the Egyptian calendar. However, since the calendar only had 365 days, the missing quarter day would soon add up. The result was that the date of the beginning of the year, with its observance of the heliacal rising of Sothis and the flooding the Nile, was occurring weeks before the actual events. Once in a while, the Egyptian year of 365 days and the solar year matched the date and events perfectly.

$$\text{The Egyptian Year} = 365 \text{ days or } \frac{1{,}460}{4}$$

$$\text{The Sothis Year (the Solar Year)} = 365\tfrac{1}{4} \text{ days or } \frac{1{,}461}{4}$$

1,460 Sothis Years = 1,461 Egyptian Years. That means that after 1,460 solar years of 365¼ days, the events of the heliacal rising of Sothis and the rising of the Nile will occur on the date they are supposed to according to the Egyptian calendar of 365 days. Every 1,460 years this happens. This period is called the Sothic Cycle. The oldest date we have in history is the year 4241 B.C. This date happens to be the beginning of a Sothic Cycle. The two calendars fit that year.

Our calendar shares its history with other calendars. It is the result of the effort of many people and various cultures. Originally it was a basic lunisolar calendar with all the strengths and problems that come with using the different rhythms of the Sun and the Moon. By the time it reached Rome, it looked like the calendar listed under Roman in the Months of the Year chart.

The Chinese Calendar   The Chinese calendar is one of the world's oldest. While it may not have been the first, the Chinese calendar was thriving by the year 2357 B.C. More people past and present have used the Chinese calendar than any other calendar, including the Gregorian one. The Chinese divided their lunisolar calendar into 24 half-months. The New Year began on the first new Moon after the Sun entered the zodiac constellation of Aquarius.

The Julian Calendar   Julius Caesar (102–44 B.C.) made the most far-reaching and long-lasting reforms in the calendar. The ideas suggested to Caesar by the astronomer Sosigenes from Alexandria in Egypt included some of the ideas put forth almost 200 years earlier by **Ptolemy II Euergetes**. One of them was his idea of a **leap year**. Caesar inserted the extra day between February 23 and 24, 6 days before the Calends of March. He also rearranged the months to start with Januarius instead of Martius. Januarius is the month sacred to the god **Janus** who has two faces, one looking ahead and one looking behind. In 44 B.C., 2 years after Caesar's death, **Mark Antony** renamed the 5th month **Quinctilis**, the month in which Caesar was born, **Julius** in honor of this great Roman leader. Caesar's calendar served humanity faithfully for over 1,600 years. It was only 11 minutes and 14 seconds too long.

The next emperor, **Augustus Caesar** (63 B.C.–14 A.D.), moved some of the days around from one month to another. He shortened February by one day and increased Sextilis by two. Sextilis was the month that had the most dates celebrating the great deeds of the emperor Augustus. For that, the Senate renamed it Augustus. They took a day from September and added it to October. They also took a day that was in November and added it to December.

In 321 A.D. the emperor **Constantine** (288–337 A.D.) changed the day of rest from Saturday to Sunday. He also made the 7-day week official.

The Gregorian Calendar   In 1582 people used an analemma to show **Pope Gregory XIII** (1502–1585) that the equinox and solstices did not occur on the dates given for them on the calendar. The extra 11 minutes and 14 seconds in Julius Caesar's calendar had been steadily adding up at the rate of one day extra in 128 years.

THE MONTHS OF THE YEAR

Egyptian 4000 B.C. (Lunisolar)		Maya (Lunisolar, Planetary)		Jewish (Lunar)		Moslem 622 A.D. (Lunar)	
Thoth	30	Pop	20	Nisan	30	Muharram	30
Paophi	30	Uo	20	Iyyar	29	Safar	29
Tybi	30	Zip	20	Sivan	30	Rabi 1	30
Mechir	30	Zotz'	20	Tammuz	29	Rabi 2	29
Pachons	30	Zec	20	Av	30	Jumada 1	30
Payni	30	Xul	20	Ellul	29	Jumada 2	29
Athyr	30	Yaxkin	20	Tishri	30	Rajab	30
Choiak	30	Mol	20	Heshvan	29	Sha'ban	29
Phamenoth	30	Ch'en	20	Kislev	30	Ramadan	30
Pharauithi	30	Yax	20	Tevet	29	Shawwal	29
Epiphi	30	Zac	20	Shevat	30	Dhu al-Qa'dah	30
Mesore	30	Ceh	20	Adar	29	Dhu al-Hijjah	29
Total Days	360	Mac	20	*Total Days*	354	*Total Days*	354

Egyptian (continuation): Plus 5 days added to the end of 1 year and the beginning of the next to celebrate the birthdays of the gods:
1. Osiris
2. Horus
3. Set
4. Isis
5. Nepthys

Maya (continuation): Kankin 20, Muan 20, Pax 20, Kayab 20, Cumku 20, *Total Days* 360. Plus a month of 5 unlucky days (Uayeb) used with another calendar of 28 weeks with 13 numbered days each

Moslem (continuation): Designed by Muhammad to replace the old lunisolar calendar of the Arabs. The Moslem calendar is totally lunar and does not relate to the Sun or the seasons.

Roman 746 A.D. (Lunar)		Julian/Augustan (Lunisolar)		Gregorian 1582 (Lunisolar)	
Martius	31	Januarius	31	January	31
Aprilis	29	Februarius	29/30	February	28/29
Maius	31	Martius	31	March	31
Junius	29	Aprilis	30	April	30
Quinctilis	31	Maius	31	May	31
Sextilis	29	Junius	30	June	30
September	29	Julius*	31	July	31
October	31	Augustus*	30/31	August	31
November	29	September	30/31	September	30
December	29	October	30/31	October	31
Januarius*	29	November	30/31	November	30
Februarius*	28	December	30/31	December	31
Total Days	355	*Total Days*	365/366	*Total Days*	365

*Added in 712 B.C. by King Numa. Even numbers were unlucky, so the months had odd numbers of days. The names of the months from Quinctilis through December begin with the Latin word for the numbers 5 through 10.

*Names given by the emperors Julius and Augustus Caesar. Sosigenes of Alexandria designed the Julian calendar by order of Julius Caesar. This calendar replaced the lunar calendar and made the calendar function regularly by itself. The solar year had 365¼ days. The civil year had 365 days. Each fourth year had an extra day.

Designed by Pope Gregory XIII. Pope Gregory removed 10 days from the Julian calendar that was in use in order to restore the vernal equinox to March 21. This calendar omits leap year three times in four centuries, provided that you can divide the century by 400. Each year begins on a different day of the week. After 400 years, the pattern repeats itself.

By 1582, the extra days meant that spring began around March 11 instead of March 21. By papal decree, Pope Gregory removed 10 days from that year's calendar. The result was that October 4, 1582, was followed by October 15 instead of October 5! This restored the vernal equinox to March 21. In addition to having a leap year every four years, the Pope decreed that people should omit the leap year three times in four centuries.

> Thirty days hath September, April, June, and November.
> All the rest have 31,
> Except February with 28 and no more,
> 'Till Leap Year comes and it gets one more.

Say the names of the months in order, counting on your left hand while you point with your right (do the opposite if you are left-handed). Point to the tips of your fingers for the long months and in between for the short ones. February has the shortest journey for your pointing finger. Start again with August on the tip of your third finger and count backward ending with December on the tip of your first finger.

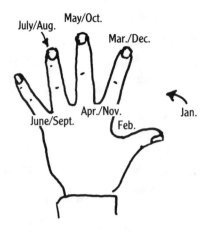

A Handy Month Reminder

The Julian Period

Joseph Justus Scaliger (1540–1609), a French chronologist living at the time of Pope Gregory XIII, took three different calendar cycles of time and calculated when they would all begin together and when they would meet again. He found the interval between these two dates to be 7,980 years. This period he called the **Julian Period** after his father **Julius Scaliger** (1484–1558). Using the Julian Period, Joseph Scaliger established the date January 1, 4713 B.C., as the beginning point of time reckoning. The end of the first Julian Period will be December 31, 3267. In the Julian system, there are no weeks, months, or years, only day numbers, a day being from noon to noon. Parts of a day appear as decimals carried to as many places as needed depending on the degree of precision required. Individual day numbers show the number of days that have passed since the beginning of the period, that is, since January 1, 4713 B.C. Here's how to figure out a particular day, for example, September 21, 1988, a day of Mars's close approach to Earth.

1. Multiply $4,713 \times 365.24798 = 1,721,413.7$.
2. Multiply $1,988 \times 365.24798 = 726,112.98$.
3. Calculate the number of days since December 31, 1988 = 265.
4. Add all three figures together.
   The Julian Day for September 21, 1988 = 2,447,791.7.

Today, astronomers use Julian Day numbers to list computer-calculated dates of ancient eclipses and other astronomical events, because by using simple subtraction you can find the interval between dates in different months and years.

A.D., B.C., A.U.C., Etc. In the United States we abbreviate dates by writing day, month, year (e.g., October 7, 1991, is 10/7/91). In Europe the date is abbreviated month, day, year (or 7/10/91). The A.D. we sometimes add at the end stands for the Latin words **Anno Domini** = "Year of Our Lord" or the Christian Era. The earliest known use of A.D. was on a document written by **Reginald**, King of the Isle of Man, in 1219. B.C. simply means **before Christ**. Dates in B.C. are numbered backward.

Julius Caesar lived from 102 to 44 B.C. That means he was born 102 years before the Christian Era and died 44 years before it. Some people refer to B.C. as B.C.E. or **Before the Common Era** and A.D. as C.E. or **the Common Era.**

The Romans numbered their years after the founding of Rome, which occurred in 753 B.C. The letters A.U.C., which stand for the Latin term *ab urbe condita* = from the founding of the city, appeared at the end of the year number showing how long after the founding of the city the date occurred.

The Islamic calendar gives dates for the Moslem Era starting from the Hegira or the date of the Flight of the Prophet Mohammed from Mecca in 622 A.D.

Counting the years from some point in the past to the present is called a **long count.** The Native Americans often used long counts to record their history.

Maya and Inca Calendars   In our 20th-century long counts, we use four counting positions: **Weekday** (name of the day)—one of seven names for a 7-day period; **day number** (day of the month)—number from 1 to 31; **month** (name of the month) one of 12 names; and **year** (number of years in the Christian Era).

The Maya people of Central America had a unique calendar that calculated long counts. In this next project you can see how these calendars worked by making one for yourself.

★ ★ ★ ★ ★ ★ ★ ★ ★ ★**Project 12: Making a Maya Calendar** ★ ★ ★ ★ ★ ★ ★ ★ ★ ★

MATERIALS

three circles from book	colored string
stiff paper	scissors
two metal eyelets	glue
colored pencils or watercolors	access to a photocopier

PROCEDURE

1. Photocopy the three circles on the opposite page (a–c), enlarging each of them 200%. Glue them onto stiff paper and cut them out.

2. Color in the designs using colored pencils or watercolors.

3. Cut a 7½-inch (17 cm) circle from stiff paper. This is the *plate.*

4. Use the point of the scissors to cut a hole in the center of each circle. Attach the three circles to the plate with a metal eyelet. Make sure the circles can move freely.

5. Loop a piece of colored string through the plate. Loop the middle yarn around the metal eyelet and bring both ends up to the top of the plate.

6. Put a metal eyelet near the top of the plate. Thread both ends of the string through the metal eyelet and tie them in a knot. You will be lining up the circles using the string as a marker.

7. Tie the loose ends of the string together a little way from the edge of the plate so that you can hang up your calendar.

USING YOUR MAYA CALENDAR

Line up the three circles so that the date shown in the book (11 Ix 8 Yaz) lines up at the top of your calendar. To change the date, move each circle clockwise, one space for each day. To read the date, start with the day number circle, then the day name, then the month. The arrangement of a 260-day lunar cycle and a 360 + 5–day solar cycle is similar to the two Egyptian calendars, the 360 + 5–day lunar cycle and the 365¼ day Sothis/solar period. With all the combinations possible, the same exact combination would recur only every 19,980 days (52 years). See if you can line up the date 7 Imix 14 Zec (May 7, 755 A.D.).

OBSERVATIONS

The Maya calendar has two main cycles: 260 days (the two inner circles on your calendar) and 365 days (the large circle). The 260-day calendar has been in existence at least since 800 B.C. and is still being used by the Quiche Maya. When **Hernando Cortez** (1485–1546) arrived in Mexico in 1518, the Spaniards were amazed that the Maya could measure time so well. The Maya calendar agreed precisely with the Spaniards' calendar except that the Maya calendar was missing 10 days!

The World Calendar   There is no calendar today that keeps perfect time. Somewhere along the line the differences between lunar and solar time are going to cause problems and require adjustments in the calendar. In 1914 the International Congress of Commerce asked that people study the possibility of a new calendar. What this study came up with was the **world calendar. Elizabeth Achelis** has been a leading supporter of this calendar in which the days of the month are the same every year. Holidays and birthdays fall on the same day of the week every year. Easter is always on Sunday, April 8. The world calendar has not been accepted yet. Some people feel that the world calendar doesn't show a living

260-day cycle circles

a. The 13 day numbers

b. The 20 day names

360 + 5 day circle

c. The 18 months of 20 days each, numbered 0–9, moving counterclockwise from the long line to the short line

Stone carving of a Mayan astronomer-priest from the temple in Copal, showing the date 6 Caban 10 Mol (July 1, 763 A.D.)

relationship with the rhythms of nature and the sky. The festivals and the seasons no longer shape the mood and course of the year; they are simply dates. Others feel that the calendar would make it much easier to serve religious, business, and community needs. Take a close look at the calendar yourself and see what you think.

THE WORLD CALENDAR

First Quarter

	S	M	T	W	T	F	S
Jan.	1	2	3	4	5	6	7
	8	9	10	11	12	13	14
	15	16	17	18	19	20	21
	22	23	24	25	26	27	28
	29	30	31				
Feb.				1	2	3	4
	5	6	7	8	9	10	11
	12	13	14	15	16	17	18
	19	20	21	22	23	24	25
	26	27	28	29	30		
March						1	2
	3	4	5	6	7	8	9
	10	11	12	13	14	15	16
	17	18	19	20	21	22	23
	24	25	26	27	28	29	30

Third Quarter

	S	M	T	W	T	F	S
July	1	2	3	4	5	6	7
	8	9	10	11	12	13	14
	15	16	17	18	19	20	21
	22	23	24	25	26	27	28
	29	30	31				
August				1	2	3	4
	5	6	7	8	9	10	11
	12	13	14	15	16	17	18
	19	20	21	22	23	24	25
	26	27	28	29	30		
Sept.						1	2
	3	4	5	6	7	8	9
	10	11	12	13	14	15	16
	17	18	19	20	21	22	23
	24	25	26	27	28	29	30

Second Quarter

	S	M	T	W	T	F	S
April	1	2	3	4	5	6	7
	8	9	10	11	12	13	14
	15	16	17	18	19	20	21
	22	23	24	25	26	27	28
	29	30	31				
May				1	2	3	4
	5	6	7	8	9	10	11
	12	13	14	15	16	17	18
	19	20	21	22	23	24	25
	26	27	28	29	30		
June						1	2
	3	4	5	6	7	8	9
	10	11	12	13	14	15	16
	17	18	19	20	21	22	23
	24	25	26	27	28	29	30*

*Leap-year day follows June 30 in leap years.

Fourth Quarter

	S	M	T	W	T	F	S
Oct.	1	2	3	4	5	6	7
	8	9	10	11	12	13	14
	15	16	17	18	19	20	21
	22	23	24	25	26	27	28
	29	30	31				
Nov.				1	2	3	4
	5	6	7	8	9	10	11
	12	13	14	15	16	17	18
	19	20	21	22	23	24	25
	26	27	28	29	30		
Dec.						1	2
	3	4	5	6	7	8	9
	10	11	12	13	14	15	16
	17	18	19	20	21	22	23
	24	25	26	27	28	29	30†

†Year-end day follows December 30 every year.

In this next project you can use all that you have learned about calendars to design one of your own. You may want to design a calendar that doesn't use the traditional 7-day week or 12-month year.

★ ★ ★ ★ ★ ★ ★ **Project 13: Designing Your Own Calendar** ★ ★ ★ ★ ★ ★ ★ ★

MATERIALS

13 sheets of drawing or painting-
   quality paper
pencil
ruler
drawing and painting supplies
magazines
fine-point felt-tip pens (several
   colors)

scissors
glue
hole punch
a copy of next year's calendar
almanac
yarn
access to a photocopier

PROCEDURE

1. Using your pencil and ruler, make a grid for 35 days (7 across and 5 down) with the names of the week at the top but no month name or dates. Make 12 photocopies of the grid. Photocopy onto the drawing or painting paper if you can. Otherwise glue the photocopies onto the paper.

2. Label each page with the name of the month. Use the copy of next year's calendar to fill in the dates.

3. Put all of the months in order, with the blank sheet on top. Punch three holes in the tops and one hole exactly in the middle of the bottom. Tie the pages together loosely with yarn so you can flip them.

4. Illustrate each month:

    a. Pick a color for each season and use it to shade the outer edges of the three months that are in that season.

    b. Check the almanac to find out the Moon phases and draw them on the days they occur.

    c. Write in the names of the major festivals of the year on the dates they occur. Include a drawing or symbol for each, if you wish.

    d. Write in important events (births, deaths, discoveries, etc.) on the dates they occur.

e. Illustrate the months using the blank page on the back of the calendar for the previous month. Cut out pictures from magazines, take your own photographs, or make drawings of things that happen during that month, either where you live or somewhere else in the world.

OBSERVATION

What else can calendars do for you besides simply recording dates? (For one thing, calendars make welcome gifts.)

READING MORE

Chase, William D. and Helen M. *Chase's Annual Events.* Chicago: Contemporary Books, published for each year.
Irwin, Keith G. *The 365 Days: The Story of Our Calendar.* New York: Thomas Y. Crowell, 1963.

Horsehead Nebula (*photo courtesy of Observatoire de Haute Provence*)

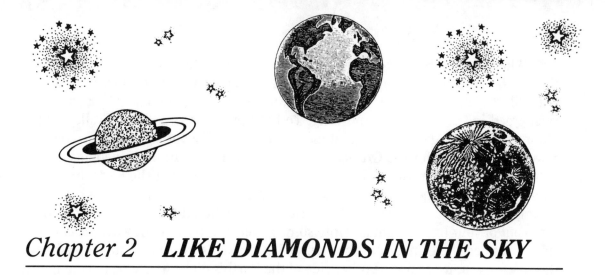

Chapter 2 LIKE DIAMONDS IN THE SKY

Section 1 THE ZODIAC

The Path of the Sun   The apparent path of the Sun passes across the celestial hemisphere and therefore in front of some of the stars on it. When the Sun is "high" in the summer, it passes in front of the higher stars; in the winter, the lower ones; and at the equinoxes, the middle ones. The star groups visited by the Sun remain the same year after year. The ancients recognized 12 of them, and because they alone are hosts to the visiting Sun, they have the honor of belonging to a unique collection of star groups. This band of stars is the **zodiac**. Stars that form a group we call a **constellation**.

The zodiac constellations form the backdrop against which the Moon and planets also travel. The orbits of the Moon and planets appear alongside the apparent path of the Sun. Each of these orbits crosses or intersects the Sun's path in two places. When the Moon reaches one of these places in its orbit at the same time that the Sun is at the other crossing point, we have an **eclipse**. For this reason, we call the Sun's path the **ecliptic**.

Zodiac comes from the Greek word ζωος (*zoos*) = living, since the Sun brings life.
Constellation comes from the Latin words *con* = with and *stella* = star. There are 12 zodiac constellations and 76 other constellations, 88 in all.
Ecliptic comes from the Greek word ἐκλειπω (*ekleipo*) = to leave out.

♈	Aries	April
♉	Taurus	May
♊	Gemini	June
♋	Cancer	July
♌	Leo	August
♍	Virgo	September
♎	Libra	October
♏	Scorpius	November
♐	Sagittarius	December
♑	Capricornus	January
♒	Aquarius	February
♓	Pisces	March

Armillary sphere, Middle Ages

Where do the Sun, Moon, planets, and stars go when they set and where do they come from when they rise? People once believed that the heavenly bodies entered the mountains in the west at night, traveled under the Earth, and reemerged in the east in the morning. To the Egyptians, a goddess swallowed the Moon at night and gave birth to it at moonrise. For the Egyptians, a boat carried the Sun across the sky; for the Greeks, a chariot carried the Sun. Soon people came to believe that the sky must be larger than half a sphere and that the Earth must also be more vast than one's own country. These ideas inspired the picture of the sky as a complete globe surrounded by stars. The stars set when the celestial sphere moved them out of your line of sight and into someone else's. In the same way, the celestial sphere carried the Sun across the sky, which caused sunrise and sunset. When it was day for you, those on the other side of the Earth's globe would be having night.

In this new picture, the zodiac was a band of constellations wrapped around the inside of the celestial sphere. The ecliptic passed along this band, right in its center. This next project will show you what the zodiac looks like as the celestial sphere moves it across the sky.

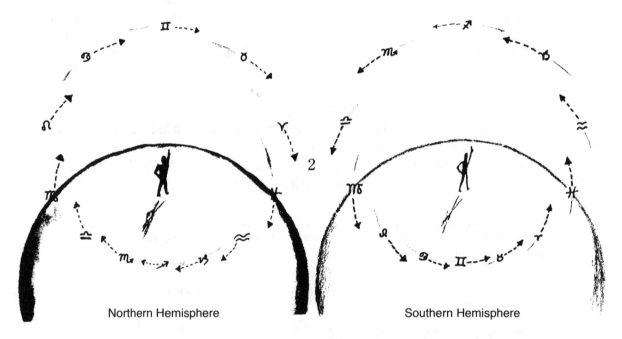

Northern Hemisphere   Southern Hemisphere

★ ★ ★ ★ ★ ★ ★ ★ **Project 14: Sketching the Daily Movement** ★ ★ ★ ★ ★ ★ ★ ★
of the Zodiac*

MATERIALS
zodiac grid   pen
seven sheets of tracing paper   colored pencils or crayons

*This project is adapted from *Sterne Schauen Dich An* by Heidi Keller-von Asten. Dornach: Verlag Walter Keller, 1973. Used with permission.

PROCEDURE

1. Place a sheet of tracing paper over the zodiac grid on the following page.

2. Draw the horizon line using a colored pencil or crayon. This line does not represent the whole Earth. It shows only the part you are on so don't draw it as a complete circle.

3. Draw yourself standing just below the horizon line so your feet are above the center point of all the concentric circles and your head is below the two concentric circles close together above the horizon line.

4. Write the symbol for Gemini at the top where the seventh circle crosses the vertical line.

5. Write the symbol for Sagittarius where the first circle meets the vertical line.

6. Write the symbol for Taurus on the right where the sixth circle crosses the line on the right of the vertical line and for Cancer on the left where the sixth circle crosses the line on the left of the vertical line.

7. Continue on in this way until you have written all the symbols as shown: Leo and Aries on the fifth, Virgo and Pisces on the fourth, right where the circle meets the horizon line. Libra and Aquarius go below the horizon line on the third circle and Scorpius and Capricornus on the second.

8. Draw little arrows from each constellation to the next, pointing counterclockwise. This is the daily east-to-west movement you saw in chapter 1. Label this drawing 1.

9. Make six more drawings, but each time you make a new chart, move each constellation counterclockwise to the next line on the grid. Don't change the constellations from the circles they are on, just imagine that the circles are moving, carrying the constellations to a new spot.

10. For the Southern Hemisphere, start with Sagittarius at the top, and draw all symbols as shown in the illustration. Your arrows should point *clockwise.*

11. Place all seven sheets in front of you and observe what has happened.

OBSERVATIONS

You have just made a record of the passage of the zodiac constellations in one 24-hour period. What has happened? The little figure of yourself is looking south into the daytime sky. Below the horizon line it is night. When a constellation is straight over your head, it is noon. Notice the difference between when Gemini is in the noon position and when Sagittarius is there. If the Sun is passing in front of the constellation Gemini, it will be straight overhead at noon, high in the sky, and it will be summer in the Northern Hemisphere. In the Southern Hemisphere, Gemini will be low in the sky, and it will be winter. In the Northern Hemisphere, when the Sun is "in" Sagittarius, it is at its lowest angle at noon rather than shining down directly on us. It will be winter. In the Southern Hemisphere Sagittarius will be high in the sky at noon, and it will be summer. The positions of the Sun at its midheight occur when the Sun is either in Pisces or Virgo. At these times we have our in-between seasons, spring and autumn.

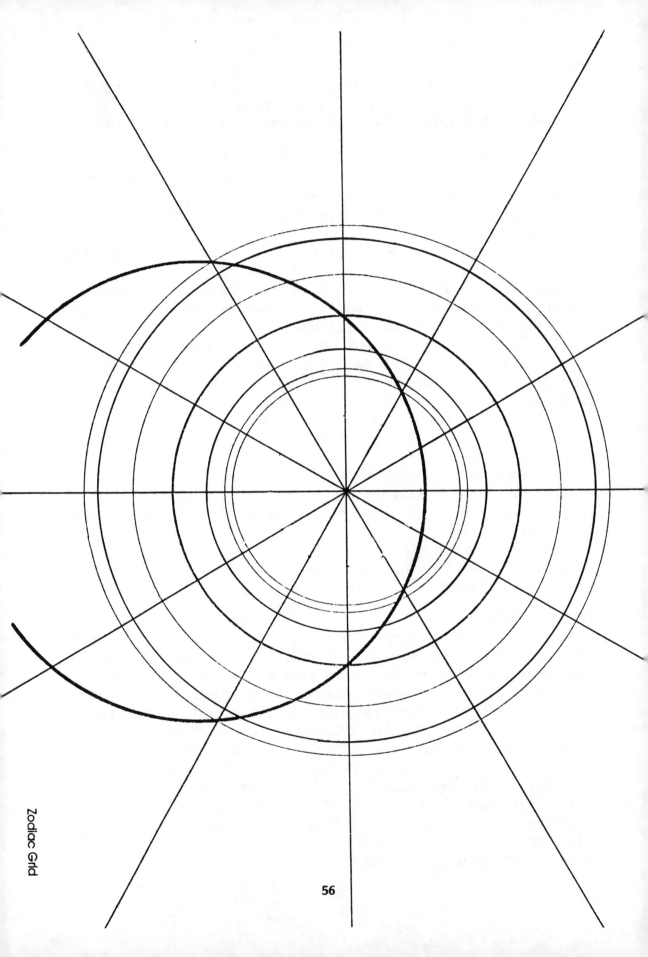

The Zodiac Constellations   Sometime before 3000 B.C., Akkadian astronomer-priests moved into Syria bringing with them their ideas of the celestial sphere and the zodiac. The Babylonians absorbed these ideas into their teachings and writings such as the Babylonian Tablets, the oldest written records we have. The Egyptians may have had a zodiac as early as 5000 B.C., although the earliest example we have is from 250 B.C. The Chinese zodiac is also quite ancient.

The Chinese zodiac

The constellations of the zodiac vary in size and brightness. Virgo is the largest; Cancer is the smallest. Leo and Taurus are the brightest; Cancer and Aquarius are the dimmest. Each constellation can just about fit into a space of 30°, or ¹/₁₂ of the complete circle around the inside of the celestial sphere. Thus, the Sun spends about one month (or ¹/₁₂ of a year) in front of each of these 12 constellations.

From your project you can see that the sphere of the heavens and the sphere of the Earth each have a northern half and a southern half. Both halves are equal. The line that divides them into two hemispheres (half spheres) is called the **equator**, which means *equal*. In chapter 3 you will find out how you can further divide and map the Earth and the sky.

The Earth's equator is in the middle of our globe. It is 90° from the north part of the world, which we call the **North Pole** and 90° from the south part of the world, which we call the **South Pole**. Imagine that these poles point to the north and the south of the celestial sphere, which also has a north and a south pole. **Polaris**, the North Star, marks the North Pole of the sky, and Octanis marks the South Pole. Constellations that travel in small circles around these poles are called **circumpolar constellations**. They never set, and you can always see them from your location. Ursa Major (which contains the Big Dipper) is a circumpolar constellation for most Northern Hemisphere observers, and Crux (which contains the Southern Cross) is a circumpolar constellation for most observers in the Southern Hemisphere. The illustrations in Projects 2 and 3 are of the circumpolar constellations.

Looking at Orion on the celestial equator

If you were on the opposite hemisphere, your view of Orion would appear upside down.

Circumpolar comes from the Latin word *circum* = around and the Greek word πολος (*polos*) = pivot around which something turns.

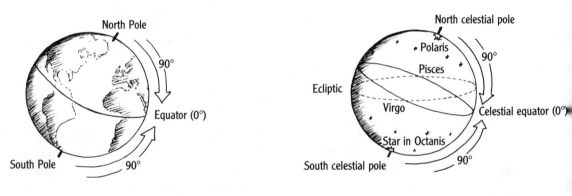

The Earth

The celestial sphere

If you move 90° from the polestars, you will find the **celestial equator**. Pisces and Virgo are on that part of the ecliptic that crosses the celestial equator. Gemini is north of the celestial equator, and Sagittarius is south of the celestial equator.

You can track the Sun and Moon in the zodiac by using the hands of a clock. Imagine that each number on the face of the clock is a zodiac constellation, and that they mark months instead of hours. The hour hand is the Sun, the minute hand is the Moon. In your clock model of the zodiac, it takes the Sun one hour (month) to go through one zodiac constellation and 12 hours (year) to go through all 12 zodiac constellations. How long does it take the Moon to do the same?

To help you understand the combined motions of the daily movement of the zodiac as the celestial sphere turns and the monthly or yearly movement of the Moon and the Sun in front of the zodiac, you can make a moving model of the zodiac.

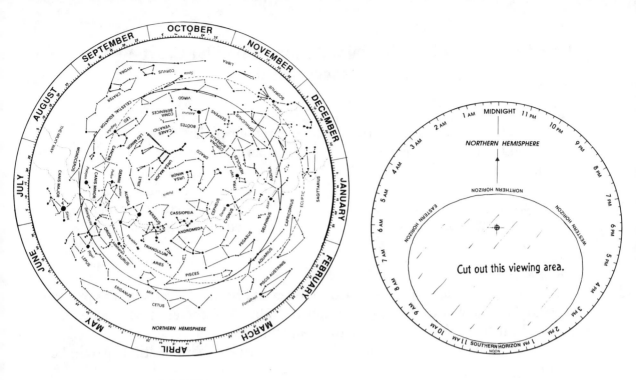

STAR CIRCLE

HORIZON CIRCLE

HORIZON CIRCLE

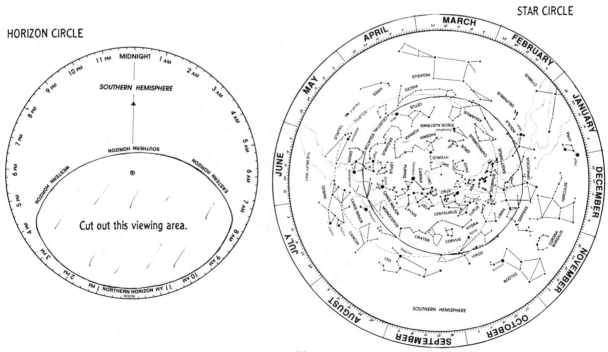

STAR CIRCLE

★ ★ ★ ★ ★ ★ ★ Project 15: Making a Moveable Star Chart ★ ★ ★ ★ ★ ★ ★
(Planesphere)

MATERIALS

star circles and horizon circles
  on the previous page
metal eyelet
scissors
2 clear plastic sheets
cardboard or stiff paper
glue

grease pencil
paper towel or rag
permanent ink felt-tip pens
access to photocopier
flashlight covered with paper bag
  or red plastic (or red cloth)

PROCEDURE

1. Photocopy and enlarge the star circles and horizon circles on the previous page to the size you want your planesphere to be. A diameter of 8¾ inches (22.2 cm) to 10 inches (25.4 cms) seems to be a popular size.

2. Glue the *star circles* back to back onto the cardboard or stiff paper and cut them out.

3. Cut out the *horizon circles* and remove the viewing areas.

4. Glue each *horizon circle* onto a separate plastic sheet.

5. Poke a hole through the center of all the circles and attach them as shown using the metal eyelet. *Make sure that the horizon circle for each hemisphere appears with the star circle for the same hemisphere.*

USING YOUR PLANESPHERE

TO RECOGNIZE THE CONSTELLATIONS

1. Use the covered flashlight so you can look at the planesphere without losing your night vision.

2. Line up the time (Standard Time) on the horizon circle with today's date on the star circle.

3. Hold the planesphere straight up and down in front of you with the direction of the horizon you are facing printed below the viewing area on the planesphere. The stars you see in the lower half of the planesphere will look like the stars you see in the sky in front of you.

TO VIEW THE MOON AND THE PLANETS

1. Find the ecliptic by facing the *southern* horizon if you live in the Northern Hemisphere.

2. Find the ecliptic by facing the *northern* horizon if you live in the Southern Hemisphere.

TO DETERMINE SUNRISE AND SUNSET

1. Set the horizon circle to noon for today's date. The Sun's position today will be on the ecliptic straight overhead.

2. Use the grease pencil to mark the Sun's position (or remember what star the Sun is near).

3. Turn the horizon circle until the Sun's position on the ecliptic for today's date touches the eastern horizon (for sunrise) or the western horizon (for sunset).

4. The horizon circle will now point to the time for today's sunrise or sunset.

OBSERVATIONS

You can mark the positions of the Sun, Moon, or planets with the grease pencil. Erase your marks with a paper towel or rag when you are finished observing. Use your planesphere to show why the longest day occurs in June and the shortest day occurs in December. You can also find what time of year and at what time of night you can see your favorite constellations.

Remember, we tell time by the position of the Sun, not the Moon.

Constellations and Signs   You may have heard the term **signs of the zodiac** and have wondered if they were the same as the **constellations of the zodiac**. They were the same once. In ancient Greece, spring began when the Sun reached the vernal equinox point. In those days, this point was in the constellation Aries. Today this point is in Pisces. What happened?

In its apparent yearly journey around the zodiac the Sun does not return to the exact place where it began the journey one year ago. The Sun stops a little short of a complete 360-degree passage around the zodiac by about 50 arc seconds. In 72 years, the Sun has fallen back in the zodiac by 1 degree. One degree in the sky is about the size of two full Moons side by side. The Babylonians gave each zodiac constellation the ideal boundaries of 30 degrees ($12 \times 30° = 360°$). In ancient recorded zodiacs spring began in the constellation Taurus. Since that time, the number of degrees the Sun has fallen back has been adding up. After 2,160 years the vernal equinox falls back one whole constellation. Later it appeared in Aries. By late Greek times, the vernal equinox point had entered Pisces. Today it is approaching the end of Pisces as it moves slowly toward Aquarius. This change to ever earlier constellations for the vernal point is the **precession of the equinoxes.**

Precession comes from the Latin word *praecedo* = to go before. We associate each period in history with the constellation in which the vernal equinox occurred. That is what people mean when they talk about the dawning of the Age of Aquarius.

March 21 now occurs in Pisces. The constellation Pisces that is visible to us in the night sky does not fit neatly into a boundary of 30 degrees as it did on the Babylonian charts. For these reasons, when people speak of the **signs** of the zodiac, they mean the ideal arrangement in which there are 12 equal zodiac constellations of 30 degrees each and the first point of Aries is the beginning of spring. This zodiac is also the one we use to map the Earth as you will see in the next chapter.

Notice that the names of the **signs** Scorpio and Capricorn are different from the **constellations** Scorpius and Capricornus. People sometimes use these names for the constellations.

Star Wisdom, Astrology, and Astronomy   Almost every civilization ancient and modern has practiced some form of **star wisdom.** Although it is barely remembered or understood, star wisdom is the original source for most seasonal celebrations, many national customs, and a number of words in several languages. Star wisdom is the great-grandmother of astronomy and the mother of astrology.

Astrology came about as a calculating and interpreting task of the priesthood of ancient cultures who became the official representatives of what was then known about star wisdom. These astronomer-priests considered time sacred: the time of birth, the time of death, the time of founding a city or beginning a battle. These times were sacred because the gods were present at all important events. The priests could detect the presence of the gods at human events by making a chart showing exactly how the signposts of the gods (the stars and planets) were arranged at any moment in the past or the future. This chart is a **horoscope.**

The chart of a horoscope is similar to the planesphere you made. Preparing such a chart required careful mathematical reckoning, an understanding of the sky, and a sensitivity to the information it revealed. The three wise men or Magi who visited the Christ child were astronomer-priests.

Casting a baby's horoscope in ancient Rome

Horoscope comes from the Greek word ὥρα (*hora*) = time and σκοπεω (*skopeo*) = to look at.
Magi comes from the Greek word μαγος (*magos*) = wise man, seer.

The astronomer-priests made the information they gathered from the stars available only to the king; the pharaoh; or in China, the emperor. It was very late in the history of astrology, around 400 B.C., that this information became available to the general public.

The practice of astrology spread from Babylonia and Egypt into Greece and the rest of Europe. People also practiced astrology in China, India, and Central America. Today astronomer-priests are not the only ones engaged in the ancient practice of astrology. Computers often prepare the charts that an astrologer interprets and that used to require considerable work to calculate. Many astrologers are no longer familiar with the night sky. Some astrologers, however, have helped advance the continued growth and relevance of their art and have helped many people understand their lives better in the process.

Astronomy is among the "things fit to be learned" according to the ancient Greek definition of mathematics. These "things fit to be learned" were **arithmetic** (numbering), **geometry** (measuring the Earth), **astronomy** (classifying the stars), **optics** (light), and **harmonics** (the theory of music and therefore sound).

Over the years astronomy has grown from being the daughter of astrology to become a separate scientific discipline that includes within it the other "things fit to be learned." As a science astronomy makes use of experiments, technology, and intelligent guesses called hypotheses and theories. Many astronomers no longer go out and look at the night sky. Much of their information comes to them from telescopes, cameras, and computers. Modern astronomy is concerned with

63

examining the physical nature of the objects in the universe to increase humanity's understanding of them. The work of astronomers has greatly advanced our knowledge of the physical makeup of our own planet and others.

READING MORE

Branley, Franklyn M. *Age of Aquarius*. New York: Harper and Row, 1979.

Knox, Richard. *Experiments in Astronomy for Amateurs*. New York: St. Martin's Press, 1977.

Section 2   CONSTELLATIONS

Stories in the Sky   By 270 B.C., people in Europe and the Middle East knew 44 constellations by specific names and two more that were unnamed. When knowledge of what lived behind the constellations faded from memory, the starry sky became a connect-the-dots puzzle. Naming the shapes you found depended on when and where you lived. In early Judaeo-Christian lands, people chose biblical names like Camelopardalis (the camel that brought Rebecca to Isaac) and Columba (Noah's dove). In Renaissance times, explorers brought back descriptions of new creatures from the Southern Hemisphere to name constellations such as Tucana (the Toucan) or Volans (the Flying Fish). People honored their leaders by naming stars after them: Scutum Scobiescianum (the shield of **John Scobiesci III**, king of Poland). Enlightenment France selected names from the tools of the arts and sciences: Pictor (the painter's easel) and Fornax (the chemist's furnace). **Augustin Delporte** (1844–1891) drew the boundaries of all the constellations.

In 1930 the International Astronomical Union (IAU) declared that no one could name any more constellations. The IAU would only recognize the names and boundaries of the 88 constellations known at that time. Astronomers still use this system of charting the constellations.

In early star maps, artists drew the constellations as you would see them on the *outside* of the celestial sphere instead of how they would look if you saw them from inside the celestial sphere. That is why their drawings appear backward from the view you have from Earth.

To find your way through the maze of constellations, you can group them into smaller sections. One way to group them is by seasons. The star charts on pages 67 through 70 show the constellations as they appear each season. Another grouping is to keep those constellations together that share a common story or origin. The lists that follow divide the constellations into six groups. Groups one through five contain the constellations whose stories come from the great myths and religions of Asia Minor, Egypt, Greece, and Rome. The sixth group contains all the constellations that people have added since classical times. Therefore, most of their names and shapes are from the imaginations of individuals rather than the stories of whole cultures. Most of them are also located in the skies of the Southern Hemisphere. The early inhabitants of Australia, New Zealand, South Africa, and Polynesia saw in those same skies their own star patterns long before the Europeans arrived and gave them the names we use now.

The constellation Leo, shown backward on old star maps

There are several familiar groups of stars in the sky that make shapes that are easy to recognize. These groups are not separate constellations; they are parts of one or more constellations. We call them **asterisms.** Here are some asterisms you can find in the night sky.

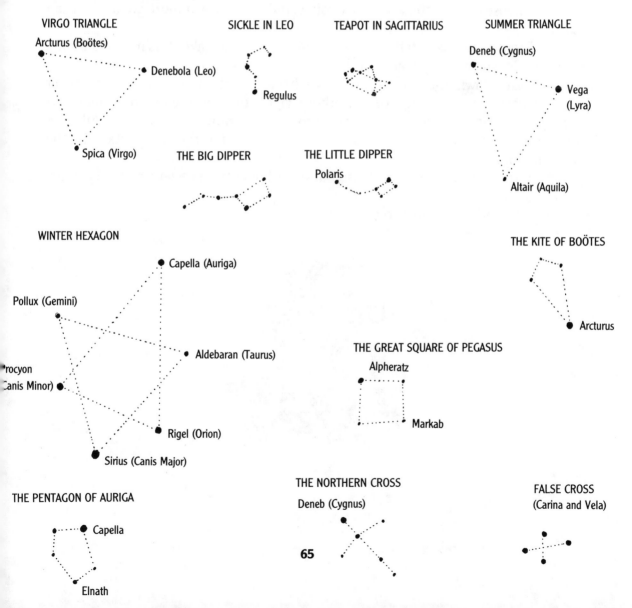

VIRGO TRIANGLE
Arcturus (Boötes)
Denebola (Leo)
Spica (Virgo)

SICKLE IN LEO
Regulus

TEAPOT IN SAGITTARIUS

SUMMER TRIANGLE
Deneb (Cygnus)
Vega (Lyra)
Altair (Aquila)

THE BIG DIPPER

THE LITTLE DIPPER
Polaris

WINTER HEXAGON
Capella (Auriga)
Pollux (Gemini)
Aldebaran (Taurus)
Procyon (Canis Minor)
Rigel (Orion)
Sirius (Canis Major)

THE KITE OF BOÖTES
Arcturus

THE GREAT SQUARE OF PEGASUS
Alpheratz
Markab

THE PENTAGON OF AURIGA
Capella
Elnath

THE NORTHERN CROSS
Deneb (Cygnus)

FALSE CROSS
(Carina and Vela)

65

★ ★ ★ ★ ★ ★ ★ ★ ★Project 16: Learning the Constellations ★ ★ ★ ★ ★ ★ ★ ★ ★

MATERIALS

star group charts in this book
star chart without connecting lines
   (in Sky Files)
colored paper (or gummed stars)
paste or glue

sheet of black or dark blue
   construction paper
colored pencil (white or yellow)
scissors

PROCEDURE

1. Choose the star group you can see in the night sky this month.

2. Study the constellations in the star group. Try to find them in the star chart that has no connecting lines. (see Sky Files in the back of this book).

3. Choose one constellation that you would like to learn more about. You can learn one a day.

4. Find out that constellation's story and information about its individual stars from the Constellations Catalog in the back of this book.

5. Paste down the main stars of each constellation onto the black sheet of paper using small squares (or any other shape) cut from the colored paper. Use the lightest colors of paper. (You can also used gummed stars.) You could use one color for the main stars and a different color for the other stars in the constellation.

6. Write the name of each constellation at the bottom of your picture using a light-colored pencil.

7. Make other star pictures from the same group.

Aquarius

OBSERVATION

Look for your constellations in the night sky and as many other constellations as you can see from your latitude.

Star Groups   The numbers after each constellation refer to its alphabetical rank in the Constellations Catalog in Sky Files at the back of this book. (Also in Sky Files see the list of Gods and Goddesses.) An alpha (α) by a star name indicates it is the brightest star in the constellation.

1. THE ANDROMEDA GROUP (visible October–January)

ANDROMEDA (1) Andromeda
CASSIOPEIA (18) Cassiopeia
CEPHEUS (20) Cepheus
PERSEUS (63) Perseus
PEGASUS (62) The Winged Horse
CETUS (21) The Sea Beast
ERIDANUS (36) The River
TRIANGULUM (80) The Triangle
ARIES (7) The Ram
PISCES (66) The Fishes

The Andromeda Group

2. THE OSIRIS GROUP (visible January–March)

ORION (60) Orion
LEPUS (48) The Hare
CANIS MAJOR (14) The Great Dog
CANIS MINOR (15) The Lesser Dog
TAURUS (78) The Bull
AURIGA (8) The Charioteer
GEMINI (38) The Twins
CANCER (12) The Crab

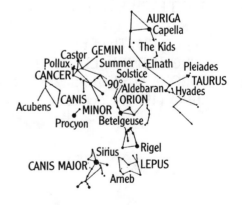

The Osiris Group

3. THE HARNESSING AND HARVESTING GROUP
(visible March–June)

LEO (46) The Lion
HYDRA (42) The Sea Serpent
CORVUS (28) The Crow
CRATER (29) The Cup
VIRGO (86) The Young Woman
BOÖTES (9) The Ploughman
URSA MAJOR (83) The Great Bear
URSA MINOR (84) The Lesser Bear
THE SHIP ARGO
   VELA (85) The Sail
   PUPPIS (68) The Stern
   CARINA (17) The Keel

The Harnessing and Harvesting Group

4. THE HERO AND HEALER GROUP (visible May–September)

OPHIUCHUS (59) The Serpent Holder
SERPENS (76) The Serpent
SCORPIUS (73) The Scorpion
CENTAURUS (19) The Centaur
LUPUS (50) The Wolf
ARA (6) The Altar
SAGITTARIUS (72) The Archer
HERCULES (40) Hercules
DRACO (34) The Dragon
CORONA BOREALIS (27) The Northern Crown
CORONA AUSTRALIS (26) The Southern Crown
LIBRA (49) The Scales

The Hero and Healer Group

5. THE BIRDS AND SEA DWELLERS GROUP (visible August–November)

CYGNUS (31) The Swan
AQUILA (5) The Eagle
SAGITTA (71) The Arrow
LYRA (52) The Lyre
DELPHINUS (32) The Dolphin
PISCIS AUSTRINIS (67) The Southern Fish
AQUARIUS (4) The Watercarrier
CAPRICORNUS (16) The Sea-Goat

The Birds and Sea Dwellers Group

6. THE MODERN AND SOUTH POLAR GROUP

LYNX (51) The Tiger
LEO MINOR (47) The Lesser Lion
VULPECULA (88) The Little Fox
SCUTUM (75) The Shield
CANES VENATICI (13) The Hunting Dogs
MONOCEROS (55) The Unicorn
MUSCA (56) The Fly
APUS (3) The Bird of Paradise
CRUX (30) The Southern Cross
COMA BERENICES (25) Berenice's Hair
OCTANS (58) The Octant
PICTOR (65) The Painter's Easel
DORADO (33) The Goldfish
RETICULUM (70) The Net
HYDRUS (43) The Water Monster
TUCANA (82) The Toucan
PAVO (61) The Peacock
TRIANGULUM AUSTRALE (81) The Southern Triangle
CIRCINUS (23) The Compasses
CHAMAELEON (22) The Chameleon
VOLANS (87) The Flying Fish
PYXIS (69) The Mariner's Compass
ANTLIA (2) The Air Pump
NORMA (57) The Level
TELESCOPIUM (79) The Telescope
MENSA (53) The Table

Modern and South Polar Group (Part I)

SEXTANS (77) The Sextant
SCULPTOR (74) The Sculptor
LACERTA (45) The Lizard
FORNAX (37) The Chemist's Furnace
HOROLOGIUM (41) The Clock
COLUMBA (24) The Dove
CAELUM (10) The Engraving Tool
CAMELOPARDALIS (11) The Camel
EQUULEUS (35) The Foal
MICROSCOPIUM (54) The Microscope
GRUS (39) The Crane
INDUS (44) The American Indian
PHOENIX (64) The Phoenix

Modern and South Polar Group (Part II)

Hydra takes up the most area of all the constellations. Which constellation do you think takes up the least?

When he was seven years old, the British astronomer **Sir Patrick Moore** set himself the task to learn one new constellation every night. He soon discovered that the task was not as hard as it may sound and that it only took a few minutes each clear evening. What the job did require was patience. As you become more familiar with the constellations, they will become like old friends who come back to visit every year. You will find yourself looking forward to their arrival and the season that brings them. Use the star chart on the next page to help you recognize any constellation in the sky at any time of the year.

READING MORE

Allen, Richard Hinkley. *Star Names: Their Lore and Meaning.* New York: Dover, 1963.
Raymo, Chet. *365 Starry Nights: An Introduction to Astronomy for Every Night of the Year.* Englewood Cliffs, NJ: Prentice-Hall, 1982.

SEPTEMBER
Sun in Virgo,
Sept. 16–Oct. 30
Astrological Sign Libra,
Sept. 22–Oct. 23

OCTOBER
Sun in Libra,
Oct. 30–Nov. 22
Astrological Sign Scorpio,
Oct. 23–Nov. 22

NOVEMBER
Sun in Scorpius,
Nov. 22–Dec. 17
Astrological Sign Sagittarius,
Nov. 22–Dec. 21

DECEMBER
Sun in Sagittarius,
Dec. 17–Jan. 20
Astrological Sign Capricorn,
Dec. 21–Jan. 20

JANUARY
Sun in Capricornus,
Jan. 20–Feb. 16
Astrological Sign Aquarius,
Jan. 20–Feb. 19

FEBRUARY
Sun in Aquarius,
Feb. 16–Mar. 11
Astrological Sign Pisces,
Feb. 19–Mar. 20

MARCH
Sun in Pisces, Mar. 11–Apr. 18
Astrological Sign Aries,
Mar. 20–Apr. 19

APRIL
Sun in Aries, Apr. 18–May 13
Astrological Sign Taurus,
Apr. 19–May 20

MAY
Sun in Taurus, May 13–June 21
Astrological Sign Gemini,
May 20–June 21

JUNE
Sun in Gemini, June 21–July 20
Astrological Sign Cancer,
June 21–July 22

JULY
Sun in Cancer, July 20–Aug. 10
Astrological Sign Leo,
July 22–Aug. 22

AUGUST
Sun in Leo,
Aug. 10–Sept. 16
Astrological Sign Virgo,
Aug. 22–Sept. 22

STAR CHART FOR THE WHOLE YEAR*

Magnitudes
- 0
- 1
- 2
- 3
- 4
- 5
- 6

Month	Visibility
AUGUST	February's daytime sky
JULY	January's daytime sky
JUNE	December's daytime sky
MAY	November's daytime sky
APRIL	October's daytime sky
MARCH	September's daytime sky
FEBRUARY	August's daytime sky
JANUARY	July's daytime sky
DECEMBER	June's daytime sky
NOVEMBER	May's daytime sky
OCTOBER	April's daytime sky
SEPTEMBER	March's daytime sky

*Visibility is given for 9:00 P.M. For 8:00 P.M., choose the date on the chart that is 2 weeks (½ month) earlier. For 10:00 P.M., choose the date on the chart that is 2 weeks (½ month) later.

Section 3 *INDIVIDUAL STARS*

What makes a constellation are its individual stars. Many of them have their own stories and particular qualities. Many stars have their own names given to them by Arab astronomers hundreds of years ago. These names describe the position of the star in the picture of the constellation.

Remember how important the star Sirius was for the Egyptians? Other stars were just as important for other peoples. Arcturus in Boötes and Aldebaran and the Pleiades in Taurus were favorite planting-time reminders. "When the Pleiades, children of Atlas first arise, begin your harvest: when they leave the skies, plough" (Hesiod, 8th century B.C.).

Some stars, including the North Star, are well-known orientation markers for navigators (see chapter 3). The Constellations Catalog, appearing in Sky Files in the back of this book, tells briefly about the names of the brighter stars.

The Apparent Brightness of Stars   As night falls, the brightest stars come out first. The term for the brightness of a star is **stellar magnitude**. This term refers to the brightness of a star and not its size. This idea came from the Greek astronomer **Hipparchos** (190–120 B.C.). Hipparchos set out to catalog the brightness of all the stars he could see (about 1,028 of them). He categorized all the stars by their brightness, calling the brightest stars the **first magnitude**. There were about 21 of these first magnitude stars, including Sirius (Canis Major) and Castor (Gemini). Stars that were half as bright as these Hipparchos called **second magnitude**. These included Polaris (Ursa Minor) and most of the stars in the Big Dipper and Cassiopeia. Those stars half as bright as the second magnitude stars Hipparchos called **third magnitude** and so forth until he reached the limit of his vision at the sixth magnitude.

In 1603 the Bavarian astronomer **Johann J. Bayer** published his own star catalog in which he used the Greek alphabet to name the stars in order of brightness. The brightest star was α *(alpha),* the next brightest was β *(beta),* and so on. After the Greek letter came the constellation name in Latin written in the possessive, or *genitive,* case. The name for Sirius would be **Canis Majoris**, meaning that Sirius *belongs* to Canis Major. Star catalogs often abbreviate the names of constellations. Canis Major becomes **C Ma**, for example. A complete listing of the genitive case endings and abbreviations for *all* constellations and a listing of the Greek letters for the stars appears in the Constellations Catalog Sky Files at the back of this book.

The German astronomer **Friedrich Argelander** (1799–1875) and his associates used an interesting method in preparing the great star catalog, the *B.D. Catalogue.* (*B.D.* is the abbreviation of the German title of the catalog, *Bonner Durchmusterung [The Bonn Catalogue]*). You can use the same method that Argelander used to measure the brightness of stars. Compare the apparent brightness of a star in a constellation that has two or more nearby stars whose magnitudes you already know. A star that appears somewhat fainter than a neighboring star of 2.4 magnitude and somewhat brighter than another neighboring star of 2.6 magnitude you will say has a magnitude of 2.5.

Make sure that

(a) the star you are measuring and the star with the known magnitude are at about the same height above the horizon, (b) the known magnitude stars are as close as possible to the star you are measuring, and (c) one of the known magnitude stars is somewhat brighter and the other is somewhat dimmer than the star you are measuring.

Do you think this method is very accurate? Check your findings with the Constellations Catalog in Sky Files at the back of this book.

A helpful magnitude guide for people in the Northern Hemisphere is to use the stars in the head of the constellation Draco (The Dragon) and the stars in Ursa Major. For those in the Southern Hemisphere, Centaurus contains stars from − 0.27 to 5. Look at the Star Chart for the Whole Year (earlier in this chapter). Also consult the Constellations Catalog in Sky Files for magnitudes in these constellations.

In this next project you can make a handy device to measure magnitudes just by looking at a star through it.

★ ★ ★ ★ ★ ★Project 17: Making a Brightness Measuring Tool*★ ★ ★ ★ ★ ★

MATERIALS

a piece of cardboard, 2 × 10 inches   glue
   (5 × 25 cm)   scissors
a pencil   ruler
a small coin
five clear cellophane strips 1¼
   inches (3 cm) wide

PROCEDURE

1. Divide the cardboard into five 2-inch (5 cm) sections.
2. Trace a circle in the center of each section by drawing around the coin.
3. Cut out the five circles.
4. Glue a strip of cellophane onto the cardboard so that it covers all five of the holes. Be sure to keep the glue away from the cellophane where the holes are.
5. Glue the second cellophane strip onto the first strip so that it only covers four of the holes in the cardboard.
6. Glue the third cellophane strip onto the second strip so that it only covers three of the holes in the cardboard, and so on until the last strip only covers one hole in the cardboard.
7. Write the number *1* in the space on the cardboard next to the hole with the five layers of cellophane.
8. Write the number *2* in the space on the cardboard next to the hole with the four layers of cellophane, and so on until the last hole, *5,* with only one strip.

USING YOUR BRIGHTNESS MEASURING TOOL

Look at a star through your brightness measuring tool. If you can see the star through the hole marked *1,* it is a first magnitude star. If you can see a star through

*This project is adapted from *The Night Sky Book* by Jamie Jobb. Boston: Little, Brown, 1977. Used with permission.

the hole marked *2*, that star is a second magnitude star, and so on down to the fifth magnitude.

OBSERVATION

How accurate is this tool compared to the method used by Argelander?

Today we still measure the magnitude of stars using Hipparchos' system. The **apparent visual magnitude** of a star is how bright it appears to us when we look at it from Earth. We have had to modify Hipparchos' system since we have found stars brighter than his brightest stars of the first magnitude. Following his magnitude scale, the brightest stars now range from 0 magnitude to −1 (see the Brightest Star list in Sky Files). The dimmer stars still range down to sixth magnitude and lower (see the Constellations Catalog in Sky Files). As you move from one magnitude to the next, the brightness increases or decreases by 2½ times.

Visibility of Stars   Side (peripheral) vision can make stars visible for some people down to sixth and seventh magnitudes, but those below fourth magnitude will usually disappear when you stare directly at them. They will come back out once you look slightly away from them. This happens because the parts of your eye that are most sensitive to dimly lit objects are found in greater numbers away from the center of your eye. If you want to see a dim star, don't look *at* it, look *around* it and it will pop into view.

Peripheral comes from the Greek word περι *(peri)* = around. See chapter 5, section 2 for more about the eye and how you see.

You may not always be able to see even the sixth magnitude stars. When the Moon is bright, your eyes will not become very dark-adapted, so you will not see these stars. Nor will you see them if there are any bright streetlights nearby. A slight haze will also hamper visibility, even on a moonless night.

Starwatchers everywhere have been concerned about the "shrinking sky" made smaller and dimmer by street lamps, city lights, and smog. One famous research observatory has closed because of this. Many people are joining the efforts of starwatchers to control pollution and the amount of vision-hampering light. The International Astronomical Union met in 1988 to discuss the problem and make recommendations.

If the night is really dark and clear, you have from 1,500 to 2,000 stars to choose from. If you had binoculars, you could see many thousands. With a small telescope, almost half a million. If you took a photograph through a large professional telescope, you could find millions upon millions of stars. On a dark, clear night, try counting the stars in a small area of the sky. (See chapter 5, sections 2 and 3 for more about telescopes and cameras.)

This next project has three parts. Do all three if you can to learn some important characteristics about the brightness of stars that will help you understand how astronomers measure distances to stars.

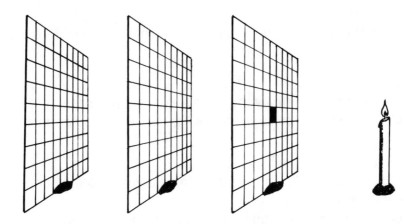

★ ★ ★ ★ ★ ★ **Project 18: Comparing Brightness and Distance*** ★ ★ ★ ★ ★ ★

MATERIALS

a sheet of dark glass or plastic   pencil
two lamps   ruler
one 25-watt light bulb   scissors
two 60-watt light bulbs   clay
one 75-watt light bulb
three cardboard sheets, 9 × 9 inches
    (23 × 23 cm)

PROCEDURE

PART 1

1. Place two lamps with 60-watt bulbs next to each other on a table and turn them on. From a distance of several feet, observe the two lamps through the dark glass.

2. Move one of the lamps about a foot closer to you. Look at both lamps through the dark glass.

3. Place one of the lamps at least halfway between you and the other lamp.

OBSERVATION

By looking at both lamps through the dark glass at different distances, what do you notice about their brightness compared to one another?

PART 2

1. Place a lamp with a 25-watt bulb on a table next to a lamp with a 75-watt bulb. Turn the lamps on and observe them through the dark glass from a distance of several feet.

*This project is adapted from *Science Experiments for the Space Age* by Sam Rosenfeld. Irvington, NJ: Harvey House, 1972.

2. Place the 25-watt bulb closer to you so that when you look through the glass both lights appear equally bright.

OBSERVATION

If you had no way of knowing the actual brightness and distance of each bulb and could see them only through the dark glass, would you be able to tell which one was closer?

PART 3

1. Draw 81 1-inch (23 cm) squares (nine across and nine down) on each of the three cardboard sheets.

2. Cut out the middle square from one of the sheets of cardboard.

3. Stand up each cardboard sheet using a piece of clay as a base. Arrange the cardboard sheets so that they are exactly 6 inches (15 cm) from each other.

4. Set a lamp exactly 6 inches (15 cm) from the first cardboard sheet so that its light is directly in line with the hole in the middle of the cardboard.

5. Notice how bright each square inch of light is on the first cardboard sheet. Now look at the second cardboard sheet. Notice that the light that passed through the 1-inch square hole has spread out on the second cardboard sheet so that it covers four squares. Compare the amount of brightness (intensity) of a square inch of light on the first cardboard sheet with the intensity of a square inch of light on the second cardboard sheet.

6. Remove the second cardboard sheet so that the light passing through the hole in the first cardboard sheet lights up the third cardboard sheet. Notice that the light has spread out even more and covers about nine squares.

7. Move the third cardboard sheet another 6 inches away. Upon how many squares does the intensity of the light *decrease* as you *increase* the distance of the cardboard sheet from the light?

OBSERVATIONS

If you didn't know that both light sources were the same distance from you, which would seem closer? If you didn't know the brightness of each light source and could only see them through the dark glass, would you be able to tell which was closer?

If two stars that give off different quantities of light were the same distance from the Earth, would they appear equally bright in the sky?

If two stars appear to be equally bright in the sky, does it mean that they are the same distance from the Earth?

Why does a star appear dimmer the farther away it is?

Absolute Magnitude

When you describe the brightness of the stars based on what you see, you are referring to its **apparent visual magnitude**. The apparent visual magnitude does not necessarily tell you which light source is actually brighter, which one is dimmer, which one is really closer, and which one only appears to be closer. In order to compare the true brightness of stars, you would need to have them side by side so that when you viewed them, they would each be the same distance from you. This is what you did when you looked at the lamps. To put stars side by side, you need to set up an imaginary location in space, determine that location's distance from the Earth, and calculate how bright a star would be if it was shining from there. Every star whose brightness you want to measure will be measured as if it was at this one location. The distance from Earth to this location becomes the standard distance for comparing the magnitudes of all stars.

Astronomers have chosen the distance of about 190 trillion miles (306 trillion km) away. They use the apparent visual magnitude of a star to calculate how bright it would be if you viewed it from this distance. The brightness of a star at that distance is its **absolute magnitude**. The apparent magnitude of the Sun is -26.8. The apparent magnitude of Sirius is -1.43, which means that to our eyes, the Sun appears to be 14,000 million times brighter than Sirius. The absolute magnitude of the Sun is 4.8, while Sirius is 1.3. According to this measurement, the Sun is only about $1/25$ as bright as Sirius. At a distance of 190 trillion miles, the Sun would barely be visible to the naked eye. This means that the Sun is really 21 times dimmer than Sirius.

The distance for absolute magnitude = 10 parsecs (see chapter 7, section 1). The symbol for absolute magnitude = M, for apparent magnitude = m.

In the third part of the last project, you noticed that the farther the square inch of light traveled, the more it spread out and the dimmer it became in the process. On the second cardboard sheet the light covered four squares. Each square received a quarter of the light. On the third cardboard sheet (3 units of 6 inches, or 23 cm) the light covered nine squares. Each square received one-ninth of the light. When you double the distance from the lamp, the light on each square is a quarter of the original amount of light; when you triple the distance, the light is one-ninth. Do you see the pattern that is emerging? The bottom number in the fraction is the distance times itself. Twice as far away = 2×2 or 4. Each square is a quarter of the original amount of light. You can see that the change in the amount of light is the opposite of the distance the light changes multiplied by itself. The way the law of distance states this is that *light varies inversely as the square of the distance*. This is the **inverse square law**.

The Color of Stars   Not all of the stars shine with the same bright white light. Stars actually glow with hues from white to yellow, blue, orange, and red. These colors depend on the star's size, temperature, and distance from us.

The colors of stars, like their apparent magnitude, will differ according to the sensitivity of your own eyes. For real stellar beauty, look for Sirius, Algol, and Arcturus. Not only are they bright and colorful, but their colors flash and glisten like sparkling gems.

The Constellations Catalog in Sky Files lists the colors for all of the visible stars. Here is a short list of the brighter ones. See how many of these you can find in the night sky. (You can find out more about the colors and temperatures of stars in chapter 7, section 2.)

- **Red**—Betelgeuse (α Orionis), Antares (α Scorpii)
- **Reddish**—Aldebaran (α Tauri); μ Cephei is the reddest
- **Orange**—Arcturus (α Boötis), Pollux (β Geminorum)
- **Yellow**—The Sun, Capella (α Aurigae)
- **Yellowish**—Procyon (α Canis Minoris)
- **White**—Canopus (α Carinae)
- **Greenish**—β Librae
- **Blue-White**—Sirius (α Canis Majoris), Vega (α Lyrae), Rigel (β Orionis), Spica (α Virginis)
- **Bluish**—Altair (α Aquilae)
- **Blue**—Mintaka (δ Orionis)

THE STAR

Twinkle, twinkle, little star,
How I wonder what you are!
Up above the world so high,
Like a diamond in the sky.

When the blazing sun is gone,
When she nothing shines upon,
Then you show your little light,
Twinkle, twinkle all the night.

Then the traveler in the dark
Thanks you for your tiny spark;
He could not see which way to go,
If you did not twinkle so.

In the dark blue sky you keep,
And often through my curtains peep,
For you never shut your eye
Till the sun is in the sky.

As your bright and tiny spark
Lights the traveler in the dark,
Though I know not what you are,
Twinkle, twinkle, little star.

—Ann and Jane Taylor

READING MORE

Burnham, Robert, Jr., *Burnham's Celestial Handbook.* New York: Dover, 1978.
Ronan, Colin. *The Practical Astronomer.* New York: Macmillan, 1981.

Section 4 THE MILKY WAY

NAGACORK'S GOODBYE*

And the old man Nagacork, the Creator, went on a long walkabout to see all the tribesmen, the birds, animals, fish, and reptiles.

And as Nagacork traveled through all the different countries of the tribes he sang:

"Allo, allo, allo, allo, allo, cha nallah, wirrit, burra burra, cubrimilla, cubrimilla. Bo bo!" This means, "Oh well, all you people who belong to me have changed into men, animals, birds, reptiles, fish, sun, moon, and stars. I go now. I go forever. You will see me no more. But all the time I will watch about you."

And the tribesmen say that you can see the old man Nagacork lying among the stars. His lubral [woman] is lying near him with one arm behind her head. And the tribesmen say that the stream of stars that the white man calls the Milky Way is the smoke of Nagacork's campfire drifting across the night.

Stories of the Milky Way   Seeing the **Milky Way** with its wisps of faint stars suggests far distances and the clouds of mystery between us and what lies beyond. It is not surprising that for so many centuries people have seen the Milky Way as a path or road from Earth to the heavens.

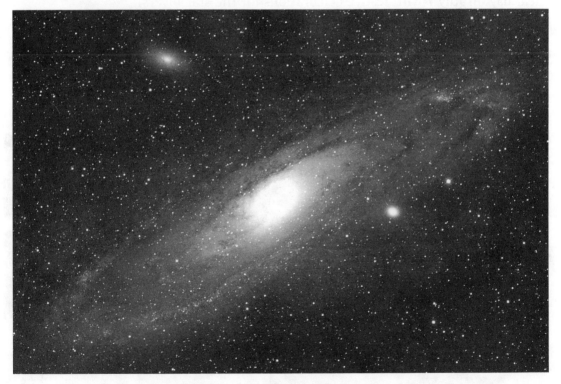

The Andromeda Galaxy (M31) (*photo courtesy of Observatoire de Haute Provence*)

*From *Aboriginal Myths and Legends: Age-old Stories of the Australian Tribes.* Selected by Roland Robinson. London: Paul Hamlyn, 1969.

The name **Milky Way** comes to us from the ancient Greeks. Their title for this band of star dust was Γαλακτικος or Γαλαξιας (*galactic* or *galaxy*) = milk. The Romans called it *Via Galactica*, which means "Milky Way." The milk is from the breast of the goddess Hera (Juno), spilled while nursing the infant Herakles (Hercules).

According to a French tale, the stars in the Milky Way are lights held by angel spirits to show mortals the way to heaven. The Native American Algonquins believed that this was the path of souls leading to the villages in the Sun. As the spirits travel along the pathway, we see their blazing campfires as bright stars.

An old Chinese tale tells of the Spinning Maiden (the star Vega in Lyra) and the Herd Boy (the star Altair in Aquila) who live on opposite sides of the Milky Way, the "Silver River of the Sky." The lovers are free to cross the Silver River of the Sky by a bridge made of magpies and visit each other only on one night of the year: the 7th day of the 7th month. If it rains on that day, the birds will look for shelter and not form the bridge. The Spinning Maiden and the Herd Boy must spend another year separated from each other. The people on Earth send their wishes skyward for a clear day on July 7 with festive celebrations for the star lovers.

Arabic and African traditions tell of a heavenly path strewn with straw. In Mexico the Milky Way is the "Sister of the Rainbow." In Nepal the Milky Way is the "Sky River."

This is our galaxy, and all the stars, planets, the Sun, and the Moon dwell and move within it. In this next project you can make a glittering picture of what the Milky Way looks like from Earth.

★ ★ ★ ★ ★ ★ **Project 19: Creating a Picture of the Milky Way** ★ ★ ★ ★ ★ ★

MATERIALS

map of the Milky Way (above)
black or dark blue paper or poster
   board
pencil

silver glitter
glue
paper cup

PROCEDURE

1. Go outside and look at the Milky Way before making a picture of it. The best times of year for this are January, July, and November.

2. Sketch the outline of the Milky Way lightly onto the black paper using a pencil and the map on the previous page. Although the exact outline of the Milky Way is unclear, its general shape is thicker in some areas and thinner and broken in others.

3. Put glue on all the areas where the stars of the Milky Way are.

4. Sprinkle silver glitter onto the glued areas, being very careful to put less glitter around your outline so the stars appear to fade out around the edges of your illustration as they do in the night sky.

5. Spread the glitter around using your finger or a stick.

6. Clean up while your picture is drying. When it is completely dry, tip the paper sideways and collect the extra glitter in a paper cup so you can use it again.

OBSERVATIONS

In which part of the Milky Way do you think there are the most stars? Look at chapter 7, section 3 for another view of our galaxy.

Early Ideas About the Universe When you look at the Milky Way, you see the border of our galaxy. We live inside it surrounded by planets and stars. What does our neighborhood look like? How is it arranged? The ideas, beliefs, and theories that attempt to explain the layout of our universe come from as many places and times as the constellation stories. We call such an explanation a **cosmology.**

Cosmology comes from the Greek word κοσμος (*cosmos*) = order, and therefore the **universe,** because of its perfect arrangement. *Cosmology* = layout, or the way the universe looks. How the perfect order of the universe came to be is the subject of **cosmogony.** *Cosmogony* = beginnings or the origin of the universe. You pronounce the *g* in cosmogony like the *g* in beginnings. In the adjective *cosmological,* you pronounce the *g* like a *j.*

The early cosmological ideas of the universe were thought pictures, meant to create an image or impression rather than a map. Here are some thought pictures based on the cosmological stories of several ancient cultures:

India The great serpent biting its own tail surrounds the universe. Resting on the coils of the great serpent is the tortoise, symbol of force and creative power. On the back of the tortoise stand four elephants supporting the lower region, the Earth (Mt. Meru) and the upper region (shown by a triangle, symbol of creation). Considering all of the various religions and philosophies in India, there is an impressive collection of cosmological models.

China The sky was like an upside-down bowl turning around the polestar. The sky carried with it the other stars fixed to the inner surface of the bowl. The Earth was a cube with the four seas coming from the four cardinal directions and lapping at its sides.

Babylonia   A wall supported the dome of the sky under which all the celestial bodies lived. The oceans surrounded the flat Earth, which rested on a water chamber.

Egypt   The star-covered sky goddess Nut arched over Earth to form the universe. Below lay her leaf-covered husband Geb, the Earth. Shu, the god of the air, floated in between his two parents Nut and Geb. A later Egyptian thought picture showed the universe in the shape of a rectangular box. Egypt was at the bottom center surrounded by great mountain ranges. Four tall peaks supported the flat sky. Gods stood on top of the sky and lowered the stars through holes in the sky when it was night. Night came when the Sun, traveling on the sky river through the mountains, went behind a mountain peak.

Greece   The Greeks had the biggest collection of cosmological ideas that have survived in the Western world. Astronomy was required study for all learned people, so it was a subject much on the minds and in the hearts of all the great thinkers. Instead of a single Greek picture of the universe, there are many. Let's look at three of them.

The Pythagorian Brotherhood   The Pythagorean Brotherhood followed the teachings of the great mathematician and philosopher **Pythagoras**, the best-known demonstrator of the theorem for measuring right triangles. The brotherhood experimented with geometrical shapes. For their experiments they chose those shapes that had equal sides and equal angles. We call these shapes **regular polygons**. They include the **triangle** (3 sides, 3 angles), the **square** (4 sides and angles), the **pentagon** (5 sides and angles), the **hexagon** (6 sides and angles), and so on.

Polygon comes from the Greek words πολι (*poly*) = many and γουυ (*gonu*) = the knee or angle.

The Pythagoreans used these polygons to make regular solids in which all edges, faces, and angles were equal. We call these solids **regular polyhedra**. Four triangles connected together form a pyramid called a tetrahedron (τετρα [*tetra*] = 4). Six squares connected together make a cube, which is a hexahedron (ἑξα [*hexa*] = 6). Two tetrahedra placed together form an eight-faced figure called an octahedron (ὀκτα [*octa*] = 8). The Egyptians had known about these three shapes since ancient times.

Polyhedra comes from the Greek words πολι (*poly*) = many and ἑδρα (*hedra*) = base.

The Pythagorean Brotherhood had the pentagram for its symbol. By putting together five **equilateral triangles** they discovered they could construct a hollow, dome-shaped figure whose open base formed a perfect pentagon. The next step was to combine more equilateral triangles in order to make a solid. After much experimenting, the brotherhood found that they could use two of the dome-shaped figures, one for the top and one for the bottom. For the sides they constructed a band of 10 equilateral triangles based on an old Babylonian pattern. It took exactly 20 triangles to construct this new regular polyhedron, so we call it an **icosahedron** (έικοσα [*eikosa*] = 20).

Equilateral comes from the Latin words *equí* = equal and *lateral* = side.

In their further explorations of regular solids and pentagons, the Pythagoreans put together a flower-petal form composed of a central pentagon with five others around it, one on each of the five sides. By connecting the edges of the outer pentagons, they created a hollow, dome-shaped form. Placing this dome on top of another upside-down dome produced a completely new regular polyhedron, the **dodecahedron**, made from the faces of 12 pentagons (δωδεκα [*dodeka*] = 12).

The great geometer **Euclid** devoted the last 13 books of his famous work *Elements* almost entirely to these solids, including proof that only five of them existed. Today there are still only five regular polyhedra: tetrahedron, hexahedron, octahedron, icosahedron, and dodecahedron. As Lewis Carroll (1832–1898), the author of *Alice in Wonderland,* once commented, they are "provokingly few in number."

To the Pythagoreans (and later to Plato) these five solids contained the building blocks of all creation: earth, air, fire, and water. The cube, which stands so firmly on its base, imitates the solidity of the Earth. The octahedron, which rotates freely when held by its two opposite ends, resembles the freely moving air. The tetrahedron, which has the smallest volume for its triangular size, is related to the tongues of fire. The almost spherical icosahedron is connected with water. The dodecahedron, with its 12 faces, mirrors so much of the cosmos (the 12 signs of the zodiac, the 12 months, etc.) that it was clearly the image of the whole universe.

All five of these remarkable shapes can fit inside a sphere and inside each other. You can draw them within a circle, within themselves, and within each other. Many examples of these regular polyhedra appear in nature. Over the years people have called them the "dice of the gods" and the "Platonic solids." In this next project you can make your own models of these beautiful shapes.

★ ★ ★ ★ ★ ★ Project 20: Making Models of the Platonic Solids ★ ★ ★ ★ ★ ★

MATERIALS

tape	scissors
drinking straws	toothpicks or small dowels
string	glue or modeling clay
ruler	paint
stiff paper	access to a photocopier
pencil	

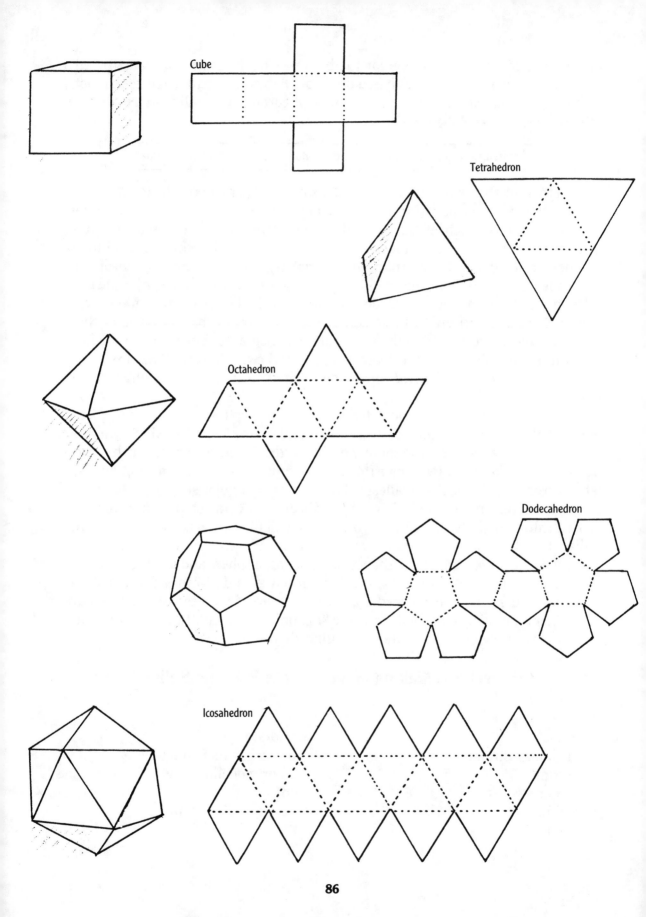

Cube

Tetrahedron

Octahedron

Dodecahedron

Icosahedron

86

PROCEDURE

In this project you can construct models that will let you see either the edges or the faces of each solid.

EDGES

1. Cut equal lengths of drinking straws, toothpicks, or small dowels 2 inches (5 cm) or longer.
2. Thread string through straws and tie them together to form six squares and 31 triangles. You can also make these shapes by attaching toothpicks or dowels together with glue or modeling clay.
3. Tie, attach, or glue squares together to form a cube. Use triangles to make a tetrahedron, octahedron, and icosahedron.
4. Attach or glue toothpicks or dowels together into 12 pentagons. (You can't make a small dodecahedron using straws.)
5. Attach or glue pentagons together to make a dodecahedron.

FACES

1. Photocopy the drawings of the "unfolded" shapes and glue them onto stiff paper.
2. Cut out the shapes.
3. Fold as necessary along the dotted lines of the polygons.
4. Tape the solids into place.
5. Paint your completed Platonic solids.

OBSERVATIONS

To find out what **Johannes Kepler** (1571–1630) decided to do with these shapes, see chapter 5, section 1.

Aristotle (384–322 B.C.)   Aristotle was a friend of Plato and a student at Plato's Academy for 20 years. Aristotle founded the Lyceum in Athens. **Alexander the Great** was one of his students.

Using the observable world as his starting point, Aristotle wrote about and analyzed the work of those who had previously contributed their ideas about the structure of the universe. He reasoned that

1. the Earth was round because the stars appeared at different heights from your horizon if you traveled north or south.
2. the Earth was at the center of the universe.
3. the Sun was farther from the Earth than the Moon because during a solar eclipse, the Moon completely blocked the Sun.
4. the crescent phases of the Moon proved that the Moon was between the Earth and the Sun.

In this project you can make a working model of the universe according to Aristotle.

SPHERE OF THE FIXED STARS
THE PRIME MOVER
THE REALM OF THE GODS, GODDESSES, AND THE ELECT

★ ★ ★ ★ ★ ★ ★ ★ ★ ★ **Project 21: Making a Moveable Plan** ★ ★ ★ ★ ★ ★ ★ ★ ★ ★
of the Earth-Centered Universe

MATERIALS

polar graph paper (from Sky Files at
    the back of this book)
stiff paper or posterboard
sheets of clear plastic (from report
    covers)
drawing and painting supplies
glue (household or contact cement)

scissors
paper fastener
large nail
ruler
access to a photocopier
almanac

PROCEDURE

1. Cut the paper or posterboard into a circle with a 12-inch (30½ cm)
diameter. Find the center of the circle and mark it.

2. Draw 10 concentric circles beginning with a 2-inch (5 cm) diameter, then
a 3-inch (8 cm) diameter, and so on until 11 inches (28 cm).

3. Color the first seven circles lightly following the list below:

    a. 2-inch (5 cm)—purple (the Moon)

b. 3-inch (8 cm)—white (the Sun)
c. 4-inch (10 cm)—yellow (Mercury)
d. 5-inch (13 cm)—green (Venus)
e. 6-inch (15 cm)—red (Mars)
f. 7-inch (18 cm)—orange (Jupiter)
g. 8-inch (20 cm)—blue (Saturn)

4. Photocopy the polar graph paper and use it to mark 360° around the outside edge of the 8-inch (20 cm) circle with 0° on the top.

5. Divide the 9-inch (23 cm) circle into 12 30° sections for the 12 zodiac constellations. Label each section with its zodiac symbol starting with Pisces on the right and moving counterclockwise so that Gemini is at the top and so on. You might want to draw a picture for each constellation.

6. Title the 10-inch (25½ cm) circle *"The Fixed Stars."* Draw stars around the rest of the circle. Color the space in between the stars blue.

7. Title the 11-inch (28 cm) circle *"The Prime Mover"* and color the circle purple.

8. Title the 12-inch (30½ cm) circle *"The Realm of the Gods"* and color the circle gold.

9. Measure and cut out seven circles from the plastic sheets with the same diameters as the colored paper circles and mark the center of each plastic circle.

10. Label the outer edges of each plastic circle with their planetary symbols. Use paint or write the symbol on small pieces of paper and glue them onto the plastic circles.

11. Put the plastic circles together in order, largest on the bottom, and place them on the paper circles, lining up the center marks. Make a large hole with the nail through the center of all the plastic circles and the posterboard.

12. Put a paper fastener through the hole with the head under the posterboard and the metal prongs on the plastic side. Spread the prongs out so that they lie flat but do not prevent any of the plastic circles from turning freely, especially the smallest one on the top.

13. Draw a circle 1 inch (2½ cm) in diameter on a separate piece of posterboard. Divide it into four sections with a cross in the center. In each section draw a representation of one of the four elements: earth, air, fire, and water. This circle is the Earth. Glue or tape the Earth onto the prongs of the paper fastener.

14. Illustrate or decorate the rest of your model as you see fit. It needs to be beautiful, but not cluttered. Decorate only the Earth itself and the area beyond Saturn, nowhere in between.

OBSERVATIONS

You now have a "model of a model." Arrange the daily positions of the Sun, Moon, and planets from an almanac, ephemeris, or astronomical calendar. Use your model to demonstrate the daily east-to-west movement of the stars in one direction while the planets move west to east in their yearly paths.

The Ptolemaic Picture   Claudius Ptolemy (ca. 90–165 A.D.) lived and worked nearly 200 years after Hipparchos. During that time there had been a serious decline in Greek astronomy. Ptolemy's first task, as Aristotle's had one been, was to review the work of those who had come before him. Ptolemy lived in Alexandria long after Alexander the Great had established a great library and world center there.

Ptolemy. Relief by Giotto and Andrea Pisano on the Campanile of the Duomo in Florence, Italy

Ptolemy's two important books were *Tetrabiblos* (on planetary influences and astrology) and *Syntaxis Mathematica* (called in Arabic *Al Majisti* or the *Almagest*, meaning "The Greatest"). In these books Ptolemy (a) used a star-measuring instrument for accurately determining the positions of the stars, Moon, and planets and (b) extended the star catalog of 1,022 stars, correcting older star positions to compensate for changed positions due to the precession of the equinoxes.

History remembers Ptolemy for the following statement and how he chose to put it into practice:

> We believe that the object which the astronomer must strive to achieve is this: to demonstrate that all the phenomena in the sky are produced by uniform and circular motions. Having set ourselves the task to prove that the apparent irregularities of the five planets, the Sun and Moon can all be represented by means of uniform circular motions because only such motions are appropriate to their divine nature, we are entitled to regard the accomplishment of this task as the ultimate aim of mathematical science based on philosophy and is to be considered a great thing, very difficult and as yet unattained in a reasonable way by anyone. —from the *Almagest*

Ptolemy's solution to the problem of how to "save the appearances" of uniform circular motion was to use mathematical explanations. He refined a theory introduced around 150 B.C. by Hipparchos that stated that the planets traveled along their orbits on orbiting circles called **epicycles**. Ptolemy's mathematical model included

40 circles and epicycles, which enabled anyone to accurately predict planetary positions. Ptolemy's system was the generally accepted world view for the next 1,400 years.

READING MORE

Diggins, Julia E. *String, Straightedge and Shadow: The Story of Geometry.* New York: Viking, 1965.

Tauber, Gerald. *Man's View of the Universe: Evolving Concepts of Astronomy from Babylonian Times to Present.* New York: Crown, 1979.

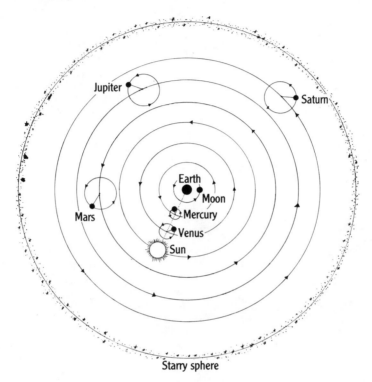

Ptolemy's system, showing the Earth in the center and the planets traveling around in smaller circles (epicycles) on their orbits

Chapter 3   *MEASURING THE SKY*

Section 1   MAPPING THE SKY

The Celestial Sphere   When Hipparchos and Ptolemy compiled their star catalogs, they had several ways of telling other watchers of the stars exactly where each star in the catalog could be found in a sky full of millions of stars. One way was to say how far a star was above the horizon and how far it was from a fixed position somewhere in the sky. If they wanted to point out a planet in the sky, they could say where it was located on the ecliptic. The catalog readers could also determine a star's position at some particular distance from one of the two poles of the celestial sphere. To find the star or planet, you would need to know how far it was from the poles and how far along the celestial equator. Finding exact positions was simply a matter of tracking down where the imaginary lines of the measurement of up and down crossed those that measured the distances from side to side.

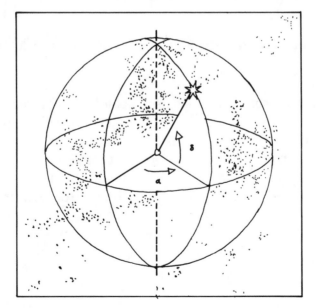

When two roads cross each other, we call the crossing point an **intersection**. On maps, these intersecting lines of measurement are **coordinates**. Coordinates form a grid on which you can pinpoint the object you are trying to locate. In the next project you can make a model of the celestial sphere that will help you see how the ancients imagined the universe.

Intersection comes from the Latin words *inter* = between and *sector* = one who cuts.
Coordinates comes from the Latin words *co* = together with and *ordo* = a row or line.

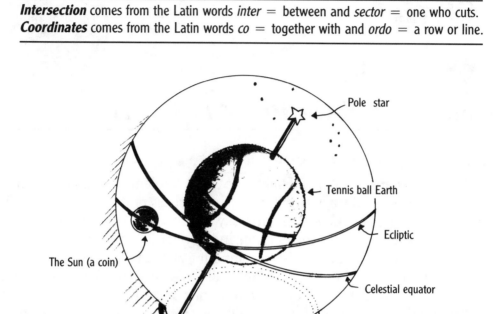

★ ★ ★ ★ ★ **Project 22: Making a Model of the Celestial Sphere** ★ ★ ★ ★ ★

MATERIALS

clear glass globe (from a light fixture)
tennis ball
knitting needle
three rubber bands
protractor
lamp
scissors
gummed stars

paints, or colored felt-tip pens (of various colors, particularly orange and blue)
grease pencil
modeling clay
thick cardboard (from a grocery box)
tape
small coin

PROCEDURE

1. Draw a map of the Earth on the tennis ball, using paints or felt-tip pens.

2. Put a rubber band around the middle for the equator. Color it blue with a felt-tip pen.

3. Push the knitting needle through the north and south poles of the tennis ball *Earth*.

4. Cut a piece of thick cardboard the same size as the opening on the glass globe.

5. Mark the top center of the glass globe with the grease pencil. Put the protractor inside the globe and mark the outside of the globe at a point 23½° below the top mark. Glue a star on this spot. This is the *polestar*.

6. Reach inside the globe and place a small ball of modeling clay where the star is.

7. Put a rubber band around the globe from the top to the bottom. Use this rubber band and the protractor to find and mark 23½° near the bottom of the globe. Place another rubber band on the outside of the globe 90° below the top mark. Color this rubber band orange with a colored marking pen. This is the *ecliptic*.

8. Mark the solstice and equinox points and indicate the month names for each.

    a. **Summer Solstice**—where the ecliptic is farthest north (above) the celestial equator.

    b. **Autumnal Equinox**—where the ecliptic crosses the celestial equator, moving counterclockwise around the celestial sphere from the Summer Solstice point.

    c. **Winter Solstice**—where the ecliptic is farthest south (below) the celestial equator.

    d. **Vernal Equinox**—where the ecliptic crosses the celestial equator, moving counterclockwise around the celestial sphere from the Winter Solstice point.

9. Move the rubber band on the outside of the glass globe so that it lines up with the rubber band on the tennis ball. Color this rubber band blue just like the one on the tennis ball. This is the *celestial equator*.

10. Remove the tennis ball Earth. Push the knitting needle through the thick cardboard circle so that the needle stays lined up with the 23½° line. Put the tennis ball Earth back on the knitting needle. Tape the cardboard in place.

11. Mark the circumpolar stars using the grease pencil.

12. Place a coin (the *Sun*) under the orange rubber band to show the different seasonal positions of the Sun.

13. Shine the light through the celestial sphere onto the Earth from each solstice and equinox position.

14. Turn the knitting needle so that if you were on the Earth you would

experience day and night: the Earth would turn clockwise if you are looking at the North Star, counterclockwise if you are looking at the Southern Cross.

OBSERVATIONS

How does the amount of sunlight and darkness compare at different times of the year where you live? How does it compare at other places on the Earth? Is there any place that receives sunlight all the time? Is there any place that receives no sunlight?

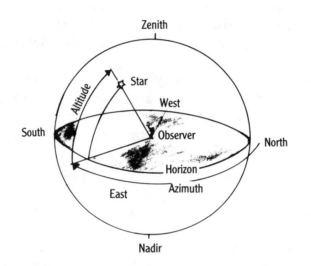

The horizon system

The Horizon System   Start with the horizon. Find your meridian. Remember, the meridian is the north-south line in the sky overhead. The point on the meridian directly overhead (90° above the horizon) is the **zenith**. The point directly below you on the other side of the world is the **nadir**.

Zenith comes from the Middle English spelling *senyth* of the Arabic word *samt* = direction above the head.
Nadir comes from the Arabic word *nazir* = opposite.

To find the coordinates of a star, first measure the star's height above or below the horizon. Use the meridian or another vertical circle like it drawn around the celestial sphere, crossing through the zenith and nadir and passing through the star you are measuring. The height of the star on this vertical line in degrees above or below the horizon is the **altitude**. Since the altitude of the zenith is 90° above the horizon, 90° minus the altitude of a star will give you the number of degrees from the star to the zenith.

> **Altitude** comes from the Latin word *altitudo* = height or elevation.

The other coordinate is the distance from the north point on the horizon eastward (clockwise) along the horizon to the vertical circle that passes through the star. You measure this in degrees from 0° to 360°. This is the **azimuth**.

> **Azimuth** comes from the Arabic word *as-sumut* = the way, direction.

When it comes to finding coordinates using just your eyes, it is easier to come up with an estimate of the altitude and azimuth than it is to use the other coordinate systems. In this next project you can make a simple degree-measuring device.

★ ★ ★ ★ ★ ★Project 23: Measuring Degrees Between the Stars★ ★ ★ ★ ★ ★ (Star Bow)

MATERIALS

yard- or meterstick
twine
dowel, ¾ inch (2 cm) × 2 feet (61 cm)

saw
hammer
nail

PROCEDURE

1. Cut the yardstick down to 2 feet or the meterstick down to 61 centimeters.
2. Nail the dowel to the center of the measuring stick.

97

3. Tie both ends of the measuring stick with twine to form a bow. The string of the bow should be 2 inches (5 cm) from the center of the measuring stick.

USING YOUR STAR BOW

Put the end of the dowel on your cheekbone and beside your nose, just below your eye. Look down the dowel at the measuring stick and aim at a group of stars. Line two stars up with the marks on the measuring stick. Read how far apart the stars appear on the stick, then divide that number by 2 to find how many degrees apart the stars are.

OBSERVATION

Your star bow can work for planets, the moon, and objects on Earth. *Never use it to look at the Sun!*

The Ecliptic System   Ptolemy and those before him generally used the ecliptic system. The ecliptic system uses the path of the Sun or the ecliptic as its starting point for measuring. Imagine each of the 360° around the ecliptic as a point where a huge circle around the celestial sphere crosses the ecliptic. Zero degrees on the ecliptic is the circle that passes through the **first point of Aries,** the place where the vernal equinox occurs. This is also the place where the ecliptic crosses the celestial equator. This place is 0° **celestial longitude.** Celestial longitude tells you how far away east or west an object is from 0°. **Celestial latitude** tells you how far above or below the ecliptic an object is. As described earlier, the precession of the equinoxes means that today the ecliptic crosses the celestial equator in Pisces. We still call this crossing place the first point of Aries.

Longitude comes from the Latin word *longitudo* = length.
Latitude comes from the Latin word *latitudo* = width.

PLOTTING STARS USING THE ECLIPTIC COORDINATE SYSTEM

The constellation Leo as it appears in the night sky   The constellation Leo as it appears on a grid with the ecliptic as the center

To indicate celestial latitude above the ecliptic, you write the word *north* (N) or a plus sign (+). To indicate celestial latitude below the ecliptic, you use the word *south* (S) or a minus sign (−). To write parallels of longitude, you use the Greek letter λ in front of them. Parallels of longitude start with 0° at the first point of Aries and move eastward along the ecliptic forming 12 groups of 30° each. Parallels of latitude have the Greek letter β in front of them starting with 0° at the ecliptic.

Using the grid showing the constellation of Leo, fill in the coordinates for the stars listed on the chart below.

Star	λ	β
α		
β		
γ		
δ		
ε		
ζ		
η		
θ		
λ		
μ		
ο		

λ is the Greek letter for *l* in our word *longitude.*

The Equatorial System   The equatorial system uses the celestial equator as its reference point. It is the 0° marker like the ecliptic was in the ecliptic system. In the equatorial system you measure positions above and below the celestial equator in degrees up to 90°, which is the celestial pole. This distance is the **declination.** You measure declination north of the celestial equator from 0° to N 90° (+ 90°). South of the equator you measure declination from 0° to S 90° (− 90°). Declination resembles the celestial latitude in the ecliptic system.

The east-west coordinate in the equatorial system that is similar to celestial longitude is the **right ascension.** You measure it along the celestial equator in degrees or time eastward from the vernal equinox. There are 24 major divisions in the 360° of right ascension. Each division is equal to 15° and is also equal to 1 hour of time. This is how far (space) the sky moves as it turns in 1 hour (time). You found this out when you measured the star trails in chapter 1. As you noticed from your measurement of sidereal time, 1° of arc is equal to 4 minutes of time. Ninety degrees minus the declination of a star gives its distance to the celestial pole. A star changes its altitude or its distance from the horizon, but it does not change its declination. Its distance above the celestial equator always stays the same.

As a result of the precession of the equinoxes the position of the vernal equinox moves slightly every year. Since this is the starting point for the equatorial system, the precession means that over the years declinations and right ascensions of all the stars will shift gradually. The stars stay in their same places in the sky. The grid we use to map them changes. That means that approximately every 50 years astronomers must adjust their star charts to keep them precise. They calculate new right ascension and declination positions that are accurate for a particular year or **epoch.** This book uses the epoch 2000 for its star charts, which means the star positions are accurate for the year 2000. The last remeasuring occurred in the year 1950.

> ***Epoch*** comes from the Greek word ἐποχη (*epoche*) = fixed point in time.

Parallels of *right* *a*scension or hour angles have the Greek letter α or the abbreviation **R.A.** in front of them. Parallels of declination have the Greek letter δ or the abbreviation **Dec.** in front of them.

Look at the star chart on the preceding page and fill in the coordinates of right ascension and declination.

Star	α	δ
α		
β		
γ		
δ		
ε		
ζ		
η		
θ		
λ		
μ		
ο		

Equatorial system coordinates

> The letter α, which stands for right ascension, is the Greek letter alpha, the first letter of the Greek alphabet. It stands for the *a* in our term *right ascension*. The letter δ is delta, the Greek letter for *d* in our word *declination*.

How do these coordinate measurements compare with those using the ecliptic coordinate system? In the next project you can do what many astronomers have done and plot your own star chart.

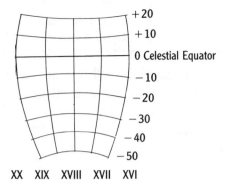

+20
+10
0 Celestial Equator
-10
-20
-30
-40
-50

XX XIX XVIII XVII XVI

★ ★ ★ ★ ★ ★ ★ ★ ★ ★ ★ **Project 24: Mapping Stars** ★ ★ ★ ★ ★ ★ ★ ★ ★ ★ ★
(Equatorial Coordinate System)

MATERIALS

star chart grid (at top of this box)   pen or pencil

PROCEDURE

1. Plot a star map using the star chart grid and the coordinates given in the list below. Your map should accurately show

a. the positions of all stars listed, including their Greek letter names,

b. the names of the constellations, and

c. the location of the ecliptic and the positions of the Sun on it, showing the dates for each position.

STAR POSITIONS

No.	Star	α		δ		No.	Star	α		δ	
1	α Sct	18	35	−8	14	18	η Sgr	18	17	−36	45
2	β Sct	18	47	−4	44	19	λ Sgr	18	27	−25	25
3	γ Sct	18	29	−14	33	20	σ Sgr	18	55	−26	17
4	δ Sct	18	42	−9	03	21	τ Sgr	19	06	−27	40
5	α Ser	15	44	+6	25	22	α Cr A	19	09	−37	54
6	δ Ser	15	34	+10	32	23	δ Cr A	19	08	−40	29
7	η Ser	18	21	−2	53	24	θ Cr A	18	33	−42	18
8	ξ Ser	17	37	−15	23	25	η Cr A	18	48	−43	40
9	α Oph	17	34	+12	33	26	α Sco	16	29	−26	25
10	β Oph	17	43	+4	34	27	β Sco	16	05	−19	48
11	ζ Oph	16	37	−10	34	28	δ Sco	16	00	−22	37
12	η Oph	17	10	−15	43	29	ε Sco	16	50	−34	17
13	κ Oph	16	57	+9	22	30	θ Sco	17	37	−42	59
14	γ Sgr	18	05	−30	25	31	κ Sco	17	42	−39	01
15	δ Sgr	18	20	−29	49	32	λ Sco	17	33	−37	06
16	ε Sgr	18	24	−34	23	33	π Sco	15	58	−26	06
17	ζ Sgr	19	02	−29	52						

SUN POSITIONS

Date	α		δ	
Nov. 7	14	46	−16	02
Nov. 17	15	27	−18	47
Nov. 27	16	09	−20	58
Dec. 7	16	52	−22	31
Dec. 17	17	36	−23	19
Dec. 27	18	20	−23	22
Jan. 6	19	04	−22	37
Jan. 16	19	48	−21	08
Jan. 26	20	30	−18	58

OBSERVATIONS

How does this system compare with the others for accuracy and your ability to read it?

The Chinese astronomer-priests practiced a pole-oriented astronomy. In this book you will be using the equatorial system since it is the one that people generally use in astronomy today.

The Galactic System   If you want to locate an object on or beyond the Milky Way, you can use the galactic system of coordinates. It is similar in some ways to the equatorial system. Instead of the equator of the celestial sphere, the galactic system uses the line that marks the middle of the Milky Way or the "equator" of the galaxy. The "equator" of the galaxy is the **galactic plane** or **galactic circle**. It is 90° above and below the galactic poles. You measure **galactic longitudes** eastward along the galactic plane from the point where it crosses the celestial equator. This occurs at 18 hours, 44 minutes according to the equatorial system. You measure galactic latitudes north (+) or south (−) of the galactic plane toward the galactic poles. The galactic plane is inclined 62° from the celestial equator. The north pole of the galaxy is in the constellation Coma Berenices; the south pole is in the constellation Sculptor. People use galactic coordinates only in the three-dimensional study of the universe. You can look into this kind of measurement further in chapter 7, section 3.

Locating Positions and Measuring Degrees   Since you can't see any of the coordinate grids that are in the sky, you need to find ways to help you locate positions and measure degrees.

Locating the Celestial Equator   The following stars are on the celestial equator. The first season is for the Northern Hemisphere, the second for the Southern Hemisphere.

Spring/ γ in Virgo   α in Sextans   ι in Hydra   δ in Monoceros
Autumn η in Virgo   β in Sextans
              ζ in Virgo
Summer/α in Aquarius
Winter   ζ in Aquarius
Autumn/ λ in Pisces   α in Aquarius
Spring   κ in Pisces   ζ in Aquarius
                                  η in Aquarius
Winter/   δ in Orion   δ in Cetus
Summer δ in Monoceros   10 in Taurus

Locating the Ecliptic   The following stars are on or near the ecliptic. The first season is for the Northern Hemisphere, the second for the Southern Hemisphere.

Spring/   β in Virgo   α (Spica) It is not as close to the ecliptic as the other
Autumn   stars in Virgo, but it is easier to find.

              η in Virgo
              λ in Virgo
Summer/β in Scorpius   θ in Capricornus
Winter   π in Sagittarius
Autumn/ λ in Aquarius   ε in Pisces
Spring   ζ in Pisces
Winter/   δ in Gemini   δ in Cancer
Summer η in Gemini   α in Leo
              μ in Gemini
              (between the Pleiades and Hyades in Taurus)

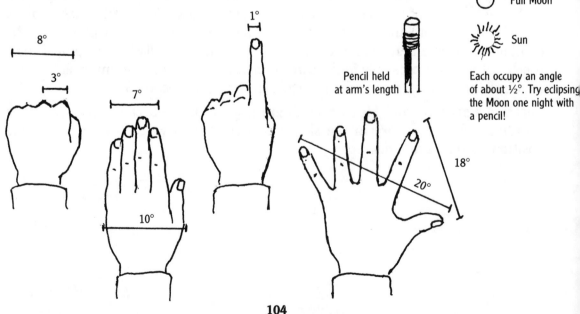

8°

3°

7°

1°

10°

Pencil held
at arm's length

18°

20°

○ Full Moon

Sun

Each occupy an angle
of about ½°. Try eclipsing
the Moon one night with
a pencil!

104

Although all of these stars may not be listed in the Constellations Catalog, you can find them (unnamed) on a star chart near the celestial equator.

Measuring Degrees with Your Hand   Hold your hand out at arm's length. Remember that these measurements are approximate and depend on the size of your hand. Compare these measurements with the size of the Moon, whose disk takes up ½°.

NightStar   The newest and most practical kind of star map is **NightStar**, an invention of **Bruce King**, an engineer and guitar maker from New Zealand. When Bruce was 12 years old, a friend pointed out the star Alpha Centauri. Twenty years later King decided to make a star map that looked and acted like the sky dome. It took 15 years to realize his dream. NightStar is a soft, moveable star map that you can easily adjust to match what the sky looks like for any place and any time in the world without distorting any of the constellations.

NightStar, a new kind of star map

READING MORE
Hirsch, S. Carl. *The Globe for the Space Age.* New York: Viking, 1963.
Rand McNally. *The Rand McNally New Concise Atlas of the Universe.* Chicago: Rand McNally, 1974.

Section 2   MAPPING THE EARTH
Map Coordinates   You have seen how people charted the sky using coordinate systems. Since the Earth is round like the celestial sphere, some of the same problems and solutions exist when you try to map it.

The words **map** and **chart** describe the materials people first used to make them. Map comes from the Latin word *mappa* = cloth. Chart comes from the Latin word *charta* = paper. Throughout history people have drawn maps on birch bark, blocks of wood, animal skins, iron, and clay. Today we usually use the word *map* when we are showing positions on the land (like a road map). Charts usually show positions in the sea or sky (like "charting the seven seas" and the star charts in this book).

Maps usually begin with a small area with your location as the central point. On some maps there is an arrow that points out, "You are here." That is the main task of a map: to indicate where you are and to show others how to get there.

The Jewish astronomer Masha Allah from the eighth century measures a globe. (*Etching by Albrecht Durer, De Scientia Motus Orbis. From* Space Time Infinity *by Charles Phillips, © Smithsonian Institution.*)

To map their country of many tiny islands, the Polynesians displayed the patterns of waves around the islands. The natives of the Marshall Islands used sticks made of narrow strips from the center ribs of palm leaves. They tied these sticks together with coconut fiber cords. To show where the islands were, the natives attached shells or coral at the crossing points of the sticks. The sticks themselves represented the places where the waves driven by the trade winds met the wave crests formed by breakers near the shore. These maps helped the Marshall Islanders find islands they couldn't see. To feel the effect of the waves, the navigators would lie down in their canoes, pointing their boats toward the more active waves that led toward the shore.

For their maps, the native North Americans drew pictures of what you would see on your way from one place to another.

Because the Nile River flooded every year, washing away most of the boundary markers, the ancient Egyptians had to resurvey their land and remap it every year.

The ancient Greeks gave us the first map of the entire world that we know of. This map was the work of **Anaximander** (ca. 600 B.C.). Through the work of another Greek, we have the first accurate measurement of the size of the Earth.

Geography in Greek means "Earth writers (or describers)" from the Greek words γεο (*geo*) = earth and γραφος (*graphos*) = to write. Today **Earth science** includes the parts of geography that have to do with what the surface and interior of the Earth are made of. You can find out more about the structure of the Earth in chapter 4.

A stick chart from the Marshall Islands

A Babylonian world map on a clay tablet

Eratosthenes (276–192 B.C.) was a geometer, geographer, mapmaker, and chief librarian at the museum in Alexandria, Egypt. He knew that at noon on June 21 every year in the town of Syene the Sun's rays shone right to the bottom of a deep well without casting any shadows. Eratosthenes also knew that on the same day at noon in his city of Alexandria, the Sun cast a slight shadow from the tall gnomon outside the library where he worked. Eratosthenes figured that he had enough information to calculate the size of the Earth.

Eratosthenes set up a geometry problem using the information he had:

1. He imagined the tall gnomon in Alexandria and the deep well at Syene both to be pointing to the center of the Earth.

2. He assumed that Alexandria and Syene were on the same meridian circle (Syene is actually 3° east of Alexandria).

3. He knew that Syene was 5,000 stadia or 500 miles (800 km) south of Alexandria. He assumed that Syene was in the tropics (it was actually 37 miles [63 km] north of being exactly under the Sun in the tropics).

4. He assumed that the rays of the Sun that reach the Earth are parallel because the Sun is so far away. (Sunlight shining through pinholes in a curtain or through dust in the air appears as parallel rays.)

5. The shadow cast from the gnomon indicated that the Sun's rays formed a 7° angle with the top of the gnomon.

6. He also knew from geometry that when a straight line cuts across two parallel straight lines, it makes equal angles with both of them, so the 7° angle could also be the distance between Alexandria and Syene.

7. A circle has 360°. The distance around a circle is the circumference.

8. 360 ÷ 7 will tell you what part of a complete circle the distance from Alexandria to Syene is. It is close to $^1/_{50}$ of a circle.

9. If $^1/_{50}$ of the circle of the Earth is 5,000 stadia, then 50 × 5,000 = the number of stadia completely around the Earth. It is 250,000 stadia.

10. Most people agree that 1 stadia = close to 500 feet (158 m). Since 1 mile = close to 5,000 feet and 1 kilometer = 1,000 meters,

  1 stadia = 500 feet/5,000 feet (0.10 mi) or 158/1,000 meters (0.16 km);
  250,000 stadia × 0.10 mile = 25,000 miles; and
  250,000 stadia × 0.16 kilometer = 40,000 kilometers.

Therefore, according to Eratosthenes 2,200 years ago the Earth was 25,000 miles (40,000 km) around. The current figure given for the circumference of the Earth is 24,902 miles (40,075 km).

According to the Chaldeans, if a person walked at a steady pace of 30 stadia an hour (about 3 mi or 5 km), it would take a year to go completely around the Earth. This would make the circumference of the Earth 263,000 stadia—a figure very close to the 250,000 stadia calculated by Eratosthenes.

Using the formula diameter = circumference ÷ 3.14159, what is the diameter of the Earth based on Eratosthenes' value for the circumference?

The ultimate authority in map making and astronomy from Greek times to the Age of Exploration was another Greek, Ptolemy, who wrote the first known world atlas in history. Ptolemy used the two main coordinates in making maps of the Earth: **latitude** and **longitude**. In this next project you can make a clay model of the Earth showing the lines of latitude and longitude.

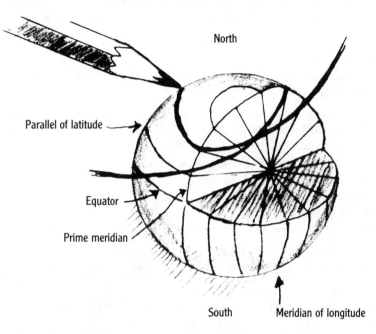

★ ★ ★ ★ ★ **Project 25: Demonstrating Latitude and Longitude** ★ ★ ★ ★ ★

MATERIALS

modeling clay	pencil
string	index card
table knife	scissors
protractor	ruler
drawing compass	

PROCEDURE

1. Make a ball of clay about 3 inches (8 cm) in diameter.

2. Cut out a quarter section from the clay ball.

3. Draw a circle on the index card (using the compass) with the same diameter as the ball.

4. Divide the circle (using the protractor) into 36 10° sections, drawing lines through the center of the circle for each section.

5. Cut out the circle and fold it in half along one of the lines and fit it into the cut out portion of the clay ball.

6. Continue the lines from the file card onto the clay ball using the string and pencil.

OBSERVATIONS

Lines of **latitude** are really circles around the Earth parallel to the equator. Their measurements come from the angles they make from the center of the Earth to a point above (north) or below (south) the equator. The equator itself is 0° latitude.

Lines of **longitude** are circles around the Earth that all pass through the North and the South Poles. Their measurements also come from the angles they make from the center of the Earth to a point east or west of the prime meridian. The prime meridian is 0°. In Ptolemy's day, the prime meridian passed through the Canary Islands. Today it passes through **Greenwich, England.**

When you combine latitude and longitude lines, they form a grid. You can use this grid to find any place on the Earth.

Before Ptolemy, the Egyptians had the reputation of the greatest land measurers. As early as 2800 B.C., using precise astronomical observations, they
1. could measure latitude to within a few hundred feet,
2. could measure longitude almost as accurately,
3. knew the length of the circumference of the Earth very precisely, and
4. knew the length of their country almost to the cubit (about 1 yd or 1 m).

Maps of a Sphere   How do you make a map of a sphere? One way is to make a sphere and put the map on it like you did when you made your tennis ball sky dome (Project 3, Making a Tennis Ball Sky Dome) and the model of the celestial sphere (Project 22, Making a Model of the Celestial Sphere). **Martin Beheim (1459–1509)** of Nurnberg, made the earliest globe of the Earth to survive to the present. It was 20 inches in diameter and made of wood. Beheim called his globe the **erdapfel.** He divided it into 12 spearhead-shaped sections of 30° each called **gores.** To make his globe, Beheim arranged his 12 gores like an unraveled orange peel, as if he had peeled away the skin of the Earth.

Martin Waldseemuler made a world map in 1507. His maps were the first to use the name *America.* Waldseemuler suggested the name America for the New World in honor of his colleague, Amerigo Vespucci, who explored and named the Venezuelan coast in 1499.

Every flat map of the round Earth distorts the true picture of the world. One-eighth of the globe is about as much as you can show flat without distortion. Distortion can be a serious problem for a navigator who depends on maps to give an accurate picture of size, shape, distance, and direction of land and water areas. No flat map can show all four of these accurately. A big step in making a flat map of the spherical Earth came about through the work of **Gerhart Kramer (1512–1594)**, whose name in Latin was **Gerardus Mercator.** In his time Mercator was the most honored mapmaker in Europe. He called his collection of maps an **atlas**, and people have used that word ever since to describe a book of maps.

Mercator used the idea of projecting an image of the Earth's sphere onto a flat surface as if the Earth was transparent and a light was inside it. Mercator invented two map projections: the **Mercator** and the **conic.** Today people use the projection named after him for nearly all sea charts. Depending on where the light is inside the globe of the Earth, you will get a different projection.

When you try to show large areas of the Earth you have to imagine that you are projecting the image of these areas onto a shape other than a sphere, which can be more easily "unpeeled" and opened out flat. Three popular shapes are the cylinder, the cone, and the flat plane.

A **cylinder** touches the globe around the equator, so cylindrical projection maps are most accurate for areas around the equator. They are not very accurate for showing size or distance. Mercator's map is a variation of the cylindrical projection.

A **cone** touches the globe at 40° latitude. This latitude passes through the United States. Conic projection maps are most accurate for the Northern

Hemisphere and the United States. They are not very accurate for direction. Ptolemy's map is a variation of the conical map.

A flat plane can touch the globe at any one point. Because maps made from flat plane projections are accurate in one area we call them **azimuthal projections**. Mapmakers often use azimuthal projections in maps of the North or South Poles. They are very accurate at showing direction.

Conic projection

Mercator cylindrical projection

Azimuthal projection

Triangulation   Gemma Frisius Regnier (1508–1542), a German surveyor, perfected a system for measuring far distances. The system uses the observer's knowledge of triangles from trigonometry, so we call it **triangulation**. Gemma Frisius did not invent triangulation. It probably came from ancient Egypt.

A triangle has six parts: three sides and three angles. If you know the sizes of three parts of a triangle, one of which must be one of the sides, then you can figure out each of the three other parts.

Jacques Cassini (1678–1756) of the French Academy used the method of triangulation to measure and map all of France. His son, Cesar François, and his cousin, Maraldi, assisted him in this massive undertaking. They completed their measurements and in 1744 published a map based on them. In triangulation you make triangles out of the distances you are going to measure. Then you find out the angles and lengths that you can measure and calculate the distances that are too far to measure just as you would with any triangle.

This method also works when you want to measure the distance to stars.

Topographic Maps   Some maps actually show both the height of various points on the map compared to other features around these points, and the elevation or the height of a feature above sea level. These measurements are **contours**, and the kind of map that shows them is a **topographic map**. Topographic maps give you a very good idea of the shape of the land and where the high and low spots are. We use topographic maps today to plot the surface features of Mars, Venus, and the moons of the planets. In radio astronomy (see chapter 5, section 4) we measure intensities and map them in a fashion similar to topographic maps.

Part of Cassini's triangulation map of France, 1744

Topographic comes from the Greek words τοπος (*topos*) = place or spot and γραφος (*graphos*) = to write.

Benjamin Banneker (1731–1806) was an American mathematician, surveyor, astronomer and inventor. In 1790 President George Washington appointed him to the survey team that was to lay out the plans for Washington, D.C. Banneker determined the longitude, latitude, and boundaries by using the stars. He also published several astronomical almanacs.

READING MORE

Dicks, Brian, consultant editor. *The Children's World Atlas.* Milbrae, CA: Celestial Arts, 1981.

Kjellstrom, Bjorn. *Be an Expert with Map and Compass.* New York: Charles Scribner's Sons, 1976.

The Pleiades (M45) *(photo courtesy of Observatoire de Haute Provence)*

Star Positions and Degrees in Between   Knowing how to read the map of the sky can help you get around on the Earth. Explorers, adventurers, and sailors all over the world have known this for thousands of years. Even with all of the technology available to them today, navigators still carry star-reading tools and charts on board. These items never break down.

To travel on the Earth using the sky as your guide you need to know the altitude of several important stars, when they will cross the meridian, and what time they rise and set. You also need to know exactly where they are. In the 16th century, **Tycho Brahe** (1546–1601) and others used an instrument to help answer these questions. Because this instrument was in the shape of a quarter circle, these astronomers called them **quadrants**. In this next project you can build the same instrument.

Quadrant comes from the Latin word *quatuor* = four.

★ ★ ★ ★ ★ ★ Project 26: Making a Quadrant and Azimuth ★ ★ ★ ★ ★ ★ Measuring Instrument

MATERIALS

drinking straw
bolt with wing nut and washer
wood   *base:* 12 × 12 × ¾ inches
           (30 × 30 × 2 cm)
       supports: 1 × 1 inch
           (2½ × 2½ cm)
       pointer: 1 × ½ inches
           (2½ cm × 12 mm)
hand drill and bits
red thread

small lead weight (fishing
   sinker)
flat-head screw with washer
sheet of stiff paper
bubble level (optional)
compass (optional)
access to a photocopier
quadrant and azimuth circles,
   above

PROCEDURE

1. Cut the wood pieces as they appear in the drawings, drilling holes where needed.
2. Photocopy the quadrant and azimuth circles (on the next page).
3. Assemble as shown in the drawing.

USING YOUR QUADRANT AND AZIMUTH MEASURING INSTRUMENT

1. Place on a level surface.
2. Sight Polaris through the straw. Line up the base so it reads 0° at the north pointer.
3. Keep the base stationary and move the sighting instrument to find a star. The pointer on the instrument will point to a number on the circle on the base. This is the **azimuth** of the star. See section 1 of this chapter for an explanation of the

azimuth as part of the horizon coordinate system. The weighted string on the protractor will indicate the **altitude** of the star above the horizon.

OBSERVATIONS

You can remove the quadrant from its base and use it by itself to find altitudes. The altitude and azimuth measurements depend entirely on your local horizon and the time of your measurements. Measurements of the same star made from another location and time will be different.

The Sun and the North Star are the two most reliable sources with which to determine direction and location. In 1607 John Davis published a description of his astronomical device that he called the **backstaff**. It was a version of another astronomical instrument that was popular for a long time, the **cross-staff**. The cross-staff used the line of the horizon and the position of the Sun. To use it meant that you had to look right at the Sun. You also had to look at both ends of the crosspiece at the same time while one end touched the horizon and the other the Sun. The backstaff placed the back of the observer to the Sun, sighting along the staff at the line of the horizon. At the end of the staff was a small screen; the observer moved the crosspiece until its top cast a shadow on the bottom of the screen. The crosspiece now lined up with a number on the staff that gave the altitude angle between the horizon and whatever you were observing in the sky.

In this next project you can build a model of the cross-staff designed for measuring degrees in the night sky. *Do not use it to look at the Sun.*

Using the backstaff, 1681   A backstaff   Using the cross-staff, 1681

★ ★ ★ ★ ★ ★ ★ ★ ★ ★ ★ **Project 27: Making a Cross-Staff** ★ ★ ★ ★ ★ ★ ★ ★ ★ ★ ★

MATERIALS

wood: *staff:*
    1 × 1 × 30 inches
    (2½ × 2½ × 76 cm)
    crosspieces:
    1½ × ½ × 12 inches
    (3¾ × 1¼ × 30 cm)
    1½ × ½ × 6 inches
    (3¾ × 1¼ × 15 cm)

flat black paint
dark brown stain or paint
protractor
white pencil
ruler
rubber band
small piece of cloth

117

PROCEDURE

1. Cut out all the pieces of wood.

2. Paint the staff flat black, and stain or paint the crosspieces brown.

3. Draw a line on the crosspieces using the white colored pencil to mark the middle of each crosspiece.

4. Lay the large crosspiece on top of the staff. Loop one end of the rubber band around one end of the crosspiece, pass the rubber band under the staff, and loop it around the other end of the crosspiece.

5. Adjust the crosspiece so that the staff is under the exact middle mark of the crosspiece. If you have difficulty sliding the crosspiece up and down the staff, wrap the rubber band with the small piece of cloth.

6. Hold the end of the staff on your cheek and against the side of your nose, next to your eye. Slide the large crosspiece (also called a *transversal*) until it fits in between your horizon and a star whose altitude you already know (e.g., Polaris). Let's say that distance is 38°. Using the white colored pencil and the ruler, carefully mark a line and the number 38° on the staff right where the side of the crosspiece nearest you crosses the staff.

7. Use the stars and their degree measurements listed at the end of the first section of this chapter (and the protractor if necessary) to mark more lines and degrees on your staff.

8. Replace the large crosspiece with the shorter one for smaller distances, and sight with the opposite end of the staff. Make your marks for the shorter crosspiece on the other side of the staff.

USING YOUR CROSS-STAFF

To measure the degrees between two stars, hold the end of the staff on your cheek and against the side of your nose, next to your eye. Slide the crosspiece along the staff until the ends of the crosspiece fit in between the stars. Look at the staff and see what line and degree number the crosspiece is near. This will tell you how many degrees apart the two stars are.

OBSERVATIONS

You can measure distances above the horizon, distances between stars, and the changing position between planets and stars. Some cross-staffs had four crosspieces with scales on each side of the staff.

Around 170 B.C. Hipparchos developed a way to draw the celestial sphere onto a flat surface: the stereoscopic projection. Using this projection he invented a device called the **astrolabe**. It served as a portable combination altitude/azimuth measurer, planesphere, sundial, and device for telling time by the stars.

Astrolabe comes from the Greek words ἀστηρ (*aster*) = star and λαβω (*labo*) = to take hold of.

With this instrument you could "take hold of the stars" for surveying, timekeeping, charting the skies, and casting horoscopes. Its use developed and spread during the time of the Islamic Empire. It was a way to find out the correct date from the stars so that you could celebrate the required religious festivals. Every citizen who could afford one owned an astrolabe. It helped them know the correct time to pray and the direction of the city of Mecca toward which they were to pray.

The Moors reintroduced the astrolabe to Europe when they conquered Spain in the Middle Ages. European instrument makers produced astrolabes for scholars, noblemen, freemasons, and astronomers. In the 14th century, the English poet **Geoffrey Chaucer** (ca. 1342–1400) called it the "noble instrument." He wanted to teach his 10-year-old son how to use one, but the only texts on the astrolabe were in Latin. Chaucer thus translated a Latin instruction text into English.

In this next project you can make your own astrolabe.

★ ★ ★ ★ ★ ★ ★ ★ ★ ★ ★ **Project 28: Making an Astrolabe** ★ ★ ★ ★ ★ ★ ★ ★ ★ ★ ★

MATERIALS

astrolabe plans and computer
    instructions from Sky Files
rubber cement
plastic sheet (from report covers)
colored yarn or rope
flashlight with paper bag covering
cardboard

stiff paper
paper fastener
metal ring
gummed paper reinforcements
scissors
access to a photocopier

PROCEDURE

1. Photocopy the astrolabe sheets and glue them onto a piece of cardboard.
2. Use a computer program* to determine the measurements for your particular latitude, or use the one shown here.
3. Cut out the parts.
4. Assemble as shown.
5. Attach the ring through the circle on the top of the mater.

USING YOUR ASTROLABE

FINDING THE ALTITUDE AND AZIMUTH OF A STAR

Hold the astrolabe by the ring on the top with the back of the astrolabe facing to your right. Sight a star through the two viewing holes in the alidade, moving the alidade as needed. The alidade will now be pointing to a number on the altitude scale (inside circle) of the mater. This is the altitude angle of the star above the horizon. Use the flashlight to read this angle or go inside to complete your calculations.

If the star you are sighting is Arcturus, for example, and you find it to be 30° above the eastern horizon, you turn the rete until the tip of the Arcturus star finder on it lines up with the almucanter, which shows an altitude of 30° above the eastern horizon.

*The computer program in Sky Files that allows you to construct your astrolabe to be accurate in your latitude was programmed especially for this book by David Schaefer.

Cut on 3 sides of this square (not on dotted line).

back pointer (alidade)

Cut on these three sides (not on dotted line).

front pointer

rete

★ : First Point of Aries

ecliptic circle

Azimuth measurements showing number of degrees east of north/south meridian.

East

Eastern Horizon

Western Horizon

Western Horizon

North

Tropic of Cancer

Equator

Meridian

almucanter

Tropic of Capricorn

Mater (front)

Grommet
Pointer
Rete
Almucanter
Metal ring
Mater
Alidade
Grommet

Mater (back)

121

You can now check the position of the rete to find the azimuth of Arcturus as well as the altitude and azimuth of the other stars that have pointers on the rete (as long as they are above the horizon).

You can also find the azimuth by holding the astrolabe sideways so that the mater is horizontal. The 0°/360° marker on the top of the back of the mater must point to the north.

Calculating star positions, 1533 (*engraving by Petrus Apianus,* Instrument Buch, *1533, from* Space Time Infinity *by Charles Phillips,* © *Smithsonian Institution*). Note the nocturnal, cross-staff, quadrant, platonic solids, and even a hand being used!

FINDING THE RISING AND SETTING TIMES OF A STAR

You can tell the hour when a star will rise, cross the meridian, or set for any time of the year. Locate the star finder in the rete for the star whose rising time you want to know. Set the tip of the star finder to the eastern horizon (for rising), meridian (for crossing), or western horizon (for setting). Line up the pointer with the Sun's position on the correct date as shown in the ecliptic circle. The pointer now points to a time on the rim of the mater which is the rising, crossing, or setting time of the star.

FINDING THE RISING AND SETTING TIMES OF THE SUN

Set the rete so that the Sun's position on the ecliptic for the date you want touches the eastern horizon (for sunrise) or the western horizon (sunset). Set the pointer to line up with this point. The pointer points to the hour on the rim of the mater.

FINDING THE TIME USING THE STARS

Using the steps described in *Finding the Altitude and Azimuth of a Star* (above) locate the position of a star visible in the sky at some unknown time at night. Set the pointer to line up with the first point of Aries, marked on the ecliptic circle. The end of the pointer will point to the hour of star time on the rim of the mater. You may or may not need to add 12 to this hour, depending on how many degrees the first point of Aries is from the meridian.

OBSERVATIONS

You can also use the astrolabe to locate positions of the Moon and the planets. Both the cross-staff and the backstaff were far more practical on board ship than the astrolabe proved to be. An astrolabe needed to be held in a level position. Such conditions were rare at sea. However, if you knew how to use it, an astrolabe was like having an observatory on board.

The invention of the printing press in 1454 by **Johann Gutenberg** (ca. 1398–1468) was a major event in history. For mapmakers it meant the possibility of producing many copies of maps for a wide audience. Artistic skill blossomed forth in both charting and decorating maps of the sky, seas, and Earth. Librarians no longer needed to have scribes recopy these highly detailed documents. Printed copies as accurate as the originals were available. Navigators used the new presses to print up their own charts and tables with which to calculate star positions. These calculations were far more accurate than those their astrolabes could offer.

Navigators soon altered the appearance of the astrolabe. They added mirrors and later telescopes to the alidade and the mater so they could sight the Sun, a star, or the Moon and the horizon at the same time, much like a backstaff. With each change in the astrolabe, there was a change in its name.

In 1669 **Jean Picard** (1620–1682) added a telescope to the sighting portion of the staff of the quadrant. By 1678 **Robert Hooke, Johannes Hevelius,** and **Edmond Halley** had all tried the same idea. Halley's improvement was to add to the telescope a piece of glass, half mirror and half clear, with which to both view the horizon (with the clear part) and to reflect the light of the Sun (the mirror part). You could move the reflected light to line up with the horizon. Sometime before his death, **Sir Isaac Newton** (1643–1727) had worked on variations of the quadrant using mirrors. In 1730 two men working independently developed a variation of the quadrant that relied on one-sixth of a full circle for its measurements. They called their instruments **sextants.**

Sextant comes from the Latin word *sex* = six.

Both **John Hadley** from England and **Thomas Godfrey** of the United States designed a sextant with two mirrors. The sextant makes use of the principle that the angle that a ray of light makes when it reflects off two mirrors in a row is two times as big as the angle between the two mirrors. The sextant is an instrument that navigators still prize and use today.

As you pursue your study of astronomy, you will find a number of examples of discoveries made by two people at about the same time who didn't even know who the other person was or what he or she was doing. In some cases, after their discoveries, they met.

Here's where having a nondigital watch comes in handy. Hold your watch level or lay it on the ground and stand a thin stick straight up beside it. Turn the watch until the shadow of the stick falls across the hour hand in a straight line to the time on the opposite side. Halfway between the shadow and the number 12 on the watch is the direction of north. (See also Project 6 in Chapter 1, Finding Directions from a Shadow Stick.)

Time and Place   Clocks have teamed up with navigators to help find directions and locations. People have generally measured time from the transit of the Sun across the meridian (see chapter 1, section 3). The upper transit occurs at noon, the lower transit at midnight. Since 1925, the lower transit has been the standard measuring point. This means that a new day starts at midnight. When we map the Earth with a global grid we find that the Sun crosses the various meridians at different times. This means that you can measure the differences between any two places on the Earth both in distance and in time.

It is inconvenient, however, to have people in the same town using different times just because they live at different meridians. One way to solve this problem is to divide the world into time zones and pretend that, for the sake of convenience in telling time, all the meridians within a particular time zone are compressed into one. Each of these zones is more or less 15° wide and runs from east to west across the globe. These zones have irregular shapes to conform to national boundaries.

If you compare the Sun's crossing of your local meridian with its crossing of your standard time zone meridian, it probably won't be exactly at 12:00 noon. You will have to add or subtract a few minutes on your observation time. The additional minutes you added, or the difference between the two times, will give you the number of degrees of longitude you need to adjust your standard time meridian by. The way to figure your calculations is to remember that the Sun appears to travel a distance of 15° for every hour of time, or 1° every 4 minutes. If the Sun crosses your meridian before noon, you need to add the degrees eastward from your standard time meridian. If the Sun crosses your local meridian after noon, you measure the difference in longitude west from your standard time meridian.

To measure time and longitude, you need a starting point that everyone agrees to use. Hipparchos had chosen Rhodes as his prime meridian or zero point. For Ptolemy, it was the "Fortunate Isles" (the Canary Islands), which were the western boundary of the then-known world. Other astronomers and mapmakers have chosen some city in their native land.

In 1634 **Cardinal Richelieu (1585–1642)** called together mathematicians and astronomers in Paris to decide on a prime meridian. They based their decision on Ptolemy's suggestion and chose the island farthest west in the Canary Islands, called Ferro or Isle de Fer. In the 1700s many people had been using the meridian passing through the Royal Observatory outside London in the suburb of Greenwich (pronounced "greń-itch"). At that time the two most important observatories for navigators in Europe were the one in Paris and the one in Greenwich.

A geographic conference in 1884 chose Greenwich as prime meridian. At this same conference, the members made the decision to begin the day at midnight on the prime meridian instead of noon. It wasn't until 1925 that all the nations (except parts of Saudi Arabia) accepted the recommendations for the prime meridian midnight starting time and worldwide time zones all based on the meridian at Greenwich.

In one hour the Sun appears to move $1/24$ of a complete circle around the Earth traveling west. Since there are 360° in a circle, $1/24$ would be 15°. If the Sun starts in Greenwich, which is 0°, in 1 hour the Sun will be over the meridian that is 15° west of the prime meridian. When this happens and it is noon at 15°W, it is 1:00 P.M. at Greenwich. If you are sailing west and it is noon at Greenwich and the time where you are is 3:30, you are 3½ times 15° or 52° 30′ west. (With this information you find your longitude in part 2 of the next project.)

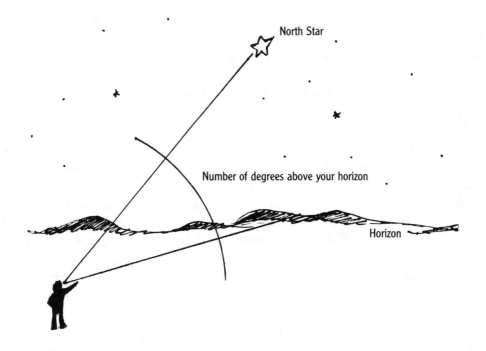

North Star

Number of degrees above your horizon

Horizon

★ ★ ★ ★ ★ ★ **Project 29: Finding Your Latitude and Longitude** ★ ★ ★ ★ ★ ★

MATERIALS

altitude/azimuth measurer (from
   Project 26)
list of stars on the celestial equator
   ("Locating the Celestial Equator"
   earlier in this chapter)

pencil and paper
time zones chart (later in this
   chapter)
watch or clock

PROCEDURE

PART 1: FINDING YOUR LATITUDE
Northern Hemisphere
   1. Facing north at night, use your altitude/azimuth measurer to determine the altitude of the North Star. Since the North Star is almost directly above the Earth's North Pole, the altitude of the North Star above the horizon is the same as your latitude.

Southern Hemisphere
   1. There is no easily visible South Pole star, so you need to look for the stars on the celestial equator.
   2. See the list of stars on the celestial equator. Pick one of these stars when it appears highest in the sky for you (due north). Use your altitude/azimuth measurer to determine its altitude.

3. Subtract the altitude of the star you measured from 90°. That will be your latitude.

PART 2: FINDING YOUR LONGITUDE

1. Consult the time zones chart to find how many hours different your time zone is from Greenwich (12 noon).

2. Multiply the difference by 15°, which is the number of degrees in each time zone and the number of degrees the sky moves in 1 hour. The answer will be your longitude east or west of Greenwich (which is 0°).

OBSERVATION

In order to find your exact longitude you need to know the corrected Sun time for your location at local noon and the Greenwich mean time at that same moment.

How are you going to know what time it is in Greenwich? People asked this question at a point in history when sundials, sand clocks, and huge, unreliable timepieces were the only ways of keeping time. The other problem was that, as you saw in chapter 1, Sun time and clock time are not always the same. On November 2, the Sun passes the meridian around 11:42 A.M., local mean time, while on February 9, it passes at 12:13 P.M. The equation of time corrects this difference between the real Sun time (apparent) and the local time (mean). Tables showing these corrections were carried on board ship.

In 1530 Gemma Frisius said that you should be able to carry an accurate clock with you to sea, keeping it set so that it always told you the time at the port from which you left. You could find your local time from the Sun. With this information you could change the difference in the time between two places into the difference in longitude between them.

In 1714 the British Parliament offered a prize of £20,000 "for providing a Publick Reward for such Person or Persons as shall discover the Longitude at Sea." As you can see from the amount of the prize money, this was a difficult contest. To win you had to try out your method on a voyage to the West Indies and back with a total error of less than 30' or 2 minutes of time. Up until that date, people kept time on board ship with a sand clock measuring half-hour intervals. The job of keeping track of the sand clock also included writing down the intervals and ringing a bell each half hour in 8-hour shifts. This is the origin of telling time at sea by bells: one for the first half hour, two for the first hour, two close together, a pause, and then a single one for the third half an hour, and so on. When the bell tolled, someone else had the task of marking the ship's position with a peg on a huge board. The board had holes in it at various points along the ship's course at half-hour intervals.

The two most common ways of finding longitude were by observing eclipses and occultations of the planets by the Moon's disk, then comparing differences in local apparent time and converting to longitude.

John Harrison (1693–1776), a carpenter from Yorkshire, England, won the contest by building the first accurate sea-going clock. Altogether it took him 43 years and six different versions to perfect his timepiece. The final version was about the size of a large stopwatch. People called this unique clock a **chronometer** to show that it was different from a regular clock.

John Harrison was born in Yorkshire, England. His father had been a carpenter and John was to be one, too. John caught smallpox when he was six and had to spend quite a bit of time recuperating. A friend gave him a watch to play with to keep him occupied while he was getting better. From that day on, he was fascinated with all kinds of timepieces. As a hobby, he built and repaired clocks, building an entire grandfather clock by himself.

John Harrison's chronometer, final version, 1759 (*photo courtesy of National Maritime Museum, England*)

In 1767 the **Reverend Nevil Maskelyne**, the Astronomer Royal of England, compiled the first **Nautical Almanac**. In it were all the charts and tables, the locations of the 57 stars used for navigation—in fact, the fruits of all the labors of astronomers since their science first began. Using the Nautical Almanac, the sextant, and the chronometer, sailors, sea captains, and pilots greatly expanded their knowledge of celestial navigation and our knowledge of the world.

The Naval Observatory in Washington, D.C., also publishes an American version of the Nautical Almanac. In 1842 **Matthew Fontaine Maury** (1806–1873) started this work. A young naval lieutenant, Maury had broken his leg in a stagecoach accident. Assigned to a land-based job at the navy's Bureau of Navigation in Washington, D.C., at age 36 because he could no longer carry out sea duty, Maury set out to make the best use of his situation. Maury was in charge of the Depot of Charts and Instruments. He published a book for sea pilots, listing wind and sea currents based on the vast amount of records and logbooks stored at the depot. He established the Naval Observatory and the Hydrographic Office. Maury was the first head of the Naval Observatory. He also started the Weather Bureau, suggested building the Panama Canal and the port of Norfolk, Virginia, recommended the use of steamer lanes at sea 25 miles (40 km) apart, called for lighthouses on the Gulf Coast, recommended close observation of the rise and fall of the waters of the Mississippi River, and encouraged the use of circle sailing and the reclaiming of drowned lands. He was decorated and honored by many countries for the international usefulness of many of his ideas.

The Naval Observatory, like the one in England, told time for its nation and tested and corrected all nautical instruments used by the navy. Both observatories once used a bright red ball on a long shaft sitting on top of the observatory where ships at sea could easily spot it. At noon the ball would be dropped down from the top of the spire. When it reached the bottom of the shaft (like the ball in Times Square on New Year's Eve), it would be precisely 12 noon. Ship captains would adjust their clocks and set sail. Both observatories have transit sighting telescopes and very sophisticated timekeeping devices. They both continue to publish Nautical Almanacs and other useful documents.

Rhumb Lines   Another important document that came out earlier, in 1569, was Mercator's world map. In it Mercator tried to make a chart that could locate places by their longitude and latitude and in which the straight traveling line between any two places would be represented as a straight line whose angle from every meridian would be the same. If a person in London and another person on the 180th meridian were to both point to the north, to an observer on the celestial sphere above the Earth's North Pole, both people would be pointing in the same direction. The same would be true if both people pointed south. If, however, they pointed east, to the observer on the celestial sphere, they would be pointing in opposite directions. The same would be true if they pointed west.

If you and a friend could walk to the North Pole from two different places on the Earth, you both would always be heading north. Both of you would meet at the North Pole. Once you got there, if you kept walking, you would pass each other and would be heading south. Now, suppose both you and your friend are standing together right at the North Pole. Which direction is east? What about north and west?

Suppose you and your friend start your journeys from the same points where you began but instead of venturing north, you head slightly south and a little east of north. As you both travel, stick to your north-east course, crossing each meridian you come to at the same angle. What will happen? What you will see from the celestial sphere point of view is two people walking in an ever-tightening spiral around the globe until they meet at the North Pole. Anytime you travel on the globe in any direction other than the four cardinal points—north, south, east, west—you will be traveling in a spiral. This pattern is a **loxodromic curve**. It is also called a **rhumb line**.

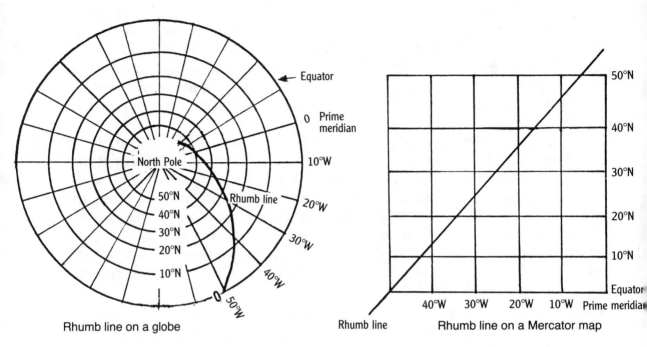

Rhumb line on a globe

Rhumb line   Rhumb line on a Mercator map

The straight-traveling line or rhumb line is the direction you would sail without altering your course and without being thrown off course by any causes. On a globe map, rhumb lines are not straight. They tend to spiral gradually. Mercator's map shows the rhumb lines as straight, which makes it much easier to plot your course on a flat map and to stay on it at sea.

Loxodromic curve comes from the Greek words λοχος (*loxos*) = slanting, crosswise and δρομος (*dromos*) = a course. **Rhumb** comes from the old Spanish word *rumb* = room, space, hold of a ship and the Greek word ρομβος (*rombos*) = anything that may be spun or whirled around.

Great Circle Maps   Look at a flat map of the world and plan the shortest possible voyage from San Francisco to Yokohama, Japan. Now do the same planning using a globe. Would you pick the same route that you did with the flat map? On a globe, the shortest distance between two points is a line cut out on the globe by a plane intersecting the Earth's center. This line is called a **great circle**. Airplane pilots know about the great circles and use them often. They have maps based on the **gnomonic projection**. In this projection, great circles appear as straight lines. The captain looks at a gnomonic chart, plots a course, and transfers it to a Mercator chart that he or she will use.

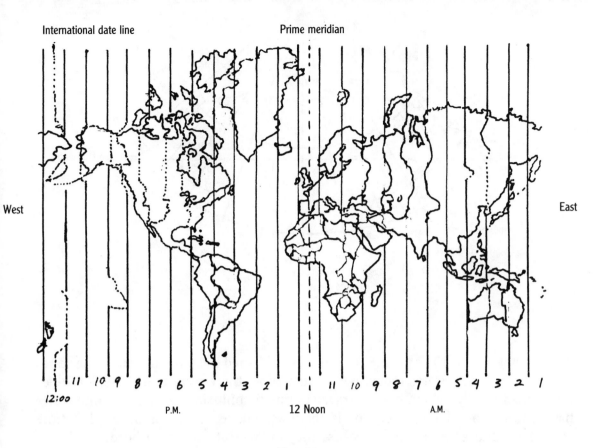

International date line

Prime meridian

West

East

11   10   9   8   7   6   5   4   3   2   1 | 11   10   9   8   7   6   5   4   3   2   1

12:00

P.M.   12 Noon   A.M.

Time zones

MAPS OF THE EARTH AND THE SKY
(seen from the Southern Hemisphere)

MAPS OF THE SKY
(seen from the Northern Hemisphere)

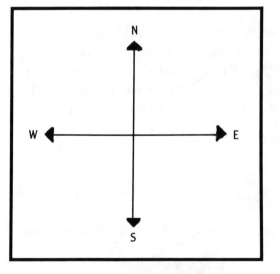

Looking down onto the earth
◄— Sunlight and time move in this direction

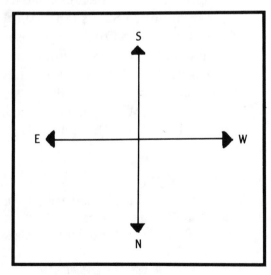

Looking up into the sky
Stars and planets move in this direction —►

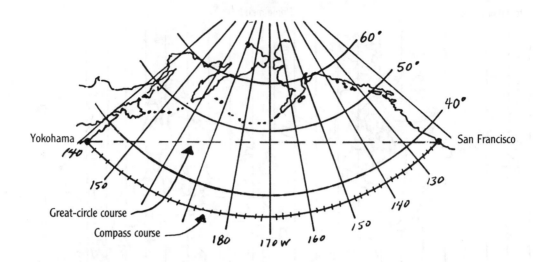

Yokohama ... San Francisco

60°
50°
40°
140
150
130
140
Great-circle course
Compass course
180 170 W 160 150

Time Zones   In 1918 the U.S. Congress established the four standard time zones used in the United States today. Before that time, there were many smaller zones established locally, which caused travelers much confusion. While the time zones have uneven boundaries, each one is about as wide as 15° of longitude. The time zones have uneven boundaries because they follow state and river borders.

Standard time rarely agrees with Sun time. According to Sun time, noon is when the Sun is highest in the sky. But noon standard time hardly ever finds the Sun at its highest point. The farther you are from the center of your time zone, the more difference you will find between what Sun time tells you and what standard time tells you. Sun time and standard time agree only along four longitudes in the continental United States (75°W, 90°W, 105°W, and 120°W).

Halfway around the world from Greenwich is the 180th meridian. When it is noon at Greenwich, it is midnight at the 180th meridian. A new day has begun. For this reason, the 180th meridian is called the **international date line**. It can be written either as 180°E or 180°W, since it is the same distance each way from the prime meridian. When you cross the international date line, people usually give you a certificate marking the moment.

READING MORE

Bauer, Commander Bruce A. (USN, retired). *The Sextant Handbook: Adjustment, Repair, Use and History.* Annapolis, MD: Azimuth Press, 1986.

Hale, John R., and the editors of Time-Life Books. *Great Ages of Man: Age of Exploration.* New York: Time, 1966.

Hirsch, S. Carl. *On Course! Navigating in Sea, Air and Space.* New York: Viking, 1967.

Veil Nebula (NGC 6990-92-95) (*photo courtesy of Observatoire de Haute Provence*)

Section 4 POLES AND MAGNETISM

Magnets   You are used to seeing magnets and watching how they "stick" to certain metals. Most of the magnets you have seen were probably flat pieces of metal in the shape of a bar or a horseshoe. Magnets come from minerals that have had many names down through the ages: magnes, magnetis, heraclion, sideritis, and lodestone. The minerals are naturally occurring iron ore that we call **magnetite**.

Most researchers seem to think that the ancient Chinese were the first to notice the unusual features or properties of these minerals around 3000 B.C.

Magnet comes from the Greek words λιθος Μαγνητις (*lithos magnetis*) = stone from Magnesia, an ancient city in Asia Minor, near the Ural Mountains. There was a huge stone near this ancient city that used to "pull" at the iron tips of shepherds' staffs and the nails in their boots.

If you placed a piece of iron next to the magnetic mineral, the mineral would somehow "pull" the iron toward it and "hold" on to it. The piece of iron would then hold on to another piece of iron placed on it. The same thing would happen if you put two magnets near each other. However, if you turned one of them around, the two would "push" each other apart. Imagine what an impression such a stone would make on the first people to observe it. Clearly the stone was magic.

One magnet   Two magnets, same ends   Two magnets, opposite ends

Opposite ends of the magnets attract each other, joining their lines of force or force fields together to make one larger magnet. Like ends of the magnets repel each other, keeping their own force fields separate.

Magnets also line up in a certain direction with one end always pointing the same way. From what you have just observed about the properties of magnets, why do you suppose they always line up and point in a certain direction? What is it that they are lining up with and to what are they pointing?

The Compass   The ends of a magnet are the **north seeking end** and the **south seeking end**. These ends are also called **poles**. Opposite poles attract each other; similar poles repel each other because magnetized pieces always take up a position of minimum blockage to the flow of the magnetic field. The north seeking end of a magnet is really the magnet's south pole. Because it is the opposite of Earth's North Pole, the two magnet ends attract one another, causing the magnet's south pole to seek the North Pole of the Earth.

Long ago someone discovered this curious relationship between the Earth and magnets. The piece of magnetite that people used as a magnet pointed north to the Earth's pole and thus to the polestar. The polestar was called the **lodestar.**

Lodestar comes from the Anglo-Saxon word *lad-steorra* = leading star, so the mineral that pointed to it was named **lodestone** or leading stone.

The ancient Chinese used magnets to line up people's graves to help them enter the afterlife. By 900 B.C. people began using magnets to tell directions. Soon people were navigating, led by the forces of the leading stone.

> By means of this instrument you will be able to direct your steps to cities, islands, and to any places whatever in the world, wherever you may be on land or sea.
> —Petrus Perigrinus, 1269

When people dug up the pirate loot of Captain Kidd in the year 1699, the list of buried treasure included "one large lodestone." For many years, a lodestone remained one of the most important items aboard a sailing vessel, kept under lock and key in the captain's quarters. In this next project you can use a piece of lodestone to make a copy of the first **compass**.

Compass comes from Middle English word *compas* and the Middle French word *compasser* = to go around, measure or divide.

★ ★ ★ ★ ★ **Project 30: Making a Water Compass (Stella Maris)** ★ ★ ★ ★ ★

MATERIALS
a sliver of lodestone or magnetized   bowl
    needle   water
drinking straw or piece of cork

PROCEDURE
1. Fill the bowl with water.
2. Place the sliver of lodestone through the straw at right angles to it to form a +.
3. Float the straw and the lodestone gently on the surface of the water.

OBSERVATIONS
One end of the lodestone will point to the north, the other to the south. The two ends of the straw point to the east and west. The stella maris is the ancestor of the compass. The early sagas of the Faroe Islands mentions the use of a stella maris; so do other sources concerning the Norsemen, Italians, Persians, and Arabs.

Stella maris = "star of the sea" in Latin. It served as an all-weather, day and night guide.

When people found out that they could magnetize a thin piece of metal or a needle by rubbing it in one direction against a magnet, they decided to replace the floating lodestone in the stella maris. In time, people also removed the water in the stella maris, put a small dent under the center of the magnetized needle, and set it on a pivot. The needle was now free to float, balanced on the pivot, and to point out the north-south directions even on board a rocking ship. The needle and pivot were mounted on a card that had the cardinal directions written on it. Later still, people again placed the disk and needle in a container filled with water. The card floated on the water. The water cushioned the movement of the tossing ship like shock absorbers in a car. The container also had a cover to keep the water from spilling out. The name for the container was "the box," and in some parts of the Mediterranean people still call a compass "the box" (*bussola*) rather than "the needle."

Another improvement was to replace the needle itself. Instead, the compass maker glued magnetized wires under the compass disk and pivoted the whole card. The compass card is also known as the **wind rose** because the points on it show the directions from which the winds blow and because the pattern of the card resembles the petals of the rose. The rose pattern also resembles the pattern of a star.

The stellar rose pattern appears in a variety of places in nature, particularly in members of the rose family: rose hips, hawthorn, apples, strawberries, raspberries, meadow sweet, acrimony, blackberries.

Wind rose

In the early days of sailing, navigators spoke of direction at sea in terms of following a certain wind: "from Crete to Carpathus is 60 miles with the wind Favorius (the west wind)."

> Remember, remember the circle of the sky
> The stars and the brown eagle
> The supernatural winds
> Breathing night and day
> from the four directions . . .
> —*from the Pawnee, Osage Omaha*

The Earth as a Magnet   Why does a magnet hanging by a string point in a certain direction? To find the answer, **William Gilbert (1544–1603)**, the first great researcher in the field of magnetism, put together his observations with an experiment to try out an idea he had. Gilbert thought that the Earth itself was a giant magnet. Like a magnet, the Earth had a great concentration of its magnetic fields at its two poles. The Earth's magnet attracted other magnets and compasses, lining them up with the north-south magnetic field of the Earth, where there is the minimum blockage of the flow. To pursue his idea, Gilbert worked with a piece of lodestone, which he shaped into a globelike magnetic ball. He called this ball the **terrella** (little earth).

The terrella had a north and south pole, with a magnetic field lining up along the meridians. It also had an equator that actually indicated the natural division between the two poles. At the equator, the compass needle pointed horizontally; at the poles it pointed vertically. Gilbert published the results and methods of his experiments in his book *De Magnete: On the Magnet, Magnetick Bodies Also and on the Great Magnet the Earth; A New Philosophy Demonstrated by Many Arguments and Experiments.* This was the earliest and most comprehensive work on magnetism. The first section was about the lodestone and the properties of magnets, the second section was about navigation, and the third about astronomy.

The open seas now became less of a threat. You could leave the security of the familiar Mediterranean and head out westward. **Christopher Columbus (1451–1506)** relied heavily on the truth of this possibility. He wanted to do what seemed perfectly believable on a globe—to reach the east by traveling west. Don Christobal de Colon (Columbus's full name in Spanish, not Latin) of Genoa, Italy, "sailed the ocean blue in 1492" and "found" the New World. The voyage of Columbus was an important one for the development of geography and astronomy.

Columbus also learned some important characteristics about compasses. One was that the compass points to the Earth's **North Magnetic Pole**, not the North Geographic Pole. The two aren't the same. The focal point of the Earth's magnetic field moves every year. The point on the globe 90° above the equator doesn't. As you might imagine, this could cause some real problems for navigators. The difference between compass (magnetic) directions and true (geographic) directions is known as **variation**. From his experiences with the compass at sea, Columbus came to the conclusion that the variation was different in different parts of the globe.

The angle of magnetic variation is also called the **magnetic declination**. It can vary from 0° to a full 180°. Compasses always show north as an arrowhead. Magnetic north is only a half an arrowhead. Only when both the North Magnetic Pole and the North Geographic Pole are in line on a meridian will the compass needle point to true north.

If you hang a compass needle straight up and down, it will come to rest parallel with the lines of magnetic force surrounding it and passing through it. We call this instrument a **dip needle**, and we use it to measure magnetic inclination. At the magnetic equator, the dip needle shows no dip. It is parallel to the surface of the Earth. At either magnetic pole, the needle follows the lines of force and points straight up and down, perpendicular to the surface of the Earth.

The North Magnetic Pole is in northwest Canada, about 750 miles (1,200 km) south of the North Geographic Pole.

The South Magnetic Pole is in southwest Antarctica, about 1,250 miles (2,012 km) north of the South Geographic Pole.

Map by Edmond Halley showing lines of equal magnetic inclination

In this next project you can make a model of Gilbert's terrella and use a dip needle to check the magnetic variations on the Earth.

North Geographic Pole

South Geographic Pole

★ ★ ★ ★ ★ ★Project 31: Making a Model of the Magnetic Earth★ ★ ★ ★ ★ ★ (Terrella)

MATERIALS

alnico magnet (regular bar magnet)　　rubber band
tennis ball　　scissors
compass
dip needle (follow the description in
　　the paragraphs above to make one)

PROCEDURE

1. Put a hole in the tennis ball with the scissors and place the magnet inside to act as the Earth's Magnetic North and South Poles.

2. Use a compass to check for magnetic declination.

3. Use the dip needle to check for magnetic inclination.

4. Use a rubber band to indicate the magnetic equator.

OBSERVATIONS

This model, like Gilbert's terrella, comes close to explaining how the Earth acts as a magnet. The current theory (see Chapter 4, section 2) is that the center or core of the Earth is a hot and partly molten mass of iron. This fluid moves with the Earth, generating electric currents that in turn produce the magnetic fields around the Earth. As the strength and direction of the magnetic fields change, so do the Earth's magnetic poles. It is thought that the Earth's magnetic poles reverse every 500,000 years.

Keeping up with the shifting magnetic fields is part of the responsibility of mapmakers and those who use the maps, the navigators.

READING MORE

Ley, Willy, and the editors of *Life. The Poles* (Life *Nature Library*). New York: Time, 1962.

Trifid Nebula (Sagittarius) (*photo courtesy of Observatoire de Haute Provence*)

Chapter 4 THE SKY ABOVE AND THE EARTH BELOW

Section 1 LIFE ON EARTH

Beginnings   "In the beginning. . . ." With these three words cultures from all over the world have told the story of the Creation. It is a basic part of being human to want to know where we came from and where we are going. We also want to know how the universe began and how the planets, especially the Earth, came to be. As you read the following stories, you can listen to people speaking across the ages about the most human of all questions. Perhaps the answers we have today will seem strange to a future generation with answers of its own.

Babylonia   There was only Apsu (Sweet-Water), Tiamat (Salt-Water), and their son, Mummu (the Mist). From the mingling of these waters came the gods. Tiamat was angry at the gods, who were restless inside her. She sent monsters to destroy the gods once they were born. Filled with fear, the gods were unable to defend themselves, except for the brave Marduk, son of Ea. He killed Tiamat with his arrow and created the heavens and Earth from her body. A mountain towered upward from her head, and from her eyes flowed the Tigris and Euphrates rivers. Marduk changed the monsters into statues to hold up the gates where the Sun rises and sets. Marduk became the supreme god. He set up the zodiac, determined the length of the year, assigned three constellations for each of the 12 months, caused the Moon to shine with her different phases to measure the days and months, and created the first people to live on the Earth.

Scandinavia (The Norsemen)   There was nothing but a huge gulf, Ginnunga-gap. This Yawning Void stretched from Niflheim, the northern realm of ice, darkness, and mist, to Muspelheim, the southern realm of fire. Deep down within Ginnungagap lay Hvergelmir, the Well of Life whose waters flowed into the Yawning Void. These waters joined those the fire and icy mist had made as they came together. The cold of Niflheim turned the waters into blocks of ice; the fires of Muspelheim turned them into masses of ice and slush. This half-frozen water filled in the once empty gulf. As more warmth came up from Muspelheim, the blocks of ice began to melt. This first trickle of water was the ancestor of everything that lives, because the drops formed the body of the first giant, Ymir. Ymir was soon joined by Audhumla, the cow. From Audhumla's udders flowed four rivers of milk with which to nourish Ymir. For her food, Audhumla licked the ice around her and found in it the Salt of Life, from the Well of Life. On the first day she licked the ice, the warm drops made by her tongue on the ice formed the hair of a man. On the second day, the head took shape, and on the third day, the whole man was there. His name was Buri. Buri created a son, Bor, who married the giantess Bestla, one of Ymir's descendants. Bor and Bestla were the parents of the great Aesir gods Odin, Vili, and Ve. Ymir fathered a race of giants that constantly fought against the Aesir.

The sons of Bor killed Ymir and set to work to form the world from his body. From the blood of Ymir, the gods made the seas. From his body, which they threw into the gap, the gods made the Earth. From his bones, they made the mountains; from his hair, the forests and plants. His teeth became the gravel and stones. His brains became the clouds. The ice-blue skull of the giant became the dome of the heavens. From his eyebrows the gods made Midgard (middle Earth) the land between Niflheim and Muspelheim. Gathering the sparks that constantly flew out from Muspelheim, the Aesir placed stars into the sky and set their course.

They also brought molten gold from Muspelheim and made a glowing Sun chariot. The horses Early-Waker and All-Strong drew the chariot with the goddess Sol controlling the reins. Before her went the Moon chariot drawn by the horse All-Swift. In the chariot was the boy Mani. In this way, night came first, followed by day, and the Aesir caused time to exist. Odin created the first man from the ash tree, calling him Ask, and created the first woman, Embla, from an elder tree. These people and their descendants lived in Midgard, protected from the giants by the wall of mountains made by Ymir's bones. The world of humans was connected to Asgard, the world of the gods, by the Bifrost Ridge, made from the rainbow.

Mexico (The Toltecs)   The world lay in darkness. All things were orderless, and water covered the slime and ooze that the world was then. When the waters parted, land, forests, and mountains appeared. Tloque Nahuaque, the Lord of All Existence, created the universe. He made the first man and woman. After 676, on the date 4 Tiger, this first Earth was destroyed. The Sun disappeared. Tigers ate the people. Another Sun followed. After 364 years on the date 4 Wind, the Sun disappeared. Mighty winds swept the people away. Another Sun followed. After 312 years on the date 4 Fire-Rain, the Sun disappeared. Fire rained down on the people. Another Sun followed. After 676 years on the date 4 Water, the Sun disappeared. A flood destroyed the world, and only one man and one woman survived. Another Sun followed. This is our Sun. In time, earthquakes will destroy our world.

Marduk

Tonatiuh, one of the Aztec Suns

Japan   There appeared above the great swirling ocean mass a pair of gods, Izanagi and Izanami. They stood on the Rainbow Bridge of Heaven, and Izanagi thrust his jeweled spear into the ocean mass. Water dripping from its tip thickened and formed an island. This island became the Earth. Izanagi and Izanami came down to Earth where they married and became the parents of the world, including islands, seas, rivers, herbs, trees, mountains, and wind.

After his wife's death, Izanagi gave birth to the Sun goddess Amaterasu (Heaven-Illumining Lady) from his left eye. From his right eye, he gave birth to the stars and Tsuki-yami-no Mikoto (the Moon). From Izanagi's nostrils came the storm god Susanowo (the Impetuous Male), who dwelt in the seas.

The Sun goddess and the storm god often quarreled. Once Susanowo ruined his sister's fields and frightened her so much that she accidentally cut herself while weaving. Extremely angry and ashamed, Amaterasu left the sky and hid herself in a cave. There was darkness on the Earth. The gods assembled and discussed how they might persuade the Sun to come out from her hiding place and bring her light to Earth. The gods welded stars together to form a mirror and hung it in front of the cave with jewels and other offerings. Night birds sang at the entrance to Amaterasu's cave. The goddess of laughter, Ama-no-uzume (Heaven-Alarming Female), put on a headdress, stood on top of an upturned tub, and danced to please the gods. They roared with laughter. Curious, Amaterasu peeked out from the cave. She was so fascinated by her reflection in the mirror made by the gods that she came out of the cave. Normal day and night returned to the Earth.

New Zealand (The Maori)   There was Rangi (Heaven) and Papa (Earth). Although Rangi and Papa had created many human beings, the gods had never seen them because Rangi and Papa clung tightly to each other, keeping the humans and all the light from view. The gods met to plan a way to separate their parents, Rangi and Papa. Tane-mahuta, the god and father of forests, birds, and insects, decided that Papa should remain below as their mother and that Rangi should be pushed far above. It was Tane-mahuta who was able to put his head on Papa and with his feet push Rangi away. Now there was darkness *and* light. People lived on the Earth below, and the sky was above.

Greece   There was Chaos (Space). From Chaos came Gaea (Earth) and Eros (Love). Next came Erebus (Darkness) and Nyx (Night). Erebus and Nyx brought forth Aether (Light) and Hemera (Day). Gaea gave birth to Ouranos (the Starry Heavens) as a covering for herself. Next Gaea brought forth the mountains, fields, plains, sea, plants, and animals. Then she gave birth to Pontus (the Deep Waters that surround the Earth). Eros brought Ouranos and Gaea together. They became the parents of the 12 Titans. Ouranos banished three of his children. Gaea pleaded with her other children to help rescue their brothers. Cronos (Time), the youngest Titan, responded and seriously wounded Ouranos with his sharp sickle.

Cronos now reigned as lord of Heaven and Earth with his wife, Rhea. Cronos did not free his brothers as he promised, so his mother, Gaea, vowed that he would know the fate that befell his father. To prevent one of his own children from rising up against him, Cronos swallowed each of them as they were born. Rhea decided to save her sixth child, Zeus, so she went to Crete where Zeus was born and raised him in secrecy. In Zeus' place, Rhea brought Cronos a stone wrapped in swaddling clothes, which he ate. When Zeus came of age, he gave Cronos a potion that caused him to vomit up the children he had swallowed. Zeus and his brothers and sisters went to Mount Olympus after defeating Cronos. Out of the eastern side of the world rose Eos (Dawn), Helios (Sun), and Selene (Moon). Each had a place that they left each day to ride in their chariots, bringing day and night to the world of mortals.

"And God saw everything that He had made, and behold, it was very good." —Genesis

---

Origin of the Universe

The Big Bang (1930s, Abbe Georges Lemaitre; 1967, Robert Wagoner and William Fowler)   There was a vast fireball, the **primeval atom** or primeval cosmic egg. This contained all the material of the universe in the form of radiation. There was nothing outside the fireball—it *was* the entire universe. There was tremendous temperature and enormous pressure on this dense cloud of burning gas. Ten or 15 billion years ago, the fireball exploded, breaking into billions of pieces and ejecting them into space at tremendous speeds. These pieces also broke into smaller pieces. When the fireball exploded, it exploded to everywhere from everywhere. The exploding material created the space in which it expanded. No one knows how or why the primeval fireball came to be or even what happened before it exploded.

As the primeval fireball expanded, its temperature dropped from the original 100 billion degrees. More and more of the radiation became matter, mostly hydrogen, about 25% helium, and a trace of deuterium. Three seconds after the explosion, the temperature fell from 1 trillion degrees to about 5 billion. After 3 minutes, the temperature cooled to about a billion degrees. After about 1 million

Big Bang Theory: explosion, formation, and expansion of galaxies

years, the temperature fell to about 5,000° absolute, and there was more matter than radiation in the universe. The width of the universe then was less than 1/1,000 of its present size. For the next few hundred thousand years, the fireball was like the inside of a star.

Large concentrations of matter developed and grew by attraction and collecting more material as they moved through space. This broke the universe up into large masses of gas. About 1 million years after the big bang, galaxies began to form from these clouds of gas. Thermonuclear reactions began taking place in certain gas clouds, and stars were born. Our Sun was one of those stars. From within the gas cloud where the Sun was born, a smaller gas cloud flattened and its dust and gas condensed into the planets. One of these became the Earth. The material of our bodies comes from material in the fireball. According to the Big Bang Theory the universe will last more than 10 billion years.

Arno A. Penzias and Robert Wilson received the Nobel Prize in 1978 for detecting and identifying the hum of the cosmic background radiation left over from the big bang explosion.

Steady State (1950s, Hermann Bondi, Thomas Gold, and Fred Hoyle)   The universe had no beginning and it will have no end. The way it appears now is the way it has always appeared and will always appear no matter where in the universe you are looking. Its condition (state) remains steady. There are always the same number of galaxies. As some galaxies move away into the distance, new ones move in to take their place. Aging stars give off the materials (gases, dust, and energy) needed to produce new stars, as old trees in the forest give material to produce new trees. As it is needed, hydrogen comes into existence through continuous creation.

Oscillating Universe (1940s to present, a version of the Big Bang Theory)   At some point in the future after the big bang, the gravitational force exerted by the combined masses of the galaxies will stop the universe from expanding. The universe will then reach its maximum possible size and begin to contract, bringing back all the material to the original fireball. This is the "big crunch" (a term that **John A. Wheeler** made up). When the universe reaches its maximum possible density level, a second big bang will occur and the universe will start to expand. The universe will continue to expand and contract, almost like breathing (oscillation).

Nebular hypothesis

Formation of the Solar System

Nebular Hypothesis (1796, Immanuel Kant and Pierre Simon La Place)   The protosun (original or first sun) contracted to form a huge rotating gas cloud (primeval solar nebula). As the gas cloud cooled, it contracted even more and the size of the Sun became smaller. The decrease in size caused an increase in the speed at which the Sun was turning and thus increased the accelerating forces coming from the Sun. When the accelerating force from inside the Sun became stronger than the Sun's forces of attraction, a ring separated from the main body of the Sun. As the Sun continued to contract and cool, more rings of matter, like ripples in a pool of water, moved out from the Sun. These gaseous rings gradually condensed into spheres that became the planets.

Tidal Theory (1785, Georges Louis de Button)   A passing star raised a great tide on the Sun and released the gas that later formed the planets due to forces of acceleration.

Planetesimal Theory

Planetesimal Theory (1900, Forrest Moulton and Thomas Chamberlain)   The tidal action of a passing star released matter from the Sun. This matter cooled and, by the forces of acceleration large enough to overcome the gravitational pull of the Sun, formed small particles (planetesimals). These grew in size by picking up scattered material nearby and formed the planets.

Combination/Accumulation Protoplanet Hypothesis (1950, G. P. Kuiper)   The protosun formed at the center of the protosolar nebula. Rotation supported this nebula as it collapsed. Dust grains flew through the nebula and collected into a thin disk of material. Gravitational instability caused the disk to break up into small particles (planetesimals). Over time, the planetesimals formed the planets. Near the Sun, only the rocklike materials could survive the high temperatures; farther away from the Sun, the icy material could condense. For this reason, the inner planets are small, heavy, and rocky, while the outer planets are large, light, and icy. The thin disk of material from the collapsed nebula caused the orbits of all the planets to lie in a flat plane around the equator of the Sun and all the planets except Venus and Uranus to rotate in the same direction.

The accumulation theory predicts that the moons around a planet should resemble a solar system in miniature. They should all lie within the equatorial plane of the planet, have circular orbits, and revolve and spin in the same direction.

In this next project you can make a simple model that can show you the various ways people think the universe might be expanding.

★ ★ ★ ★ ★ ★ ★ ★ ★ ★ ★ **Project 32: Making a Model** ★ ★ ★ ★ ★ ★ ★ ★ ★ ★ ★
of the Expanding Universe

MATERIALS

a round balloon   pencil and paper
paper   ruler
rubber cement   hole punch
felt-tip pen

PROCEDURE

1. Punch holes in the paper and save the small paper circles. Glue the paper circles all over the balloon at different distances apart using the rubber cement. These circles represent the **galaxies**. The balloon represents the size of the universe.

2. Measure and write down the distances between several pairs of galaxies. Mark the paper circles that you measured with a letter or number. Refer to these letters or numbers in your record keeping.

THE BIG BANG UNIVERSE

3. Blow up the balloon without knotting it and notice what happens to the galaxies when you keep the balloon inflated.

4. Measure the distances between the marked galaxies.

THE STEADY STATE UNIVERSE

5. Make several very small dots with the felt-tip pen in between the paper galaxies on the slightly inflated balloon. Try to make the dots so small that you can't see them when the balloon is completely deflated. Each dot in between is new matter forming to take the place of the old.

THE OSCILLATING UNIVERSE

6. Blow up the balloon, stop, then slowly let the air out until the balloon is empty. Blow the balloon up again, stop, then slowly let the air out until the balloon is empty, and so on.

OBSERVATIONS

In "The Big Bang Universe" did any new galaxies appear? Did the galaxies themselves grow larger? Was the universe any more dense after it expanded? What happened to the speed at which the galaxies moved the farther apart they were from one another? Did two galaxies that were twice as far apart as two others move away from each other twice as fast? Check your results again. In "The Steady State Universe" did everything stay the same at all times? Did "The Oscillating Universe" "breathe"?

Your balloon project is a model of how the universe appears to be expanding. Many current creation stories describe an expanding universe. Right now astronomers are trying to find out how much mass there is in the universe. This will help them figure out how big the universe is and whether it is opened or closed (continually expanding or not). One of the biggest events in this research occurred in 1920 in the form of a debate between **Harlow Shapley** and **H. D. Curtis** held at the National Academy of Sciences.

Life on Earth   All of the ancient creation stories tell of the variety of life on Earth. There are 1.7 million known species of plants and animals and another 5 to 30 million we don't know. The smallest group of organisms includes the 4.4 billion animals we use for food and work. Humans are the next largest group with 5 billion. Following us in size are the 580,000 billion water animals, then the 1,667,000 billion wild animals. Then come the worms and termites, the insects, the protozoa and algae, the land plants, and, lastly, bacteria. The numbers in these groups range from 92,428,683,600,000,000,000 billion (worms and termites) to 2,165,105,198,325,000,000,000 billion (bacteria).

All of these different plants and animals (**organisms**) have managed to live and work together wherever they are within an **ecosystem**. The living beings within an ecosystem may gather together in **populations** (groups of individuals of any one kind of organism) or **communities** (all of the populations living in one place). Where an organism lives is its **habitat**, this is its address. What the organism "does for a living" is its **ecological niche**.

Ecosystem, ecological, ecology, and even the word *economics* all come from the Greek word οικος (*oikos*) = home.

Rhythms   Several rhythms or cycles in nature bring about regularly occurring changes within the plant and animal communities:

1. *Daily rhythms* of day and night and the temperature changes that this brings about.

2. *Seasonal rhythms* of the different lengths of day and night, the temperature, and amount of rainfall. In some cases, early and late spring and early and late summer are as different from each other as autumn and winter.

3. *Lunar rhythms* during which time the ocean level rises and falls. The high and low ocean levels are called *tides,* and their rhythm is 12½ hours from one high tide to the next. This means in most places, high tides occur twice daily, 50 minutes later each day. Approximately every two weeks, unusually high tides and unusually low tides occur. See chapter 6, section 2 for more detail on the tides.

The Nereis worm on the Atlantic coast of North America spawns twice each lunar month during the summer. This worm normally lives in burrows on the bottom of the sea and swims out in huge numbers at the full moon and again at the quarter moon.

4. *Internal rhythms* that tell an organism when to sleep or wake up, etc.

5. *Community rhythms* that occur within a specific group of plants or animals.

Water Life   The Earth, like our bodies, is three-quarters water. Life extends to all depths of the ocean. There is more life in the oceans than in all the land and fresh water combined. The most intensive study of the oceans began in 1872, with the voyage of the HMS *Challenger,* one of the first ships to be specifically equipped to study the sea. The study of the physical, chemical, geological, and biological parts of the sea is **oceanography.**

The ocean is in continual circulation, so the temperature range is small. **Warm currents** flow especially in the Indian Ocean and in those parts of the Atlantic and Pacific around the equator from the Americas to Africa and across to Asia. **Cold currents** flow in the Arctic and Southern oceans.

In 1845 a biologist named **Johannes Müller (1801–1858)** used fine-meshed silk nets to catch very young starfish to help him study the life cycle of this sea animal. He was excited to find all kinds of sea life captured in his nets that no one had really noticed before. He told the biologist **Ernst Haeckel (1834–1919)** about his find. Haeckel, Müller, and other biologists began to use similar nets and study what they found in them. In this way, they all became pioneer students of the places and ways people, plants, and animals live together. Haeckel himself made up the word ecology 24 years later in 1869.

We're All in This Together

The Biosphere   Life on Earth extends only a few feet below and above the Earth's surface. This includes the thin outer shell of the Earth, the oceans, and the atmosphere. Only one-fifth of the Earth's total land surface, or less than 40 million square miles (64 million sq. km), can support a permanent standing crop of some kind of vegetation. This is home for all the people on Earth and an even larger number of species of plants and animals. Here chemical and physical changes occur through the interaction of the Sun, air, water, soil. These changes help make it possible for organisms to exist. We call this "realm of life" the Earth's **biosphere.** In the biosphere all life is interrelated. For this reason, it is essential that we come to know who we are sharing life with on the Earth and how we can live together.

Biosphere comes from the Greek words βιος (*bios*) = life and σφαιρα (*sphaira*) = ball, globe.

The Earth's natural landscapes and life forms are the result of processes that have been occurring for billions of years. If left alone, the same processes would continue indefinitely to shape and to reshape the land, plants, and animals. When human beings arrived, we gradually put ever greater demands and stresses upon the rest of creation. Humans change the landscape by farming, mining, building, etc. We grow food and we use energy. Sometimes the energy we use to power our cars and to manufacture things in our factories causes pollution. Because of our presence, some animals no longer exist, they have become **extinct**. Also because of our presence, some desert areas are now rich in vegetation, they have become fertile.

One way to help is to use other forms of energy that don't pollute or use up natural resources. We call these **renewable resources.**

"Go to Nature's School — the one true University." — John Muir

Energy Sources and Resources *Sunlight* and *wind* are renewable resources. To make electricity we can use wind-driven turbines and generators. Concentrated sunlight can boil water.

Oil, natural gas, and *coal* are fossil fuels and nonrenewable resources. Two-thirds of the coal mined is used to make electricity. The largest coal reserves in the world are in the United States.

Biomass is a renewable resource to make electricity. You can burn things to make steam to drive turbines and generators.

Hydroelectricity is renewable. The force of falling water turns the blades of a turbine, which in turn runs a generator and makes electricity.

Nuclear fusion/fission are controlled reactions to make electricity indirectly. Nuclear energy boils water to make steam. Steam turns the blades of a turbine.

Geothermal energy is renewable and will not run out. A turbine operates a generator.

Electricity is a secondary energy source that we get from other energies: oil, gas, water, atoms, wind.

Ocean thermal energy conversion (OTEC) is renewable. Surface water from tropical oceans is warm enough to boil liquid ammonia. Steam produced from boiling ammonia spins the blades of a turbine. The turbine runs a generator that makes electricity. Cold ocean water cools the steam, which condenses back into liquid ammonia. You can then reuse the liquid.

Hot dry rock energy is renewable and comes from volcanoes. It is a form of geothermal energy. In 1960 a scientist named **Robert Potter** got the idea while he was reading a science fiction book, *At the Earth's Core* by **Edgar Rice Burroughs**

(the author of *Tarzan*). Potter's idea developed into the hot dry rock energy process that people are trying out at an experimental plant in Tenton Hill, New Mexico. Engineers drilled deep pipelines into the hot rock below ground. They pump water into the pipe that travels through the hot rock. The hot rock heats the water far above its boiling point. When the heated water returns to the surface through another pipe, steam from the boiling water spins the blades of a turbine which operates a generator to produce electricity.

Generators turn large loops of wire. When the wire moves near a magnet, electricity flows in the wire. Power lines carry this electricity to wherever it is needed.

In this next project you can try your hand at heating water with the Sun instead of using gas, oil, or electricity.

★ ★ ★ ★ ★ ★ **Project 33: Testing an Alternative Energy Source** ★ ★ ★ ★ ★ ★
(Solar Collector)*

MATERIALS

shoe box	paperback book (like this one)
flat black paint	medium-sized jar
newspaper	plastic food container
scissors	clothespin
¼ × 36 inches (6 cm × 1 m) rubber	plastic wrap
or plastic tubing	thermometer
funnel to fit into tubing	water
masking tape	paper and pencil

PROCEDURE

1. Paint the inside of the shoe box and several sheets of newspaper black.
2. Fill the shoe box halfway with crumpled black sheets of newspaper.
3. Cut holes the width of the tubing at each end of the shoe box.
4. Arrange the tubing as shown and tape it in place.
5. Cover the box tightly with plastic wrap.
6. Fill a jar with water and measure and record its temperature.
7. Place the shoe box in direct sunlight. Put a paperback book under one end. Face the opposite end toward the south.
8. Clamp the clothespin on the tube at the south-facing end. Put an empty container under the tube.
9. Place the funnel into the tube at the north end and pour water into it. Open the clothespin and allow the water to flow through the tubing until it starts to come out at the other end. Then clamp the tube closed with the clothespin.

*This project is adapted from **Heath Physical Science** by Louise Mary Nolan and Wallace Tucker. Lexington: D. C. Heath, 1984. Used with permission.

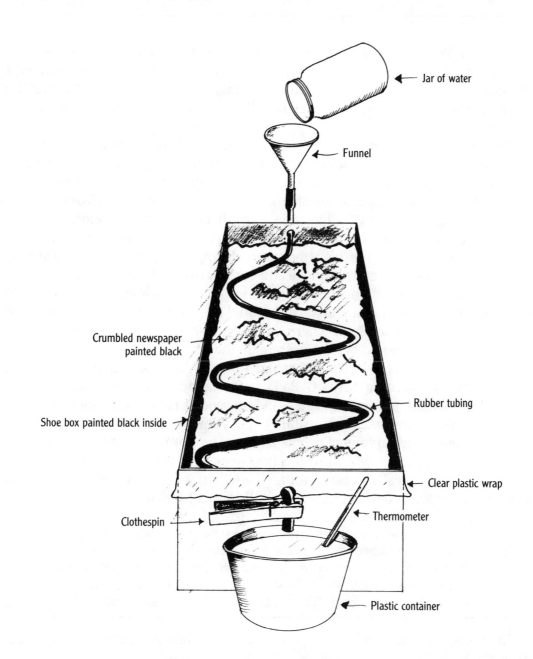

Jar of water

Funnel

Crumbled newspaper painted black

Rubber tubing

Shoe box painted black inside

Clear plastic wrap

Clothespin

Thermometer

Plastic container

10. Let the water sit in the tube for 15 minutes. Open the clothespin and let the water flow into the empty container.

11. Measure and record the temperature of the water.

OBSERVATIONS

How did your solar collector affect the water temperature? What would happen if you left the water in the tube longer?

Nuclear Winter   Of all of humanity's many inventions, nuclear weapons are the most useless and destructive. One of these weapons is too many, but we have tens of thousands. We are in the unfortunate predicament of having made something before we really knew what we were getting into. As research into nuclear weapons continues, we find ourselves up against the biggest challenge ever to face the human race. We have the power to destroy all life on this planet. We can make the human race extinct.

No one wants to do this. For this reason, many people would like to believe that it is not possible. In 1971 research began on the planet Mars using the *Mariner 9* spacecraft (see chapter 6, section 4). The huge dust storms that rage frequently on the planet blew into the upper atmosphere, blocking most of the light from the Sun. The planet received very little light and warmth because of this blockage. As a result, the surface of Mars became a "chilly desert." A research team looked into what would happen to the Earth's atmosphere during a nuclear war. They came to the startling realization that the smoke and dust caused by fires and explosions set off by only 5% of the world's nuclear weapons would create a Mars-like condition in the Earth's atmosphere. Light and warmth would not reach the Earth. Winds would carry these dark clouds to places where the weapons hadn't even been. In a matter of months, the Earth would begin to resemble the frozen, lifeless surface of Mars. Ecological systems and food webs and chains would break, causing many plant and animal species to become extinct. Radioactive fallout, lack of food, dramatic temperature changes, poisonous fumes, and ultraviolet rays in this **nuclear winter** would combine to eliminate the possibility of anyone surviving, anywhere.

Fortunately, there are many people all over the world who are determined to keep this from happening. We all realize how important it is, now more than ever, to see the world as it really is: home for all life. When we see our home from space, it becomes so clear, so obvious that we are all in this together.

"Think of it. We are traveling on a planet, revolving around the Sun, in almost perfect symmetry. We are blessed with technology that would be indescribable to our forefathers. We have the wherewithal, the know-it-all, to feed everybody, clothe everybody, give every human on Earth a chance. We dwell instead on petty things. We kill each other. We build monuments to ourselves. What a waste of time. . . . Think of it. What a chance we have. . . ." — Buckminster Fuller

---

In this next project there are many suggestions for things you can do to take care of the Earth and its resources.

★ ★ ★ ★ ★ ★ ★ ★ ★ ★ **Project 34: Looking After the Earth** ★ ★ ★ ★ ★ ★ ★ ★ ★ ★

MATERIALS
    a little thoughtfulness

PROCEDURE
    Try as many of these ideas as you can. In a friendly way, mention some of them to others.

1. Turn the lights, radio, and TV off when no one is in the room.
2. Recycle cans, glass, and paper in your home and school.
3. Don't accept junk mail—tell your post office or have mail returned to sender.
4. Bring your own shopping bags to stores, especially grocery stores.
5. Put a brick in the tank of your toilet—it raises the water level and lowers the amount of water you use.
6. Put a water-saving shower head on your shower. (Showers use less water than baths.)
7. Use paper bags instead of plastic ones for garbage.
8. Eat lower on the food chain (more vegetables, less beef, more poultry).
9. Walk, bicycle, or use public transportation instead of cars.
10. Close closet doors so there is less space to heat or cool.
11. Don't throw trash on the ground or out of the car window.
12. Pick up trash, even if it's not yours.
13. Throw metal soft-drink tabs and plastic can carriers in the trash.
14. Dry your clothes on the line whenever possible instead of using the dryer.
15. Wait until your dishwasher or washing machine is full before you use it. Use shortest cycle and air-dry dishes. Wash clothes with cold water.
16. Plant trees to shade your house in summer and to protect against wind in winter.
17. Don't play your radios and tapes loudly outside (or at all in scenic places).
18. Replace mechanized recreation (motorcycles, dune buggies, snowmobiles, power boats, trail bikes, and jeeps) with quieter, nonpolluting, less destructive alternatives (bicycles, skates, skiis, canoes, windsurfers, surfboards, sailboats, etc.).

19. Use a living, potted Christmas tree.

20. Consider giving gifts that encourage creativity and increase concern for the environment: gardening sets; tool kits; art and craft materials; cooking equipment; camping equipment; cameras; sports equipment; books (especially about nature); subscriptions to nature magazines; new games; pets; "rain checks" for trips to the beach, zoo, or mountains; contributions to nature and environmental organizations.

21. If you really want to wrap the gifts you give reuse wrapping paper or be creative with pages from newspapers or magazines.

22. Become a volunteer at a wildlife protection agency.

23. Insulate the attic and walls of your house, including hot-water heater and pipes.

24. Examine and compare the efficiency ratios of several similar appliances before you buy.

25. Keep a record of everything your family consumes in 1 week (food, water, electricity, gasoline, etc.). Use meters to check electricity and water. Also keep a record of how much garbage your family throws away in 1 week. Consider yours an average family and multiply your consumption and garbage by the population of your town or country to get an idea of your impact on the environment.

26. Fix leaky faucets.

27. Lower the temperature on your hot-water heater.

28. Open and close the refrigerator as little as necessary.

29. Use a microwave or toaster oven.

30. Use the lowest possible setting on the stove.

31. Don't preheat the oven for more than 10 minutes.

32. Clean furnace and air conditioner filters once a month.

33. Dress warmer in the house and turn the heat down.

34. Keep the damper closed when you're not using the fireplace.

35. Light the places where you are working (your desk, etc.) instead of the whole room.

36. Keep the coils under the refrigerator clean.

37. Air- or towel-dry your hair.

38. Install storm windows and doors and weatherstrip windows and doors.

39. Turn the thermostat down at night.

40. Close the curtains and shades at night to save heat.

READING MORE

Diagram Group, The. *A Science Digest Book: Spaceship Earth — Its Voyage Through Time.* New York: Hearst Books, 1980.

Earthworks Group, The. *50 Simple Things You Can Do to Save the Earth.* Berkeley: Earthworks Press, 1989.

Kyselka, Will, and Ray Lanterman. *North Star to Southern Cross.* Honolulu: University Press of Hawaii, 1976.

Nickelsburg, Janet. *Ecology: Habitats, Niches, and Food Chains.* Philadelphia: J. B. Lippincott, 1969.

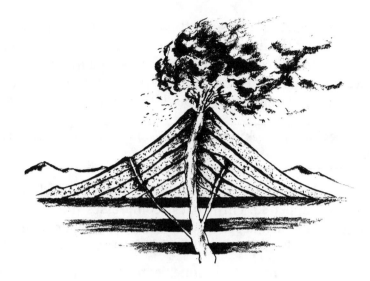

Section 2 *FROM CORE TO MANTLE*

Inside the Earth   How far down into the Earth do you think people have explored? Tens or hundreds of miles or kilometers? The answer is a surprising 10 miles (16 km), which is about twice as high as Mount Everest. No one has been to the center of the Earth. When I was very little, I would see a construction crew digging a hole, and I would wonder, Are they going to dig down as far as hell? When I got a little older, I wondered, Are Chinese people going to come out of the hole? When I got even bigger, I wondered, Are they going to make a hole right through the Earth so you can see the sky on the other side? A favorite question when I was in college was, If you did manage to dig a hole through the Earth and you dropped something into it, where would it go?

The French writer **Jules Verne** (1828–1905) had his own answers to these questions. He wrote a great adventure story entitled *Journey to the Center of the Earth.* At the center of the Earth in Verne's world were vast caves and oceans. His description of the center of the Earth sounds a bit like that of the Roman writer **Seneca** (ca. 4 B.C.–65 A.D.), who said

> Be assured that there exists below, everything that you see above. There are vast caverns, immense recesses and vacant spaces with mountains overhanging on either hand. There are yawning gulfs, stretching down into the abyss, which have often swallowed up cities that have fallen into them. These retreats are filled with air, for nowhere is there a vacuum in nature; through their ample spaces stretch marshes over which darkness ever broods. Animals are also produced in them but they are slow-paced and shapeless.

From our study of earthquake waves we have put together our own picture of the interior of the Earth. The Earth has three main spheres. The word *sphere* means a ball, but it can also mean an area of activity or influence. In the case of the Earth's spheres, it means both. There is a sphere for each of the three forms of matter: **solid, liquid,** and **gas.**

Lithosphere   The solid part of the Earth, that part upon which we live, is mostly rock and soil, so we call it the **lithosphere.** The lithosphere encloses the four-layered interior of the Earth: the **inner core,** the **outer core,** the **mantle,** and the **crust.** As you move toward the center of the Earth from the crust, the temperature increases 1°C per 100 feet, 96°F per mile, or 30°C per kilometer.

Lithosphere comes from the Greek words λιθος (*lithos*) = stone and σφαιρα (*sphaira*) = globe or ball.

The Inner Core   The pressure is so great in the inner core (close to 9 million lb. per sq. in. [4 million kg per sq. cm]) that it compresses the nickel-iron material, raising its boiling point which keeps it solid. Still, the temperature at the center of the Earth is estimated to be about 9,000°F (5,500°C).

The Outer Core   Surrounding the inner core is an outer layer of liquid iron. This liquid metal is believed to circulate at 0.008 inches (0.02 cm) per second. This motion sets up electric currents that create the Earth's magnetic field.

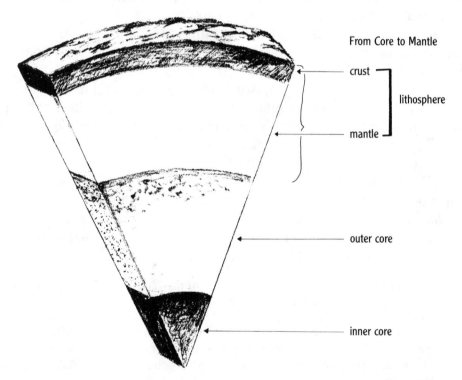

From Core to Mantle

crust ⎤
        ⎥ lithosphere
mantle ⎦

outer core

inner core

The Mantle   The mantle is a semimolten layer that wraps itself around the outer and inner core of the Earth. We have never seen the mantle, even though it lies fewer than 50 miles beneath our feet. Most of what we know about what the mantle is made of has literally come up to us from it by way of deep volcanoes. This material is made of dense, solid rocks. These rocks are rich in iron and minerals made of oxygen, silicon, magnesium, iron, and calcium. The part of the mantle closest to the core we sometimes call the **mesosphere** because it is between the center and the surface of the Earth.

Mantle comes from the Latin word *mantele* = a towel, napkin, or covering.
Meso- comes from the Greek word μεσος (*mesos*) = middle.

The upper part of the mantle is a soft layer of nearly molten rock about the consistency of asphalt. This is the **asthenosphere** (= without strength). The study of waves coming from quakes on the Earth or any planet we call **seismology**. People have charted the boundary between the next layer, the crust, and the mantle based on seismology. The speed of a wave depends on how dense the material is that it is traveling through. The speed of these waves increases as the density of the material increases. Primary waves (P waves) can travel through both solid and liquid materials. Secondary waves (S waves) can only travel through solid material. If a layer of one material with a particular density and composition lies above another layer whose density and composition are different, the direction of the earthquake waves will change sharply as they pass from one material to another.

By careful studies of seismograms, you can locate the depths at which these abrupt changes occur. This is what **Andrija Mohorovicic**, a Yugoslavian, did in 1909. He detected a sharp change in the path of earthquake waves at a depth of 25 miles (40 km) below the continents. At this level he noticed that the waves met a zone of increased density. In this zone they could travel 25% faster than they could above it. Their travel path had changed or discontinued their previous wave pattern. The waves had entered the mantle. To this dividing line at 25 miles (40 km) below the Earth's surface that marks the end of the crust and the beginning of the mantle we have given the name **Mohorovicic discontinuity** or simply the **Moho**. Earthquakes can occur at depths of no more than 435 miles (700 km) within the mantle.

Asthenosphere comes from the Greek word ἀσθενος (*asthenos*) = without strength. The lithosphere technically includes all of the crust and part of the upper mantle above the asthenosphere.

In this next project you can put all of this information together in a model of what the Earth looks like inside.

★ ★ ★ ★ ★ ★ ★ ★ **Project 35: Making a Model of the Inside** ★ ★ ★ ★ ★ ★ ★ ★
of the Earth

MATERIALS

four different colors of modeling clay	paper
thin wire	colored pencils (four different colors)
string	glue

PROCEDURE

1. Make a ball of the first color of modeling clay. This is the inner core.
2. Flatten out a piece of the second color of modeling clay 1½ times as large as the inner core. This is the outer core.
3. Flatten out a piece of the third color of modeling clay twice as large as the inner core. This is the mantle. Roll it around the other two layers without losing the shape of the sphere or thinning out the clay.
4. Flatten out a very thin piece of the fourth color of modeling clay. This is the crust. Cover the sphere keeping it round and without thinning out the clay.
5. Take the thin wire and carefully cut the sphere in half. Write the names of each part of the Earth's interior on a small piece of paper using the same color of pencils as the parts of the Earth. Connect each name to the model using string with one end stuck into the modeling clay and the other end glued onto the paper.

OBSERVATIONS

Use your model while you reread about the inside of the Earth. Does it help you get a better picture of the different parts? You may want to add the asthenosphere and the Moho.

The Crust   This is the layer we know the best. Under the continents, it is about 30 miles (48 km) thick, under the oceans only about 3 miles (5 km). Overall, the ocean floor sinks farther below sea level than the continents rise above sea level. The average depth of the oceans is about 2½ miles (4 km) below sea level, whereas the average height of the continents is about ½ mile (0.8 km) above sea level. In some places, such as the Marianas Trench in the Pacific, the ocean is almost 7 miles (11 km) deep. By comparison, the highest mountain on the land, Mount Everest, is only a little more than 5½ miles (9 km) high. Compared to the entire Earth, the thickness of the crust is like the thickness of the skin of an apple. Its wrinkled surface even resembles the skin of an old apple. These wrinkles (which create the mountains, valleys, and flatlands) are due to the activity of the crust, whose several segments are always on the move. We call the segments of the Earth's crust **plates**.

There are about 10 large plates and several small ones, each only about 30 miles (50 km) thick.

Sir Francis Bacon (1561–1626), and others after him, suggested that the continents had drifted apart. Rock samples from both continents were of similar type and age and in the same order in layers at those places where the continents would have been joined. Fossil remains showed similar plant and animal life. Mountains lined up with each other.

In 1869 **Antonio Snyder Pellegrini**, a meteorologist (a person who studies the weather), helped develop the idea of **continental drift**. In 1912, in his book *The Origin of Continents and Oceans*, **Alfred Wegener** (1880–1930), a German geologist, meteorologist, and explorer, presented as much evidence as he could concerning the theory of continental drift. People considered him to be the founder of this theory, although the idea did not originate with him.

Alfred Wegener began his scholarly career as a historian of astronomy, studying the 13th-century Alfonsine tables of planetary motions.

In 1965 **J. Tuzo Wilson** took the theory of continental drift and the concepts of magnetic studies and sea-floor spreading and combined them into one theory, the **theory of plate tectonics**. According to this theory, seven major plates and several smaller plates make up the Earth's surface.

If Earth's plates are moving, then where they are now is not where they have always been. Under the Earth's hard crust there is a general temperature increase of about 1°F for every 60 feet (18 m) you go down toward the center (or 10°C for every 98 ft. [30 m]). While not hot enough to melt the rock under the crust, this heat flow does make the material under the crust slightly soft. This slightly soft layer is the asthenosphere. From within the asthenosphere (60–120 mi. [100–200 km] deep), over time the material "flows" in currents.

The hard plates of the Earth's crust that "float" on top of the soft rock are carried around the surface of the Earth by the movement going on underneath. The speed that the plates travel is a few inches per year. The continents, which are attached to a certain plate, move whenever the plate moves.

When one plate meets another, there is no empty space in which to move, so they jam into each other and burrow under each other, sliding right into the mantle. The places where this happens are called **trenches**. A good example of a trench is the Japan Trench along the coast of that country. The process of pushing underneath to form trenches is called **subduction**. The continents, however, don't usually get shoved under. Instead they crash head-on into each other and either join together or force the land to push upward at the boundaries to form mountain ranges. Mount Everest and the Himalaya Mountains came about when India joined Asia. Sometimes plates collide with each other without sliding underneath. Then they buckle up to form mountains just as continents do. These are called **ridges**. The Mid-Atlantic Ridge upon which Iceland sits is an example of this activity.

Earth's plates and the direction of their movement

Subduction comes from the Latin words *sub* = under and *duct* = to lead.

The boundaries of plates look like cracks in the surface of the Earth. A good way to imagine them is to look at a crack in a rock or a mountain. The cracks in the Earth's crust are **faults**. A famous fault line in the United States is the San Andreas Fault from the west of San Francisco in the north to the Gulf of California in the south. The fault line or boundary between two plates is also a place where new material for the crust can flow up from the mantle. The material may come gradually or be thrust out from volcanoes in the form of lava. The new material joins on to the edge of the plate, and in this way the Earth replenishes its surface. Knowing where the greatest amount of volcanic activity is occurring can help you locate the boundaries of the plates.

If Sir Francis Bacon and Alfred Wegener were right, the continents were once joined together. What would that have looked like? Wegener made up the name **Pangaea** for this land mass.

> **Pangaea** comes from the Greek words π$αν$ (*pan*) = all and γαια (*gaia*) = Earth.

According to Wegener's theory in the first separation of the lands, Pangaea divided into two large areas, almost along the equator. To the north was **Laurasia,** which was to become North America, Europe, and Asia. To the south was **Gondwanaland,** which included present-day India, Australia, Africa, South America, and Antarctica.

> **Laurasia** = combination of North America, Europe, and Asia.
> **Gondwanaland** = a province of India of geological interest.

| Pangaea | Laurasia and Gondwanaland | Approaching the present position |

The drifting continents

Tectonic activity, cratering, and volcanoes have all been found to occur on many planets and their moons. Studying this activity on other bodies in space helps us understand what happens on our own planet.

The Earth's crust is rich in rock and mineral deposits. New material is constantly working its way up from the Earth's interior. New Hampshire farmers will tell you that their first crop of the season is always rocks. Residents of Rockland County, New York, make a similar boast. Most of these "crops" consist of silicate—rich granitic rock types. The rocks below the oceans and mountains are mostly basaltic rock, volcanic in origin. The crust is composed of 46.6% oxygen, with 27.7% silicon, 8.1% aluminum, 5.0% iron, 3.6% calcium, 2.8% sodium, 2.6% potassium, and 2.1% magnesium (and 1.5% miscellaneous). "Soil" is usually not more than 20 feet (6 m) deep. We also call soil "earth." Sometimes we call it dirt. Our idea of "dirty" or "earthy" being unclean probably comes from Aristotle's picture of the planet Earth as that place farthest from the gods.

Water on the Earth   The oceans contain 97% of all the water on Earth. The largest of these is the Pacific Ocean, whose surface area is greater than that of all the continents put together. The Atlantic Ocean is the next largest ocean, followed by the Indian Ocean and the Arctic Ocean.

There are many lakes, streams, rivers, ponds, and creeks. The water in these places usually comes from melted snow in mountain peaks and is fresh. The water in the oceans and some seas is salty; sometimes we call it **brine**. The freshwater bodies hold less than 1% of the Earth's water. The remaining 2% of the total is frozen into ice in glaciers and around the North and South poles.

Water seeks to take the shape of a sphere. When moving, it creates spirals and curled shapes. In the crest of a wave or the wavy-lined shape of riverbanks, we see the signature of the forces of form and movement. In this next project you can see these shapes yourself as you make the signature of form and movement visible in water.

★ ★ ★ ★ ★ ★ **Project 36: Interpreting Patterns of Movement** ★ ★ ★ ★ ★ ★
in Water*

MATERIALS

long, flat cooking dish	fine powder (e.g., lycopodium)
ink or food coloring	pencil
eyedropper	water
glycerine	camera with ASA 400 film

PROCEDURE

1. Fill the cooking dish with water.
2. Fill the eyedropper with ink or food coloring.
3. Squirt the ink into the water from one end of the cooking dish with the eyedropper under water. Squirt slowly at first, then faster. Observe the patterns the ink makes in the water.
4. Empty the container and refill it with water.

*This project is adapted from the work of Theodor Schwenk appearing in his book *Sensitive Chaos: The Creation of Flowing Forms in Water and Air*. London: Rudolf Steiner Press, 1965.

5. Add enough glycerine to make the water thicker.
6. Sprinkle the surface of the water with the fine powder.
7. Hold the pencil straight up in the water at one end of the cooking dish.
8. Move the pencil straight across the water. Photograph what you see.
9. Move the pencil faster across the water. Photograph what you see.
10. Move the pencil twice through the water. Photograph what you see.
11. Repeat steps 8 and 9 with your thumb. Photograph what you see.

OBSERVATIONS
Where in nature have you seen these forms before? Compare your photographs with photographs of the surfaces of Jupiter and Saturn.

READING MORE
Beiser, Arthur, and the Editors of Time-Life Books. *The Earth.* New York: Time-Life Books, 1970.
Clayton, Keith. *The Crust of Earth: The Story of Geology.* Garden City, NJ: The Natural History Press, 1967.

The Orion nebula *(from* The Story of the Heavens *by Sir Robert S. Ball. London: Cassel, 1886)*

Section 3   FROM ATMOSPHERE TO EXOSPHERE
The Air Around the Earth   When you look up at the blue sky, you are looking at a blanket of air that surrounds and protects our Earth. This blanket filters out the harmful ultraviolet rays from the Sun and helps balance out extremes in temperature. We call this protective air blanket the **atmosphere**. The atmosphere contains six layers: the **troposphere**, the **stratosphere**, the **mesosphere**, the **thermosphere**, the **ionosphere**, and the **exosphere**.

Atmosphere comes from the Greek word ἁτμος (*atmos*) = smoke or vapor.

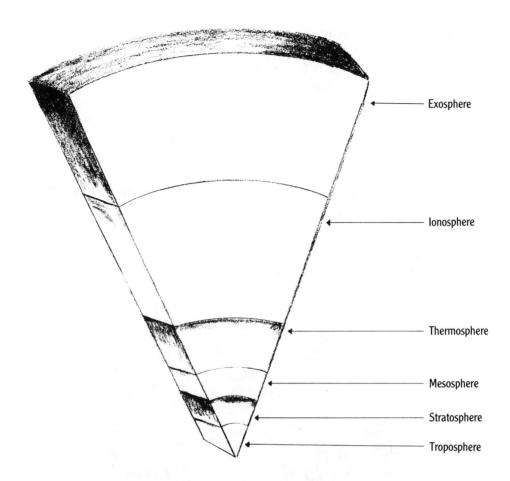

From atmosphere to exosphere

The Troposphere   The troposphere contains about $9/10$ of the atmosphere's total mass and all the constantly changing elements that cause the weather: water vapor, dust, smoke, clouds, and winds. All of our weather occurs within this sphere. The air currents sweep up and down, causing winds, storms, clouds, snow, and rain.

Troposphere comes from the Greek word τροπος (*tropos*) = a turn, direction, or way.

If you move upward through the troposphere, the temperature of the air decreases steadily at a rate of 1°F for every 300 feet (90 m). When you reach the top of the troposphere, the temperature begins to rise again. The temperature at the top of the troposphere is warmest just above the Earth's poles where the air is almost always 50° below zero. Here the troposphere extends to a height of about 5 miles (8 km). Above the equator where the troposphere layer reaches the highest, about 11 miles (18 km), the temperature at the top of the troposphere normally remains near −100°F or −86°C. The average height of the troposphere is 10 miles (16 km), about twice the height of Mount Everest. Practically all of the moisture in the atmosphere is in the troposphere. About 90% of all the gas in the atmosphere is also within the troposphere. The air you breathe is 78% nitrogen, 21% oxygen, and 1% argon, with traces of water (as a gas), carbon dioxide, and other gases. The boundary between the troposphere and the stratosphere is the **tropopause.**

The Stratosphere   Above the ever-changing troposphere is the stratosphere. Here the air is calm and almost completely free from water vapor, dust, and gases. A few thin clouds sometimes appear here, but there is no turbulence. The air currents flow in horizontal layers rather than in vertical columns as in the troposphere. For all of these reasons, airline pilots prefer to fly their large jets in the stratosphere. Since the air outside the plane is too "thin" to support life, the plane must supply air for people to breathe. Temperatures in the 25 miles (40 km) of the stratosphere remain constant from 70°F to −45°F (21°C to −43°C) in the lower half to about −30°F (−35°C) in the upper half. In 1942 V2 rockets launched at White Sands, New Mexico, first recorded above-freezing temperatures in this region.

Stratosphere comes from the Latin word *stratum* = covering or layer.

Within the stratosphere layer are winds that blow usually from west to east at speeds of up to 300 miles (480 km) per hour. This narrow band seems to follow roughly the southern edge of the large cold air mass that covers much of the northern parts of the North American continent. We call it the **jet stream.** During the winter when this air mass is large, the North American jet stream passes directly over the center of the United States. In 1944, U.S. pilots discovered the jet stream when they attempted to fly westward above the troposphere. They met the jet stream head-on, blowing from the opposite direction with such a force that the planes, the largest and highest flying aircraft ever built at that time, could hardly move.

The boundary between the stratosphere and the mesosphere is the **stratopause.**

The Mesosphere   The stratopause marks the beginning of a sharp increase in the temperature of the air, within the 25 miles (40 km) of the mesosphere. In the lower levels of the mesosphere, temperatures climb to +170°F (77°C). At the upper limit of the mesosphere, the temperature plunges to −150°F (−101°C). The lowest temperatures in the atmosphere occur here.

Mesosphere comes from the Greek word μεσο (*meso*) = middle.

The boundary between the mesosphere and the thermosphere and ionosphere is the **mesopause.**

The Thermosphere and the Ionosphere   When you reach beyond the mesosphere you encounter four layers of gases whose names come from the chief elements that they contain: the **nitrogen layer** (about 70 mi. or 112 km thick), the **oxygen layer** (almost 575 mi. or 925 km thick), the **helium layer** (about 150 mi. or 240 km thick), and the **hydrogen layer** (about 20,000 mi. or 32,000 km thick). The air in this sphere is very hot because of the energy from the Sun that collects here. For this reason, we call this sphere the **thermosphere**. The air is also very thin in this sphere.

Thermosphere comes from the Greek word θερμος (*thermos*) = warm or hot.

Overlapping the mesosphere and the thermosphere are several layers of electrically charged particles. The Sun seems to be responsible for creating these charged particles from material in the air. The particles are **ions**. The ionosphere reflects radio waves. These waves do not follow the curved shape of the Earth but follow straight lines. (For more information about radio waves, see chapter 5, section 4.) Since some of the waves are reflected back, we can send them around the world. **Guglielmo Marconi** (1874–1937) recognized this possibility on December 12, 1901, when he sent the code letter *S* using radio waves from Cornwall, England, across the Atlantic to St. John's on the coast of Newfoundland. His Nobel Prize–winning work led to the discovery and further use of the layers of ionized particles in the upper atmosphere.

Working apart but at the same time, an Englishman named **Arthur Edwin Kennelly** (1861–1939) and an English electrical engineer named **Oliver Heaviside** (1850–1925) concluded that there must be an electrical reflecting layer high in the atmosphere that reflects certain radio waves back to the Earth while letting others pass through. We call this "radio roof" the **Kennelly-Heaviside layer** after its discoverers. Auroras or Northern and Southern Lights occur here. Here too is where meteoroids burn up and produce meteors.

Ion comes from the Greek word ιον (*ion*) = to go.

The Exosphere Above the ionosphere, 300 miles (480 km) above the Earth's surface, the air is very, very thin. This final layer of the Earth's atmosphere reaches right out into space. For that reason we call it the **exosphere**.

Exosphere comes from the Latin word *ex* = out of.

The atmosphere protects us from the Sun's full energy by absorbing the ultraviolet rays while letting some of the light and warmth reach us. The atmosphere also provides us with two unique and beautiful features of living on Earth: blue skies and sunsets. How? The next project, based on the work of the German poet and scientist **Johann Goethe** (1749–1832), will help you answer this question.

Light from back

Light from side

★ ★ ★ ★ ★ ★ ★ ★Project 37: Demonstrating How the Colors ★ ★ ★ ★ ★ ★ ★
of the Sky Are Made

MATERIALS

an aquarium or large, clear container   liquid detergent, milk, or powdered
slide projector   coffee creamer
                                                                   water

PROCEDURE

1. Fill the tank with water. Add enough liquid detergent, milk, or powdered creamer to the water so that it is semitransparent.

2. Shine the projector on the *side* of the tank. Look through the front of the tank. What color is the water?

3. Shine the projector on the *back* of the tank. Look through the front of the tank at the light behind it. What color is the water?

OBSERVATIONS

The presence of an atmosphere around the Earth creates a "dusty" layer of material through which light must pass: air, tiny droplets of water, and dust particles. The bluing and reddening of the sky is due to the spreading out of the sunlight through this dusty layer. We call it **diffusion**. The blue light reaches us from all directions, while the red is more focused.

Diffusion comes from the Latin word *diffussus* = spread abroad, extended.

The moist particles of dust and smoke in the atmosphere act as tiny mirrors sending the reflection of light back to the Earth. This happens before sunrise when the Sun's light is reflected and after sunset, thus providing additional daylight and daytime. City lights at night often light up the sky. You can look at light and the effects the atmosphere has on it in more detail in chapter 5, section 2.

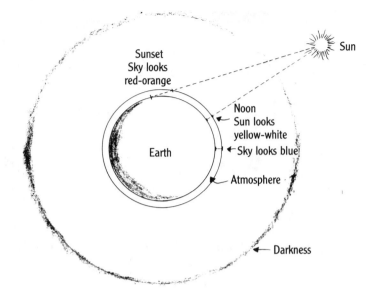

The Magnetosphere   The **magnetosphere** is a blanket of particles surrounding the Earth. It extends about 4,000 miles (6,500 km) out from the Earth. Radiation from the Sun, also invisible, sweeps out into space with the force of an air current. For this reason we call the Sun's radiation the **solar wind**. When the solar wind hits the Earth's magnetosphere, it pushes the magnetosphere in at one side while stretching it out on the other.

The U.S. satellites *Explorer I* (1958), *Pioneer III* (1959), and later *Explorer III, Explorer IV,* and *Pioneer I* included radiation-detecting instruments designed by **James A. Van Allen**, a physicist at the State University of Iowa. The satellites detected two belts of very strong radiation within the magnetosphere. These belts had a shape like two doughnuts, a small one inside a large one. We call these belts **Van Allen belts**, after their discoverer.

WEATHER

Whether the weather is cold
or whether the weather is hot,
We'll weather the weather
whatever the weather
whether we like it or not!

Weather   Climate is the average yearly and seasonal pattern of weather conditions that you find in any location. Climate limits the growing season and restricts the crops that you can grow. Because of its effects on the soil, the climate is responsible for how fertile the land will be. This helps explain why people are spread so unevenly over the Earth. They're looking for places where the climate will let them grow food.

Weather is how we describe what is happening to the air and the water in it at a specific time and in a specific place. It is what the climate is right here, right now.

Climate comes from the Greek word κλιμα (*klima*) = inclination or slope of the Earth toward the pole, in ancient geography. A climate was one of seven astrological belts or zones on the Earth. Each of the seven planets had a zone that it looked after.
Weather comes from the Middle English word *weder* = weather.

Air is constantly moving where there are differences in temperature and therefore pressure. The greater the differences in pressure, the stronger the winds will blow. In an effort toward balance, hot air is sent toward the poles, cold air toward the tropics. When each reaches its goal, the temperature it meets changes the temperature of the air causing it to move again.

Winds are named according to the direction from which they are coming.

In 1680 Sir Edmond Halley (1656–1742), the British Astronomer Royal, published a paper in which he made the first attempt to show that the flow of cold, dense air toward regions of warmer, lighter air caused the different wind patterns around the globe.

Edmond Halley's chart of the wind patterns, 1686

How can you tell whether the air pressure is high or low? In 1643 a student of Galileo named **Evangelista Torricelli** (1608–1647) invented an instrument to do just that. He called his instrument a **barometer**. When Torricelli made his barometer, he used liquid mercury in a thin glass tube standing above a glass dish. The column of mercury stopped moving down the glass tube and into the dish when the pressure due to its weight was balanced by the pressure of the air pushing down on the mercury in the dish. The level of mercury in the tube in this balanced position was 30 inches (76 cm) above the surface of the mercury in the dish. When the air pressure gets heavier, it pushes down on the surface of the mercury in the dish, sending the mercury higher up in the column. Thus, you can actually see the pressure rising. A pressure of 30 inches (76 cm) is equal to 1,016 millibars, the unit of measurement that the U.S. Weather Bureau prefers to use. (To change from inches to millibars, multiply the pressure in inches by 33.87.)

Barometer comes from the Greek words βαροσ (*baros*) = weight or pressure and μετρον (*metron*) = to measure.

Warm air is lighter, and cold air is heavier. When you hear the expression "the barometer is falling," it means that the pressure is below 30 inches (76 cm). Keep checking with the weather bureau. "When the glass falls low prepare for a blow, when it rises high let all your kites fly."

"We live submerged at the bottom of an ocean of the element air."
—Evangelista Torricelli, 1644

In 1843 **Lucien Vidie**, a French scientist, invented a barometer that was less expensive, smaller, lightweight, and portable. He removed the air from a tiny accordion-like box. Changes in air pressure caused the little box to collapse or expand slightly. These changes were indicated by a needle and a dial on the box. Because this barometer has no liquid in it, we call it an **aneroid barometer**.

Aneroid comes from the Greek words ἀ (*a*) = without and νηρον (*neron*) = liquid.

In 1612 Galileo constructed an instrument to measure the temperature of the air. He called his instrument a **thermometer**.

Thermometer comes from the Greek words θερμος (*thermos*) = warm and μετρον (*metron*) = to measure.

Moisture   The amount of moisture in the air contributes to its pressure. There is dry, hot air in low-pressure areas. Wet, cold air is in high-pressure areas. This moisture is what you hear people complain about when they say, "It's not just the heat, it's the **humidity**."

Humidity comes from the Latin word *humidus* = moist, damp.

In 1783 the Swiss geologist **Horace Bénédict de Saussure** (1740–1799) invented a method to measure the moisture or humidity in the air. He called his invention the **hair hygrometer**. De Saussure used strands of human hair attached to a dial. When the air was moist, the hair stretched. When the air was dry, the hair shrank. A dial showed the change.

220	110	400	
200	100	373	Boiling point
180	90		
160	80		
140	70		
120	60		
100	50		
80	40		
60	30	300	
40	20	273	Freezing point
20	10		
0	0		
-20	-10		
-40	-20		
-60	-30		
-80	-40	200	
-100	-50		
-200	-60		
-300	-80	100	
-400	-100		
-460°	-200		
	-273		Absolute zero

Fahrenheit   Celsius   Kelvin

Comparing Fahrenheit, Celsius, and Kelvin temperatures

Hygrometer comes from the Greek word ὑγρός (*hygros*) = wet, moist.

In 1714 **Gabriel Daniel Fahrenheit** (1686–1736), a German scientist, invented the familiar **Fahrenheit** scale. On his scale, the boiling point of water is 212°, and the freezing point of water is 32°. In 1742 **Anders Celsius** (1701–1744), a Swedish astronomer, invented the **centigrade** scale. On this scale, the boiling point of water is 100°, and the freezing point of water is 0°. In 1850 the Scottish mathematician and physicist William Thomson, **Lord Kelvin** (1824–1907), developed the **Kelvin** or **absolute** scale. In this scale, absolute zero is the lowest possible temperature.

The Water Cycle   Water is always present in the air, even in the desert. About 9/10 of it is in the air above the Earth. This moisture constantly recirculates in what we call the **water cycle**.

Rain and Storms   From the clouds come rain and snow, returning moisture to the Earth. In order for this to happen, a cloud must contain water droplets and ice crystals. Water vapor gathers into clouds by collecting onto tiny particles of dust, dirt, and salt spray in the air. The cloud droplets around these dust particles are about 1/2,500 inch (0.0010 cm) in diameter. They contain water or ice crystals or both. Water forms around the ice crystals, making them heavier. When they are too

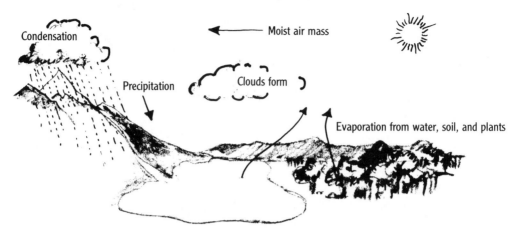

The water cycle

heavy to float in the air, they fall. If they pass through a warm sky, the ice crystals melt and fall as **rain.** If the air is cold, the crystals fall to the Earth as **snow.** If the ice crystals pass back and forth in a large thunderstorm cloud between freezing and nonfreezing air levels, onionlike layers of ice gradually fall as **hailstones** at about 7 miles (11 km) per hour.

Raindrops range in size from about 1/100 to ¼ inch (¼–6 mm) or less in diameter. They start round but end up flat at the bottom and round at the top, like a mushroom. No two snowflakes are alike, but they all have six sides. The largest hailstone found was more than 5 inches (13 cm) across.

Thunderstorms occur when warm rain is pulled straight up into cold skies where it condenses into a cloud. Because of the heat of the day, more and more air is pulled upward and heated. The cloud grows taller and taller as more moist air is pulled into it. Droplets of water form at the top of the cloud where it meets the very cold air of high altitudes. The raindrops that fall carry positively charged particles with them, leaving the cloud overly full of negatively charged particles. These negatively charged particles are attracted to the positive ones wherever they can be found in another part of the same cloud, in another cloud, a tree, a house, a living creature. The negatively charged particles make a great leap through the air to get to the positively charged particles. The air in their path crackles and glows as it expands violently from the heat of the charged particles passing by. The sounds of this violent expansion are **thunder,** and the glow is **lightning,** traveling 20,000 miles (32,000 km) a second.

About 2,200 thunderstorms are going on almost constantly all over the Earth.
Lightning strikes the Earth about 100 times per second, which adds up to about 3.15 billion times a year. Lightning is about 54,032°F (30,000°C), more than five times the temperature of the Sun's surface.

There are three conditions needed for water vapor to condense into a cloud:
1. Warm moisture
2. Dust particles on which the water vapor can condense
3. Drop in pressure at the same time that the moisture cools

You can combine all three of these to make your own clouds in this next project.

★ ★ ★ ★ ★ ★ ★ ★ ★ ★ ★ ★ **Project 38: Forming Clouds** ★ ★ ★ ★ ★ ★ ★ ★ ★ ★ ★ ★ ★

MATERIALS

wide-mouth glass jar   hot water
chalk dust or fine talcum powder   drinking straw

PROCEDURE

1. Fill the glass jar with hot water; let it stand for a while. Pour out the water and leave a small amount in the bottom.

2. Sprinkle chalk dust or powder into jar.

3. Cover the opening of the jar with your hand, leaving enough room between your thumb and fingers for the straw. Blow air through the straw into the jar several times. Then stop suddenly, lift your hand, and let outside air enter the jar.

4. Repeat as often as you need to until you form a cloud inside the jar.

OBSERVATION

What happens to the cloud when pressure is increased compared to when it is decreased?

Hurricanes (also called typhoons in the Western Pacific, cyclones in the Indian Ocean, or willy willys in Australia) occur when a very warm mass of air over the southern part of tropical oceans filled with water meets a cold air mass. The cold air is warmed as it sits over the ocean and lifts both masses higher into the southern skies. The warm air on top meets the cool air high in the southern skies and wants to come back down again. The pushing and pulling that follows sends out rain from a whirlpool-shaped mass of air 10 miles (16 km) above the sea. The winds are moving at about 200 miles (320 km) an hour in a circle about 500 miles (800 km) across, heading north. The center or "eye" of the hurricane is calm. There is no rain and almost no wind in the area of low pressure and humidity but high temperatures. A hurricane may last for several weeks.

Hurricane comes from the Spanish word *huracan* = winds.

Tornadoes (or twisters) come about much like hurricanes do. They may last only 8 minutes but they are highly destructive. The twisting effect caused by the Earth's spinning creates funnels made of sets of powerful whirling masses of warm and cold air.

Predicting the weather is tricky—and very important. When will it rain? Is a hurricane coming?

Meteorology, the study of weather, comes from the Greek word μετεωρολογος (*meteorologos*) = talking or treating of the heavenly bodies.

Weather forecasters rely on information provided by nearly 3,000 weather stations throughout the world on land, ships at sea, and satellites circling the Earth. Four times a day these stations send information to the National Weather Bureau, which makes a map of the information. Meteorologists read these maps and predict what may happen in a certain location. Usually weather travels from west to east at about 15 miles (24 km) per hour in the summer and about 25 miles (40 km) per hour in the winter. In the summer, today's weather for people 400 to 500 miles (650–800 km) west of you will probably be your weather tomorrow. In the winter, today's weather 700 miles (1,125 km) west of you is likely to be your weather tomorrow. If there is warm air behind cool air, there is usually rain 500 miles (800 km) ahead. Still, with all the charts, maps, and satellite pictures available, predicting what the weather will actually do is not always easy or accurate. The planets also have weather, including storms.

READING MORE

Donnan, John A., and Marcia Donnan. *Rain Dance to Research.* New York: David McKay, 1977.
Milgrom, Harry. *Understanding Weather.* London: Crowell-Collier, 1970.

(photo courtesy of NASA)

Section 4 THE EARTH IN SPACE
Our Point of View

> Once a photograph of the Earth, taken from the outside, is available . . . a new idea
> as powerful as any in history will let loose. —Sir Fred Hoyle, 1948

Such a photograph *is* available. It is the one above. When it first appeared in 1969, it startled many people. Imagine looking at the Earth and not being on it! It certainly changes your perspectives about the Earth, the people, plants, and animals on it, and our relationship to each other when you can see the whole world in a glance.

Mapmakers often have relied on brass or wooden globes to represent the Earth. Globes of the sky showed the Earth in the center giving you an "extraterrestrial" point of view, looking down through the celestial sphere.

Extraterrestrial comes from the Latin words *extra* = outside and *terra* = the Earth.

Point of view makes a big difference. In the Middle Ages, when people tried to understand the stars and planets and their relationship to the Earth and the Sun, they had a point of view that they considered "acceptable." This was the view that your own eyes could prove: the Earth stood still in the center of the universe while everything else, including the Sun, Moon, and planets, circled around it. The Sun rose, moved across the sky, and set. The stars changed seasonally. The Sun, Moon, and planets moved in front of the zodiac constellations in predictable rhythms.

This was the view that your own feelings could prove: the Earth was the home of people, the peak of creation. Where else would God or the gods place our home? The variety of life on Earth and the ever-unfolding mental powers of the human being proved that the inhabitants of the Earth were unique. The gods and goddesses of every religion visited or cared for these inhabitants, entrusting them with enormous responsibilities. Clearly the Earth was the center of some great plan and those living on it were destined to carry out this plan.

This was the view that the most reliable and knowledgeable scholars could prove. Aristotle, Ptolemy, and Thomas Aquinas had all written about it in great detail. With your common sense, religious conviction, and scientific thoroughness, you had formed a standpoint.

Nicolaus Copernicus (1473–1543)   In 1506 a young Polish priest, Nicojac Koppernigk (Nicolaus Copernicus in Latin), looked over the same Earth-centered ideas. As an astronomy and mathematics teacher, he was looking for ways to explain things better and more simply both to himself and his students. He found the ideas of Ptolemy fascinating but cluttered up with all the additional circles that Ptolemy used to explain the motions of the planets. On paper, Copernicus worked out a much simpler way of showing how the planets moved. He set out to simplify the geocentric system of Ptolemy because it did not succeed in showing uniform motion of the planets in space. Copernicus still used extra circles to explain planetary motion. All orbits still followed perfect circles.

The way Copernicus managed to unclutter the dance of the heavens was to have two of the dancers change places. Where one had stood motionless in the very center of the dance (the Earth), that one was now dancing around the new center (the Sun). The dance itself and the other dancers stayed the same. With the Sun in the center, you could much more easily account for the movement of everything. Copernicus declared that the sky doesn't move overhead, nor does the Sun rise and set. These motions only *seem* to occur. What is really happening is that the Earth is moving. It is turning around itself while it circles the Sun.

So the Sun sits as upon a royal throne ruling his children, the planets, which circle around him. —Copernicus

Copernicus arrived at his conclusions by using mathematics and rational thought and far less accurate observing equipment than Ptolemy used. In fact, Copernicus only made 27 recorded observations.

The Copernican System
(*from the original copy of* De Revolutionibus)

Nicolaus Copernicus

The young teacher circulated descriptions of his ideas to his friends. They encouraged him to publish his work so that others could read it and think about it. He was not very excited about doing this. The more he thought about the idea, the more Copernicus realized what problems it was creating inside him and what problems it would surely create inside others. It is not surprising, then, that he waited 36 years to publish his six-volume work, which was patterned after Ptolemy's *Almagest*. (Pythagoras had waited 9 years before fully presenting his ideas.) The first published copy of *De Revolutionibus Orbium Coelestium* [*Concerning the Revolutions of the Heavenly Spheres*] was handed to its author in 1543 as he lay dying.

Copernicus is the father of the **Scientific Revolution** (from the title of his book). He had turned the Earth into a planet and made his own picture of the Earth available. His idea is the basis of our own picture of the universe today. In it we place the Sun at the center of what we call the **solar system**. We have stopped the celestial sphere from turning. The Earth turns, not the starry sky. The Earth turns, the Sun doesn't rise and set. The planets circle around the Sun—so do we. Nothing but the Moon circles around the Earth.

We have all grown up with these ideas. Imagine, however, hearing them for the first time, maybe as one of the students in Copernicus's class. How would you feel? How would you feel about yourself and your place in the universe? If you carefully consider these feelings, then you will be able to understand why it was that people fought so hard not to believe or accept Copernicus's ideas.

In the model that Copernicus suggested, the Earth moves as one of the planets around the Sun, which is in the center. For this reason, we call his model the **heliocentric** system. In the system represented by Ptolemy and the ancients before him, the Earth is at the center. We call this arrangement the **geocentric** system.

Heliocentric comes from the Greek words ήλιος (*helios*) = Sun and κεντρυμ (*kentrum*) = center.

Geocentric comes from the Greek words γεω (*geo*) = Earth and κεντρυμ (*kentrum*) = center.

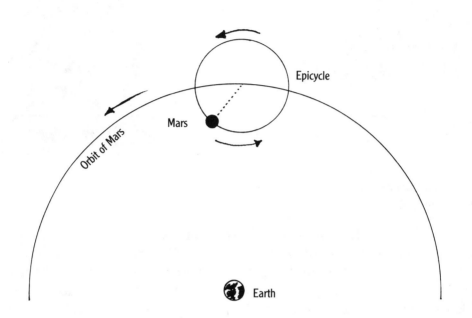

In Ptolemy's geocentric picture of the universe, the apparent backward (retrograde) motion of Mars could be explained by the use of epicycles. Remember, in Ptolemy's system everything in space had to travel in a perfect circle and in the same direction. Mars moved along its orbit, traveling in one direction. Mars also moved along its epicycle in the same direction (counterclockwise). When Mars passed by Earth at a time when its epicycle motion was nearest to us, from our point of view the planet appeared to be going backward, making loops in the sky. See page 280 for photographs that illustrate the retrograde motion of Mars.

Retrograde motion in the heliocentric system can be explained by the different speeds of two objects passing each other. You can demonstrate how this happens in the next project.

★ ★ ★ ★ ★ **Project 39: Showing How Mars "Goes Backward"** ★ ★ ★ ★ ★ ★
(Retrograde Motion) *

MATERIALS

stiff paper

knitting needle

red and green felt-tip pens

white colored pencil

black construction paper

paper glue

ruler

pencil

scissors

sheet of cardboard

straight pins

tape

light source

PROCEDURE

1. Draw the two patterns from the following page onto stiff paper. Color the longer one red for Mars and the shorter one green for Earth. Cut them out and glue each into a circle.

2. Draw a straight line down the middle of the sheet of cardboard. Draw the disk of the Sun in the middle of the line. Place the *Earth* circle in the middle so that the number four is above the line. Pin the circle to the cardboard. Pin the *Mars* circle into place on the cardboard so that the space between it and the Earth circle is even all around.

3. Stand the black construction paper up a few inches from the Mars circle in a curved position. Mark this curve on the cardboard and tape the construction paper in place.

*This project is adapted from *Everybody's Guide to Astronomy* prepared by the editorial staff of *Popular Science Monthly.* New York: Popular Science, 1934.

4. Lay the knitting needle down on the two circles so that it lines up with the slot numbered one in each circle.

5. Bring the point of the needle right up to the black construction paper and push it through the paper. Mark this hole *1* in the construction paper with the white colored pencil.

6. Repeat step 5 for all the numbered slots. (In the illustration the needle is lined up with 7.)

7. Shine a light on the black construction paper to see how the path of Mars appears to go backward.

Earth circle

Mars circle

OBSERVATIONS

We see cars traveling "retrograde" when we are driving alongside at a slightly faster speed. Even though we know they are traveling in the same direction we are, they look like they are going backward.

In this next project you will be doing an experiment invented in 1851 by the French physicist **J. B. L. Focault** (1819–1868) to prove that the Earth rotates.

★ ★ ★ ★ ★ ★ ★ **Project 40: Proving the Rotation of the Earth** ★ ★ ★ ★ ★ ★ ★

MATERIALS

PART 1

lead weight (e.g., a fishing sinker)   wire coat hanger
string

PART 2

pen or pencil   lazy susan (or something similar that
paper   can turn)

PART 3

suspension wire   chalk
bearings   scissors
string   lead weight

PART 1

PROCEDURE

1. Make a pendulum by attaching the weight to the string and tying the other end to the wire coat hanger.

2. Aim the wire hanger at an object on the wall and hold it so it doesn't move.

3. Pull the weight back and let it swing in the same direction that the wire hanger is aimed.

4. While the pendulum is swinging, slowly turn the hanger away from the object on the wall.

OBSERVATIONS

Does the pendulum change its direction? Suppose the object on the wall was a star. What would happen if the star was moving? What would it mean if the star wasn't moving but was fixed in space?

PART 2

PROCEDURE

1. Draw a circle on the piece of paper and write the four directions on it. This circle will be the Earth, seen from one of its poles.
2. Put the Earth on top of a lazy susan, record player, piano stool, or anything that can turn.
3. Hang the end of the pendulum above the Earth and start it swinging in a north-south direction. Turn the Earth in a counterclockwise direction.

OBSERVATIONS

Does the pendulum still swing in a north-south line? To an observer on Earth in the Northern Hemisphere, in what direction does the pendulum appear to be changing, clockwise or counterclockwise? How about to an observer in the Southern Hemisphere?

Focault performed his experiment in the Pantheon in Paris with a 200-foot (60-m) length of suspension wire. Pendulums will continue to swing in whatever direction you start them until they come to a rest.

PART 3

PROCEDURE

1. Attach the suspension wire to the bearings so the wire can move freely.
2. Attach the bearings to the ceiling.
3. Place the lead weight at the end of the wire. Tie one end of some string to the weighted end of the wire and pull it to one side. Tie the string to a stationary object. When the weighted wire has stopped moving, cut the string to start the pendulum swinging.
4. Mark a line with chalk on the ground showing the path made by the swinging weight.

OBSERVATIONS

Notice the path of the weight a half hour later. What do you see? What do you think happened? To obtain a complete circle in 24 hours (23 hours, 56 minutes sidereal time) you would have to perform the experiment at the Earth's North or South Pole.

Proofs of the Rotation of the Earth   Another proof of the Earth's rotation came from a discovery by **James Bradley** (1693–1762). In 1725 Bradley found that starlight moves over or shifts from the position it actually holds in the sky. If it didn't, it would travel down from the sky in a straight line and directly into the tube of a telescope. What happens instead is that you have to tilt the telescope to receive the light in much the same way as you have to tilt an umbrella while walking in the rain, no matter how vertical the rainfall is. You have to tip the umbrella because you are moving and thus meeting the raindrops as though they were coming at a slant. You have to tip the telescope because the Earth is moving and thus you are meeting the starlight as if it was coming at a slant, or from a place other than where it actually started. This apparent shift of the light from a star is the **aberration of starlight**. The tilt changes to the opposite direction every 6 months.

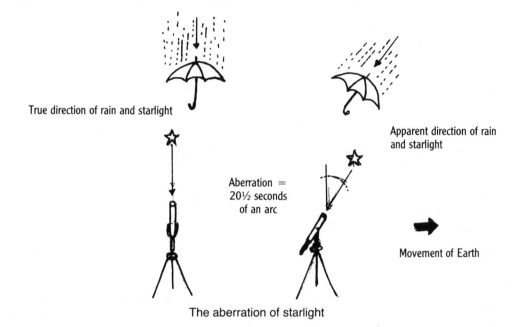

True direction of rain and starlight

Apparent direction of rain and starlight

Aberration = 20½ seconds of an arc

Movement of Earth

The aberration of starlight

Focault carried out yet another proof of the Earth's rotation in 1852 using a gyroscope. The axis of the gyroscope usually remains in its original direction. As the Earth rotates, the gyroscope swings into a north-south line over the Earth's axis, a proof of the Earth's rotation.

The spinning Earth causes
- *day and night*—the Earth turns into the Sun bringing day;
- *the direction of Earth's axis*—the Earth's axis continues to point to the North Star; and
- *flattening of the Earth at the poles*—probably caused while the Earth's surface was in a more liquid form.

Because the Earth is spinning, its roundness gets slightly distorted. The Earth bulges slightly in the middle and flattens slightly at the poles. At the equator, the Earth is about 27 miles (44 km) larger than it is at the poles.

In this project you can see for yourself what spinning does to the shape of the Earth.

★ ★ ★ ★ ★ **Project 41: Demonstrating the Bulging of the Earth** ★ ★ ★ ★ ★

MATERIALS

pencil with an eraser
thumbtack
paper

tape
hole punch

PROCEDURE

1. Cut two strips of paper about 1 × 11 inches (2½ × 27½ cm). Overlap the ends and tape them together to form a round loop about 20 inches (50 cm) long.

2. Punch a hole in the bottom of the loop. The hole should be slightly larger than the diameter of the pencil so that the paper can move freely around the pencil.

3. Push the eraser end of the pencil through the hole until the eraser touches the inside of the top of the loop.

4. Fasten the top of the paper loop to the eraser using the thumbtack.

5. Twist the pencil quickly between your hands and observe the shape of the loop.

OBSERVATIONS

What happens to the shape of the loop? Where is the widest diameter? What happens to the size of the bulge when you make the loop turn faster?

We call Earth's rapid spinning its **rotation**. The whole Earth turns at once, but because it is a sphere parts of it turn faster than others. Places on the equator travel faster than those closer to the poles. The distance around the Earth at the equator is bigger, so it has farther to travel. As the Earth turns at different speeds from west to east, the air that was traveling from the equator to the pole in a straight line gets "bent." Its path curves almost as much as 90° as it moves from the swifter rotating equator to the slower rotating poles. Everything in the Northern Hemisphere is deflected to the right, including sea currents and water. Water going down a drain enters on the right and moves in a counterclockwise spiral. In the Southern Hemisphere, everything is deflected to the left, including water. Water going down a drain enters on the left and moves in a clockwise spiral.

Rotation comes from the Latin word *rotare* = to turn.

Gaspard de Coriolis (1792–1843), a French mathematician, first explained this deflection of freely moving objects in 1835. We call this deflection the **Coriolis effect** after him. The Coriolis effect is strongest at the poles and weakest at the equator. The faster the wind, the stronger the Coriolis effect. Edmond Halley of England also suggested this idea, a hundred years earlier.

Swirls of clouds on a photograph of the Earth from space show some of the Coriolis effect. The Earth's atmosphere appears as a thin blue layer wrapped around the Earth. In this next project you can create your own Coriolis effect.

★ ★ ★ ★ ★ ★ Project 42: Showing the Effects of the Earth's ★ ★ ★ ★ ★ ★ Spinning (Coriolis Effect)*

MATERIALS

PART 1	PART 2
merry-go-round or piano stool	globe or basketball
ball	chalk
a partner	

PART 1

PROCEDURE
1. Stand or sit in the middle of a merry-go-round.
2. Have someone stand or sit in the outer edge of the merry-go-round.
3. Turn the merry-go-round counterclockwise.
4. Roll or throw the ball to that person.

OBSERVATION
What happened to the path of the ball?

---

*Part 1 of this project is adapted from *Everybody's Guide to Astronomy,* prepared by the editorial staff of *Popular Science Monthly.* New York: Popular Science, 1934.

PART 2

PROCEDURE

1. Rotate the globe counterclockwise.

2. Draw a line on the globe while it is moving, right down from the North Pole to the equator.

3. Draw a line on the globe while it is moving, straight up from the South Pole to the equator.

OBSERVATION

What happened when you drew the two lines?

Proofs That the Earth Is Round   You can prove that the Earth is round in a number of ways:

- As a ship sails out to sea, we see the body of the ship disappearing first and the top last.
- Northern stars are higher as you travel north and lower if you travel south. Southern stars are higher as you travel south and lower as you travel north.
- At the Northern Hemisphere, for each 69 miles (110 km) you travel north, the North Star appears 1° higher above the horizon. For each 69 miles (110 km) you travel south, the North Star appears 1° lower above the horizon.
- A level line that surveyors make is not straight but arched.
- Photographs taken from great heights above the Earth show the horizon to be curved.
- Navigators calculate their positions as if they were on a sphere. These calculations have also successfully located positions of ships on the Earth.
- Photographs of lunar eclipses show the shadow of the Earth's curved surface on the Moon.

- Many people have traveled around the globe in the same direction and have returned to their starting points.
- Pillars of suspension bridges (like the Golden Gate Bridge in San Francisco) are farther apart at the tops than they are at the bottoms due to the curvature of the Earth's surface between them.

The Earth has a gentle curve. In 10 miles (16 km), the curve only drops 67 feet (20 m).

As Others See Us   What do you suppose life on Earth looks like to visitors from another planet? If a team of scientists came to Earth from another planet, how would they describe what they found? In this next project you can take the part of a visiting team from another planet and see what you find on the blue planet Earth.

★ ★ ★ ★ ★ ★ ★ Project 43: Filing an Extraterrestrial Report ★ ★ ★ ★ ★ ★ ★ on the Planet Earth

MATERIALS
paper
pencil

photographs from magazines
drawing supplies

PROCEDURE
Imagine you are on a scout team from another planet. Your team's mission is to land one "manned" spacecraft on Earth and file a report after carrying out the following experiments. Use photographs from magazines or create drawings of your own. Prepare a written description to go with your photographs, or use the descriptions without photographs.

IMAGES OF EARTH AND LANDING SITE AREA

1. Photographs of Earth from space
2. Photographs approaching landing site areas from different locations in space
3. Photographs of landing area taken on the ground

NATURE OF AREA IMMEDIATELY AROUND LANDING SITE

1. Vegetation
2. Air
3. Rocks, hills, water
4. Temperature
5. Visibility

RETRIEVING SAMPLES

1. Describe natural surroundings of area where you removed the sample material.
2. Describe process of removing sample.
3. Describe experiments performed on sample.

CONTACT WITH EARTH LIFE

1. Describe life forms.
2. What tests did you perform to indicate the presence of life?
3. Describe communication ability of life form.
    a. How was it able to communicate?
    b. How would you describe the mood or intent of this communication?

LANDING SITES

Team 1: in the desert
Team 2: your neighborhood
Team 3: downtown in any large city, anytime
Team 4: on a farm, anytime
Other possible sites: at the Olympic Games, Antarctica, the Dead Sea, New Orleans at Mardi Gras, the Alps, a coral island in the ocean, the ocean.

OBSERVATIONS

Do you think the teams got a very accurate picture of what it is like on Earth from their visit? To see how people from Earth responded when they sent probes to other planets, see chapter 7, section 4 and parts of chapter 6.

READING MORE

Feldman, Anthony. *Space.* New York: Facts on File, 1980.
Sagan, Carl, F. D. Drake, Ann Druyan, Timothy Ferris, Jon Lomberg, and Linda Salzman Sagan. *Murmurs of Earth: The Voyager Interstellar Record.* New York: Random House, 1978.

The Orion nebula

Chapter 5   SKY-GATHERING TOOLS

Section 1   A NEW LOOK AT THE PLANETS

The Moving Earth   Our present concept of a heliocentric system is quite different from that of Copernicus's, yet the two seem very similar. Copernicus did not disprove the geocentric system, he simply replaced it with another system that was simpler and more accurate.

In the geocentric system, the Earth is motionless. It sits at the center of the universe while the entire heavens parade in front of it. In the heliocentric system, the Earth is active. It participates in a complex combination of at least six motions.

1. *It rotates about its axis once a day.* The Earth spins counterclockwise about its axis, making one complete turn or rotation at about 1,000 miles (1,600 km) per hour or about 1,500 feet (450 km) per second.

2. *It revolves around the Sun once a year.* The Earth travels in a counterclockwise orbit around the Sun.

3. *The axis of the Earth precesses.* The Earth's axis is not perpendicular to its orbit, but makes an angle of 23°27'. It is this tilt that causes the seasons. As the earth revolves around the Sun and spins about its axis, the pole of the Earth traces a small circle in the sky. It takes 25,800 years to trace the complete circle. In the process of making this circle, the North Pole of the Earth points to different stars, making them the North Star.

4. *The axis of the Earth nutates.* The curve that the Earth's axis traces is not a smooth circle. It has small waves due to the "nodding" of the Earth's axis from its average position of 23°27'. The period of one complete wave is 19 years, causing a nod of 9 seconds of an angle from the 23°27' angle. The main cause of Earth's nutation is the gravitational pull of the Moon.

5. *The solar system moves.* The Sun, with the Earth and the other planets, speeds through the local cluster of stars at a speed of 12 miles (19 km) per second.

6. *The galaxy moves.* The local cluster of stars takes part in the rotation around the center of our galaxy at a speed of hundreds of miles or kilometers per second.

Tycho Brahe (1546–1601)   When he was 14, Tycho saw a partial eclipse of the Sun from his native Denmark. He was so struck by this sight that from then on he devoted his life to making and recording accurate observations of the heavens. His relatives weren't thrilled with his decision, so Tycho had to struggle to finally achieve his goal without hiding what he was doing. Eventually, he became quite a well-known and respected astronomer.

Tycho was also quite a flashy character. He lost the tip of his nose in a duel and replaced it with one he made out of gold and silver. He was given an island in Denmark with a castle, which he turned into an observatory. Tycho called his castle Uraniborg, after Urania, the Greek muse of astronomy. There he lived and worked like a king for 20 years with an amazing collection of observing instruments and assistants to help him use them. Among these instruments were a 7-foot metal quadrant and a wall quadrant that he could sit in while someone measured the degrees. His favorite was a sextant.

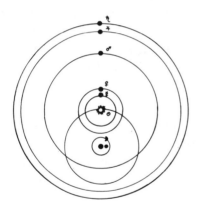

The Tychonic system, which also was suggested by Heracleides of Pontus (388–315 B.C.)

Tycho Brahe

Tycho observed supernova and several comets. He made thousands of extremely accurate observations of the positions of planets, the stars, and the Sun over a period of many years. Tycho developed a system that combined the systems of Ptolemy and Copernicus. In Tycho's system, all the planets, except the Earth, orbit around the Sun. The Earth stands still while the Sun and the rest of the solar system orbits around it.

Johannes Kepler (1571–1630)   Like Copernicus, Kepler was a successful astrologer and teacher. Like Tycho, he saw a supernova. Kepler was skinny, sickly, and suffered from multiple vision and nearsightedness, which made it impossible for him to carry out any astronomical observations. Using the ideas of the Platonic solids from Pythagoras, Kepler imagined the five Platonic solids stacked one inside the other, with a sphere in between each one. Each sphere was the orbit of a different planet. The spaces between the spheres would determine the distance between the orbits of the planets they represented.

> The earth is the sphere, the measure of all; round it describe a dodecahedron; the sphere including this will be Mars. Round Mars describe a tetrahedron; the sphere including this will be Jupiter. Describe a cube round Jupiter; the sphere including this will be Saturn. Now inscribe in the earth an icosehedron, the sphere inscribed in it will be Venus; inscribe an octahedron in Venus; the circle inscribed in it will be Mercury.
> —from *Mysterium Cosmographicum*

This idea so impressed Tycho that he wrote to Kepler inviting him to work at Tycho's observatory.

Kepler planned to spend 8 days on his assignment from Tycho, which was to figure out the orbit of Mars. It took him close to 8 years.

After Tycho died, Kepler used the records of Tycho's observations to do further studies.

Johannes Kepler

Kepler's model of the Platonic solids showing the distances between planetary orbits

Kepler wrote three laws about the orbits of planets that removed all circular motion and epicycles:

1. Each planet moves in an orbit that is an **ellipse** with the Sun at one focus.

2. The line between the Sun and each orbiting planet sweeps over equal areas in equal amounts of time.

3. The square of the speed of each planet's orbit is proportional to the cube of its average distance from the Sun.

An ellipse is like an oval. Aristotle, Ptolemy, Copernicus, and everyone before them had insisted that the planets traveled in orbits that were in the shape of a perfect circle. Ellipses have two points inside them as their focal point instead of one as in a circle. Each point is the **focus**. The plural of *focus* is *foci*. The distance between the two foci determines the shape of an ellipse. As this distance increases, the shape of the ellipse becomes more elongated. When the two foci meet at the center, you have a circle.

In this next project you can draw ellipses for the orbits of each of the planets to demonstrate Kepler's laws.

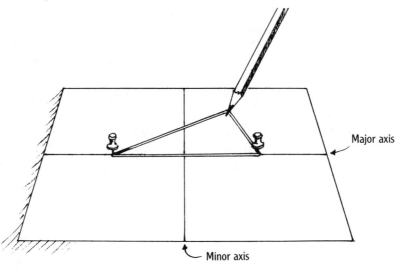

★ ★ ★ ★ ★ ★ **Project 44: Drawing Planetary Orbits (Ellipses)** ★ ★ ★ ★ ★ ★

MATERIALS

two pushpins   pencil
piece of wood   paper
string

PROCEDURE

1. Fold paper to create major and minor axes. (Always place pins at equal distances from the center point.) Place the paper on the piece of wood.

2. Stick one pin near the center of paper on the major axis fold. Label it the Sun.

3. Stick the second pin on the same fold as the focus of a planet.

4. Double the string and tie a knot 3⁷/₈ inches (9.9 cm) from the end. This will give you a loop about 3⁷/₈ inches (9.9 cm).

5. Do the same for each of the planets using the following measurements and those on the next page: 1 inch = 83 million miles, 1 centimeter = 33 million kilometers. The first measurement is in inches, and the second is in centimeters.

Planet	Distance Between Pins (in. & cm)	Size of Loop (in. & cm)
Mars	$1^1/_{16}$ (1.7)	$7^7/_8$ (19.9)
Earth	$^3/_{32}$ (0.2)	$4^3/_4$ (12.1)
Venus	$^1/_{32}$ (0.1)	$3^7/_{16}$ (8.8)
Mercury	$^3/_8$ (1.0)	$2^9/_{16}$ (6.5)

OBSERVATIONS

Which planet's orbit is closest to being a circle? Which planet's orbit is least like a circle? Which two planets could come the closest together as they travel in their orbits? Which two planets have orbits of nearly the same shape?

A circle can be said to be a special case of an ellipse where the two foci are in the same place. The ellipse belongs to a family of curves that come from taking a cut or a section out of a cone. For this reason we call them **conic sections**. In 225 B.C. **Appolonius** wrote *Conic Sections,* in which he described how you can form the ellipse, parabola, and hyperbola by passing a plane through a cone at various angles.

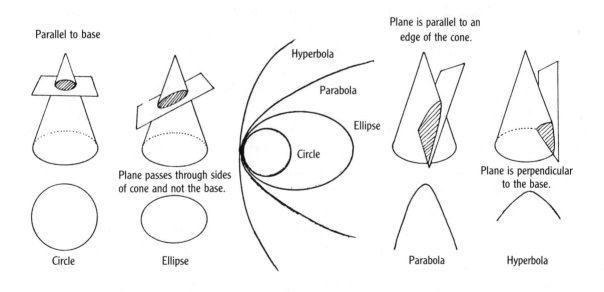

Galileo Galilei (1564–1642)   Galileo enrolled at the University of Pisa at age 16 to study medicine. His nickname in college was "The Wrangler" because he refused to accept statements that were supposed to be true simply because some famous person long ago said they were. "In questions of science, the authority of a thousand is not worth the humble reasoning of a single individual," he believed.

Galileo felt that you needed to back up what you said with proof, experiments, evidence. He spent most of his life experimenting and writing. The invention of the telescope (see the next section in this chapter) gave him a tool with which he could prove or disprove statements and observations.

Galileo Galilei

Isaac Newton

Isaac Newton (1643–1727)   According to the Julian calendar, Newton was born less than a year after Galileo died, on Christmas Day, 1642. According to the Gregorian calendar, he was born on January 4, 1643. When he died on March 20, 1727, people used only the Gregorian calendar. Newton was so small as an infant that he could fit in a cooking pot. For a while, he slept in a drawer! Like Kepler, he was nearsighted. Also, like Kepler, he wanted to know how planets moved in space. Newton changed the way people thought about the tides, mathematics (he coinvented the calculus), gravity, motion, and light. So great and long-lasting were Newton's discoveries that the poet Alexander Pope wrote

> Nature and Nature's Laws lay hid in Night:
> God said, Let Newton be! and All was Light.

Newton felt that his contributions were only possible thanks to the work of the Greek scientists and Copernicus, Brahe, Kepler, and Galileo: "If I have seen further than other men, it is because I have stood on the shoulders of giants."

Planetary Motion   Galileo said that the movement of the planets is a natural condition. His experiments showed that it is just as natural for an object to be in motion as it is for an object to be at rest.

Sir Isaac Newton put Galileo's thought this way in his First Law of Motion: *An object at rest tends to remain at rest, and an object in motion tends to remain in motion.* This tendency is **inertia**.

Inertia comes from the Latin word *inertia* = lack of skill, inactivity.

Inertia is what makes it so hard to move something when it has been standing still. Once the object is in motion, it is easier to keep it moving. Once it's moving, it is also harder to stop it. In 1687 Newton published his *Laws of Gravitation*. In this book Newton stated that two quantities that are related so that one increases when the other increases are said to be in direct relation or in **direct proportion**. If one quantity decreases when another increases, they are said to be in **inverse proportion**.

Gravitation comes from the Latin word *gravitas* = heaviness. If someone's interest is really drawn toward something, we say that person *gravitates* toward that object.

The Law of Universal Gravitation   Every particle of matter attracts every other particle of matter with a force of attraction that is directly proportional to the product of their masses and inversely proportional to the square of the distance between them.

The greater the masses of two objects, the greater the gravitational force between them. Gravitational attraction is greater when objects are close together.

Characteristics of Matter   Gravitation is the universal attraction that all objects have for all other objects. **Gravity** is Earth's gravitational force or, Kepler wrote in *New Astronomy,* "the mutual bodily tendency between material bodies toward contact; two stones for example would come together, after the manner of magnetic bodies, each approaching the other in proportion to the other's mass." We state this in units of acceleration. The farther you are from the center of the Earth, the less the amount of gravitational force. The amount of force is inversely related to the distance to the center. You weigh less on a mountaintop and even less in an airplane. Astronauts/cosmonauts get so far away from the strength of Earth's gravitational pull that they find themselves floating in the air as if they were weightless. What is happening is that they are in "free fall," falling toward the Earth. But since their spacecraft is moving, the astronauts/cosmonauts keep falling and never hit anything.

Distance from the Center of the Earth		Your Weight
16,000 miles	(25,750 km)	9 pounds
12,000 miles	(19,300 km)	16 pounds
8,000 miles	(12,900 km)	36 pounds
4,000 miles	(6,435 km)	144 pounds

Volume measures the amount of space an object occupies. **Mass** is the quantity of matter present. No matter where you are, your mass remains the same. Compare *mass* to **density**, which is the quantity of matter or the weight per unit volume of matter in terms of pounds per cubic foot or grams per cubic centimeter. **Specific gravity** is the density of an object compared with the density of water.

Weight is the measure of the force of gravitational attraction between two objects. We state this in units of weight such as pounds or grams. It is the acceleration of gravity (g) multiplied by the mass (m). Weight depends on location.

Look at a marble and a steel ball, both the same size. Do they both have the same volume? Do they weigh the same? Which has the greater density? Do they have the same mass?

How much do you weigh on other planets? With a pencil, paper, and the planetary information chart from Sky Files, look at the column on the planetary chart marked **Surface Gravity.** This number tells you how much heavier or lighter you would feel on other planets. Simply take each number and multiply by your weight on Earth to find how much you would weigh. On which planet would you weigh the most? The least? About the same?

The **centripetal force** needed to keep an object moving in a circular path increases as the speed of the object increases. If you keep the speed the same, you need less centripetal force to make the circle larger. There are other effects from applying centripetal force. Have you noticed how a runner or a bicycle racer leans inward (banks) on turns? Pilots also bank their airplanes to make turns. Banking provides centripetal force to keep you, your bicycle, or your airplane or car from skidding off into a straight line. The centripetal force needed to keep planets moving in their orbits is different for each planet. It depends on their speed and their distance from the Sun. The Sun's gravitational force is the "attraction" that pulls the planets into their nearly circular orbits. The centripetal force is just equal to this gravitational force. The centripetal force prevents the planets from flying off into a straight line.

Arrangement of the Planets   Why are the distances between the planets the way they are? Is there some pattern to them? Kepler thought the pattern might be based on fitting the Platonic solids in between the orbits. In 1772 **Johan Daniel Titius** translated the French book *Contemplation of Nature* by Charles Bonnet into German. In his translation, Titius included some of his own ideas about the distances of the planets from the Sun. **Johan Elert Bode** also published a book that year, the second edition of his book *Introduction to the Study of the Starry Sky.* Bode included as footnotes in his book the comments he had read about planetary distances by Titius in his translation of *Contemplation of Nature.* These comments became known as the **Titius-Bode Law,** even though only Titius invented them and they weren't a law. Bode later gave credit to Titius for coming up with the idea.

Titius had suggested a mathematical pattern for the planets' distances in which you start with 0, 3, 6, 12, 24, and so on (doubling the previous number), and add 4 for each planet. Taking the distance from the Sun to Saturn as 100 units,

Mercury's distance from the Sun is $4 + 0 = 4$ of these units.
Venus's distance from the Sun is $4 + 3 = 7$ of these units.
Earth's distance from the Sun is $4 + 6 = 10$ of these units.
Mars's distance from the Sun is $4 + 12 = 16$ of these units.
? (Asteroid Belt) distance from the Sun is $4 + 24 = 28$ of these units.
Jupiter's distance from the Sun is $4 + 48 = 52$ of these units.
Saturn's distance from the Sun is $4 + 96 = 100$ of these units.
By moving the decimal point one place to the left, you have the number of

astronomical units each planet is from the Sun. One astronomical unit = the distance from the Earth to the Sun.

In 1781 **William Herschel** (1738–1822) discovered the planet Uranus at 192 units or 19.2 astronomical units. In 1891 **Giuseppi Piazzi** (1746–1826) discovered the first asteroid in the empty space between Mars and Jupiter. See chapter 6, section 4, for more details.

By the time of Newton's death in 1727, the picture people had of the solar system was very much as you see it today (except that it didn't include the three trans-Saturnian planets Uranus, Neptune, and Pluto). The members of our solar system are the Sun and the planets (in order from the Sun):

1. Mercury
2. Venus
3. Earth
4. Mars
5. Jupiter
6. Saturn
7. Uranus
8. Neptune
9. Pluto

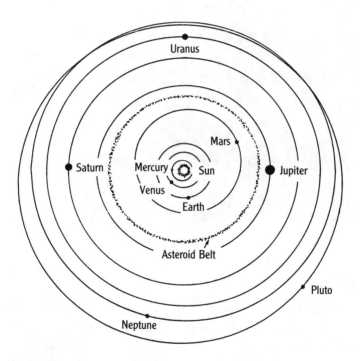

Our solar system (from *Teaching with NightStar* by Richard Moeschl)

The minor planets (asteroids) are in between the orbits of Mars and Jupiter. If there are any more planets orbiting around the Sun, they will be considered part of our solar system. Comets, meteors, stars, nebulae, pulsars, quasars, galaxies, and black holes are beyond our solar system and in most cases, outside our Milky Way Galaxy. You can find out about these other members of our solar system in chapter 7.

READING MORE
Ronin, Colin. *Man Probes the Universe.* Garden City: The Natural History Press, 1964.
Sullivan, Navin. *Pioneer Astronomers.* New York: Atheneum, 1967.

Percival Lowell (*photo courtesy of Lowell Observatory*)

Section 2   TELESCOPES

Light, the Eye, and Lenses   Most of our information about the universe comes to us in the form of radiation. Much of this radiation is the kind we are most familiar with, light that the human eye can see. Visible light is only one small form of radiation. You can find out about the other forms of radiation in section 4 of this chapter. Light is a form of energy. You can describe its speed, wavelength, frequency, and intensity. Light also has to do with how we see. Da Vinci thought that light moved in waves, much like sound does. Newton thought of light as a stream of particles.

The Eye   Light travels in a straight line from what you see (the object) to your eye, passing through these five parts:

　　1. The **cornea**, a tough, transparent layer covering the front of the eye. It helps focus the light and protect the eye.

2. The **aqueous humor,** a watery fluid between the cornea and the lens. It helps focus the light and nourishes the eye.

3. The **pupil,** a small round hole in the center of the colored **iris.** The iris controls the amount of light that enters the eye by widening or contracting, which makes the pupil larger or smaller.

4. The **lens,** a transparent, layered tissue. It helps focus light on the retina by becoming thinner or thicker.

5. The **vitreous humor,** a clear jelly filling the inside of the main portion of the eye behind the lens. It helps focus light on the retina. It also helps the eye keep its proper shape.

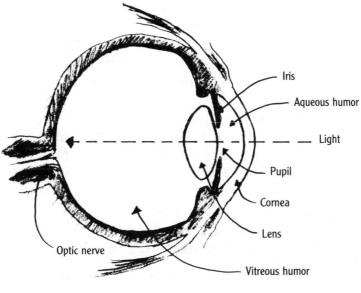

The eye

The light then shines onto the **retina,** which lines about two-thirds of the inside of your eye. An image of the object you are looking at appears on the retina. The image is upside down and backward because the lens in your eye is a convex lens and that's how the world looks through a convex lens. Your **optic nerve** and brain work together to help you see the object as it actually is and not how it appears on the retina.

The size of your pupil depends upon the amount of light your eye needs to let in so you can form a clear image on your retina — and see. When it is dark outside, your eyes need more light so your pupils open wider (about ¼ in. [7 mm]). When it is bright outside, your eyes need less light, so your pupils close together (about ³/₃₂ in. [2 mm]). Check it yourself. Look at a friend's pupils in a normal light, have your friend close his or her eyes and keep them closed for a while, then open them. What did the pupils do?

Refraction   In addition to traveling in a straight line, light can also be reflected from a smooth surface such as water or polished metals such as bronze or silver. Water and glass can carry light from one place to another through themselves.

Light will continue to travel through the air, water, or glass in a straight line if what it is passing through has the same conditions all through it. A change in temperature or thickness will break the path of the light. This change in the light's straight path is **refraction**. The different densities of the Earth's atmosphere affect any light that passes through it just as the different densities of the Earth's interior affected the path of earthquake waves (see chapter 4, section 3). When a beam of light from a star passes through the atmosphere at an angle, it bends or refracts.

Refraction comes from the Latin words *re* = again and *fractus* = break into pieces. You can get a good idea of how refraction looks by sticking a pencil in a glass of water and looking at it from the side. The light passing through the water bends so the image of the pencil looks broken. If you hold the pencil straight up in the glass, however, the image does not appear broken when you look at it from the side.

The least amount of refraction occurs when light travels in a line that is perpendicular to the places where there are changing conditions. Light from a star directly overhead goes right through the atmosphere in a straight line. The layers of different temperatures in the atmosphere are horizontal, so the starlight is not refracted. When a star is low on the horizon, its light comes through the Earth's atmosphere at an angle. As it passes through the layers of our Earth's atmosphere, the light curves downward slightly. This makes the star seem higher in the sky than it actually is.

Have you ever noticed how the Sun seems to flatten when it sets? The part of the Sun closest to the horizon has its light refracted upward. The refraction at the bottom of the Sun is greater than at the top, which makes the Sun look fatter and flatter.

Lenses By using the laws of refraction, lens makers can design lenses that bend (refract) light rays so that they can redirect the path of the light. The two main forms of lenses are **convex** and **concave**. Convex lenses are thick in the middle and thin around the edges. They bring the rays of light closer together by refracting the light toward the center. Concave lenses are thin in the middle and thick around the edges. They spread out the rays of light by refracting the light away from the center.

Convex comes from the Latin word *convexus* = arched.
Concave comes from the Latin word *concavus* = hollow.

Convex lenses

Concave lenses

Two convex lenses back-to-back or one curved on both sides resemble the shape of a lentil. (The Latin word for lentil is *lens.*)

People have known about lenses and magnification for a long time, maybe as far back as 2000 B.C. In England **Roger Bacon** (1220–1292) used lenses to help him with reading. Soon afterward, eyeglasses came into use in Italy. The country most noted for the manufacture of lenses was the Netherlands.

The Telescope   Several people claim to have invented the telescope. According to a story, **Hans Lippershey** (ca. 1570–ca. 1619), a glasses maker in the Netherlands, was the first. He found his apprentice playing with two lenses, a strong concave and a weak convex. The apprentice put the concave lens near his eye and the convex lens farther away and was looking out the window. He noticed that a weathervane on top of a distant house appeared to be much larger and closer. Lippershey placed the two lenses in a metal tube and called his invention a "looker." The name changed to "optic tube," "optic glass," and "Dutch perspectives."

Galileo called his device an *instrumentum* (instrument), a *perspicillum* (lens), or *occhiali* (eyeglass). In 1611 a Greek mathematician, **Ioannes Demisiani,** suggested the word **telescope,** which comes from the Greek words τῆλε (*tele*) = far and σκοπος (*skopos*) = to see. By 1650, *telescope* became the accepted word.

In 1609 Galileo built his own telescope based on Lippershey's model. Galileo's first telescope, which used two lenses and a lead pipe, made objects appear three times their actual size. Galileo figured the magnification by cutting out different sized circles. He compared the sizes the circles appeared through the telescope with their actual sizes. Galileo's later-model telescope had a wooden tube and made objects appear 30 times larger.

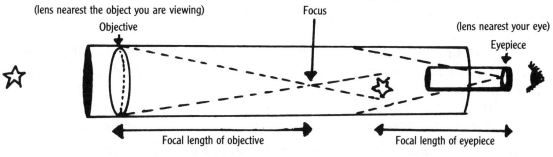

Focal length = distance between center of lens and focus

How Telescopes Work   Today, astronomical telescopes use an arrangement of lenses designed by Kepler in 1611. This arrangement uses two convex lenses instead of a convex and a concave lens. **Christian Huygens** (1629–1695) used Kepler's lens design in his tubeless telescope, which he built in 1659. With this telescope, Huygens discovered the rings of Saturn.

Since Galileo's telescope used a convex and a concave lens, the image he saw appeared right side up and the right way around. The image that resulted in Huygen's telescope is similar to the image that appears on your retina. It is upside down and backward. That is the price you pay for greater magnification. Astronomers are used to looking at the Moon, the stars, and planets upside down and backward. If they wanted to view things as they really are, astronomers would have to add an extra lens. However, with the addition of more glass and more bending of the light, the image would become dimmer and less clear. It is more important to astronomers that their images be bright and clear than right side up.

How does the telescope help you see objects brighter, clearer, and bigger? A telescope gathers the light from an *object* in one lens, the **objective**, and sends an image of the image as close to your eye as possible. The place in the telescope where the objective sends the image is the **focus**. The lens in the **eyepiece** magnifies the image formed at the focus and sends this larger image to your eye.

Focus comes from the Latin word *focus* = fireplace. The fireplace was the center of the house where the family often "focused" its attention. To get a picture of the focus and focal length, hold a convex lens (like the one in a magnifying glass) up to direct sunlight. Sprinkle some chalk dust (or other white powder) into the air on the side of the lens opposite the sun. If the background is dark enough, you will see particles of powder show how the magnifying glass causes the sun's rays to come together at the focus and then spread out again.

The telescope does three important things:

1. It increases the apparent brightness of a distant object. This is its **light-gathering power**. The greater the light-gathering power, the brighter an object appears.

2. It brings out detail on a distant object that cannot be seen with the unaided eye. This is its **resolving power**. The greater the resolving, the clearer the detail appears.

3. It enlarges the apparent size of a distant object. This is its **magnifying power**. The greater the magnifying power, the bigger or closer an object appears.

Light-Gathering Power   The objects you will want to look at in the heavens are very far away and often quite dim. It is important that your telescope gather as much light as possible from the object. What the telescope does is to take all the rays of light that the objective lens collects and concentrate them into a space the size of the eyepiece. The result of this concentration of light is that the object appears much brighter.

The light-gathering power depends on the diameter of the objective. The diameter of the objective is the **aperture**. This diameter usually tells you the size of the telescope. A 200-inch telescope has a lens that is 200 inches across. *Aperture* is often used in place of the word *objective* to describe a telescope's mirror or lens.

Aperture comes from the Latin *apertura* = to open, uncover.

To make dim objects seem brighter, you want the light coming from your telescope to fill as much of the pupil of your eye as possible. Your pupil at night is about ¼ inch (6–8 mm) in diameter. To find the diameter of the concentrated rays of light coming from the eyepiece of your telescope, divide the aperture by the magnification:

$$\text{diameter of light from eyepiece} = \frac{\text{aperture}}{\text{magnification}}$$

To find out how much more light your telescope can gather (light-gathering power) compared with your eye, multiply the square of the diameter of the objective by the number of times it is larger than the size of the pupil:

light-gathering power = (number of times the diameter of the objective is larger than the pupil)^2

For example, a telescope with a 2-inch (5 cm) diameter objective is eight times larger than the pupil. That means that 8^2 or 64 is how much more light-gathering power the telescope has compared to the human eye. With this telescope you can see stars 64 times dimmer than a star visible to your eye without a telescope.

The amount of light-gathering power of an objective is its focal ratio or f **number**. To find the f number of an objective, divide its focal length by its aperture (diameter):

$$\text{f number (or focal ratio)} = \frac{\text{focal length}}{\text{aperture}}$$

To get the most light-gathering power, you should have a telescope with a fairly short focus and low magnifying power. The more efficiently a lens collects light, the smaller its f number. An objective 6 inches (15¼ cm) in diameter has a focal length of 48 inches (122 cm). Its f number is 48/6 = 8. Focal ratios like these will make it possible for you to see fainter nebulae and star clusters.

Resolving Power   The human eye can only see as separate two objects no closer than 6 minutes of an angle apart. The eye will see objects less than 6 minutes of an angle apart as one object. A telescope makes it possible for you to see two stars that are very close together as two separate images even if the angle between them is less than 6 minutes. This is the separating or resolving power of a telescope, and it depends on the aperture.

$$\text{resolving power (in seconds of a degree)} = \frac{5}{\text{aperture (in inches)}}$$

For example, what would be the resolving power of a telescope with a 2-inch objective?

$$\text{resolving power} = \frac{5}{2 \text{ inches}} = 2.5 \text{ seconds of an arc}$$

That means that you can see two stars whose distance apart is an angle of 2.5 seconds. An angle of two seconds of an arc is the same angular size a small coin would have if you saw it without a telescope at a distance of 2 miles (3 km). Telescopes with a longer focus give you larger images and better magnification for looking at objects such as the Moon, the planets, and double stars. There is always a limit to the amount of detail that a telescope can show you. This depends on the quality of the lens, the effects of Earth's atmosphere, and the nature of light. The object lens or mirror of the telescope has a limit to its ability to show two very close stars as separate. The name of this limit is the **Dawes limit** after William Dawes (1799–1868).

Diameter of Objective		Separation	Faintest Object
(in.)	(mm)	(seconds arc)	(magnitude)
3	75	1.52	12.2
4	100	1.14	12.7
5	125	0.91	13.2
6	150	0.76	13.6
8	200	0.57	14.2

Most telescopes will enable you to see stars to about 12th magnitude.

Magnifying Power   The magnifying power of a telescope increases or modifies how much space an object appears to take up measured in degrees. We call this **angular modification**, and it makes the object seem bigger and therefore closer. The angular modification of a telescope depends on the focal lengths of both the objective and the eyepiece.

$$\text{angular modification} = \frac{\text{focal length of eyepiece}}{\text{focal length of objective}}$$

To get the most magnification from a telescope, the objective should have as long a focal length as possible and the eyepiece as short a focal length as possible. There is a limit to how much you can enlarge any image. You reach this limit when the magnification is about 50 times the size of the aperture. A 2-inch objective can usually magnify an object about 100 times ($2 \times 50 = 100$).

The bigger a telescope makes an object appear,

1. the less clear and distinct the object appears. Stars twinkle more.

2. the less bright the object appears, because you are spreading the same amount of light over a larger area.

3. the less you see of the object, because it fills up more of the view in the telescope. This is the **field of view** or how many degrees of an arc you can see.

Check the side effects of magnification by looking at something under a magnifying glass or with a telescope and see what happens to clearness, brightness, and amount of object you can see.

Types of Telescopes   There are several styles of telescopes, but they all use one of two ways of collecting light: **refracting** and **reflecting**.

Galileo's refracting telescope

Eyepiece

Objective

Light from a star

Newton's reflecting telescope

Eyepiece

Flat mirror

Light from a star

Objective (concave mirror)

Refracting and Reflecting Telescopes

Refracting   The telescope that Galileo built was a refractor. Such a telescope reflects or bends the path of light from a star by means of two lenses: the objective and the eyepiece. The farther apart the lenses are, the larger the focal length of the objective is and the larger the objective appears in your eyepiece. For this reason, refracting telescopes are also often very long and narrow. One of the longest in history was 123 feet. In this next project you can make a refracting telescope similar to the one that Galileo used.

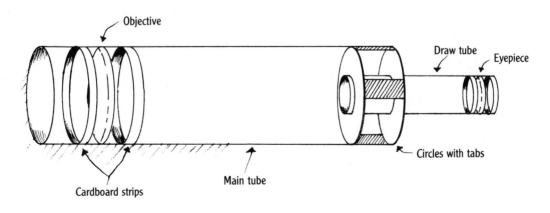

Objective

Draw tube

Eyepiece

Circles with tabs

Main tube

Cardboard strips

209

★ ★ ★ ★ ★ ★ ★ Project 45: Making a Refracting Telescope ★ ★ ★ ★ ★ ★ ★ ★

MATERIALS

two cardboard tubes or rolled sheets of stiff paper: 3¼-inch diameter × 31 inches (8¼ × 79 cm) and 1¼-inch diameter × 10 inches (3 × 25 cm)

flat black paint

3¼-inch (8¼ cm) lens (achromatic coated, 30–40 in. focal length, f number = 12.3)

½-inch (13 mm) focal length lens (coated, if possible; 40° apparent field of view)

cardboard strips

glue

black paper

scissors

pen or pencil

ruler

Look for lenses at surplus stores, secondhand shops, optometrists, and science supply stores. The lenses mentioned here will give you the exact power of Galileo's second telescope. You can use whatever lenses you can find to make your telescope. Find out the focal lengths and make the necessary changes to the size of your telescope.

PROCEDURE

1. Paint the inside of the two tubes flat black.

2. Cut out cardboard rings to hold lenses in place.

3. Draw a line around the inside of the objective end of the tube, 2 inches (5 cm) from the end.

4. Glue one of the cardboard strips for the objective so that it sits just behind the 2-inch (5 cm) line inside the tube. Place the lens in front of the strip and glue the other strip in front of the lens.

5. Repeat step 4 for the eyepiece lens, but don't set the lens back 2 inches (5 cm).

6. Cut out two cardboard circles with 1¼-inch (3 cm) holes in the center and tabs around the edges. Fold the tabs over and glue them together. When they are dry, put glue on the tabs and insert the circles in the eyepiece end of the large tube.

7. Insert the eyepiece tube into the cardboard circles.

8. Cut a ring of black paper and place it over the outer edge of the objective lens, leaving the center of the lens uncovered. Experiment with various sizes to overcome the color fringes in your view.

OBSERVATIONS

Does your telescope show you anything that you can't see at all without it? Use your telescope to demonstrate what a telescope can do as you read about it in this chapter.

Reflecting   Isaac Newton decided to improve on the design of the telescope and built the first reflecting telescope in 1668. It was about 6 inches (15 cm) long. In 1721 **John Hadley** (1682–1744) built the first professional-quality reflecting telescope.

In a reflecting telescope, the top is open and light enters and goes to the bottom of the telescope, where it is concentrated by a concave mirror. The light is then reflected back up the tube of the telescope to a flat mirror that reflects the light into the lens of the eyepiece. The concave mirror eliminates two major defects lenses often have: chromatic and spherical aberration. **Chromatic aberration** refers to colors of light not all meeting at the same point, which creates **color fringes**. Achromatic lenses help correct this problem.

In Project 46 you can make a reflecting telescope much like the kind in use in observatories around the world.

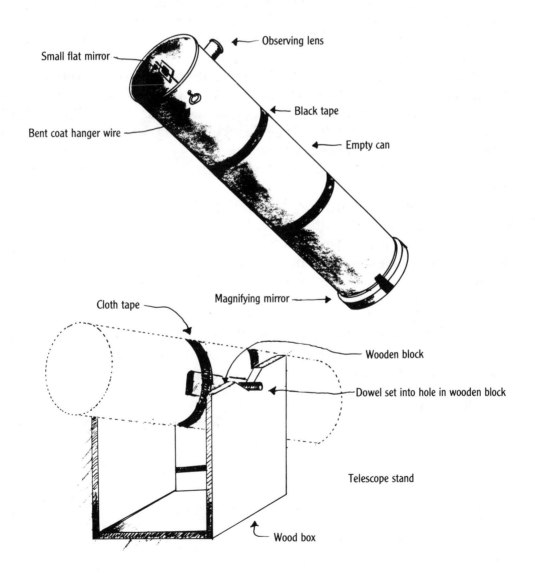

★ ★ ★ ★ ★ ★ ★Project 46: Making a Reflecting Telescope*★ ★ ★ ★ ★ ★ ★ ★

MATERIALS

three large cardboard or metal cans
   or tubes
   (from juice, oatmeal, etc.)
flat black paint
observing lens (eye loupe from a
   hardware store)
small flat mirror
coat hanger wire

electrical tape or other black tape
rubber band
ruler
nail
scissors
stiff paper tube
piece of paper
magnifying shaving mirror

PROCEDURE

1. Measure the distance from the mirror to where the Sun's rays focus on a piece of paper. This is the focal length of the mirror.

2. Remove both ends of three large cans. Paint the insides of the cans flat black. Tape them together with electrical tape.

3. Tape the magnifying mirror to one end of the cans. Put the rubber band around the opposite end. Mark on the outside of the cans the point which is 4¾ inches (7 cm) shorter than the focal length of the mirror, and roll the rubber band to this point. Measure from the rubber band to the edge of the top can to be sure it is the same distance all the way around.

4. Punch a hole with a nail at opposite sides of the top can where the rubber band is.

5. Cut a ¾-inch (2 cm) hole overlapping the rubber band and in between the two punched holes. Remove the rubber band.

6. Push the coat hanger through the two punched holes. Bend the ends of the coat hanger into handles and remove the remaining length of the wire.

7. Tape a ¾-inch (2 cm) square piece of flat mirror onto the coat hanger.

8. Insert a paper tube into hole on side of can. Tape the observing lens to the outer end of tube.

9. Turn the mirror so that light is reflected out of the hole cut into the side of the top can. Look at the mirror through the observing lens. Aim the top of the telescope at a distant object. *Never look at the sun!*

OBSERVATION

Why do most large observatories use reflecting telescopes like this one?

*This project is adapted from *Exploring Earth Science* by Walter A. Thurber, Robert E. Kilburn, and Peter S. Howell. Newton, MA: Allyn and Bacon, 1976. Used with permission.

There are many kinds of reflecting telescopes:

- *Gregorian*—designed in 1663, but not built until later. The design of this telescope inspired Newton.
- *Newtonian*—Isaac Newton designed it in 1668. There is a 98-inch (2½ m) Newtonian telescope at La Palma Observatory, Canary Islands.
- *Cassegrain*—has a small convex mirror instead of a flat one. It was designed by **Sieur Guillaume Cassegrain** in 1672. The 200-inch (5 m) Hale telescope on Palomar Mountain, California, is a Cassegrain. To observe, you sit in the telescope and move with it.
- *Prime focus*—invented by **Maurice Lowey** (1833–1907), an Austrian-French astronomer, in 1894 as an adaptation of the Newtonian and Cassegrain. The Hale telescope is an example (see above).
- *Coude focus*—a 24-inch one is in California. This type of telescope requires many mirrors. The focus does not move, only the telescope does. You can set up large observing equipment without attaching it to the telescope. The focus is in another room.

Coude comes from the French word *coude* = elbow.

- *Schmidt*—invented by **Bernhard Schmidt** (1879–1935) in 1931. Schmidt explained, "The rapid coma-free mirror system . . . offers great advantages in regard to the light-gathering power and aberration-free imagery." The size of the Schmidt telescope is the diameter of the correcting lens, which is usually two-thirds of the aperture of the objective. The 48-inch Schmidt telescope at Palomar Mountain Observatory in California has a 48-inch correcting lens and a 72-inch (1.83 meter) objective.
- *Schmidt photographic*—used for wide-angle astrophotography. Makesutov, Wright, and others changed it. It has extremely fast speeds and large fields of view. There is a 48-inch (122 cm) one in use at Siding Spring Observatory in Australia.

Uranus was the first planet to be discovered with a telescope.

Buying a Telescope   Telescopes have added so much to our understanding of the sky that many people automatically think of telescopes whenever you mention astronomy. As you have seen, a tremendous amount of what we know about the Earth, the Sun, Moon, planets, and stars we learned over the centuries *without* the aid of a telescope. There is still much you can learn with your own eyes aided only by clear thinking and your imagination.

There does come a moment when you might think about owning your own telescope. They certainly are fun and highly educational. But, *before* you buy a telescope,

1. Read and learn all you can about astronomy.
2. Learn the names and locations of the constellations and the brightest stars.
3. Use binoculars and other people's telescopes to become familiar with what these instruments can and can't do.
4. Join an astronomy club or subscribe to a good astronomy magazine.

Then, when you are ready to buy a telescope, the following suggestions should help you with your selection.

Cost   Expect to pay about $250 to $500 minimum for a quality starter telescope.

Type   The best telescope for serious amateurs is a reflecting telescope. It gives the greatest aperture for the lowest price. There are no distracting colors around the edges of the image. First choice is a 6-inch reflector or a 3-inch refractor, and second choice is a 4-inch reflector.

Aperture   Try to get at least a 3-inch (75 mm) aperture to begin with. Reflectors with larger apertures (4–10 in. and more) offer more light-gathering power.

Eyepieces   The diameter of your eyepieces should be 1¼ inches (31.75 mm). Remember that to calculate magnifying power, you divide the focal length of the objective by the focal length of the eyepiece. This will help you know what the magnification of an eyepiece will be when you use it on your telescope.

Often on the side of an eyepiece you will see a number with an *X* after it. This is the focal length of the eyepiece, not its magnifying power. You should have three eyepieces, one each for low, medium, and high power.

Eyepiece	You can see
Low power	Moons of Jupiter at 15 ×, rings of Saturn at 30 ×, comets and nebulae
Medium power	Entire Moon at 60 ×
High power	Double stars as separate at 120 ×

A Barlow lens is a handy device to have also. When you put it in front of any eyepiece, it doubles the power of the eyepiece.

Finderscope   This smaller scope mounted on the side of your larger scope helps you locate and center the object you want to view. It should have an aperture of at least 30 (preferably 50) millimeters.

Drive   This is a motor attached to your telescope that automatically moves the telescope as fast as the Earth is moving. This makes it possible to keep an image in view without having to adjust the telescope. A drive is especially useful when you want to take a long photograph without having trails.

Stand and Mount   The stand should be sturdy and not shaky. The best would be a well-made **altazimuth stand**. This kind of stand uses a fork as a mount to hold the telescope. The fork rotates on a horizontal axis. You can direct and rotate the telescope to any altitude from horizontal to zenith and any azimuth from 0° to 360°. An **equatorial mount** allows you to track the stars and planets and photograph them. A **Dobsonian mount** allows you to move your telescope very easily.

Comfort   Your telescope should be easy to carry, set up, and use. The control knobs should be big enough for you to find and turn easily.

You might consider building a reflector yourself. You can grind your own mirror and buy good eyepieces. It costs less than half what it would cost to built a refractor with the same size objective. Another possibility is to buy a high-quality pair of binoculars.

Binoculars   A **binocular** is a magnifier with two objectives and two eyepieces. It's like having two small refractor telescopes, one for each eye.

Binocular comes from the Latin words *bi* = two and *oculus* = eye.

Binoculars use prisms to fold and shift the path of light within a small space to keep the size of the instrument small. The prisms also show you the image the way it appears normally, not upside down and backward like a telescope sees it. Since there are two telescopes in a pair of binoculars, what you see has the kind of depth and three-dimensional feeling that a single telescope can't provide. Binoculars usually cost much less than a telescope. They are small, easy to carry, and very easy to use. They are good to use before buying a telescope. You can see all the planets (except Pluto) with a good pair of binoculars. You can also see the phases of Venus, the moons of Jupiter, the asteroids, comets, lunar surface features, and eclipses.

The ideal size to buy is a 7×50. The $7 \times$ is the magnifying power. The 50 is the diameter of the objective lens in millimeters. The second choice would be 10×50 or 7×35. Be sure you are buying true prismatic binoculars and not opera or field glasses or glasses made to look like binoculars. Remember that just as with a telescope, the larger the aperture, the smaller the field of view and the more noticeable your unsteady hand will be. Take your time, be picky, and be sure you can return the binoculars if you have problems.

READING MORE
Dickinson, Terence, and Alan Dyer. *The Backyard Astronomer's Guide.* Columbia, SC: Camden House, 1991.

Kals, W. S. *The Stargazer's Bible.* Garden City, NJ: Doubleday, 1980.

Maloney, Terry. *Telescopes: How to Choose and Use Them.* New York: Sterling, 1968.

The first photograph of the Moon

Section 3   CAMERAS

Photography   From the 1500s, alchemists knew that sunlight turned silver compounds like silver chloride black. Chemical experiments in the 18th century showed that it was light and not heat from the sunlight that caused the blackening. In 1822 the French artist **Joseph Niepie (1765–1833)** made a copy of an engraving using the "photographic process" of combining chemicals and the Sun. Four years later, Niepie used the same process to take the world's first photograph, a view from his window. The list of firsts continued:

- *First photograph of a living subject*—1839 by John William Draper (1811–1882)
- *First photograph of the Moon*—1840 by John William Draper
- *First photograph of a star (Vega)*—1850 by William Cranch Bond (1789–1859) and John Whipple (1823–1891)
- *First photograph of a double star*—*(Alcor and Mizar)*, 1857 by Whipple. This photo helped measure distance between stars and determine stellar magnitude

- *First astronomical discovery made with photography*—1860 by Warren de la Rue (1815–1889) and Pietro Angelo Secchi (1818–1878). Their photograph of a total solar eclipse showed that prominences and flares were attached to the Sun, not to the Moon as people had thought
- *First photographs of stars too dim for the human eye to see*—1864 by George Bond (1825–1865)

On a fine night the amount of work which can be accomplished with entire exception from the trouble, vexation and fatigue that seldom fail to attend upon ordinary observations, is astonishing. The plates, once secured, can be laid by for future study by daylight and at leisure. The record is there, with no room for doubts or mistakes as to its fidelity.—George Bond

- *First attempt to use photography in studying an astronomical object (the Moon)*—1865 by de la Rue
- *First planet discovered with photographs (Pluto):* 1939 by Clyde Tombaugh

---

Photography comes from the Greek words φωτος (*photos*) = light and γραφος (*graphos*) = to write, paint, record.

The German astronomer **J. H. Madler** (1791–1874) invented the word *photography* a few days before **John Herschel** (1792–1871) did. Herschel, also an astronomer, first used the words **positive, negative,** and **snapshot** to describe photographs.

Since astronomers have begun using photography to help them in their work, they have discovered asteroids, satellites, and rings around planets as well as studying the surfaces of planets. What began as a visual art became a scientific tool. Photographs of objects in the night sky remain a source of incredible beauty as well as information.

There are many advantages to using photography to help you study the sky.

1. Photographs can record the images of stars that are far dimmer than the eye or the telescope can see. Light from the star keeps darkening the chemicals on the plate the longer you expose it. The retina in your eye takes in all the light it can all at once.

2. Photographs don't depend on the condition of your eye for you to make them.

3. You can enlarge photographs to show more detail.

4. The image on a photograph is permanent. You can study it at any time, night or day, clear or cloudy. You can examine photographs over the years to look for any changes (that's how Clyde Tombaugh discovered Pluto).

5. You can make copies of photographs and send them to other people so that they can all see the same view.

In the next project, you can take some photographs of the sky and see for yourself what a useful tool photography is.

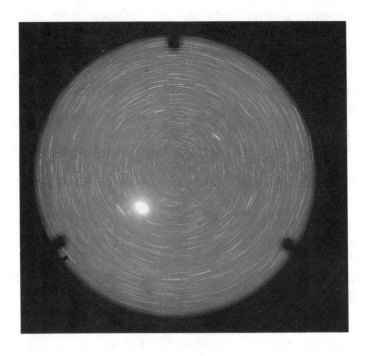

Star trails (*photo courtesy of Observatoire de Haute Provence*)

★ ★ ★ ★ ★ ★ ★ **Project 47: Photographing Stars and Planets** ★ ★ ★ ★ ★ ★ ★

MATERIALS

camera whose shutter can be left open
    (set to B for time exposure;
    preferably one that is not
    automatic)
tripod or stool
fast film (black and white: Tri-X—ASA
    400 or Plus LX—ASA 125; color:
    Ektachrome 400 or Kodachrome
    64—ASA 64. This is slide film, and
    only Kodak can process it. It may
    take a while to get it back. It works
    well for astronomical
    photographs.)

cable release
pencil and paper
watch or clock
ruler or straightedge
protractor
access to photocopier

PROCEDURE

Before you start:

1. Be patient and be prepared to shoot one role of black and white and one roll of color (12 or 24 exposures each) as a practice. You need to experiment with f-stop settings and exposure times with black and white and color. Then when a great

218

scene takes place in the sky, you'll be ready. Take practice photographs of all the subjects described here.

2. Keep track of all of your photographs in a log. Include date, object photographed, exposure time, f-stop setting, and film speed and type.

3. Start by taking one or two photographs in the daylight so the photo processing people can tell where your frames begin.

4. Tell the people where you take the film that you have photographed stars, you want all frames printed, and the sky should be black.

STAR TRAILS (LIKE YOU DREW IN CHAPTER 1)

1. Put the camera on the tripod pointing toward Polaris (in the Northern Hemisphere) or σ Octanis (in the Southern Hemisphere) or else have the polestar near the bottom of the frame.

2. Focus the camera at infinity or as far away as it will go.

3. Set the aperture (f stop) at its maximum opening.

4. Set the shutter for a time exposure (B or T).

5. Attach the cable release and open the shutter for 1 hour. Tightly screw the cable on, leave, and return in an hour.

6. Move to the next frame and open the shutter. Leave the camera for as long as you can. Before you go to bed, close the shutter and bring the camera in.

7. Write down how long you left the shutter open (exposure time).

8. Take other photographs of star trails by pointing your camera to the east, west, south, and north.

CONSTELLATIONS

1. Put the camera on the tripod pointing toward a constellation. Choose a time when the constellation is high in the sky to avoid distortion from the atmosphere. (Check for dates and times in the Constellation Catalog in Sky Files.)

2. Use the same settings (focus, aperture, and shutter speed) as in 2, 3, and 4 above.

3. Attach the cable release and experiment with shutter speeds. If you leave the camera open for a long time, you will begin to have star trails. For stars near the east, west, or the ecliptic, leave the camera open for no longer than 50 seconds. For stars nearer to the poles, your exposures can be longer. For telephoto lenses, the exposures must be only for a few seconds. For wide-angle lenses, the exposures can be longer than the time for a standard lens.

THE MOON

1. Make allowances for the brightness of the Moon.

2. Take photographs of different phases and colors (when close to horizon).

3. Photograph the Moon both in the daytime and at night.

THE PLANETS

1. Take photographs of the planets over a period of time to show their movement. Always include a few stars as reference points.

2. If you are using color film, try to show the red of Mars and the yellow of Saturn compared with the white of Venus. You can do the same with the colors of stars.

THROUGH A TELESCOPE

1. Take photographs using the clock drive on the telescope to allow you to make a longer exposure without trails.

2. Photograph the same constellations as you did before to see how many dimmer stars you can brighten.

3. Take photographs of nebulae and galaxies.

4. Photograph the Moon's craters.

5. Take photographs of Saturn's rings, Jupiter's bands and moons, and the phases of Venus.

OBSERVATIONS

What f stops, exposure times, and film type gave you the best results? Were more stars and other objects visible on your photographs than you were able to see with your eyes?

The photoelectric effect   Albert Einstein explained the photoelectric effect in 1905 and won the Nobel Peace Prize for Physics in 1921 because of it.

Photoelectric comes from the Greek words φωτος (*photos*) = light and ἠλεκτωρ (*elector*) = the beaming Sun;
ἠλεκτρων (*electron*) = metallic substance produced from amber by friction.

Electrically charged particles can blacken photographic plates. They can also generate an electrical current. The photocell is a simple light-sensitive detector in which light falls on a surface called the **photocathode**. This causes electrons to be ejected from the photocathode. The electrons then travel to a collecting electrode that causes an electric current. The current can then be used to power a motor to open doors automatically for you in a store. Look for the light by the door. It is focused on a photoelectric cell. As long as the light can reach the cell, there is enough electricity to keep the door closed. If you walk in front of the light, you interrupt the flow of electricity and the door opens.

In the spring of 1933, a beam of light from Arcturus (α Boötes) opened the Chicago World's Fair. The Century of Progress Exposition aimed its telescopes at the bright star and focused the gathered light onto photoelectric cells. These cells generated enough electricity from the starlight to turn on the switch that controlled the floodlights at the exposition grounds. The exposition planners chose Arcturus because they calculated that the light reaching the fair had left Arcturus 40 years earlier in 1893.

In 1924 astronomers began using photocells aimed at a bright star to guide their telescopes and keep the star in view, like a drive. The photoelectric effect also takes place in a video camera. Light enters the camera and releases electrically charged particles. The tube in your television has an electron beam that scans all the charged particles sent to it by the camera and translates these particles back into the original image that entered the camera. In the 1950s people aimed television cameras at the sky much as Galileo first aimed the telescope heavenward in the 1600s.

The most recent kind of image-making tube uses a phosphor screen. Electrons set the phosphor screen aglow much like a television screen. It only takes one electron to do this, which makes the phosphor screen much more sensitive than a photographic plate. The image on the screen is actually brighter than the image formed by the original light. Once collected, you can photograph the image, send it to another place by way of fiber optics, or feed it to a computer. The computer can remove any extra light around the image that you don't want, so you have a clear view of what you want to look at. You don't have to sit at your telescope out in the cold, straining your eye. Now you can control everything from a distance sitting comfortably in a room watching the results on your TV screen.

Because electronic methods can reveal very dim objects with a short exposure time (about 2/100 of a second), these methods are fast replacing photography in astronomical research.

Computers   The spectacular views brought back from the cameras of the astronauts are photographs. The pictures that we receive from spacecraft such as the *Voyager* did not come from photographic film. They came from television cameras with selenium-sulfur vidicom image tubes, 1 inch (2½ cm) in diameter. The tubes change the light entering them into electronic impulses. Radio transmitters on the spacecraft send these impulses back to Earth as black-and-white digital computer data in the form of a series of 1s and 0s. There are billions of these 1s and 0s, or binary bits, arriving on Earth from the spacecraft. Computers and their operators process this information so that an image results.

Voyager could transmit 115,200 bits per second to produce a single image that would end up containing 5,120,000 bits.

The image on the computer screen appears as a large grid. Each square in the grid stands for part of the object that the television camera in space recorded. These squares are *pic*ture *el*ements or **pixels** for short.

In the *Voyager* images, there were 640,000 pixels arranged in a grid of 800 × 800 squares. Each pixel had an 8-digit binary number signal code.

Voyager 2 space probe (*photo courtesy of Jet Propulsion Laboratory*)

As the computer processes the information, it gives a number value for light or darkness and color to each pixel. This is **digital image processing.**

What image does the computer process? On *Voyager* there are two television cameras, one with a wide-angle lens, the other with a narrow angle. The narrow-angle camera has a 60-inch (1,500 mm) focal length and a 0.4° field of view. It also has 7½ times the resolving power of the wide-angle camera. The wide-angle camera can see an area 56 times larger than the narrow-angle camera. It has a 7-inch (200 mm) focal length and a 3° field of view. Each camera has a rotating filter wheel to select the color of light the camera will see. There is also a filter to focus on wavelengths of sodium and methane. Usually the cameras take three images of the same subject, once each through the blue, green, and orange filters.

Back on Earth at your computer you can combine the images that appear on the screen to get any result you want. You can make the image have nearly the exact colors of the object the cameras looked at. The human eye is much more sensitive to colors than the lens of a camera, so your image won't be exact. You can deliberately exaggerate the brightness levels of each pixel if you want to make it easier to see certain parts of the image, especially the details. In this way, you are enhancing the contrast. You can also use false color to emphasize slight differences in color due to changes in temperature, chemicals, and land formation.

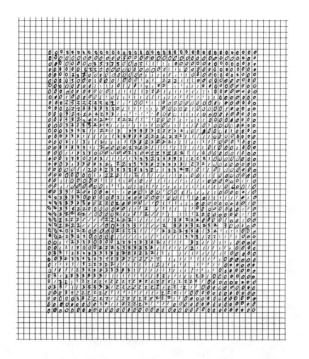

★ ★ ★ ★ ★ **Project 48: Showing How Images Are Transmitted*** ★ ★ ★ ★ ★

MATERIALS

grid on this page   access to a photocopier, one with
pencil   enlarging capabilities

PROCEDURE

A sensor on board a space probe has broken down an image of a planetary feature into pixels. A computer on board has translated each pixel into a number from 0–3 representing a brightness value from black (0) through gray (1, 2) to white (3). The space probe has transmitted the number shown on the grid above.

1. You are the ground receiver. Photocopy and enlarge the grid above. Convert the numbers back into an image by shading in each square with the brightness value assigned to it by the number.

2. Compare your image with the original object that appears in chapter 6, section 3 (Venus).

*This project is adapted from a concept appearing in *Ideas for Teaching Gifted Students Science* by Jackie Mallis. Austin, TX: Jackie Mallis, 1982.

OBSERVATIONS

Would your image have been clearer if you could have used more gradations of black, gray, and white? What advantages do you think there are in using computers instead of photographs to record images from space? What disadvantages are there?

Digital image of the Sun's corona (*photo courtesy of NASA*)

READING MORE

Burgess, E. *Celestial Basic.* Alameda, CA: Sybex, 1982.
Kals, W. S. *The Stargazer's Bible.* New York: Doubleday, 1980.
Paul, Henry E. *Outer Space Photography.* New York: Amphoto, 1976.

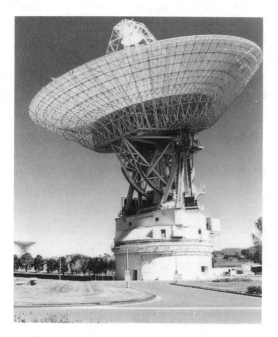

Deep space network antennae, Australia
(*photo courtesy of Jet Propulsion Laboratory*)

Section 4 *SPECTROSCOPES AND RADIO RECEIVERS*

The Color of Light   Have you ever seen a rainbow inside your house made by a crystal or a prism near your window? It's not raining, so why is there a rainbow? For centuries, people asked the same question. They figured that light from the Sun was pure, and when it went through the crystal or prism, the impurities in the glass colored the light.

> . . . in the beginning of the year 1666 (at which time, I applied myself to the grinding of Optick glasses of other figures than *Spherical*), I procured me a Triangular glass—Prisme, to try therewith the celebrated *Phaenomena of Colours*. And in order thereto having darkened my chamber, and made a small hole in my window-sheets, to let in a convenient quantity of the Sun's light, I placed my Prisme at his entrance, that it might be thereby refracted to the opposite wall. It was at first a very pleasing divertisement, to view the vivid and intense colours produced thereby. . . .
>
> —Sir Isaac Newton in the *Philosophical Transactions*
> of the Royal Society in London, 1672

The beam of light bent as it passed through Newton's prism and created a rainbow on his wall. The prism bent each color at a particular angle: violet refracted the most, then indigo, then blue, then green; yellow and orange with red refracted the least. Newton named the rainbow pattern of colors the **spectrum**, for the "ghost of light."

225

Why was the light colored? Newton tried different-sized holes in the window shutter, different-sized prized prisms, different placements of the prism, including outside the window. No change. To get only one color, he made a small hole in the screen on which the spectrum was shining right where the red light appeared. He took another prism and placed it on the other side of the screen into the path of the red light. The red light passed through the second prism and came out refracted with the same angle and red. Newton tried this with each of the other colors and had the same result. He then passed the light from the first prism through a second prism held upside down, thinking all the colors would spread out even more. Instead, the colors joined together and came out as a shaft of pure light, casting a spot of white light on the screen.

These experiments convinced Newton that white light was made up of all seven colors of the rainbow. In order to see these colors, you need a prism, glass, and water or rain to help separate the light into its parts. The prism has the ability to break (refract) white light into the spectrum of purple, blue, green, yellow, and red—the "rainbow" colors. We call the separation of light into the spectrum dispersion.

Dispersion comes from the Latin word *dispersus* = to scatter, to spread abroad.

In the late 1800s **Michael Faraday** and **Hans Christian Oersted** showed the close connection between electricity and magnetism. **James Clark Maxwell** pointed out that light is also related to electricity and magnetism and that light, electricity, and magnetism are all related to electromagnetic waves. Included in the electromagnetic spectrum are three forms of light:
- *Very long wavelengths*—infrared (invisible)
- *Visible light*—makes up only a small fraction of the electromagnetic spectrum
- *Very short wavelengths*—ultraviolet, X rays, gamma rays (invisible)

Sir William Herschel, the discoverer of the planet Uranus, conducted experiments to find how much heat each color of the Sun's spectrum carried. In this next project you can do the same kind of experiment.

★ ★ ★ ★ ★ ★ ★ ★ **Project 49: Measuring the Temperatures** ★ ★ ★ ★ ★ ★ ★ ★
of Infrared Rays

MATERIALS
prism white piece of paper
two thermometers flat black paint

PROCEDURE
1. Paint the bulbs of the two thermometers black.
2. Place the white paper on a flat surface on to which the Sun is shining. Place a thermometer on the paper and record the temperature after 3 minutes.
3. Place a prism in the path of the Sun. Place the thermometer in any color on the blue-violet end of the spectrum and record the temperature after 3 minutes.
4. Place the thermometer in the deep red and record the temperature after 3 minutes.
5. Record the temperature just beyond the red and just beyond the blue.

OBSERVATIONS
Which wavelength has greater heating effect? How far do the rays extend beyond the visible end? Herschel named the invisible radiation beyond the red end of the spectrum **infrared.**

Infrared comes from the Latin word *infra* = below.

The Spectrum Newton separated the visible light from the Sun into the spectrum. You can also separate the light coming from the stars or passing through gases of different elements. To do this you need an instrument to split up the light and spread it out into a band of colored lines representing the spectrum. **Robert Bunsen** (1811–1899), the inventor of the Bunsen burner, invented the **spectroscope** to create and view the spectra of stars. You can make photographic studies with a spectroscope using a spectrograph. Studying the spectra of stars and light passing through gases is called **spectral analysis,** an important part of astronomy.

In 1802 Englishman **William Wollaston** (1766–1828) noticed thin dark lines among the bands of color while observing the Sun's spectrum. He thought these lines were the natural boundaries between the colors. In 1817 **Joseph von Fraunhofer** (1787–1826) saw between 600 and 750 lines and assigned letters to the strongest lines, starting with "A" in the red band. We now call these lines **Fraunhofer lines.** A help in figuring out what the black lines were came when people realized that they could reproduce these black spectral lines in the laboratory. When you pass a beam of white light through a cloud of gas, the Fraunhofer lines appear in the spectrum. The spectra of light emitted from certain glowing gases also showed several separate bright lines. Each gas displayed its own pattern of spectral lines and colors.

In 1859 **Gustav Kirchoff** (1824–1887) of Germany offered the following explanation for the lines and separate colors. Any source could both emit or absorb radiation: the temperature determined which took place. When light passes through a gas that is cooler than the light source, the spectrum that results has thin dark lines crossing it. These lines represent missing colors that the gas took out of the light, or absorbed. Each chemical element in the gas selects a certain grouping of colors to absorb that no other element chooses, thus producing its own characteristic pattern of dark lines on the spectrum. It's as though each element puts it fingerprint on the light as it passes through.

When you burn an element and examine its spectral pattern against a dark background, only certain colors appear in narrow lines. Each element produces or emits its own pattern of colors. These emission lines of an element show up in the same places on the spectrum as the dark absorption lines for that element. A gas at high pressure, a liquid, or a solid, if heated to incandescence, will glow with a **continuous spectrum.** A hot gas under low pressure will produce only certain colors called bright **emission lines.** A cool gas at low pressure, if placed between the observer and a hot continuum source, absorbs certain colors, causing dark **absorption lines** in the observed spectrum.

The study of the spectra of celestial objects (**spectroscopy**) is the most powerful tool an astronomer has to find out information about the universe. So critical is spectroscopy that many astronomers devote their entire careers to it. Using Kirchoff's laws, physicists returned to the solar spectrum. Examining it carefully, they found tens of thousands of Fraunhofer lines. In their laboratories, using Bunsen burners (gas flames) or electric arcs as light sources, the physicists shone this light through gases of various compositions. They burned metal salts and examined the spectra of their flames, all in an effort to reproduce the lines in the solar spectrum. The hope was to find what elements were responsible for the Fraunhofer lines. This would reveal what the Sun and the stars were made of. **William Higgins** and **Angelo Secchi** were the first to search for the structure of stars using a spectroscope.

In this next project you can do your own spectrum studying using a spectroscope that you can make yourself, using a diffraction grating like the one invented by von Fraunhofer.

Spectroscope box

★ ★ ★ ★ ★ ★ ★ ★ Project 50: Making a Spectrum-Analyzing ★ ★ ★ ★ ★ ★ ★ ★ Instrument (Spectroscope)*

MATERIALS

spectroscope plan from book	paper clip
diffraction grating	a nail
scissors	3 × 5 inch (7½ × 12½ cm) index
rubber cement	card
ruler	access to a photocopier, one with
tape	enlarging capabilities

PROCEDURE

1. Photocopy the unfolded spectroscope plan from the next page and enlarge it so it is the size written on the plan.

2. Cut out the spectroscope. Use the edge of the ruler and the side of the scissors to help you fold up the sides and flaps of the spectroscope along the lines.

3. Glue the flaps as shown *under* the spaces where the arrows point.

4. Paper-clip the diffraction grating into place behind the square hole. Look through the grating while aiming the scale end of your spectroscope at a bright indoor light (*not the Sun*). If you do not see a spectrum on the scale, remove the grating, turn it a quarter of the way around to the next edge, and put it back in place.

*This project is adapted from *Modern Astronomy: An Activities Approach* by R. Robert Robbins and Mary Kay Hemenway. Austin: University of Texas Press, 1982. Used with permission.

5. Cut the index card to the size and shape shown. Glue it on top of the spectroscope and glue the flaps in place above the grating.

USING YOUR SPECTROSCOPE

Look through the hole while aiming the scale end of your spectroscope at a bright light (*not the Sun*). If you do not see a spectrum above the scale,

a. Remove the grating, turn it a quarter of the way around to the next edge, and put it back in place. If it works, remove the paper clip and glue the grating down.

b. Adjust the size of the opening on the scale end by placing the edges of two pieces of paper behind the slit so that their edges are in a straight line and are closer (or nearer) to each other.

Look at regular incandescent lights, fluorescent lights, street lamps, neon signs, and at the reflected light of the Sun in a piece of white paper. *Do not look at the Sun.* You might try taping the diffraction grating in front of your camera lens and photographing various light sources with color slide film. Write down what each source is. Project your slides onto the wall or a screen and use a meterstick to measure the wavelength.

OBSERVATIONS

One way of being certain that you are reading the correct fingerprint of an element as it appears on the spectrum is to measure the width of its wavelengths. A wavelength is just what the name says, the length in between the tops of two waves. This distance is extremely tiny so we use special numbers to measure it. Anders Jonas Ångstrom (1817–1874), a Swedish astronomer working in the 1860s, developed a wavelength measuring scale based on a unit equal to 1/10,000,000,000 of a meter. He called this unit "10th metre," but people preferred to call it an *Ångstrom unit* (or Å for short) after its inventor. We now use the term **nanometer**, one of which is equal to 10 Ångstroms. Using Ångstroms, wavelengths of violet light are about 4,000 Å, wavelengths of red light are about 7,000 Å. What would these be in nanometers?

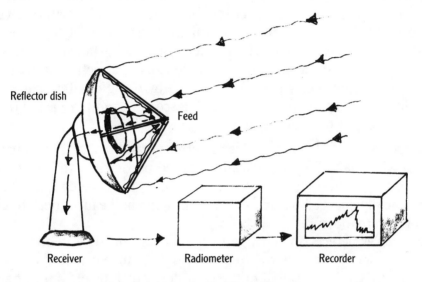

Reflector dish

Feed

Receiver

Radiometer

Recorder

A radio telescope receiving radio waves

Radio Astronomy—*"The Unseen Universe"*   American **Thomas Alva Edison** (1847–1931) and English physicist **Joseph Lodge** (1851–1940) both suggested that there might be radio waves coming from the Sun. No one could check up on their idea. The electromagnetic spectrum is vast. The visible portion of it is very small by comparison. Most of astronomy up until 1931 had focused on understanding the universe through studies of its visible light.

In 1932 an electrical engineer named **Karl Jansky** (1905–1950) was working for the telephone company trying to figure out why there was so much static on the phones from conversations sent by radio between New York and London. The usual causes such as thunderstorms were only making part of the static. A hissing sound remained. Jansky built an antenna made of wires stretched on wooden frames. Jansky made the world's first radio telescope out of eight large metal, rectangular hoops attached to a wooden frame shaped like a long rectangle. The telescope rotated slowly on a set of Model T Ford wheels. This antenna found that the hissing noise came from a point in space that 14 years before **Harlow Shapley** (1885–1972) had said was the center of the galaxy. Jansky had discovered radio waves from space. He reported his findings in 1932. Astronomers did not follow up on Jansky's discovery until almost 15 years later.

Grote Reber (b. 1911), an amateur astronomer living in Illinois, decided to listen in on these radio waves. In 1936 he built a 31-foot dish antenna to collect the radio waves the way reflector telescope mirrors collect light. Since radio waves can go through clouds, fog, and mist and light can't, Reber could use his dish anytime and in any weather. Using his **radio telescope,** Reber listened to the sky and made a contour map of the radio sky that he published in 1940. People considered this map the first and best of its kind for the next 15 years.

Radio Interferometry If you place two radio dishes some distance apart and have both observe the same source at the same time, one dish will receive the radio wave slightly before the other. By measuring the time lag in between, you can figure out the direction of the source. The farther apart the distance (baseline) between the two dishes, the more accurately you can locate the direction of the source. *Very long baseline interferometry* (VLBI) is possible by using one telescope in one part of the world (e.g., California) and another telescope in another part of the world far distant from the first (e.g., Australia).

Radio Telescopes The only device sensitive to radio waves is an **antenna,** which is simply a wire that allows electrically charged particles to move freely along it. When electromagnetic radio waves reach the antenna, they come in contact with the electronically charged particles on the antenna and cause them to change the direction they are moving.

The **receiver** detects any change in the current of the antenna. The receiver operator can select or amplify the frequency of the current just like you do with a radio. He or she sends the signal to the **recorder,** which prints out a chart of these changes. The recorder uses a pen that writes across a moving roll of paper. If you connected the receiver to a loudspeaker instead of a pen, you would hear the "cosmic hiss" that Jansky heard. When strong radio waves come across the antenna, it sounds like the radio in your car when you drive under a power line. To build up a "picture" of the source, the telescope scans back and forth across it so that it can measure its brightness and every point. The telescopic computer stores the measurements and builds up a "map" of the source. The map is usually like a topographic (contour) map (see chapter 3, section 2) with the most intense source in the center surrounded by rings of lessening levels of intensity.

A radio telescope is really a highly sensitive version of a regular radio. Radio waves come to your radio at home from a variety of radio stations. Each of these radio stations has permission to use a certain frequency of wavelength on which to send their broadcasts. The frequency is the station's number on the radio dial. If it is AM, the frequency is measured by *a*mplitude *m*odulation from 530 to 1600 kilohertz. FM is *f*requency *m*odulation from 88 to 108 megahertz. When your radio receives a broadcast, it does the opposite of what the transmitter at the radio station did: it changes radio waves back into music and voices. Radio telescopes change radio waves into images of their sources. The maps can also appear on a TV screen as a "radio photograph." In this way, using image intensifiers, false color, and computer enhancing techniques, you can build up a more detailed picture of the source. A radio telescope view of a typical radio station broadcast would show the shapes of the radio station's broadcasting antennas. Radio telescopes have their own radio dial numbers that no one else may use, especially radio stations.

In this next project you can hear how radio signals sound when you receive them using an antenna.

Aluminum foil inside

Umbrella antenna behind the radio facing the incoming waves

Umbrella antenna between the radio and the incoming waves

★ ★ ★ ★ ★ ★ ★ ★ ★ **Project 51: Receiving Radio Signals*** ★ ★ ★ ★ ★ ★ ★ ★ ★ ★

MATERIALS

FM radio
umbrella
heavy-duty aluminum foil

masking tape
pencil
paper

*This project is adapted from *Scott, Foresman Earth Science* by Jay M. Pasachoff, Naomi Pasachoff, and Timothy M. Cooney. Glenview, IL: Scott, Foresman, 1983. Used with permission.

PROCEDURE

1. Place the radio on a table. Turn the dial all the way to the left and begin to search for stations you can barely hear. Write down the dial number of five of these stations whose signals are so weak you can't tune them in clearly.

2. Open the umbrella and tape the inside of it with the aluminum foil.

3. Turn the radio to one of the five weak stations, turning the radio around until you get the best reception you can.

4. Hold the umbrella behind the radio so that the aluminum foil faces the waves going past the radio.

5. Move the umbrella slowly toward the radio or farther from it until you find the position that best improves the reception.

6. Repeat steps 3–5 for the other four weak stations. Mark each station on your list whose reception the umbrella improved.

7. Choose a station that comes in clearly. Place the umbrella in front of the radio and the incoming radio waves.

OBSERVATIONS

Your umbrella strengthened the radio waves before they reached the radio. Where did these waves come from? What happened when you put the umbrella in front of the radio with a clear station tuned in?

Radar Astronomy   Radar astronomy is the technique of sending radio waves to an object and waiting for them to bounce back to the Earth and measuring how long the round-trip took. By using the speed of light, you can figure how far away the object is. The real birth of radar astronomy, however, was in 1946, when Hungarian physicist **Zoltan Lajos Bay** sent out a beam of microwaves to the Moon and detected the return echo. Since radio waves can go through clouds, radar astronomy gave us our first views of the cloud-covered surface of Venus in 1961.

Radar = radio detection and ranging (determination of distance).

Infrared Astronomy   Infrared astronomy is like heat-sensitive photography. In infrared photographs, the red stars (like Antares and Betelgeuse) show the brightest and the blue stars (like Rigel) are dimmest. This would make Betelgeuse the brightest star in the sky. You can feel the infrared radiation from the Sun. Remember the temperature of infrared rays in Project 49, Measuring the Temperatures of Infrared Rays? Water vapor and carbon dioxide in the Earth's atmosphere absorb large amounts of infrared rays, making the infrared sky practically invisible. High-flying aircraft, balloons, and specially equipped telescopes that pass through the Earth's atmosphere can detect infrared radiation coming from the planets and stars. As a result, we have photographed a complete survey of the infrared sky. Many infrared sources are clouds of dust around very young or very old stars, warmed by the heat of the nearby star.

Microwave Astronomy   Microwave astronomy deals with the short waves in the electromagnetic spectrum between radio and infrared and overlapping radar. Radar makes use of microwave radiation. Microwave reflection has provided startling information about: Venus (its rotational period and its retrograde motion), Mercury (its rotational period), asteroids, meteors, Mars, Jupiter, and Saturn. Water absorbs microwave radiation. If you put anything moist (like meat, soup, cake batter) in a microwave oven, the moist substance will absorb the radiation and become hot very quickly. This heat comes from within the food itself rather than from the coils in the oven. That is why you can cook things very quickly in a microwave oven. You need to be careful to keep the radiation inside the oven since it can damage living tissue.

Microwave comes from the Greek word μικρος (*micros*) = small.

X-ray Astronomy   Wilhelm Konrad Röntgen (1845–1923) discovered and named X rays in 1895. In 1970 international scientists launched the first orbiting X-ray observatory from Kenya, called the *Uhuru.*

Uhuru comes from the Swahili word *uhuru* = freedom.

For three years *Uhuru* scanned the sky for X-ray sources and charted more than 200. The names of these sources come from the constellations where we find them (like Cygnus X-1, Hercules X-1). Other X-ray observatories in space include the *High Energy Astrophysics Observatory* (HEAO), the Einstein Observatory, *Exosat,* and *Rosat* (named for Röntgen). X rays are able to penetrate most materials except lead.

Optical telescopes and radio telescopes each provide an important view of the sky. Recently there has been an increasing use of radio astronomy, partly because of the many advantages it has over optical observing. You can use a radio telescope day or night, in any weather. With it you can see farther into space with no interfering background. A radio telescope is less expensive to build, uses less sophisticated materials, and does not limit you to any size. With an optical telescope you need clear skies. This is not a problem for radio telescopes.

The radio window has truly opened an unseen universe for astronomers and made us continually revise our picture of what is "out there."

READING MORE

Freeman, Ira M. *Light and Radiation.* New York: Van Nostrand Reinhold, 1981.
Learner, Richard. *Astronomy Through the Telescope.* New York: Van Nostrand Reinhold, 1981.

Chapter 6 *THE SUN-CENTERED SKY*

The "two great lights," the Sun and the Moon, are closely intertwined with the Earth. The Sun is the major source of life and light for our planet. It also gives us an idea of the size and power of a star seen closer up. The Moon gives us reflected sunlight and is a constant reminder of our place in space. To see its cratered surface with the naked eye offers us a closer view of another heavenly body, a glimpse at what a planet might look like.

Section 1 THE SUN

Pepin: What's the Sun?
Alcuin: The splendour of the universe, the beauty of the sky, the glory of the day, the divider of the hours.

—the monk Alcuin, teaching Pepin, the son of Charlemagne

Helios, the Greek Sun god (*from a Greek vase in the British Museum*)

Names People have always held the Sun in high esteem. Many cultures saw the god of life in the Sun. They watched this god's daily, monthly, and yearly movements with great care. To the Greeks, the god of the Sun was **Helios** or **Sol**, and thus we have the words *heliocentric* and *solar.* The Greeks also called the Sun Apollo. The Egyptians worshipped the Sun as Ra.

Early Observations Some cultures planned and built large cities on the basis of the Sun's movements. Such a city was Tenochtitlan, capital of the Aztec Empire. It had more people in it and was larger and better planned than many cities in Europe.

Equinox sunrise between the towers of Temple Mayor, Tenochtitlan, Mexico

Four large avenues divided the city into four sections. These four sections point to the four cardinal directions. Near the center of the city was Temple Mayor, a double temple, more than 270 feet (82 m) wide at its base and about 90 feet (27 m) tall. At sunrise on the equinoxes, the Sun would appear between the two towers at the top.

Sun observatories appear throughout the world. Chapter 1 describes some of them. Some are oriented toward the winter solstice as in the shrines at Burro Flats, Los Angeles; the Tipai Indian shelter in Baja, California; and New Grange in Ireland.

At the temple of Ramses II in Abu Simbel in Egypt is a row of baboons carved from stone. The baboon was a symbol of Thoth, god of wisdom. Baboons also have a connection with sunrise. Like roosters and birds, baboons chatter at dawn. In Abu Simbel, the first light of dawn falls upon this row of stone baboons who chatter silently to greet the day.

The View from Earth The Sun looks huge in the sky. How big is it anyway? This next project will help you find out.

★ ★ ★ ★ ★ ★ ★ ★ ★ ★ Project 52: Measuring the Sun ★ ★ ★ ★ ★ ★ ★ ★ ★ ★ ★ ★

MATERIALS

ruler   nail

two sheets of white cardboard
   or stiff paper

PROCEDURE

1. Poke a hole about the size of a small coin with the nail through the center of one of the sheets of cardboard.

2. Place this piece of cardboard at a point above you so that the Sun shines directly on it.

3. Direct the light through the hole in the cardboard onto the other piece of cardboard.

4. The Sun's image will appear on the second sheet of cardboard.

5. Measure
   a) the diameter of the Sun's image
   b) the distance between the two sheets of cardboard

6. Divide the distance by the diameter. The distance is just about 109 times bigger than the size of the Sun's image. To solve for the diameter of the Sun, diameter = distance/109. To solve for the distance to the Sun, distance = 109 × diameter.

Diameter of Sun's image/Diameter of Sun = Distance from one cardboard to the other/Distance to Sun

Distance from one cardboard to the other/Diameter of Sun's image = Diameter of Sun/Distance to Sun. Use 93,000,000 miles (150,000,000 km) for the distance to the Sun.

7. Move the pieces of cardboard much farther apart and repeat the two measurements.

8. Move the pieces of cardboard even farther apart and repeat the measurements.

OBSERVATIONS

What have you noticed about the results when you divided distance by diameter? Try using a smaller image of the Sun and a longer distance between sheets of paper. Do you still find the same diameter for the Sun? The Sun's diameter is also 109 times the diameter of the Earth.

The Sun gives you day and night. This means that as the Earth turns on its axis counterclockwise as seen from the Northern Hemisphere and clockwise as seen from the Southern Hemisphere, it turns toward or away from the light of the Sun. As it turns, dawn comes to people living on the Earth and with it, the day. In many places, the "dawn chorus" of birds singing preannounces the dawn, sweeping away the darkness and bringing light to all those along its path. Again humanity has the opportunity to participate in a shared experience. At the equinoxes, those people living in a line north and south of you experience dawn almost at the same time that you do.

The View from Space   *Skylab* in 1973 gave us our first opportunity to observe the Sun free from the distorting effects of Earth's atmosphere. It also took X-ray photographs of the Sun. The solar magnetic field of the Sun has been measured by space probes near the Earth and other planets. In 1980 the Solar Maximum Mission satellite studied variations in solar luminosity.

Composition   Like the Earth, the Sun has a core, and it grows outward from the core in layers, the final one being the atmosphere, which reaches out into space connecting with the rest of the universe.

The interior of the sun

Granulations

Chromosphere
Photosphere
Convective zone

Radiative interior

Prominence

Corona

Burning hydrogen core

Sunspots

The Core   The core is the source of most of the Sun's energy. This energy moves to the surface by both radiation and convection. Radiation carries the energy like a heater heats a room by sending it out, warming the air in front of it. As the energy travels, the air closest to the heat source remains the hottest, while the temperature drops in the air farthest away from the source. This cooling zone within the Sun meets a zone made of currents of hot turbulent gases. This convecting zone carries hot gases to the Sun's surface and sends cooler gases back down to the core. This is similar to the way heating pipes work in a house. They carry hot water to warm a room and send the cooler water back to the furnace to be reheated and recirculated.

Temperatures within the core of the Sun are as high as 25,000,000°F (15,000,000°C), the average being around 11,000°F (6,000°C). With temperatures this high, the pressure inside the Sun would have to be the same as the pressure of the gases surrounding it, otherwise the Sun would collapse. The great pressure at the Sun's core produces tremendous heat and matter that is exceptionally dense, as much as 100 times denser than water.

The Sun gets its energy from hydrogen particles joining (fusing) together in a process called **nuclear fusion.** Some of the fused hydrogen produces helium. The rest of the hydrogen changes into energy. The amount of energy produced is equal to about 500 sextillion horsepower, or, as **Hermann von Helmholtz** calculated in 1871, it is the same as having coal burning on every square foot (⅓ m) of the Sun at the rate of 1,500 pounds of coal an hour. This massive energy output has kept the Sun burning for at least 4½ billion years and will keep it burning at least another 4½ billion years.

In 1868 the French astronomer **Pierre Janssen** (1824–1907) and the English astronomers **Norman Lockyer** (1836–1920) and **Sir Edward Frankland** (1825–1899), working independently, discovered a new element on the Sun. They were observing the spectrum of the Sun's chromosphere during an eclipse and found spectral lines that indicated the presence of the unknown element. Because he first found this element on the Sun, Frankland named it *helium.* In 1882 helium showed up in the flame spectrum of Mount Vesuvius. In 1895 **William Ramsay** (1852–1916) isolated and identified helium in the laboratory and with it started a new column of gases made from liquid air in the Periodic Table of Elements.

Helium comes from the Greek word ήλιος (*helios*) = Sun.

The Photosphere   The energy carried to the Sun's surface stimulates the particles of matter it finds there. These stimulated particles give off energy in the form of heat, light, and other forms of electromagnetic radiation. This is the **photosphere,** the part of the Sun that we can see and the place that sends us sunlight.

They say that the Sun is not hot because it is not the color of fire, but is whiter and clearer. And to these people one can reply that when melted bronze is very hot and it is more like the color of the Sun, and when the bronze is less hot it is more like the color of fire.—Leonardo da Vinci

The photosphere is the boundary between the last layer of the Sun's gases and its atmosphere. This boundary is from 100 to 250 miles (160–400 km) deep and is mostly hydrogen and helium. Like the crust of the Earth, the "skin" of the Sun is neither smooth nor inactive. The hot gases that the corrective zone sends up can sometimes cause bulging bright spots in the photsphere that have a pebbly, rough grained texture. These spots are granules.

Sunspots   Powerful telescopes have made it possible for us to see the Sun's granules. The first telescope was powerful enough to reveal the first "blemishes" on the Sun's skin. Galileo and several others observed "spots" on the Sun.

Chinese observers knew about and recorded sunspots at least 1,000 years before the invention of the telescope. These observers may have suffered the same fate as Galileo, who went blind from looking directly at the Sun. You should *never* look directly at the Sun!

Sunspots are likely to be cooler than the rest of the photosphere (about 8,132°F [4,500°C]). That is why they appear dark against the Sun. If you could put sunspots out into space, they would shine brightly, like stars. The very dark central part of a sunspot is the **umbra**.

Umbra comes from the Latin word *umbra* = shadow. We call those things that give us protection from the Sun and the rain *umbrellas* from the word *umbra*.

The lighter part around the umbra is the **penumbra**. In 1908 astronomer George Ellery Hale (1868–1938) came to the conclusion that sunspots were areas of intensely powerful magnetic forces thousands of times more powerful than the magnetic field of the Earth or the Sun. Sunspots vary in size from 2,000 miles (3,200 km) across to more than 90,000 miles (144,000 km) across. Most of them are bigger than the Earth.

In this next project you can observe sunspots, the safe way, and notice what the early Chinese observers and Galileo saw.

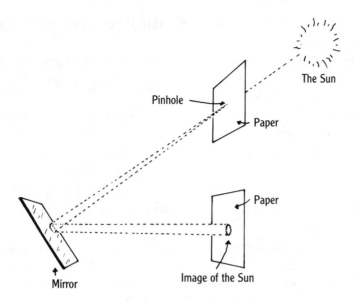

The Sun

Pinhole

Paper

Paper

Mirror

Image of the Sun

★ ★ ★ ★ ★ ★ ★ ★ ★ ★ **Project 53: Examining Sunspots** ★ ★ ★ ★ ★ ★ ★ ★ ★ ★

MATERIALS

one piece of stiff, white paper	newspaper
mirror	pencil
pin	paper
tape	

PROCEDURE

1. Tape a sheet of white paper on the wall in a darkened room below a window through which the Sun is shining. Cover the window with newspaper except for one small section. Cover this section with a piece of paper that has a pinhole cut into the center.

2. Place a mirror on the opposite wall so that the Sun hits it and is reflected onto the paper below the window.

OBSERVATIONS

Check on the positions of the sunspots every day and sketch them noting the date of your observations. Do your findings indicate that the Sun is rotating?

The Sunspot Cycle   Around 1816 the German astronomer S. H. Schwabe (1789–1875) began observing sunspots as a hobby. After keeping track of his observations for 27 years, Schwabe announced in 1843 that every 10 years the number of sunspots reaches its maximum. There may be months in between where there may be no spots. Further research has shown that this cycle is closer to 11 years than 10. In 1851 Schwabe said that there was also a greater sunspot cycle of

22 years. The following year people discovered that compass variations on the Earth follow the same 22-year cycle.

The 11-year sunspot cycle shows itself in a variety of ways in the life of the Earth. According to certain research, there is a definite 11-year pattern in nature that follows the 11-year sunspot cycle:

- earthquakes
- changes in weather
- number of icebergs in the North Atlantic
- number of famines in India due to the lack of rain
- rings of growth in trees
- fossilized layers of sand and clay formed in glacial zones

Sunspot activity also affects radio and television transmission as well as telephone connections.

During the period when there are the least amount of sunspots, the spots group around 10° from the Sun's equator. When a new sunspot cycle begins, groups of new spots appear about 30° from the Sun's equator. Sunspots often appear in pairs. The eastern spot in each Northern Hemisphere pair has a magnetic polarity—north, for example. The polarity of the sunspots in the Southern Hemisphere would be the opposite—south. The spots move across the Sun, lasting for about 4 days or less before disappearing. After a few years, the number of sunspots reaches a maximum, clustering around 20° from the solar equator. After about 11 years, the spots appear mostly around 10° from the Sun's equator again beginning another sunspot minimum cycle. This time, however, the eastern spots in the Northern Hemisphere pairs have south magnetic poles and those in the Southern Hemisphere have north magnetic poles. In another 11 years, when the poles reverse again, the Sun will have completed a full 22-year sunspot cycle and the magnetic charge of its poles will be the way they were 22 years ago. The most recent occurrence of sunspot activity was in 1991.

Since all of the sunspots move in the same direction and become visible and invisible at regular times, Galileo and others felt that the Sun moved, not the sunspots.

> Having made repeated observations I am at last convinced that the spots are objects close to the surface of the solar globe where they are continually being produced and then dissolved, some quickly and some slowly, also that they are carried around the Sun by its rotation. . . . —Galileo

Based on the slight curve of the path that the sunspots follow, observers think that the Sun is tilted 7° 10′ on its axis. In March the Sun's north pole tilts away from the Earth; in September it tilts toward the Earth.

The Chromosphere   The lower atmosphere of the Sun is about 1,500 miles (2,500 km) thick and about 110,000° kelvin. The lower atmosphere takes light from the photosphere and sends it off in a rose-colored glow that you can only see during an eclipse or with a telescope specially adjusted to block out the light from the photosphere. We call the lower atmosphere the **chromosphere** because of its rose color. The chromosphere gets its red color from the bright hydrogen alpha line in the Sun's spectrum.

Chromosphere comes from the Greek word χρωμα (*chroma*) = color.

During an eclipse, the Moon moves across the face of the Sun at some 200 miles per second; this means that the most interesting portion of the chromosphere, its lower 600 miles, shows for only 3 or 4 seconds. The upper chromosphere, which can extend for as little as 1,000 miles to as much as 10,000 miles above the photosphere, is seen for less than a minute. In the span of a century, the lower chromosphere is visible for a total of less than 10 minutes. An astronomer who observes 10 eclipses—far more than the average—may expect to observe this region of the chromosphere for no more than a minute in his lifetime, and that only if he (or she) is luckier than any other astronomer ever born.—E. Grant Athay*

When you look at the chromosphere, what you are seeing is about half a million jets of burning gases shooting out from the Sun's surface all at different times. These jets look like spikes of iron filings standing up on a magnet. For this reason their name is **spicules**.

Spicules comes from the Latin word *spiculum* = spear.

Spicules shoot out at a speed of about 72,000 miles (115,200 km) per hour. Each spicule lasts for about 2–15 minutes and can get as high as 8,000–10,000 miles (12,800–16,000 km). Spicules are about 500 miles (800 km) in diameter (the width of the state of Colorado). The spicules send matter into the Sun's upper atmosphere. Intense ultraviolet radiation travels out from the chromosphere and becomes the source of the Earth's electrically charged ionosphere.

The Corona You also can only see the Sun's upper atmosphere during an eclipse or by using special photographic equipment. People like Plutarch and Kepler who have seen it describe it as "pearly-white." The English amateur astronomer **Francis Baily** (1774–1844) first used the word **corona** to describe what he saw that looked like the Sun's crown around the Sun during a total solar eclipse on July 8, 1842.

Corona comes from the Latin word *corona* = crown.

The corona marks the boundary between the Sun and its magnetic field, which extends out into space through the entire solar system as the **solar wind**. The solar wind is a stream of magnetized particles that projects out into space from sunspots

---

*P. 89 in *"The Solar Chromosphere"* by E. Grant Athay, from *Readings from Scientific American: Frontiers in Astronomy*. San Francisco: W. H. Freeman, 1970.

and cooler places in the corona. The corona itself is millions of miles long and millions of degrees kelvin hot. It looks like a filmy white halo around the Sun.

The **chronograph** is a photograph that you take through a telescope that has a disk covering the Sun from view just as it would be during an eclipse. This makes it so you can see the corona. Using this technique, people were able to spend 8½ months observing the corona aboard *Skylab* in 1973 and 1974. Before the invention of the chronograph, the total time people were able to make photographic observations of the corona from 1839 to 1973 was less than 80 hours!

Flares   The dark ribbon you see around the edge of the Sun is the limb. Sometimes the Sun ejects huge pieces of burning gas from the chromosphere into the corona. These erruptions of energy are **flares**. Electrically charged particles from solar flares disturb the corona and reach the Earth's ionosphere within a few hours or days. They can disturb radio, television, telephones, and electricity. They also produce the aurora borealis (northern lights) and the aurora australis (the southern lights).

Prominences   Sometimes large sheets of gas fly out from the Sun twisting themselves into high arched bridges of fire before they fall back into the Sun. These are **solar prominences**. They probably happen because of the Sun's changing magnetic charge. Solar prominences may be less warm than the chromosphere or about 15,000° kelvin, which is 2,240°F (1,227°C).

During the solar eclipse of 1842, an observer who saw the corona and solar prominences exclaimed, "From the black rim of the Moon there suddenly shot forth three gigantic, purple-red tongues of flame. They paused motionless, like jagged mountain peaks in an alpine sunset. . . It was as if the Sun, behind the Moon, was flaring up in monstrous volcanic explosions." (From a journalistic account quoted in Rudolf Thiel's *And There Was Light: The Discovery of the Universe*. New York: Knopf, 1957).

READING MORE

Adams, Florence. *Catch a Sunbeam: A Book of Solar Study and Experiments.* New York: Harcourt Brace Jovanovich, 1978.

The Smithsonian Institution. *Fire of Life: The Smithsonian Book of the Sun.* New York: W. W. Norton, 1981.

The Earth seen from the Moon (*photo courtesy of NASA*)

Section 2 *THE MOON*

"Here men from the planet Earth first set foot on the Moon, July 1969 A.D. We came in peace for all mankind." —the plaque on the *Eagle's* landing stage

Names   In ancient Greece, the Moon, like the Sun, had two aspects. One was the actual moon itself as a sphere in the sky. The other was the character of the Moon and its relationship to life on Earth, particularly to nature during the night. The goddess of the sphere of the Moon in the heavens was **Selene** or **Luna**. We get most of our words about the Moon from these names. We call the "geography" of the Moon **selenography**. Things having to do with the moon are called **lunar**.

The goddess who best represents the influences of the Moon on the Earth is **Artemis** or **Diana**. Her brother is Apollo, the other Sun god. People in Greece observed that their vegetation flourished and spread the most during the cool nights with their heavy dew. The Greeks and others knew that there was more dew when the Moon was shining in a clear sky.

People said that Diana roamed by night through woods and groves, over hills and valleys accompanied by the nymphs of the fountains. People could feel her presence beside rivers, fountains, and marshes.

The Babylonians connected **Ishtar**, their Moon goddess, with springs and dew calling her the All-Dewy One. The great Sumerian city of Ur in lower Mesopotamia was especially devoted to the worship of the Moon as a male under the name of **Nanna** or **Nannor**, the father of the Sun god Shamash. The Akkadians called the Moon god, **Sin**, "the lamp of heaven and Earth," "the lamp of all gods," and "the Divine Cresent."

> If the Moon rises pale, expect rain;
> if it rises clear, expect fair.

Some Native Americans would not go hunting if the horns of the cresent Moon pointed upward. That meant dry weather, and the hunter needed moist ground where tracks would show the best.

In 1932 the International Astronomical Union standardized the naming of lunar features. There is a crater on the Moon named after the American astronomer **Maria Mitchell**. It is below Mare Frigoris and next to Aristoteles Crater at $+50°$ $+21°$.

Early Observations   In Scotland, France, and England, stone circles have been found that line the viewer up with rising and setting positions of the Moon. There is an old song called "By the Light of the Silvery Moon." For many people, the Moon's light is silvery. The Peruvian Indians said that the Moon gave mankind the gift of silver from its tears. For the alchemist, silver was the metal associated with the Moon. The Nepali word for the Moon is *chaand* or *chandra,* and the word for silver is *chaandi.* The ancient Greeks discovered that the Moon shines from the reflected light of the Sun. In some ways the "silvery" Moon acts like a mirror, which also is silvery. Similarly, the process of photography involves capturing the light reflected back to the camera from an object. The developing and printing process in the darkroom uses silver to make the photographic image visible.

The View from Earth   As you know from your own experience watching the Moon, there are times when the whole face of the Moon is illumined. There are times when just a half of the Moon appears, and there are times when only a tiny part of the moon shines back down to us. At other times, the Moon is not visible.

There are many stories that tell why the whole Moon doesn't shine all the time. An old African folktale tells of the keeper of the great shining stone who would gradually cover the box containing the stone when the sky people got tired of bringing him food. When fresh supplies came, he opened the box again and the stone sent its light down to Earth.

To the ancient Babylonians, Ishtar (the Moon) is following Marduk's command always to shine less when in the presence of the Sun. The closer the Sun and Moon get to each other, the dimmer the Moon appears until it no longer shines. When the Sun is farthest away from the Moon, then Ishtar shines in her fullest glory as queen of the night.

Phases   As the Moon travels around us, making its way around the Sun, we observe changes in the amount of sunlight reflected back to us. We call these changes the **phases** of the Moon. A phase is part of a process. Each phase lasts for about a week, so all four phases equal about a month. The Native Americans called the complete cycle of phases a *moon.* "See you in four moons" meant "see you in four months."

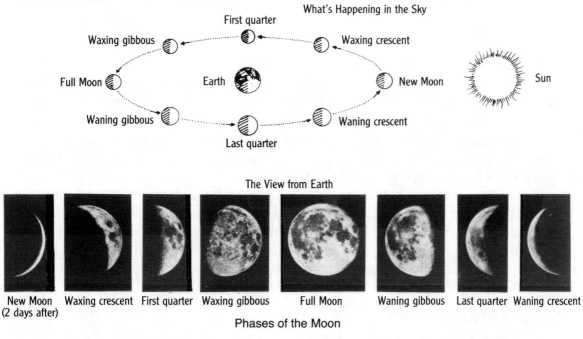

Phases of the Moon

Phase comes from the Greek word φαινω (*phaino*) = to appear, to bring to light.

In this next project you can show yourself how the Moon's phases occur and what they will look like.

★ ★ ★ ★ ★ **Project 54: Showing How the Moon's Phases Occur** ★ ★ ★ ★ ★

MATERIALS

golf ball or some other light-colored ball with a dull finish

planesphere (chart from Project 15)
modeling clay

PART 1

PROCEDURE

1. Stand facing *but not looking directly at* the Sun. Hold the ball in one hand at arm's length in front of you while pointing toward the Sun with your other hand. The ball is the Moon; your head is the Earth.

2. Move the ball through all of the phases in the photograph on the previous page. Keep looking at the ball and moving your body as necessary while keeping your other hand pointing toward the Sun.

3. Stop when you get to the Full Moon. Your body should be facing sideways from the Sun, arms outstretched. Turn and face exactly the opposite direction, put the ball in the hand farthest from the Sun, and point to the Sun with the hand nearest to it.

4. Continue to move the ball through all of the phases until you return to the New Moon position.

OBSERVATIONS

Does the changing shape of the lightest part of the ball look like the changing face of the Moon during its phases? Do the dimples in the golf ball cast shadows like Moon craters?

PART 2

PROCEDURE

1. Make a small ball out of one color of modeling clay to be the *Sun.*

2. Make a small ball out of one color of modeling clay to be the *Moon.*

3. Place the Sun and the Moon in position in the plastic circle of the planesphere to help you answer these questions.

    a. Will the last quarter Moon (June 21, Sun in Gemini) be high, medium, or low above the horizon?

    b. In what constellation will the first quarter Moon be in October (Sun in Libra) and at what time will it rise?

    c. In which season does the Full Moon appear highest in the sky?

OBSERVATIONS

Make up some questions of your own. Check your accuracy by setting up your planesphere for today and finding where the Moon should be.

Suppose you see the Moon some day or night. What phase would it be? What angle would be forming between the Sun, the Earth, and the Moon?

How can you remember which quarter moon is which, what side is lit, and which side is dark? If you speak French, you can use the words for first and last to help you. *Premier* is the word for *first,* and if you draw a line down from the first quarter Moon (**P**), it forms the letter *P* (the first letter of the word *premier*). *Dernier* is the word for *last,* and if you draw a line up from the last quarter Moon (**d**) it forms the letter *d*, the first letter in the word *dernier.* You can also turn the first quarter into a *b,* for "bigger" and "brighter," describing the Moon as it grows in size and brightness approaching its Full phase. Similarly, *d* means "dimmer" and "darker," which describes the Moon as it gets smaller and darker approaching its new phase.

You never see more than half the sphere of the Moon. When the half that you see is lit up, it is a full moon instead of a half moon because the full disk (not sphere) that you see is completely lit. The quarters refer to the moments when the Moon has completed a fraction of its journey around the Earth, either a quarter or three-quarters of the way. It just so happens that to your eyes on Earth, the Moon really is only one-fourth lit. The word *crescent* describes the growing time after the new moon and its shape. *Waxing* and *waning* are clearer terms. *Gibbous* means more than half and less than full.

Crescent comes from the Latin word *cresco* = to grow.
Waxing comes from the German word *wachsen* = to grow.
Waning comes from the Middle English word *wanien* or *wanen* = to lessen.
Gibbous comes from the Latin word *gibbus* = hump on the back.

The horns or cusps of the Moon always point away from the Sun, like the curve of a bow whose arrow is aimed at the Sun.

Go outside and look at the Moon. What quarter is it? If it is the first quarter Moon, you are looking back along the path of the Earth's orbit to the place where the Earth was 3½ hours ago.

The Moon's Distance   We had to know how far away the Moon was before we could send someone there. How did people figure it out?

The ancient Greeks used the angle the Moon's disk appears in the sky (½°), the diameter of the Earth's shadow compared to the Moon's (during eclipses), geometry, and trigonometry to calculate the Moon's distance.

Anaximander (ca. 611–546 B.C.) was the first to write about the subject of sizes and distances of planets, including the Moon. Anaximander suggested that the radius of the orbit of the Moon was 18 times the radius of the Earth. **Aristarchus** (ca. 300–250 B.C.) suggested it was 9½ times the diameter of the Earth. Hipparchus suggested the distance was 33⅔ times the diameter of the Earth. Ptolemy suggested it was 29½ times the Earth's diameter. Our current measurements put the distance of the Moon at 30⅕ times the Earth's diameter or 238,868 miles (384,404 km).

The first photograph of the Earth and Moon showing their sizes and distance from one another, from *Voyager 1,* September 18, 1977 (*photo courtesy of Jet Propulsion Laboratory*)

When Zoltan Bay sent a radar beam to the Moon in 1946, some of the radio waves bounced back to the Earth, taking about 2.6 seconds to get to the Moon and back. Radio waves travel at the speed of light. Half the time between when the radio waves are transmitted and received back is how long it takes the beam to travel. This figure multiplied by the speed of light tells you how far the beam traveled, and that figure will give you the distance to the Moon.

The Moon and the Earth travel around the center of gravity of the Earth-Moon system or barry center. They both orbit around the Sun.

Orbit comes from the Latin word *orbis* = circular path.

The Moon's Diameter   Once you know the Moon's distance, you can figure out its diameter. One interesting way is to do the same experiment for the moon that you did to find the diameter of the Sun in Project 52, Measuring the Sun. Current measurements put the diameter of the Moon at 2,160 miles (3,476 km).

Mapping the Moon   Galileo made the first sketch of the Moon in 1609 from the telescope. In 1647 Johannes Hevelius (1611–1681) made the first accurate lunar map in his *Selenographia.* In 1840 John William Draper provided us with the first detailed photographs of the Moon. A Soviet lunar probe sent back the first photograph of the "dark side of the moon" in October 1959. In 1651 Hevelius' friend **G. B. Riccioli (1598–1671)** published a two-volume work assisted by **Father Grimaldi (1618–1663).** Riccioli set the pattern for naming lunar features after great scientists and historical and political figures. In 1791 **J. H. Schroeter (1745–1818)** published the first volume of lunar studies. He discovered "rills" or "clefts," long narrow valleys in the Moon's surface. In 1879 Nasmyth and Carpenter published a beautiful book of Moon maps. In their book the authors had made models from their drawings of the Moon that they photographed in sunlight to represent the Moon's surface as accurately as possible.

FEATURES ON THE MOON

Name of Feature	East(E)/West(W)	North(N)/South(S)
1. Albategnius	0	S21
2. Aliacensis	E4	S40
3. Alphonsus	W7	S22
4. Alpine Valley	0	N46
5. Alps Mountains	W3	N45
6. Apennine Mountains	W5	N18
7. Archimedes	W8	N28
8. Ariadaeus Rille	E14	N2
9. Aristarchus	W47	N24
10. Aristillus	W2	N32
11. Aristoteles	E11	N48
12. Arzachel	W7	S28
13. Atlas	E31	N46
14. Autolycus	W2	N29
15. Caucasus Mountains	E6	N33
16. Clavius	W11	S60
17. Copernicus	W26	N6
18. Delambre	E18	S9
19. Endymion	E47	N53
20. Eratosthenes	W17	N11
21. Eudoxus	E12	N42
22. Gassendi	W45	S25
23. Grimaldi	W62	S7
24. Hercules	E20	N44
25. Herodotus	W39	N24

Name of Feature	East(E)/West(W)	North(N)/South(S)
26. Herschel	W8	S12
27. Herschel, Caroline	W31	N34
28. Herschel, John	W28	N51
29. Hipparchus	E3	S13
30. Horrocks	E4	S12
31. Julius Ceasar	E15	N5
32. Kepler	W44	N4
33. Lacus Mortis (Lake of Death)	E18	N44
34. Lacus Somniorum (Lake of Dreams)	E25	N36
35. Langrenus	E59	S12
36. Macrobius	E44	N21
37. Maginus	W8	S55
38. Manilius	E8	N10
39. Mare Crisium (Sea of Crises)	E55	N16
40. Mare Foecunditatis (Sea of Fertility)	E50	S10
41. Mare Frigoris (Sea of Cold)	W15–E25	N53
42. Mare Humboldtianum (Humboldt's Sea)	E37	N58
43. Mare Humorum (Sea of Moisture)	W41	S32
44. Mare Imbrium (Sea of Rains)	W40–E5	N30
45. Mare Nectarius (Sea of Nectar)	E35	S25
46. Mare Nubium (Sea of Clouds)	W17	S29
47. Mare Serenitatis (Sea of Serenity)	E2–E29	N25
48. Mare Smythii (Smyth's Sea)	E69	0
49. Mare Spumans (Foaming Sea)	E61	0
50. Mare Tranquillitatis (Sea of Tranquility)	E30	N5
51. Mare Undarum (Sea of Waves)	E62	N7
52. Mare Vaporum (Sea of Vapors)	E1	N10
53. Maurolycus	E12	S48
54. Mitchell	E13	N48
55. Oceanus Procellarum (Ocean of Storms)	W50	N30–S20
56. Pallus	W13	N1
57. Palus Putridenis (Marsh of Decay)	W3	N25
58. Piccolomini	E30	S37
59. Pico Mountain	W10	N45
60. Piton Mountain	W4	N40
61. Posidonius	E27	N31
62. Ptolemaeus	W8	S16
63. Pyrenees Mountains	E40	S22
64. Rheita Valley	E39	S45
65. Ricciolli	W1	S2

Name of Feature	East(E)/West(W)	North(N)/South(S)
66. Sinus Aestum (Seething Bay)	W14	N8
67. Sinus Iridium (Bay of Rainbows)	W27	N45
68. Sinus Medii (Central Bay)	W5	S5
69. Sinus Roris (Bay of Dew)	W4	N43
70. Straight Range	W18	N47
71. Straight Wall	W13	S31
72. Theophilus	E28	S18
73. Timocharis	W17	N25
74. Tycho	W13	S51

Features on the Moon

The View from Space   We have explored the Moon from unmanned space vehicles in lunar orbit, photographing and mapping our satellite's surface. Unmanned vehicles have landed and conducted simple chemical tests. From 1969 to 1972 as part of the Apollo program, a total of 12 astronauts visited the Moon and gathered samples of lunar material. This represents 842 pounds of lunar rocks and soil brought back from six different locations by six *Apollo* lunar landing missions. Three unmanned Soviet spacecrafts have also landed and returned with samples. In addition, we have placed instruments on the Moon to measure Moonquakes, meteorite impacts, and other data. These instruments operated for 8 years after they were installed.

Composition   The Moon has no atmosphere or any traces of water on its surface. The crust of the Moon appears to be thicker than the Earth's. It is covered with craters, mountains, plains, and valleys. The Moon's surface contains about 58% oxygen, 20% silicon with aluminum, calcium, iron, magnesium, and titanium. Samples from the Moon's surface contain basalt and volcanic minerals such as plagioclase and pyroxene as well as some minerals that don't exist on Earth. One of these is the mineral **armalcolite**, named for the crew of *Apollo 11*, *Arm*strong, *Al*drin, and *Col*lins.

Astronaut Alan Bean examining *Surveyor 3* on the Moon, 1969
(*photo courtesy of Johnson Space Center, NASA*)

On Earth we only see one side of the Moon. In this next project you will be sketching the "near side of the Moon" using a technique that makes your drawing look real.

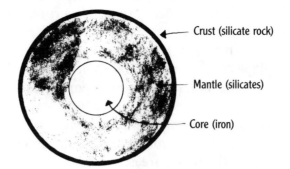

Crust (silicate rock)

Mantle (silicates)

Core (iron)

The interior of the Moon

★ ★ ★ ★ ★ ★ ★ ★ ★ ★ **Project 55: Sketching the Moon*** ★ ★ ★ ★ ★ ★ ★ ★ ★ ★

MATERIALS

telescope or binoculars
soft-lead pencil
file or fine sandpaper
tissue paper
drawing paper (smooth surface)
soft eraser
clipboard

small flashlight
dowel
three rubber bands
brown paper bag
drawing compass

PROCEDURE

1. Wedge the dowel into the hole at the top of the clipboard and mount the flashlight on it with a rubber band. Cover the light with the brown paper bag held on with a rubber band. This will be your drawing lamp.

2. Draw a circle about 3½–4 inches (10 cm) in diameter using the drawing compass.

3. File or sand your pencil so you can collect some powdered "lead." Pick up some lead with a piece of tissue paper placed over your finger. Rub the lead on the circle so it becomes an even light gray all over.

4. Put the paper onto the clipboard and take it outside on a clear night when

*This project is adapted from *Modern Astronomy: An Activities Approach* by R. Robert Robbins and Mary Kay Hemenway. Austin: University of Texas Press, 1982. Used with permission.

you can see the Moon's craters clearly through the telescope. Study the Moon for a while, noticing the light and dark areas. Use a rubber band to hold the paper down at the bottom of the clipboard.

5. Draw the outlines of the shapes you want onto the gray circle. Make sure the sizes and shapes of the craters and their positions near each other are correct. If you make a mistake, don't erase—just redraw. Use the flashlight to help you see your drawing.

6. Erase the gray background to indicate bright areas.

7. Darken the gray background to indicate dark shadows and emphasize crater edges. Don't outline the white areas.

OBSERVATION

You can use this technique later to draw the planets seen through the telescope.

Tides   We call the high and low ocean levels **tides**, and their rhythm is 12½ hours from one high tide to the next. This means in most places high tides occur two times a day, 50 minutes later each day. Approximately every 2 weeks, unusually high and low tides occur. These are the **spring tides**. The word spring has nothing to do with the spring season.

In between this 14-day period, the difference in size between high and low tides is the smallest. These are the **neap tides**.

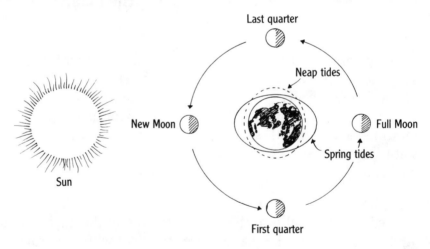

The tides

Sir Isaac Newton researched the tides and their relationship to the Sun and the Moon. It was his feeling that the Moon (and the Sun a little bit also) tugged at the Earth at different places depending on how the Sun, Moon, and the Earth lined up with each other. The water on the Earth responded to the tug. As the Moon orbited the Earth its pull was strongest when the Sun, Earth, and the Moon were in a straight line. This happens twice a month. One of these times the Earth is in between the Sun and the Full Moon, and the other time the Earth is in between the Sun and the New Moon. The water on the side of the Earth nearest the Moon feels the greatest pull and swells outward in a **high tide.** The water on the other side of the Earth feels the least attraction so that it flows away from the Moon to produce another high tide. The high tides make the water level on the remaining parts of the Earth shallower, causing **low tides.**

Many people share Newton's tide theory. Others feel that the Moon's position and the tides are related but not caused by each other. No matter what opinion you share, you can demonstrate what the bulging of the waters on the Earth looks like by doing this next project.

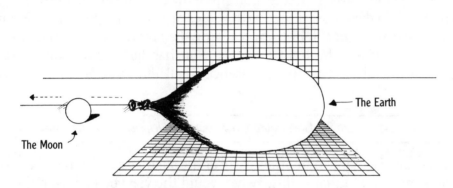

★ ★ ★ ★ ★ ★ ★ **Project 56: Showing How the Tides Occur** ★ ★ ★ ★ ★ ★ ★

MATERIALS

large balloon	paper or graph paper
water	books
stiff paper	felt-tip pen
twine	access to a photocopier

PROCEDURE

1. Fill a balloon with water and draw a rough outline of the world and oceans on it, with the opening of the balloon on one of the sides. Tie a piece of twine about 1 inch (2.5 cm) onto the end of the balloon. Set the balloon on a piece of paper. The balloon is the *Earth.*

2. Stand another piece of paper behind the balloon. Hold it up with a stack of books.

3. Draw a little picture of the Moon about 2 inches (5 cm) in diameter on the stiff paper, leaving enough paper below it so you can fold it and make a stand for the Moon.

4. Place the Moon about 6 inches (15 cm) from the Earth with the twine behind it.

5. Pull quickly on the twine. The twine is the *pull* between the Earth and the Moon.

OBSERVATIONS

The side you pull on and the side opposite will bulge and the top will go down. Mark on the paper sheets how far the balloon bulged and flattened.

Eclipses   The Earth is four times the size of the Moon. The Sun is 390 times larger than the Moon. It is also 390 times farther from us than the Moon. Because of this relationship, both the Sun and the Moon appear to us as being the same size in the sky. If the Moon passes directly in front of the Sun, it can cover the sun's disk leaving the Earth in darkness. If the Earth passes directly in between the Moon and the Sun, it blocks the Sun's light from reaching the Moon and casts the Moon into darkness. In both cases, the light from the Sun has left the sky for a brief but startling moment, taking with it the essence of all life. We call this moment an eclipse.

Eclipse comes from the Greek word ἐκκλειψις (*ekkleipsis*) = abandonment.

Eclipses can also happen in other parts of the solar system. When we on Earth are experiencing a total lunar eclipse, what would the view be like from the Moon?

Lunar Eclipse   When the Moon is full, if the alignment of the Sun, Earth, and Moon is perfectly straight, the sunlight will hit the Earth and not the Moon. The view of the Moon from the Earth will show the unlit part of the Moon as a black shadow. This is a **lunar eclipse**, and because only part of the moon is eclipsed, it is a **partial lunar eclipse**. The Earth's shadow is circular. This led the Pythagoreans in Greece to conclude that the Earth is a sphere. Because the Earth and the Moon are traveling in their orbits around the Sun, the shadow of the eclipse on the Moon will be moving at a speed of about 2,000 miles (3,200 km) an hour.

When the Earth completely blocks the path of the sunlight from the Moon, the eclipse is **total**. Instead of a black, unillumined Moon, we have a coppery-red Moon that looks like a gooseberry. The light from the Sun is refracted by the Earth's atmosphere, which acts like a lens, bending the light and focusing it on the Moon. The atmosphere absorbs some of the blue and violet in the Sun's spectrum so that the light that reaches the Moon and is reflected back to us is the orange/coppery-red part of the spectrum.

The Moon's diameter is 2,160 miles (3,476 km), and the Earth blocks out the sunlight for an area of about 5,700 miles (9,173 km). If the Moon passed straight through the area of darkness, how long would the eclipse last?

Why don't we have a lunar eclipse at every Full Moon? If the Sun, Earth, and Moon were always in a perfectly straight line with each other, we would. (Only about one sixth of the lineups of the Sun, Earth, and Moon produce eclipses.) The

Sun stays at one end of the line while the Earth and Moon take turns being in the middle and on the other end. The Moon as it travels around the Earth has its own orbit. The path of this orbit takes the Moon above and below the path of the Earth traveling around the Sun. At one point on the journey, the Moon's path is 5.2° above the Earth's path for half a month. At another, it is 5.2° below for the other half of the month. The Moon's path crosses the Earth's path (the ecliptic) twice. When it is level with the Earth's path and is about to cross it, we call that point the **node**. If the Moon is above the path, it crosses the **ascending node**. If the Moon is heading below the path, it crosses the **descending node**. When you draw a line between the two nodes, you have the **nodal line**.

Node comes from the Latin word *nodus* = knot.

In order for there to be a lunar eclipse,
- the Moon must be in its full position at one end of the line, with the Earth in the center and the Sun at the other end. This occurs every 29.53059 days.
- the Moon must be at one of the two nodes, which occurs every 13½ days.
- the nodal line must point to the Sun. This occurs once every 346.6 days.

Every 18 years and 11 days a cycle of eclipses can occur. This period is the **saros cycle**. Babylonian astronomer-priests discovered and named the saros period around 2000 B.C. The saros period is a geographic cycle that charts the regular appearance of eclipses in the same places on the Earth.

The Moon's orbit moves just like the Earth's. In chapter 1 you found that the Sun traveling on the ecliptic doesn't return to its exact starting point. It actually falls short of reaching this point by 1° every 72 years. The vernal equinox, or the point on the zodiac where the Sun's path crosses the celestial equator giving us spring, moves a little each year. We call this the precision of the equinoxes. The Moon nodes also move backward along the ecliptic, taking 18.61 years to complete one rotation. Once every 346.6201 days (18.6 days short of a full year) the nodal lines point to the Sun. We call this 346.6 day period the **eclipse year**.

Saros is a Greek word that comes from the Assyrian-Babylonian word *sharu* = repetition.

In a typical saros cycle 48 or 49 lunar eclipses occur within a period of 865 years and 70 or 71 solar eclipses in a period of about 1,200 years. This means nearly every year you can see a lunar eclipse from where you live. The next group of eclipses takes place about 120° west of the longitude where you saw the first group because the Earth has turned one-third of a revolution on its own axis during that time. After every three cycles the eclipses return to the original longitude where they were at the start of the cycle 54 years before. The latitude will be farther north or south depending on whether the series started at the Earth's North or South Pole.

Several eclipse tracks from the same saros series
(*from* Eclipse *by Brian Brewer, Seattle: Earth View Books*)

Draconic Month   The length of time it takes for the Moon to return to a node is $27^1/_5$ days. To the ancients this was the month of the dragon or the **draconic month**. The ascending node was the mouth of the dragon, the descending node was its tail. We still use the symbol ☊ for the dragon's head or ascending node and the symbol ☋ for the dragon's tail or descending node. Some people think the symbols show the head and tail swallowing the Sun.

Draco comes from the Latin word *draco* = dragon or serpent.

Solar Eclipses   The earliest record of a solar eclipse is in the ancient Chinese document *Shu Ching*. The date was October 22, 2134 B.C., when "the Sun and Moon did not meet harmoniously." The two royal astronomers **Hsi** and **Ho** failed to predict the event, which meant that people weren't prepared to make noise and shoot arrows into the sky to frighten away the Sun-eating dragon. For neglecting their duty, the emperor had the astronomers beheaded.

People all over the world have taken the idea of eclipses very seriously. Some cultures (India, Japan, China) consider the temporary loss of the Sun or Moon to be a bad omen. In the absence of the light and the forces of life, the forces of death and darkness are free to roam. Other cultures (Tahitians, Eskimos, Aleuts, and Tlingits)

262

see eclipses as the Sun and the Moon leaving their places to visit each other or to see that things are going all right on the Earth.

Solar eclipses can only occur at the time of the new moon. The minimum number of solar eclipses in any calendar year is two; the maximum is five. A total eclipse takes place on the same spot on the Earth only once every 360 years. A total solar eclipse usually lasts only 2 or 3 minutes; the longest it can last at any one place is 7½ minutes. You can only see a total solar eclipse from a point on the narrow path of totality the eclipse makes on the Earth as it passes by.

Total eclipse, July 11, 1991, Guadalajara, Mexico

Annular eclipse, January 4, 1992, San Diego, CA

10:00 A.M.

10:30 A.M.

11:00 A.M.

Partial eclipse, September 23, 1987, Okinawa, Japan

Total Eclipse   If a solar eclipse occurs when the Moon is closest to the Earth and farthest from the Sun, the disk of the moon completely covers the Sun, blocking out all its light. The stars and brighter planets come out, birds stop chirping, and the temperature drops. This is a **total eclipse.**

Annular Eclipse   If a solar eclipse occurs when the Moon is at its greatest distance from the Earth and nearest the Sun, the Moon looks slightly smaller than the Sun and does not cover it completely. The uncovered outer ring of the Sun continues to shine as a ring of light around the blacked out area. We call this kind of solar eclipse an **annular eclipse.** During an annular eclipse, the sky remains bright and you cannot see the Sun's corona.

Annular comes from the Latin word *annulus* = ring.

Partial Eclipse   When a solar eclipse occurs, the Moon is not directly in front of the Sun but very close. The Moon's disk will "bite" a little piece out of the Sun as it passes by. This is a **partial eclipse**.

Stonehenge   **Gerald Hawkins** and **Fred Hoyle** have suggested that people used Stonehenge to predict eclipses. There are 56 holes around Stonehenge called **Aubrey holes** after **John Aubrey**, a 17th-century researcher of ancient history who discovered them in 1666. These chalk-filled holes are about 3 feet (1 m) deep and were dug about 300 years before the stones of Stonehenge went up.

One complete Moon node revolution is 3×18.6 (almost 56). Moving a marker in the Aubrey holes, three holes each year equals one complete journey around the circle of 56 holes in $18\frac{2}{3}$ years. Two markers on opposite sides of the Aubrey ring would always show the position of the Moon nodes.

If a Sun marker moved two holes every 13 days, it would take 364 days ($56/2 \times 13$) or only $1\frac{1}{4}$ days less than a full year to go completely around. This would measure the length of the year. If a Moon marker moved two holes every day, it would take 28 days ($56\frac{1}{2}$) to go completely around. This would measure the length of the lunar month.

If a marker moved three holes every day until it went around the circle twice ($2\ [56/3]$), this would measure the length of the **eclipse season**. Figuring out when the Moon was at its most southern or northern part of its orbit was one of the purposes of the architecture of Stonehenge and other stone circles and lines in Scotland, France, and in other parts of England. One-fourth of a month later the Moon would be crossing one of its nodes. All of this information gave potential dates for eclipses.

Maya Calendar   Two Maya sacred rounds (see chapter 1, section 4) of 260 days each = 520 days. The line of the Moon's nodes points to the Sun every 173.31 days. Then, $3 \times 173.31 = 519.93$ days, or about 2 hours less than 2 Maya rounds. This provides another means for predicting eclipses.

The circle of Aubrey holes

264

READING MORE
Alter, Dinsmore. *Pictorial Guide to the Moon.* New York: Thomas Y. Crowell, 1973.
Brewer, Brian. *Eclipse.* Seattle: Earth View, 1991.

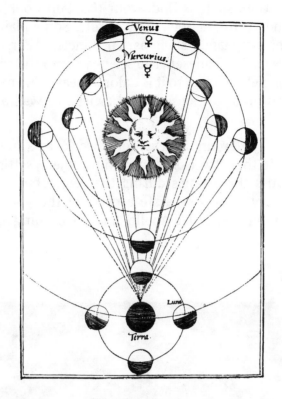

Section 3   THE INNER PLANETS

Have you ever noticed a bright object in the early evening sky, raying out with such intense light that you wondered if it was an airplane? Some people have mistaken this bright light for a spaceship from another planet. This "star" is actually a planet, the planet Venus. Together with Mercury, the planet Venus travels in between the orbit of the Earth and the Sun. For this reason, these two planets are called the *inner planets*. The closeness of these two planets to the Sun helps make them shine so brightly. Because they pass in between the Earth and the Sun, the inner planets go through phases like the Moon. While Mercury and Venus share these features in common, they are two very different planets.

Mercury

Names   The Greeks associated Mercury with the god Hermes and called it Stilbon, "the twinkler." Hermes-Thoth invented astrology, astronomy, mathematics, geometry, medicine, grammar, and music. The Polynesians called Mercury Na-holo-holo, which means "running to and fro."

The names of the cliff lines (**scarps**) of Mercury come from historic ships of discovery and exploration, such as Endeavour (Captain Cook's ship), Santa Maria (Columbus' ship), and Vostok (a Soviet spacecraft). Some plains have the name of Mercury in different languages such as Tir (ancient Persian), Odin (ancient Scandinavian), and Suisei (Japanese). The sea nearest to the spot where the Sun is overhead when the planet is closest to it is Caloris (heat). The names of craters come from nonscientific authors, composers, and artists, as well as scientists such as Kuiper (astronomer).

Early Observations Mercury appears for 8 weeks as a morning object, rising just before sunrise, and then 8 weeks as an evening object, setting just after the Sun does. This cycle occurs three times during the year. The Greeks saw these two appearances of Mercury as two separate aspects of the gods. The Mercury that appeared in the morning they called Apollo, and the evening appearing planet was Hermes.

A photomosaic of Mercury, from *Mariner 10*, 1974 (*photo courtesy of NASA*)

Since the Earth is turning at a rate of 15° an hour, the Sun always rises or sets within about 2 hours of Mercury's rising or setting. Mercury's closeness to the Sun (it's never more than 28° away) makes it difficult for us to get a good look at it. The sky is often too full of sunlight, and the planet is very close to the horizon. For these reasons, many people have never seen Mercury. Even Copernicus, who lived to be 70, sadly regretted on his deathbed that he never saw the planet. In Northern Europe where Copernicus worked, you can only see Mercury occasionally in the misty twilight.

The best time to observe Mercury is when it is farthest from the Sun (**aphelion**) and when it appears farthest east or west of the Sun (**elongation**). At these times Mercury is 28° from the Sun as seen from the Earth. The most visible eastern elongation times in the Northern Hemisphere occur in August and September when Mercury appears in the east before sunrise as the morning star. The most visible western elongation times occur in March and April when Mercury appears in the west as the evening star just after sunset. Even at these times you can only see Mercury for about a half hour.

The View from Earth   Mercury is brighter than any star, except Sirius, but among the planets it is only brighter than Saturn, Uranus, Neptune, and Pluto. Like the Moon and Venus, Mercury goes through phases from new to full. When it is full, it is farthest away from the Earth so that the brilliance you would expect becomes dimmer because of the distance. You can only see the gibbous and crescent phases of Mercury.

Except for Pluto, Mercury has the most elliptical orbit of all the planets. Mercury and Venus are both within the orbit of the Earth around the Sun. This means that as each planet travels around the Sun, it passes in between the Earth and the Sun for part of its journey. When Mercury is exactly in between, we call its location an **inferior conjunction**.

Inferior comes from the Latin word *inferior* = lower, farther down, or underneath.

As the planet continues along in its orbit around the Sun, it goes behind the Sun and out of our view. When it is exactly on the outside of a lineup of the Sun in the middle and the Earth on the other side, we call its position a **superior conjunction**.

Superior comes from the Latin word *superior* = higher, upper, or above.

Mercury is in its new phase at inferior conjunction and full at superior conjunction. Unlike the Moon, when Mercury or Venus are at the new phase, they are closer to the Earth and appear larger. At the full phase, they are farthest away from the Earth and appear much smaller.

During an inferior conjunction, Mercury sometimes crosses directly in front of the Sun. Because of the variation (inclination) of their orbits from the ecliptic, Mercury and Venus pass directly in front of the Sun only rarely. This crossing is a **transit**.

If the planet were bigger or farther away, a transit would cause a solar eclipse. Instead, you can only see a small dark spot moving across the face of the Sun. You need Sun-filtering equipment to detect this dot without harming your eyes. The complete transit of Mercury takes up to 4 hours as the planet moves from east to west across the Sun. In the United States, the Naval Observatory records transits of Mercury to accurately monitor the Earth's rotation and to correct clocks. Transits of Mercury occur either in May or November every 7 or 13 years. The next transit of Mercury will be on November 14, 1999.

Both Mercury and the Moon have thousands of craters on their surface. In this next project you can make some of those craters yourself.

★ ★ ★ ★ ★ ★ ★ ★ ★ **Project 57: Making Craters on Mercury** ★ ★ ★ ★ ★ ★ ★ ★ ★

MATERIALS

metal pie pan
plaster of paris
small stones
corn starch or white flour
water

newspaper
fine dirt or coffee granules
camera or pencil and paper
chair you can stand on

PART 1
PROCEDURE

1. Spread newspaper on the floor and place a pie pan in the middle.
2. Cover the bottom of pie pan with a layer of dirt or coffee granules.
3. Cover the dirt layer with a layer of white flour or corn starch.
4. Drop small stones one by one onto the flour while you kneel, stand, and stand on a chair.
5. Throw a stone carefully onto the flour straight down and then at an angle.
6. Photograph or draw your results.

PART 2
PROCEDURE

1. Empty the pie pan and return it to newspaper.
2. Mix enough plaster of paris to fill the pie pan almost to the top. The mixture should be as thick as syrup.
3. Fill the pie pan almost to the top with plaster of paris. Gently tap pan onto floor to remove air bubbles.
4. Repeat steps 4 and 5 from Part 1.
5. Photograph or draw your results.
6. Let the plaster of paris harden for about 10 minutes and repeat steps 4 and 5 again.
7. Photograph or draw your results.

OBSERVATIONS

Compare the photographs or drawings of your craters with photographs of the surface of Mercury. What does this project tell you about the effects of meteors on soft and hard surfaces of the planets?

The View from Space   In 1974 *Mariner 10* photographs showed us the clearest views we had ever seen of Mercury. These photographs showed craters, land features, and no evidence of plate tectonics. *Mariner 10* also provided information regarding temperatures and magnetism.

Composition   Craters cover half of Mercury's surface. The other half is mostly smooth plains. There is a covering of fine dust on the planet's surface at least several inches or centimeters deep. If you look very carefully at the craters on Mercury compared to those on the Moon, you will notice that there are several important differences. On Mercury,

1. there are plains or smooth areas between craters and basins.
2. there are not many large craters with diameters between 12 to 30 miles (20–50 km).
3. you can still see the results of early cratering.
4. there are shallow cliffs (scarps) that run for hundreds of miles or kilometers.

5. when an object strikes Mercury and makes a crater on the planet's surface, the rocks and dust that are sent out will only cover one-sixth the area they would cover on the Moon. This is because the force of gravity on Mercury is twice as strong as it is on the Moon.

6. Smaller craters tend to cluster more around larger craters than they do on the Moon.

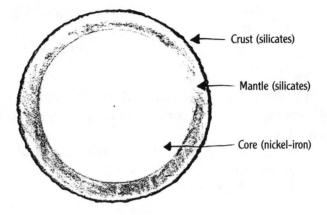

The interior of Mercury

On the Moon,

1. the highland plains show densely packed and overlapping craters.

2. there are many large craters.

3. rocks and dust scattered from recent impacts have covered much of the earlier craters.

4. there is stretching rather than cliffs.

While Mercury appears to be like the Moon on the outside, it is more like the Earth on the inside. Mercury's interior may have a core of iron that takes up about 50% of the planet's volume or 70% of its mass.

Around the planet there is a veil-like blanket of helium gas, far thinner than the atmosphere around the Earth. There is no real protective atmosphere around Mercury. There is, as around the Earth, a magnetosphere. Mercury does not rotate fast enough to create a magnetosphere, but somehow the planet generates one of its own. The solar wind is not the source.

Because one-half of Mercury faces the Sun for 176 Earth days while the other half faces away from it and is in darkness, Mercury has the strange combination of being the hottest and the coldest planet in the solar system. It lives up to its name, mercurial, which means changeable.

The sunlit side of Mercury reaches temperatures of 660°F (350°C). When the planet's orbit brings it close to the Sun (perihelion), this temperature can get as high as 775°F (412°C), hot enough to melt lead. The side of Mercury that is in darkness is not far from −459°F (−273°C). This is even colder than the temperature on the planet Pluto, the planet farthest from the Sun. These extreme temperature ranges are greater than those of any other planet.

Venus

Names   The name Venus comes from the Roman goddess of love and beauty. Her Greek name was Aphrodite. The Phoenicians called her Astarte.

The ancient Babylonians worshipped Venus first as Inanna and later as Ishtar. During the reign of **King Ammisadugua** (1646–1626 B.C.) and at the time of the great lawgiver **Hammaurabi** (1792–1750 B.C.) and his dynasty, astronomer-priests recorded regular observations of the dates when Venus was the morning and evening star.

To the Maya of Central America, Venus was the god Kukulcan or Quetzalcoatl. Certain Mexican creation stories and epic tales describe the soul of a deceased hero passing to the east. There it descends into the underworld. This visit to the land of the dead lasts for 8 days, the period during which Venus is invisible between her appearances as the evening star and the morning star. The resurrected hero then rises from the underworld to climb up the steps of the sky. Finally, the hero joins the creator in the "heart of heaven" at the zenith or noonday position of the Sun directly above the Earth. Compare this 8-day journey with the 70-day journey of the soul after death in ancient Egypt (see chapter 1, section 4).

Adjectives used to describe Venus include *Venusian, Venerian,* and *Cytherian* (from the island Cythera, where Aphrodite lived). The names of plateaus on Venus come from different titles for the goddess Venus. There is an Ishtar Terra (Babylonian) and an Aphrodite Terra (Greek).

Early Observations   In Central Mexico in the buildings at Uxmal, there are buildings directed toward Venus. The axis of the front of the Palace of the Governor is 29° east of north. Every 8 years, the astronomer-priest standing in the doorway of the Palace of the Governor would see Venus as the morning star rising at its farthest position to the south.

In 1980 archeoastronomers **Anthony Aveni** and **Horst Hartung** measured a perpendicular line to the front of the Palace. They found that their line was within 1/30 of a degree of the exact position of Venus at its maximum southern rising position.

The planet rose over the top of a pyramid nearly 100 feet (30 m) high, about 6 miles (10 km) east of Uxmal in the town of Nohpat. You can see the top of the pyramid from the doorway of the Palace. The facade of the Palace displays over 350 sculptured Venus signs like the one shown above. The two circles may represent Venus as the morning and evening stars. There are 584 X shapes between the horizontal bars on the buildings. The number 584 was important to the Maya because it was the number of days it took Venus to complete its orbit.

To the ancient Greeks, Venus as morning star was Phosphorus or Lucifer, the light bearer. To the ancient Egyptians, the morning star was Tioumoutiri, and the evening star was Quaiti. To the Quiche of Guatemala, Venus as the morning star is

Santiago, and Raskap ("thing of night" or "something late") is Venus as the evening star. To the Greeks, the evening star was Hesperus. Observers (perhaps Pythagoras was the first in the sixth century B.C.) later realized that these two stars were actually one planet—Venus.

The View from Earth   We sometimes call Venus our sister planet because of all the planets, Venus seems most like our Earth, at least in size, mass, and density. Photographs of the two cloud-covered planets often resemble each other. Venus also approaches the Earth more closely than any other planet (26 million miles or 42 million kilometers away). You can see it for a longer time than Mercury. Due to Earth's rotation of 15° every hour, you can only see Venus 3 hours before sunrise or 3 hours after sunset.

Venus commands attention. Her beauty radiates with more visible light than any star or planet in the sky except for the Sun and Moon. Venus shines with a steady white light with an apparent magnitude of −4.4. At night, light from Venus can cast a shadow. If you know where to look, you can even see Venus in the daytime.

Like Mercury, Venus goes through a complete cycle of phases. Galileo was the first to report these phases in 1610. Galileo announced this discovery, which his former pupil **Beneditto Costelli** had probably shared in making, to **Giuliano de'Medici** in Prague. He made his announcement in a code called an anagram. It said, *"Cynthiae figuras aemulatur mater amorum,"* which means, "the mother of love (Venus) imitates the shape of Cynthia (the Moon)."

Like Mercury, Venus also experiences inferior and superior conjunctions. These affect the apparent size of the planet's disk. When Venus is at full phase during its superior conjunction, you cannot see the planet because the Sun blocks your view. At the new phase and inferior conjunction, the Sun shining from behind the planet makes it impossible to see Venus. Your usual view of Venus, like that of your view of Mercury, is during its gibbous or crescent phases. Venus is at her brightest during the crescent phase about 36 days before and after an inferior conjunction. The angle between Venus and the Sun (elongation) at these times is about 39°, which gives the planet plenty of distance away from the light of the Sun. The combined movement of the Earth and Venus means that you would need almost 20 months to see Venus go through all of its phases. Venus's cloud cover makes for terrific reflection of the Sun's light. More than 70% of the light received is reflected back. At every inferior conjunction, Venus presents the same face to Earth.

Transits of Venus across the Sun are rare, occurring in 1874, 1882, and then 2004 and 2012.

The View from Space   The *Mariner 2* spacecraft launched by the United States in August 1962 passed within 22,000 miles (35,405 km) of Venus. It recorded yellowish-white clouds completely covering the planet. The *Mariner 10* came within 4,000 miles (6,400 km) of Venus in February 1974. It recorded that clouds swirl around the planet at speeds faster than 150 miles (240 km) per hour. Large convection currents also occur in the clouds on the side of Venus that faces the Sun. On October 22, 1975, the Soviet spacecraft *Venera 9* landed on Venus, sending photographs and other information back to Earth for 53 minutes. Three days later *Venera 10* landed and sent more information for 65 minutes. The photographs from these two unmanned probes were the first ever taken from the surface of another planet. In 1991 the Magellan satellite sent us dramatic views of the surface of Venus.

Two near-infrared photos of Venus: at night (left) and day (right) taken on *Galileo,* 1990
(*photo courtesy of Jet Propulsion Laboratory*)

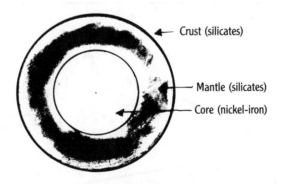

Crust (silicates)

Mantle (silicates)

Core (nickel-iron)

Composition

Interior   Most of our ideas about Venus came from the information we received from *Venera 9* and *Venera 10* and the Arecibo Radio Telescope. We know almost nothing about the interior of Venus. Astronomers assume that the mean density of Venus is similar to that of Mercury and the Earth. Because of its place in the solar system and the similarity of much of its physical characteristics to Mercury and the Earth, astronomers also assume that Venus's interior is also similar. We have looked for and have not detected much of a magnetic field around the planet.

Plateaus, canyons, mountain ranges, and volcanoes seem to make up only 5%

of the surface of Venus; most of the planet is level. There are mountains in the **Maxwell Montes** range that we have calculated to be 2.22 miles (3.6 km) taller than Mount Everest.

Exterior   The thick blanket of clouds around Venus moves across the planet's surface once every 4 days. These clouds are part of a four-layered atmosphere surrounding the planet. The tops of the clouds may be a mixture of droplets containing sulfuric acid and water.

In 1761 observations suggested that Venus had an atmosphere. Studies in 1937 suggest that the atmosphere of Venus is 98% carbon dioxide, with 0.3% of water vapor in the lower atmosphere. This combination of a thick layer of carbon dioxide and water vapor creates a condition between the atmosphere and the surface of Venus where heat energy from the Sun enters but cannot escape. This situation reminded people a little of what takes place in a greenhouse. The two conditions aren't really the same, but there is a similar quality of collecting and holding solar energy so that the temperature inside is greater than the temperature outside. This is the **greenhouse effect**. In the case of the greenhouse, short-wave energy from the Sun passes through the glass. The plants and soil inside the greenhouse absorb this energy, then give it off again. But the energy has been changed into longer waves. The glass won't allow the long-wave energy to escape, thus trapping it inside the greenhouse. This trapped energy heats the air inside, which causes it to become hotter than the air outside. In this next project you can create the greenhouse effect.

The **greenhouse effect** also takes place inside your car on a sunny day when all of the windows are up.

★ ★ ★ ★ ★ **Project 58: Demonstrating the Greenhouse Effect** ★ ★ ★ ★ ★

MATERIALS

aquarium

glass or plastic wrap to fit top of aquarium

two thermometers

light source or the Sun

plants, dirt, rocks, etc.

PROCEDURE

1. Place some dirt, plants, or rocks in the bottom of the aquarium.
2. Place a thermometer at the bottom of the aquarium near one of the sides so you can read it.
3. Cover the top of the aquarium with a glass lid or plastic wrap.
4. Place the other thermometer on top of the glass or plastic.
5. Shine a light down onto the top of the aquarium or set it in the sunlight.
6. Read and record the temperatures inside and outside.

OBSERVATION

What do the two temperatures tell you is happening?

Venus has water, light, and carbon dioxide. These are the ingredients needed for photosynthesis to occur. For this reason, some people feel that Venus could possibly support some form of life. What do you think?

READING MORE

Asimov, Isaac. *Venus, Near Neighbor of the Sun.* New York: Lothrup, Lee and Shepard Books, 1981.

Briggs, Geoffrey, and Frederick Taylor. *The Cambridge Photographic Atlas of the Planets.* Cambridge: Cambridge University Press, 1982.

Motz, Lloyd. *On the Path of Venus.* New York: Random House, 1976.

A computer-assembled mosaic of Uranus's moon, Miranda, from *Voyager 2*, January 26, 1986 (*photo courtesy of NASA*)

Section 4 THE OUTER PLANETS

Beyond the Earth, heading out away from the Sun, are the orbits of the outer planets Mars, Jupiter, and Saturn. Together with the Earth, Moon, inner planets and the Sun, the outer planets formed the boundary of the universe as people knew it from the beginning of time until as recently as 1781. We know more about these three planets than we know about any of the others. You can observe the planets Mars, Jupiter, and Saturn easily with your naked eye. The outer planets also include Uranus, Neptune, and Pluto, which were discovered after 1781.

Mars

Names   To the Greeks, Mars was Ares, the god of war and lover of strife, the son of Zeus and Hera. The Romans called the same god Mars. The Babylonians called the planet Nergal, the "star of death." The red color of Mars has added to the picture of the anger and bloodshed that war brings.

Most of the names of the canals and the dark and light areas on Mars come from **Giovanni Schiaparelli** (1835–1910), director of an observatory in Milan, who chose names of places around the Mediterranean Sea. In those days, planetary mapmakers named dark areas on the planets after bodies of water, as in the mare (seas) on the Moon, sinus (bay or gulf), lacus (lake), fretum (strait or channel), and palus (swamp).

More recently people have chosen the names of scientists for craters and even the *Mariner* spacecraft for the largest canyon: **Valles Marineris,** the Valleys of Mariner.

Early Observations   Mars was Tycho Brahe's favorite object, even without the benefit of a telescope. Tycho set Kepler to work to find a satisfactory theory of planetary motion based on observation. To do this, Kepler used Tycho's vast records of 38 years of observations of Mars.

The first person to see Mars through a telescope was probably Galileo. In 1610 he wrote that he could see the planet as a disk and that it had phases. In 1666 **Giovanni Domenico Cassini (1625–1712)** discovered the rotation period of Mars. In 1830 **Sir John Herschel (1792–1871)** noted, "In this planet we frequently discern, with perfect distinctness, the outlines of what may be continents and seas . . . (and) the appearance of brilliant white spots at its poles . . . which have been conjectured . . . to be snow."

In 1869 **Father Angelo Secchi** in Rome drew a map of Mars. On his map, Father Secchi drew streaklike markings that he called **canali.**

Canali comes from the Italian word for *channels.*

Because of the eccentricity, or degree of flatness of the elliptical orbit of Mars, Mars is almost twice as close to the Earth around August 25, and farthest away from the Earth in February. Because the close arrangement in August makes it possible to see Mars better, when an opposition occurs on or near this date we call it a "favorable opposition." Most of our information about Mars, including the discovery of its two moons, came during these favorable oppositions. These occur every 15 or 17 years. The most recent one was in September 1988.

In 1877 there was a favorable opposition of Mars which made it possible to make detailed observations of the planet. That year Schiaparelli detected what appeared to be a number of long narrow lines on the surface of Mars. These dark lines seemed to come from the "ocean" areas on Mars. They cut across the "continents" and formed a network that connected the various "seas" together. Schiaparelli popularized Father Secchi's term *canali* for these lines.

To English-speaking people, the word *canali* suggested the word *canals,* and the word *canals* suggested that someone or something had built them. The person who took this suggestion most seriously was **Percival Lowell (1855–1916).** With his own money, Lowell built an observatory in the exceptionally clear air of Mars Hill in Flagstaff, Arizona, to study Mars and to look for other planets. In his second book, *Mars and Its Canals and Mars As the Abode of Life,* Lowell put forth his ideas about the planet and the Martians who built the canals to irrigate their desert homeland. Several other observers in different locations also noted the canals. Surprisingly, the canals have never showed up in any of the photographs taken by the spacecraft that have mapped the entire surface of Mars. Like many other things about Mars, the canals remain a mystery.

Percival Lowell's map of Mars (*photo courtesy of Lowell Observatory*)

The View from Earth   Of all the planets, Mars is in the best location for observers on the Earth. Mars is the only planet whose solid surface you can see with a telescope. Mercury is too near the Sun, and the other planets are either covered with clouds or too far away. The best telescopes show Mars to be a patchwork of red, gray, white, and yellow. The red areas are probably deserts and occur mostly in the Northern Hemisphere covering about 60% of the planet's surface. The gray areas (about 40% of the planet) occur mostly in the Southern Hemisphere.

The North and South Poles take turns having a white polar cap during the winter, depending on which pole is pointing away from the Sun. The white cap builds up in several days extending 20° to 30° from the pole. Then it remains one size for the rest of the winter season. In the spring, the polar cap gradually breaks up until, in the summer, it is completely gone. The south polar cap usually becomes larger than the northern one.

Sir William Herschel (1738–1822) was the first to carefully study these polar caps. Herschel noticed that the caps were largest from 3 to 6 months after the winter solstice on Mars. They then got smaller until they reached their smallest size about 3 to 6 months after the summer solstice.

The View from Space   Exactly 7 years after the first human set foot on the Moon, the first spacecraft landed on the surface of Mars on July 20, 1976. Called the *Viking 1,* this landing probe and the one after it, *Viking 2,* have provided us with photographs and much information about the surface of Mars, its atmosphere, and temperature.

Spring   Summer

1907   1909

1924   1926

1939   1941

1954   1956

Views of Mars
(*photo courtesy of Lowell Observatory*)

November 20, 1979

December 4, 1979

December 13, 1979

January 10, 1980

The retrograde motion of Mars (*photos by Richard Moeschl*)

Composition   Mars appears like a rusty version of the Moon with fewer craters and bigger mountains. The red surface of Mars is from the iron dust that blows across the face of the planet at 100 miles (160 km) per hour. The Martian sky is pink, not blue. Every 10 years, a huge dust-filled hurricane sweeps over the planet, eroding craters, covering rocks, hiding mountains, filling in craters and valleys. Sometimes the storms expose layers of darker rocks under the red dust. There are large smooth areas on Mars where lava once flowed from one of the planet's 12 volcanoes. The largest of these volcanoes is **Olympus Mons**, the biggest volcano we know of anywhere in the universe. It is 15 miles (25 km) high and 360 miles (580 km) across. Mount Everest on Earth is about 5 miles (9 km) above sea level, and Mauna Kea, the largest volcano on Earth, would almost fit into the 42-mile (70 km) opening at the top of Olympus Mons.

The old name for Olympus Mons was **Olympus Nix** (the snows of Olympus).

Taking samples from the surface of Mars, from *Viking 1*, 1978
(*photo courtesy of Jet Propulsion Laboratory*)

Valles Marineris is a huge canyon on Mars almost as long as the width of the United States. Its branches are bigger than the Grand Canyon. Valles Marineris is only one example of many dry riverbeds, streams, and even islands that show that there may have been running water on Mars. Now the planet is dry and windswept much like the North American Southwest.

From information gathered by the *Viking* missions in 1976, the atmosphere of Mars appears to contain the following:

Carbon dioxide, 95%
Nitrogen, 2 to 3%
Argon, 1 to 2%
Oxygen, 0.1 to 0.4%
Water, 0.01 to 0.1%
Krypton, less than 0.0001%
Xenon, less than 0.0001%

The interior of Mars

Mars, from *Viking 2*, 1976 (*photo courtesy of NASA*)

The cloudiness surrounding Mars makes for incredibly high humidity. The thin atmosphere is almost saturated. Ground fog is everywhere. Because of this thin atmosphere, the temperature plummets very quickly after sunset to well below zero.

The maximum temperatures at the Martian equator are about 86°F (30°C). The temperatures at the equator are much lower, around −40°F (−40°C) at sunrise and −4°F (−20°C) at sunset. At night the temperature drops to nearly −104°F (−75°C). The temperature at the south polar cap is about −238°F (−150°C). These conversions are accurate but seem odd to those of us who are accustomed to using only Fahrenheit. You can make the conversions yourself by using the formula on the first page of Sky Files, which follow Chapter 7.

In some ways the seasons on Mars are like those on the Earth. Venus, Earth, and Mars share many qualities. These have earned them the name **terrestrial planets,** since they are in many ways Earth (*terra*)-like.

Moons   Two small moons travel around Mars. Kepler predicted they were there in 1610. **Jonathan Swift (1667–1745)** described them in 1726 in his book *Gulliver's Travels,* and the French author **Voltaire (1694–1778)** wrote about them in 1752 in his book *Micromegas.* All of this is amazing since the two satellites weren't discovered until 1877! In August 1877 **Asaph Hall (1829–1907)** of the U.S. Naval Observatory found the satellites when he was looking through what was the largest telescope in the world, a 66-centimeter refractor. He named the moons for the two sons of Mars: **Phobos** (Fear) and **Deimos** (Panic). (The other children of Mars are Terror, Trembling, and Ruiner of Cities.) Hall also named the largest crater on Phobos, **Stickney,** after his wife's maiden name.

Phobos is 5,800 miles (9,380 km) from the center of Mars and takes 7 hours and 39 minutes to travel once around the planet. Phobos rises in the west and sets 4½ hours later. An unevenly shaped, pockmarked rock, Phobos is about 10 miles (25 km) wide. Phobos goes around Mars three times in the time it takes Mars to turn around once. This appears to be the only place in the universe where such a relationship exists. For every complete journey of the Moon around the Earth, the Earth rotates 27 times. Even the Sun rotates several times before even the fastest moving planets have orbited once around the Sun.

Deimos is 14,600 miles (23,500 km) from the center of Mars and takes 30 hours and 18 minutes to circle the planet. Deimos rises in the east and goes through two complete phases before it sets in the west. Like Phobos, Deimos is a slightly elongated, pockmarked rock made of dark materials and is very old. Deimos is 7 miles (13 km) wide.

Mariner 9, launched in November 1971, is also a satellite of Mars. The first man-made satellite to orbit a planet other than Earth, *Mariner's* orbit ranges from 1,025 to 10,610 miles (1,640–16,976 km) above the surface of Mars.

Kepler was the first to use the word ***satellite*** as a name for a moon going around a planet. Satellite comes from the Latin word *satelles* = attendant or bodyguard.

The Asteroids

Names   There are other orbiting bodies in our solar system. Because they look starlike, John Herschel named them **asteroids**. They are not stars. They are more like small planets, which makes their other names **planetoids** or **minor planets** more accurate.

Asteroid comes from the Greek word ἀστερ (*aster*) = star.

Most asteroids lie in the **asteroid belt** between the orbits of Mars and Jupiter. Others have their own orbits that cross the orbits of the Earth and Mars. Some are in two swarms along Jupiter's orbit. An asteroid has two parts to its name: a number for the order in which it was discovered and a proper name. The proper names come from Greek and Roman mythology, heroines from **Richard Wagner's (1813–1883)** operas, wives of discoverers, friends, flowers, cities, colleges, pets, even favorite desserts and a computer (NORC). There are over 2,300 named minor planets. There are probably 100,000 more waiting to be charted and named.

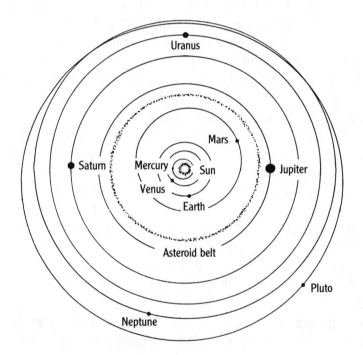

The asteroid belt
(*from* Teaching with NightStar *by Richard Moeschl*)

Asteroid 2005 is named in honor of **Karl Hencke (1783–1866)**, postmaster and amateur astronomer who discovered the fourth asteroid, **Astraea**, in 1845. Asteroid 1000 is named **Piazzia**, number 1001 is **Gaussia**, and 1002 is **Olbersia**. Olbers also has a crater on the Moon named after him. Vesta is the only minor planet you can see without a telescope.

Early Observations   According to the Titius-Bode Law, there "ought" to be a planet in the space between Mars and Jupiter, two astronomical units from the Sun. In 1800 **Baron Francis Xaver von Zach (1754–1832)** assigned a team of astronomers their own sections of the zodiac to search for the "missing planet." One of the astronomers, **Guiseppi Piazzi (1746–1826)**, hadn't received his assignment yet when he discovered a new object on January 1, 1801. Piazzi felt certain that the object was moving and thought he had found a new comet.

Since the object was 2.8 astronomical units from the Sun, von Zach was sure the moving object was the "missing planet." He needed to know the object's orbit, but to do that would take nearly a year of continued observation. The object moved in the sky near the Sun and wouldn't be visible again for 8 months. Everyone was afraid that it would never be found again. A young mathematician in Germany named **Karl Friedrich Gauss (1777–1855)** invented a new way to calculate orbits and in November sent his results to von Zach. Using these calculations, von Zach saw the object on December 7 and again on December 31, right where Gaus said it would be. On January 1, 1802, 1 year after Piazzi had first seen the new object, a doctor and amateur astronomer in Prussia named **Heinrich Wilhelm Mattias Olbers (1758–1840)** also found the object. The object was clearly not a comet; it was a small planet. At Piazzi's request the object received the name **Ceres**, the goddess of agriculture and the protecting goddess of Piazzi's native Sicily.

While tracking Ceres, Olbers discovered a second asteroid on March 28, 1802. He named it **Pallas**. In 1803 **Carl Harding (1765–1834)** discovered **Juno**. All three of these asteroids are about 2.8 astronomical units from the Sun. For this reason Olbers thought they might be the remains of a planet that had exploded. Astronomers today challenge this theory because asteroids contain different minerals, and there don't seem to be enough pieces to form a planet. Some observers believe instead that these particles were going to combine to become a planet and didn't.

Jupiter

Names   Jupiter is the Roman name for the Greek god Zeus. The Romans also called him Jove. It is by this name that the British swear when they say, "By Jove!"

Early Observations
In 1610 Galileo was the first to see the face of Jupiter through a telescope. Robert Hooke (1635–1703) first recorded the Great Red Spot in 1664, and in 1672 and 1691 drawings by Cassini showed the Great Red Spot. The first time anyone saw the Great Red Spot through a telescope was in 1831.

The View from Earth   Moving at a slow, regal pace, shining with a dazzling white brilliance, Jupiter was obviously the king. Jupiter is the second brightest planet after Venus. It reflects back a little more than half of the light it receives even though the amount it receives is far less than what Venus receives. Jupiter radiates out about 2½ times as much energy as it receives from the Sun. If Jupiter were as near to the Sun as Mars, it would be the brightest planet in the sky and we could see it in the daytime. Because it is so far from the Sun, Jupiter appears fully lit to us, even though it has a gibbous phase.

Jupiter spins around faster than any of the other planets. We can tell this by timing the movement of certain patterns in the outer clouds. Jupiter's quick rotation has caused the planet to flatten at the poles and to spread out at the equator. You can notice this flattening when you look at the planet through a telescope.

The View from Space   Views from *Pioneer II* in 1974 suggested that there might be a moon or ring orbiting Jupiter. The *Voyager* space probe took many images of Jupiter from 1977 to 1981. These images have provided us with our most recent and detailed glimpses of the giant planet. Jupiter appears to be a world of swirling clouds of gases and molten metals. These clouds get thicker as you approach the center, gradually forming into a mushy "soup." The storms that create the swirls appear to occur regularly. They form the bands on the planet with distinctive markings of blue, orange, green, red, white, yellow, and gray.

The surface of Jupiter, including the Giant Red Spot, from *Voyager 1,* March 1979
(*photo courtesy of Jet Propulsion Laboratory*)

Voyager 1 revealed much information about Jupiter, including a few surprises. One of the surprises was that Jupiter did in fact have a thin ring around it, an honor previously reserved only for Saturn. Jupiter's ring is much thinner and narrower, about 18 miles (29 km) thick and apparently made up of very tiny particles. The most notable marking on Jupiter is the Great Red Spot, which received its name in 1887. It is about 8,400 miles × 18,000 miles (13,500 km × 29,000 km). It is thought to be a giant storm center circulating counterclockwise, which travels around the planet at its own rate, in 6 days. It is 3°C (37°F) cooler than the surrounding atmosphere.

Composition   Jupiter is the biggest of the gas planets. With its size, physical properties, and numbers of satellites, Jupiter is its own solar system, with a "Sun" of gas and liquid rather than fire.

Jupiter gives off more heat energy than it receives from the Sun. The center of the planet seems to be very hot, about 54,000°F (29,982°C), or five times the temperature of the surface of the Sun. It is not clear whether this center is solid or liquid. The core may be about the size of the Earth and made from molten iron silicate. Above the core are two thick layers composed mainly of hydrogen. We don't really know what is happening in the interior of Jupiter. Some of the conditions that people have suggested, such as liquid metallic hydrogen, do not exist on Earth.

We know more about the wildly swirling clouds of Jupiter's multicolored atmosphere. We can copy some of these conditions in the laboratory. There are a great number of charged particles around Jupiter as part of the planet's magnetic field. Jupiter also has radiation belts, much like the Van Allen belt around the Earth. Jupiter has an extremely large and complex magnetosphere that extends 450 million miles (724 million km) around the planet. Jupiter's magnetic field is about 20 to 30 times more powerful than that of the Earth. Like the Earth's magnetic field, Jupiter's north and south magnetic poles are tilted from the planet's axis. We call the bright horizontal bands around the planet **zones**. They are usually light tan or yellowish. The dark horizontal bands are **belts**. They are usually brown, reddish, or greenish.

The interior of Jupiter

Jupiter has several layers of clouds, possibly containing hydrogen, helium, methane, and ammonia. The amounts of hydrogen and carbon (in various chemical combinations) compared to each other are very close to the ratio of the same elements found in the Sun. Clouds swirl around the planet in a continuous 435 miles (700 km) per hour storm. The colors and patterns are so bright and so large you can see them through a telescope.

Jupiter's atmosphere is more like the oceans on Earth rather than its winds. Jupiter's atmosphere includes the following gases:

Hydrogen, 60%
Helium, 36%
Water, 0.9%
Ammonia, 0.05%
Argon, 0.03%
Methane, 0.02%

Views from *Voyager* of Jupiter's dark side showed auroras and giant lightning bolts. In mythology, Zeus (Jupiter) often hurled lightning bolts.

The planet's outer atmosphere is quite cold, about $-184°F$ ($-119°C$).

The Galilean Satellites of Jupiter, from *Voyager 1,* 1979 (*photo courtesy of Jet Propulsion Laboratory*)

Moons   In 1610 Galileo observed Jupiter through his telescope and found four satellites. They were traveling around Jupiter like planets around the Sun, like a miniature solar system. This discovery supported the heliocentric model of the Sun and the planets that Copernicus had suggested. In it, the Earth was not the central point for all revolutions.

> I had now decided beyond all question that there existed in the heavens three stars wandering around Jupiter just as Venus and Mercury do around the Sun . . . there were not only three such stars; four wanderers complete their revolutions around Jupiter.—Galileo in *The Starry Messenger*

Simon Marius (1517–1624), a German astronomer, also observed the four moons of Jupiter. He gave these satellites their present names: **Io, Europa, Ganymede,** and **Callisto** after friends and lovers of Jupiter (Zeus). See the Chart of Gods and Goddesses in Sky Files. We call these four largest of Jupiter's moons the **Galilean Satellites** after Galileo. These moons are equal to or larger than our Moon. You can easily see them with binoculars as a string of tiny pearls next to the giant planet. Jupiter has at least 11 more moons, which you can only see with a telescope or with the aid of cameras on a space probe.

The views that the *Voyager* cameras made of the Galilean Satellites provided us with incredible sights and perplexing mysteries, including active volcanoes on Io. Voyager also found three more moons.

Jupiter has 16 moons. They are, in order of distance from the planet, closest first, Adrastea, Metis, Almalthea, Thebe, Io, Europa, Ganymede, Callisto, Leda, Himalia, Lysithea, Elara, Ananke, Carme, Pasiphae, and Sinope.

In this next project you can do what Galileo and Marius did and watch Jupiter's moons circle around the great planet.

★ ★ ★ ★ ★ ★ ★ ★ ★ ★ **Project 59: Charting the Movement** ★ ★ ★ ★ ★ ★ ★ ★ ★ ★
of Jupiter's Moons

MATERIALS
telescope or binoculars   colored pencils and paper

PROCEDURE
1. Draw a chart like the one shown on the next page, one line for every day of the month, with a band in the middle for Jupiter.

2. Number each starting point from left to right beginning with Roman numeral I.

3. Choose a color for each number (use the ones suggested below or choose your own):

I = blue   III = purple
II = brown   IV = green

The Movement of Jupiter's Moons

I II 4 III IV

4. Observe the movements of each moon every night for a month. Use colors to indicate the moons' position every day compared to Jupiter (the vertical black band). If it's cloudy, skip that date.

5. Draw the pattern or trail made by the movement of each moon as it appears on the chart at the end of the month. Use the same colors and lightly connect the changing positions of each moon. If you can, show where the moon went in front or behind Jupiter.

6. Write the names of each moon next to the number that shows its path based on what you know about these four satellites.

OBSERVATION

Charts like this one often appear in astronomy magazines like *Sky and Telescope* for all the planets and Earth's Moon as well as the moons of Jupiter.

Saturn

Names   Saturn is the father of Jupiter in Roman mythology. The Greeks knew him as Cronos. Saturn or Cronos ruled over time. To the ancients, Saturn or Cronos was the great grandfather of all the gods, the farthest of all the planets from the Earth and the nearest to heaven.

Early Observations   Through his telescope, Galileo observed two strange shapes on either side of Saturn. Either the planet's face had ears or else there were two large moons, one on each side.

I have discovered a most extraordinary marvel, which I want to make known to their Highnesses and to your Lordship, but I want it kept secret until it is published in the work which I am going to have printed. . . . The fact is that the planet Saturn is not one alone, but is composed of three, which almost touch one another and never move nor change with respect to one another. They are arranged in the form o𝗢o , as I will show their Highnesses this autumn, when it will be very easy to observe the celestial object with all the planets above the horizon. —Galileo, July 30, 1610

Galileo was astonished when he saw Saturn 2 years later. The two satellites on either side had vanished.

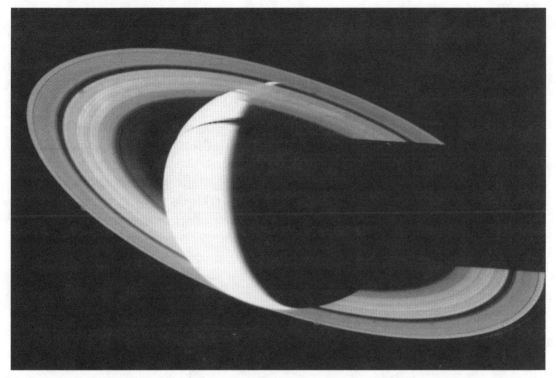

Saturn from *Voyager 1*, November 16, 1980 (*photo courtesy of Jet Propulsion Laboratory*)

In 1655 **Christian Huygens** (1629–1695), using a more powerful telescope than Galileo had, announced that Saturn's two large moons were in fact one large ring that surrounded the planet. Huygens also discovered the first satellite of Saturn, **Titan. Giovanni Domenico Cassini** noticed a division that separated the ring into two unequal parts. We still call this division **Cassini's division**. Cassini also discovered the second, third, fourth, and fifth satellites of Saturn before becoming blind in 1710.

The sight of Saturn surrounded by its rings is a strangely beautiful one. Even though the ancients knew and saw Saturn well, they never shared this view that requires a telescope.

The View from Earth   From the telescope, Saturn's rings appear to have three sections, called the A (outer), B (middle), and C (inner) rings. Cassini's division is between the A and B rings. The rings are thin and probably mostly ice. Because of the planet's tilt, you see the rings either from above or from below as Saturn makes its 29-year journey around the Sun. The rings are so thin (about 2 miles [3.6 km]) that when they are facing you edge-on as they do every 15 years, you can't see them. This is what happened when Galileo was watching them. Saturn is inclined 27° to its orbit, giving the planet seasons with a temperature of $-292°F$ ($-180°C$). Saturn glows as a bright yellowish spot, the size of a star. At opposition, Saturn shines as bright as a 0.7 magnitude star.

The View from Space   *Pioneer II* in 1979 was the first unmanned space probe to Saturn. From the *Voyager* spacecraft in 1980 and 1981, we have seen five ring sections, A through E. Each ring has many thousands of tiny ringlets and spaces in between. The surface of Saturn shows the same kinds of swirls that we saw on Jupiter. (See Project 36, Interpreting Patterns of Movement in Water.) In 1991 the Hubble Space Telescope revealed a Great White Spot on Saturn.

Composition   The inside of Saturn is very similar to that of Jupiter, probably with a rocky core. Saturn's atmosphere is also very similar in chemical composition to that of Jupiter and the Sun.

Like Mercury, Earth, and Jupiter, Saturn has a magnetic field. Space exploration has taught us that Saturn's field is stronger than Earth's and weaker than Jupiter's. As with Jupiter, Van Allen belts of radiation surround the planet.

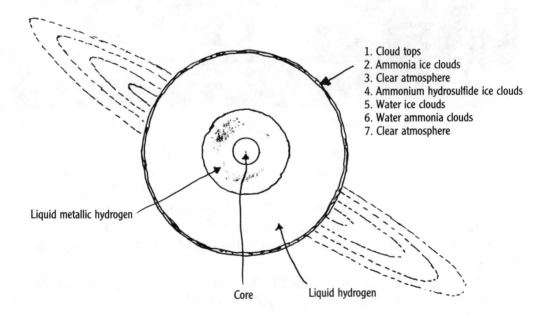

1. Cloud tops
2. Ammonia ice clouds
3. Clear atmosphere
4. Ammonium hydrosulfide ice clouds
5. Water ice clouds
6. Water ammonia clouds
7. Clear atmosphere

Liquid metallic hydrogen

Core   Liquid hydrogen

The interior of Saturn

Winds blow across Saturn at 870 miles (1,400 km) per hour, which is two times faster than on Jupiter. The atmosphere contains hydrogen, helium, methane, and ammonia. The whole planet is so light that it could float on water.

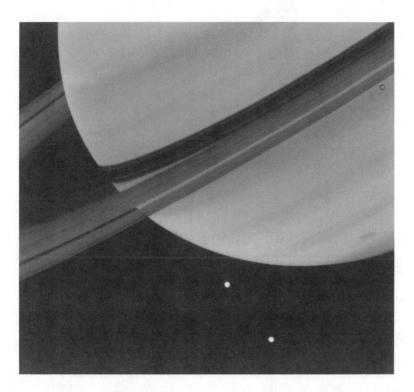

Saturn with two of its moons, Tethys (above) and Dione (below), from *Voyager 1,* November 3, 1980 (*photo courtesy of Jet Propulsion Laboratory*)

Moons   Saturn has 20 moons. The 17 most visible are, in order of distance from the planet, closest first, Atlas, Inner F Ring Shepherd Moon, Outer F Ring Shepherd Moon, Epimetheus, Janus, Mimas, Encledaus, Tethys, Telesto, Calypso, Dione, 1980 S6, Rhea, Titan, Hyperion, Iapetus, and Phoebe. *Voyager* examined many of these moons and found most of them heavily cratered.

Saturn is such a fascinating planet to look at that its picture appears everywhere. Everyone knows what Saturn looks like with its famous rings. In this next project you can build a model of this amazing planet to hang from the "sky" in your room.

★ ★ ★ ★ ★ ★ ★ ★ ★ **Project 60: Making a Model of Saturn** ★ ★ ★ ★ ★ ★ ★ ★ ★ ★

MATERIALS

hollow ball about 4 inches in diameter
acrylic paints
felt-tip pens
plastic sheet
thin fishing line
thumbtack

scissors
rubber band
protractor
straight pin
drawing compass

PROCEDURE

1. Divide the ball in half using the rubber band as a marker. Make sure the rubber band is even all around. Make a mark ⅛ inch (3 mm) above and below the rubber band all the way around. Cut through both of these lines as carefully as you can so your cuts are straight.

2. Paint the ball to look like Saturn. Use a photograph of the planet as a guide.

3. Cut out an 8-inch (20 cm) diameter circle from the plastic sheet.

4. Place one of the halves of the ball on a piece of paper and trace its outline. Remove the ball. Draw another circle around the first circle with a 5½-inch (15 cm) diameter.

5. Place the clear plastic circle on the paper with the outline of the ball in the center. Saturn's rings occupy the space between the outer edge of the plastic circle and the 5½-inch circle on the paper.

6. Mark the divisions between the rings and draw concentric circles on either side of the divisions.

7. Leave the paper under the plastic circle while you paint the rings lightly. Use thinner colors to fade toward the 5½-inch circle on the paper. There should be no color from this circle to the circle where the ball (Saturn) will be.

8. When the planet and rings are dry, put a protractor next to the top half of the ball and make a mark on the top, 27° from the center. Push a straight pin through the 27° mark. Remove the pin.

9. Poke a hole through the center of the plastic circle and the bottom half of the ball. Thread the fishing line through the top half of the ball, through the plastic rings, and out through the bottom half. Tie several knots in the end of the fishing line to keep everything together.

10. Hang Saturn from your ceiling using the fishing line and thumbtack.

OBSERVATION

Notice that when the rings are facing you edge-on, you can't see them. The same thing happens when viewing Saturn through a telescope from Earth.

Uranus

Discovery Starting in the year 1690, people noticed the planet and marked it on their star charts, thinking it was a star. In 1781 William Herschel was "sweeping the skies" with his telescope as part of a project to examine the whole sky. By March, he had reached the Gemini section. On March 13 he spotted an object that appeared as a disk rather than as a glowing star. Herschel thought it was a comet and followed it for several weeks. After a few months and several calculations of its orbit, Herschel decided that the orbit was circular and his object was not a comet but a planet. This made William Herschel the first person we know of to discover a planet.

Herschel suggested that the name of the new planet should be **Geogium Sidus** (George's Star) in honor of the king of England, George III. Some people wanted to name the planet Herschel in honor of its discoverer. Johann Bode was very excited about the discovery because it was further proof of his law based on Johann Daniel Titius' series of numbers. (See chapter 5, section 1 for more about the Titius-Bode Law.) Bode suggested the name **Uranus** for the new planet in keeping with the Roman names of gods and goddesses.

> It has generally been supposed that it was a lucky accident that brought this new star to my view; this is an evident mistake. In the regular manner, I examined every star of the heavens, not only of that magnitude but many far inferior, it was that night its turn to be discovered . . . had business prevented me that evening I must have found it the next, and the goodness of my telescope was such that I perceived its visible planetary disc as soon as I looked at it; and by the application of my micrometer, determined its motion in a few hours. —William Herschel

Names   In the Greek story of the origin of the universe, **Ouranos** (the Greek word for Uranus) was heaven. His wife was Gaea, the Earth. Their children included the Titans, among whom was Cronos (Saturn), the father of Zeus (Jupiter). (See chapter 4, section 1.)

The View from Earth   You can see Uranus on a clear night with your unaided eyes. It looks like a dim star. Binoculars help to show it more clearly. Through the telescope, Uranus looks greenish. Generally, Uranus has a magnitude of 5.5. Uranus is tilted 82° from its orbit. This means that Uranus is practically lying on its side. When you look at the planet, at different times during its orbit you are seeing either its north or south pole.

The rotation of Uranus and the revolution of its satellites are in the opposite direction of all the other planets except Venus. This arrangement could make for extreme seasons. When the north pole is pointing toward the Sun, the Northern Hemisphere has a 21-year summer of continual light and heat while the Southern Hemisphere experiences 21 years of cold and darkness. In between would be 21-year periods when the Sun would be shining on the planet's equator, bringing day and night to the whole planet every 23 hours much like we experience on Earth. Compare this to the 6 months of light followed by 6 months of dark in the northern parts of the Earth.

In March 1977, 196 years after Herschel discovered the planet, observers planned to watch Uranus move in front of a bright star. When this happens, astronomers can use the star's dimming light to reveal information about the atmosphere of the planet. When Uranus came near the star, the star dimmed and then brightened again before dimming once more. This happened several times at an equal distance on both sides of the planet's disk. Why? The observations suggested that there might be a ring around Uranus that passed in front of the star before the planet did, causing the star to dim. When the ring passed, it uncovered the star.

Unlike the rings of Saturn, which are wide with narrow gaps in between, the rings of Uranus appear to be narrow with wide gaps in between. These rings are invisible to Earth-bound telescopes. Their diameter is about 63,382 miles (102,000 km).

The View from Space   *Voyager 2* showed us views of the 11 rings of Uranus and glimpses of the planet's moons, discovering 10 of them. *Voyager 2* detected a comparatively strong magnetic field. There is strong evidence from *Voyager* that a huge cauldron of water with small amounts of methane and ammonia lurks beneath Uranus' thick atmosphere. This liquid could be more than 4,992 miles (8,000 km) deep and as hot as several thousand kelvins.

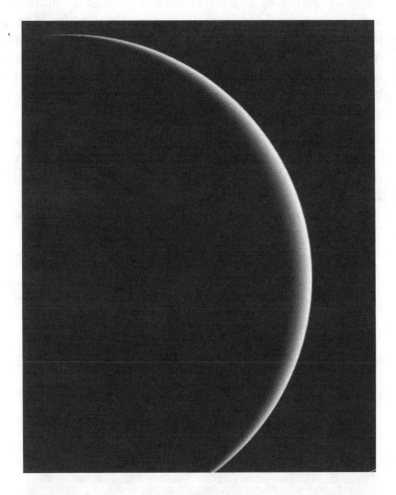

Uranus, from *Voyager 2,* January 25, 1986 (*photo courtesy of Jet Propulsion Laboratory*)

The interior of Uranus

Composition   The ability of Uranus to reflect a large amount of light could mean that there is a reflective cloud layer or mist around the planet. The atmosphere contains hydrogen, helium, and considerable amounts of methane. The interior is probably similar to Jupiter and Saturn. It seems that the atmosphere around Uranus is clearer than Jupiter's. A rocky and icy core could make up about half of the planet's interior. The outer layers are probably most hydrogen. The temperature is below 90°K, which is −298°F (−183°C).

Moons   William Herschel found the first two moons in 1787. Two more were found in 1851. Kuiper found the smallest in 1948. Uranus has 15 moons. The largest five, in order of distance from the planet, closest first, are: Miranda, Ariel, Umbriel, Titania, and Oberon.

Miranda has places on its surface called **ovoid regions** that contain strange features that do not exist anywhere else in the solar system.

The names of the moons of Uranus come from Shakespearean characters from *The Tempest* and *A Midsummer's Night's Dream*. William Herschel's son John started this tradition.

Neptune and Triton, one of its moons

Neptune

Discovery   The mathematical calculations of Kepler and Newton did not fully explain the motions of Uranus. Some people suggested that there might be another planet pulling at Uranus. In 1840 two young scientists set out independently to find this "unknown planet." One of the two scientists was a French mathematician, **Jean Joseph Leverrier (1811–1877)**; the other was an English astronomer, **John Couch Adams (1819–1892)**. Both hoped the unknown planet would be where the

Titius-Bode Law said it would be, but it wasn't because the original figures used to calculate the planetary distances weren't completely accurate.

In 1913 **Mary Blagg** (1858–1944) used a slightly different number combination to revise the Titius-Bode Law. Using these revised figures, the unknown planet follows the Titius-Bode Law almost exactly. The same is true of all of the other planets including the asteroid belt, Uranus, and Pluto.

Adams finished his calculations first in September 1845. He had neither the equipment nor the skill to check out his calculations with a large telescope. When he went to those who had both, they were either not there or only slightly interested. Two months after Adams completed his calculations, Leverrier finished the first part of his own and published them. The following August Leverrier completed his final calculations and like Adams, he needed the instrument and skill of others to test his mathematical predictions. Unable to get help in France, he wrote to the assistant at the Berlin Observatory in Germany. The young director of the observatory, **Johann Gottfried Galle** (1812–1910), agreed to let Leverrier search for the unknown planet the very night he received Leverrier's letter. That was September 23, 1846. With the help of a young student astronomer, **Heinrich Louis d'Arrest** (1822–1875), Galle looked into the predicted position. D'Arrest looked at a star chart while Galle looked through the telescope, calling out stars and their positions. D'Arrest searched for the stars Galle described. Finally Galle called out an eighth-magnitude star that d'Arrest couldn't find on the charts. They had found the unknown planet after more than 2 years of research and half an hour at the telescope. The honor of the discovery belongs to both Adams and Leverrier.

Names Neptune is the Roman name for the Greek god Poseidon, God of the Sea. He is the son of Cronos (Saturn) and brother of Zeus (Jupiter).

The View from Earth Joseph Lelande had seen Neptune on May 8 and 10, 1795, but he didn't recognize the object as a planet. It is also possible that Galileo observed Neptune in 1613 while he was looking at Jupiter and its satellites. Galileo recorded seeing an eighth-magnitude star near Jupiter and it appeared to be moving. Through a telescope, Neptune looks greenish, a bit like Uranus. Neptune has an apparent magnitude of 7.8.

The View from Space *Voyager 2* revealed strong winds swirling around in Neptune's atmosphere. Images sent from *Voyager* show an enormous whirlwind storm system turning counterclockwise called the Great Dark Spot. It is as wide as the Earth and resembles Jupiter's Great Red Spot. *Voyager 2* also found that Neptune has a complex magnetic field, with auroras spread over large areas around the planet. Auroras on Earth are concentrated only at the poles.

Composition Neptune's strong light-reflecting ability suggests that the planet has a reflecting atmosphere of clouds or gas like Uranus. Hydrogen, helium, and methane help make up this atmosphere. Inside Neptune there is probably a rocky core like the one inside Uranus, with large amounts of water surrounded by liquid hydrogen and helium. The temperature on Neptune is around 60°K, or −353°F (−251°C).

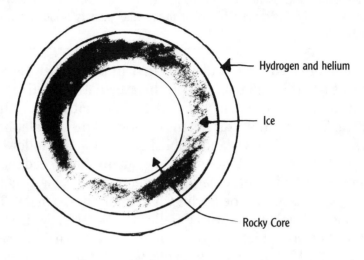

The interior of Neptune

Moons   Neptune has eight moons that we know of. **Triton**, the largest of them, takes its name from the son of Neptune. It is about 211,800 miles (340,850 km) from Neptune and travels from east to west. **Nereid**, the smaller of the two moons, is named for the Nereids, which were sea nymphs. Discovered in 1949, Nereid has the most eccentric orbit of any satellite in the solar system. Its distance from Neptune varies from 6 to 12 million miles (10–20 million kilometers).

Pluto

Discovery   The discovery of Neptune helped explain some of the peculiar movements of Uranus. There were still some unanswered questions. Once again, people considered the pull of another planet beyond Neptune. Three scientists in the early years of the 20th century set out to find this new, unknown planet, Planet X: **Gaillot** in 1909, **Percival Lowell** in 1915, and **W. H. Pickering** in 1928.

Lowell searched for the missing planet for 10 years (1906–1916) using the telescopes at his observatory in Arizona. After Lowell died in 1916, his brother gave the observatory a 13-inch (33 cm) photographic telescope that could record on a single photograph a 12 × 14 inch (31 × 36 cm) area of the sky. Observers began using the new camera in 1929 to continue the search for "Planet X." Lowell had suggested that the unknown planet was in the Gemini region of the sky. This area is rich in stars, so the photographs contained about 300,000 star images on each plate. If a planet was among the stars, it would look the same as every other speck of light. You would have to compare several photographs of the same part of the sky taken several days apart. If one of the 300,000 specks appeared in a different place on the plates, it meant that it had moved and was not a star. How can you do this without going crazy?

Fortunately, someone invented a device called the blink comparator or the blink microscope. To use this instrument, you place side by side two photographs of the same part of the sky taken a few days apart. Looking through the two eyepieces of the blink microscope, you see first one photograph then the other. If nothing has changed position on the plates since the two photographs were taken, what you see appears to be one photograph. If something has moved in the sky, what you will see through the blink microscope is a speck of light jumping back and forth as your eye moves from one photograph to the next.

This is just what **Clyde Tombaugh** saw in February 1930. He was looking at two plates, one made on January 23 and one on January 29, and saw an object move very near the area where Lowell had predicted Planet X would be, following an orbit like the one Lowell had calculated. "There it was, a most unimportant-looking dim, starlike object, which had moved from its plate position of the night before," he said. On March 13, 1930, the observatory announced the discovery of the ninth planet. Percival Lowell was born on this date 75 years before. On March 13, 1781, Sir William Herschel had discovered Uranus in the same constellation (Gemini) where Clyde Tombaugh found Pluto 149 years later.

The photographic plates Clyde Tombaugh used to discover Pluto (*photo courtesy of Lowell Observatory*)

Names   Pluto is the Roman name for the Greek god Hades. Hades is the brother of Jupiter (Zeus) and Neptune (Poseidon). He is the Lord of the Underworld and ruler of the spirits of the dead. Pluto had a helmet that made him invisible. He also had a fork, like Neptune's, but Pluto's fork had only two prongs, not three. An 11-year-old girl, **Venetia Burney**, the daughter of an Oxford astronomy professor, suggested the name Pluto for the new planet. At school, she had learned about the old Greek and Latin mythologies and the distances of the planets. Her grandfather's brother had named Deimos and Phobos, the two satellites of Mars. The initials *Percival Lowell* and the first two letters in the planet's name *Pl*uto appear in the symbol for the planet: ♇ .

Venetia Burney, the 11-year-old girl who gave the planet Pluto its name

The View from Earth   To see Pluto you need a good telescope and you need to know exactly where the planet is. Even in a highly enlarged photograph, Pluto looks more like a smudge than a disk. Pluto's brightness varies every 6.39 days with a magnitude of 15.1.

The View from Space   The *Infrared Astronomical Satellite* (IRAS) revealed that there is a dark band around Pluto and that there are polar caps of frozen methane. Pluto has the most irregular (eccentric) orbit in the solar system. It is tilted 17° from the ecliptic compared to the Moon's 5°. Pluto's orbit brings it 2,800 billion miles (4,500 billion kilometers) close to the Sun (perihelion) and as far away as 4,350 billion miles (7,000 billion kilometers) at its greatest distance from the Sun (aphelion).

One theory about Pluto's wild orbit is that Pluto isn't really a planet. It was once one of Neptune's moons that was pushed out of orbit by the giant satellite Triton. This may also explain why Triton has such an unusual orbit. Once freed from orbiting around Neptune, Pluto was "captured" into an orbit around the Sun where it has remained.

Pluto's orbit crosses in front of Neptune's orbit, at one point carrying the planet in front of Neptune's orbit for about 20 years. That is where Pluto is right now. In 1999 Pluto will reach the part of its orbit that continues beyond the orbit of Neptune, which will return Pluto to its position as the farthest planet from the Sun. You can see for yourself why Pluto and Neptune don't crash into each other by making a three-dimensional model of their orbits in this next project.

★ ★ ★ ★ ★ ★ ★ ★ Project 61: Making a Model of the Orbits ★ ★ ★ ★ ★ ★ ★ ★
of Uranus, Neptune, and Pluto

MATERIALS

stiff paper

pencil or marking pen

drawing compass

paper glue

small paper circles

scissors

drawings from this book

tape

access to a photocopier

PROCEDURE

1. Draw three complete circles the same sizes as the ones included with this project. Use the compass. Draw a dark line on the outer rim of each circle for the planet's orbit. Glue or draw the circles onto stiff paper and cut them out.

2. Photocopy the orbit lines from this project and glue the photocopied sheet onto stiff paper. Cut out the dark parts of the lines.

3. Slide one end of each orbit circle into its proper slot on the photocopied sheet. Feed the orbit circle through to the slot. Tape the ends of the orbit circles together.

4. Make planets from two small paper circles. Slice each circle *slightly* more than halfway through. Slide the two circles together and glue one of the halves of the circles down onto the outer part of an orbit circle.

OBSERVATION

Pluto doesn't crash into Neptune when they cross each other's orbit because the high inclination of Pluto's orbit never brings it closer to Neptune than 240 million miles (385 million kilometers).

Composition   We know very little about Pluto. Our best guesses come from observations made from Earth in 1980. These suggest that Pluto is a small planet, probably 1,600 miles (2575 km) across or 2½ times smaller than Mercury. The surface of Pluto is most likely covered by a frost of frozen methane with a very thin atmosphere of methane. Pluto's temperature is 40°K, which is -235°F (-113°C).

Moons   On July 2, 1978, **James W. Christy** of the U.S. Naval Observatory in Flagstaff, Arizona, saw a strange "bump" on a photograph of Pluto. Checking on the photographs of the planet, Christy noticed that the bump appeared in some of them and wasn't there in others. Christy concluded that the bump was a moon orbiting around Pluto. The satellite's orbit takes 6 days, 9 hours, and 17 minutes, or 6.39 days, the same amount of time that Pluto's brightness varies. Now people know why.

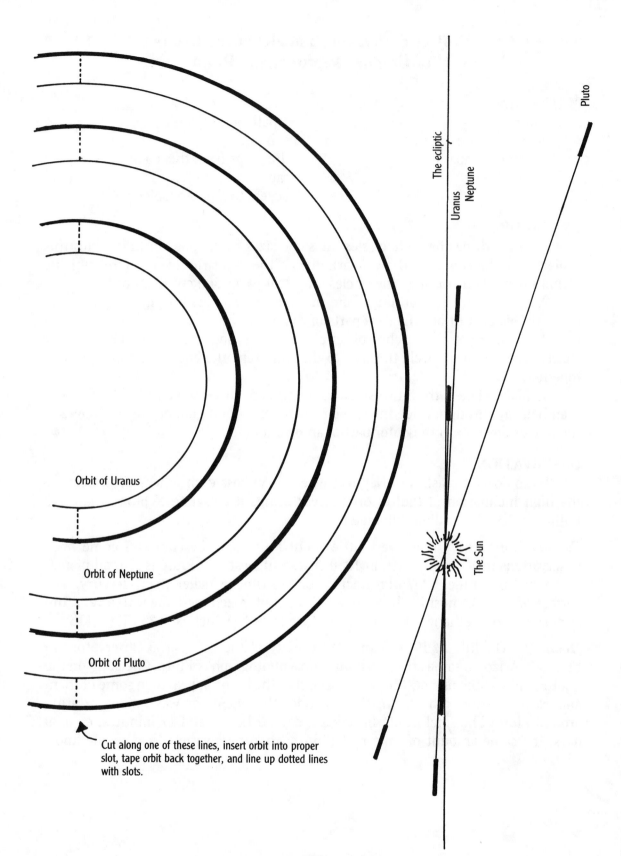

Orbit of Uranus

Orbit of Neptune

Orbit of Pluto

Cut along one of these lines, insert orbit into proper
slot, tape orbit back together, and line up dotted lines
with slots.

The ecliptic

Uranus

Neptune

Pluto

The Sun

A sketch of Pluto and its moon, Charon, taken from the photograph

The name of Pluto's moon is **Charon**, the boatman who ferried the souls of the dead across the river Styx. Charon travels from east to west (backward) around Pluto and is about one-third the size of the planet.

The moons of Uranus, from *Voyager 2*, January 24, 1986 (*photo courtesy of Jet Propulsion Laboratory*)

READING MORE

Simon, Tony. *The Search for Planet X.* New York: Scholastic Book Services, 1969.

Washburn, Mark. *Distant Encounters: The Exploration of Jupiter and Saturn.* New York: Harcourt Brace Jovanovich, 1983.

North American nebula: NGC 2000

Chapter 7 *CHANGING VIEWS OF THE SKY*

Section 1 SPACE AND TIME

The Chinese term **yu-chou** for the universe is similar to the modern idea of space-time. "All time that has passed since antiquity is called *chou;* all space in every direction is called *yu.*"

> From this hour on, space as such and time as such shall recede to the shadows and only a kind of union of the two retain significance. —H. Minkowski (1908)

Measurement of Distance How far away are the stars? The ancients thought the stars occupied the farthermost regions of the celestial sphere, beyond the planets. When you look at stars through the most powerful telescopes they are still too far away to look like anything but points of light. Their distances are truly "astronomical." How can you possibly measure an object that far away?

Parallax Look at something that is as far away as possible, like a distant hill, tree, or building. While looking at this object, quickly blink from one eye to the next. Does the object seem to move from one side to another? Now hold your finger at arm's length in front of the object. Quickly close one eye and then the next. What did your finger do? Try blinking again with your finger closer to you, then closer so your finger is almost touching your nose. How would you describe what you saw each time?

This changing position of your finger in front of a distant object whenever you blink your eyes we call **parallax**. The Sun, Moon, and planets are close enough to the Earth to change their position in front of the much more distant stars. The Greeks observed this change and made allowance for it in their calculations. Aristotle knew that if the Earth moved through space, nearby stars ought to show parallax.

Parallax comes from the Greek word $\pi\alpha\rho\alpha\lambda\lambda\alpha\xi$ (*parallax*) = alternately.

Tycho Brahe also searched for parallax among the stars. Galileo pointed out in 1632 that "by extremely accurate observations of [the fixed stars] there may be discovered those tiny changes that Copernicus took to be impossible to detect."

Copernicus knew that the stars were so far away that you couldn't notice any parallax with your eyes.

Friedrich Wilhelm Bessell (1784–1846) believed that the stars nearer to us would appear to move slightly in front of the more distant background stars if you compared observations made from opposite sides of the Earth's orbit. Your observations would be 186,000,000 miles (297,600,000 km) and 6 months apart. Bessell chose the star 61 Cygni since he figured it was very close to the Earth. He made a series of photographs 6 months apart and found that the star actually showed a change in its position.

That changing position of your finger in front of a distant object when you blink represents a nearby star. Your right eye represents the view from Earth at one phase in its orbit. Your left eye represents the view from Earth 6 months later in its orbit.

The parallaxes of stars are extremely small angles. The nearest star angle, α Centauri, has a parallax of only 0.756 seconds of a degree. This is much smaller than the angle a small coin would make at a distance of 1 mile (1.6 km).

Triangulation   The most direct method for measuring the distance to the stars is the one the Egyptians and Greeks used and the one used to map the city of Paris. (See chapter 3, section 2.) This method requires constructing a triangle from the star to a baseline the width of Earth's orbit around the Sun and then back to the star, similar to the parallax triangle. Can you see how triangulation makes it easy to measure long distances including the stars without having to leave your room?

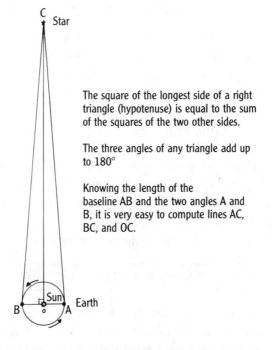

The square of the longest side of a right triangle (hypotenuse) is equal to the sum of the squares of the two other sides.

The three angles of any triangle add up to 180°

Knowing the length of the baseline AB and the two angles A and B, it is very easy to compute lines AC, BC, and OC.

Baseline of 186,000,000 miles (297,600,000 km).

The distances to stars are so great that our ordinary units of miles and kilometers are impractical. The nearest star is 25,000,000,000,000 miles (40,000,000,000,000 km) away. These numbers are difficult to write, remember, and use. Instead, you can use three other ways of measuring:

1. the astronomical unit
2. the light-year
3. the parsec

The Astronomical Unit   This is the distance from the center of the Earth to the center of the Sun—93 million miles (150 million kilometers). The abbreviation for astronomical unit is AU. You use astronomical units when you are measuring a distance within the solar system.

The Light-Year   This is the distance a beam (ray) of light travels in 1 year. One light-year = 6 trillion miles (9.6 trillion kilometers). α Centauri = 4.2 light-years away. You use light-years to measure distances to stars.

The Parsec   This is equal to 19.2 million, million miles (30.7 million, million kilometers) or 206,265 AU. *Parsec* means *par*allax of 1 *sec*ond (1/3,600 of a degree). This is about the angle a coin ¾ inch (18 mm) in diameter would appear to make from a distance of 2.3 miles (3.7 km). You use parsecs to measure extremely large distances. One parsec = 3.26 light-years. For extremely large distances, you use megaparsecs or red-shift.

Sirius is 8.6 light-years away. How far away is Sirius in parsecs? In AUs? In miles? In kilometers?

The Doppler Effect   What would you have to do to your voice to make it sound like a car coming from far away, getting closer, and zooming by? For which direction do you make your voice lower? Higher?

By making the pitch (not the volume) of your voice higher, you made the car sound like it was far away, but getting closer. The sound waves for such a pitch are compressed. The closer together they are, the higher the pitch. The longer the wavelength is, the lower the pitch. As the car approaches you, the distance between you and the car (including its sound waves) is constantly getting shorter. The sound waves become more and more compacted, striking your ear at a faster rate than if the car were not moving. When the car passes you, the distance between you and the car (including its sound waves) is constantly getting longer. The sound waves spread out, striking your ear at a slower rate.

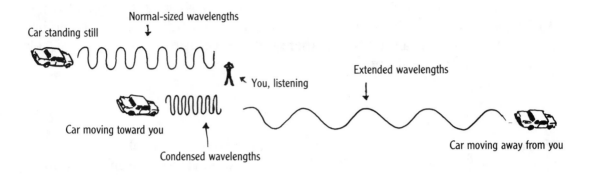

Normal-sized wavelengths

Car standing still

You, listening

Extended wavelengths

Car moving toward you

Condensed wavelengths

Car moving away from you

The Doppler Effect

In 1842 **Christian Doppler** (1803–1853) noticed this effect when listening to trains approaching and passing by. The changing wavelength due to motion is called the **Doppler Effect**. This term also applies to light waves as well as sound waves. Light waves from a moving object shorten as the object moves toward you and lengthen as the object moves away. You can *hear* the sound change, but how can you *see* the light change? To make the light waves visible you look at the spectrum they create. If the object is moving toward you, a given line in the spectrum will condense. This will make the line in the spectrum appear to shift from its normal position to a position closer to the blue end of the spectrum. We call this a **blue-shift**. If the object is moving away from you, a given line in the spectrum will lengthen. This will make the line in the spectrum appear to shift from the normal position to a position closer to the red end of the spectrum. We call this a **red-shift**. If the object is a star, you can tell by looking at its spectrum whether the star is approaching or moving away from you and how fast it is traveling. The amount the wavelength changes on the spectrum depends on how fast the star appears to be traveling, seen from Earth.

The Speed of Light   During a thunderstorm, the sky flashes with a jagged bolt of lightning. Moments later, "Crack!" comes the sound of thunder. What you saw came to your eyes almost the moment it happened. What you heard took longer to arrive. To find out how many miles away a lightning bolt is, you count the seconds after you see it until you hear the thunder. Then multiply by 5. Mach One, the speed of sound, is about .211 miles (0.34 km) per second. The French mathematician **Marin Mersenne** (1588–1648) came close to finding that out in 1640, by timing echoes over a known distance. In 1710 Englishman **William Derham** (1657–1735) refined Mersenne's calculations by comparing the time between the sight and sound of cannons firing 12 miles or 20 kilometers apart.

How did we figure out how fast light travels? In 1638 Galileo suggested having two people stand about a mile away from each other, each holding a covered lantern. As soon as one person uncovered his or her lantern, the other person would immediately uncover theirs. The amount of time it took should be the speed of light, except that Galileo realized that light moved too fast for someone to measure it this way.

In 1676 Ole Romer (1644–1710) from Denmark used the times in between the eclipses of Jupiter's moons to come up with 141,000 miles (226,916 km) per second as the speed that light travels. After centuries of very imaginative experiments, we have clocked the speed of light to 186,290 miles (299,792.458 kilometers) per second. We usually round it off to 186,000 miles per second.

How long does it take light from the Moon to reach us? Earth-Moon distance = 238,857 miles (384,392 kilometers)/186,000 miles (299,000 kilometers) = 1.3 seconds.

How long does it take light from the Sun to reach us? Earth-Sun distance = 93,000,000 miles (150,000,000 km)/186,000 miles (299,792 km) = 500 seconds, and 500/60 = 8.3 minutes. It takes 8.64 years for the light from Sirius to reach us.

Relativity   What would happen, the 16-year-old Einstein wondered, if I could move at the speed of light and catch up with a beam of light? Since we were both traveling at the same speed, when I looked at the beam of light it would seem to be standing still.

Einstein's way of looking at the light beam is something you take for granted. Galileo came up with the idea, about 300 years ago, that all motion depends on its relation to something else. This is the **principle of relativity**, and it all depends on your frame of reference.

In 1905, when he was 26, Einstein published his thoughts on the speed of light in a paper entitled "The Special Theory of Relativity." Eleven years later, he developed his general theory of relativity.

Albert Einstein

When you ride in a car or train next to another car or train moving at the same speed, it looks like you are both standing still, like Einstein's light beam. If one of you goes a little faster or slower, it is hard to tell just from looking whose speed has changed or if one of you is going backward. While all of this motion is going on outside the car, inside all is motionless. You can toss a ball straight up into the air and catch it just as if you were standing still. You have no sense of motion.

The same is true of your experience of the much faster speed of the Earth traveling through space at 18 miles (29 km) per second. You don't feel it. Your hair doesn't blow back in the strong wind created by this motion. Neither do the trees. For these reasons, people long ago found it difficult to accept that the Earth was moving.

There has been research into the possibility of a particle that can travel faster than light. It is called a **tachyon.**

Einstein added time to the three dimensions of length, width, and height. A point of space at a point of time he called a "world-point," and all the possible world-points put together he called the "world." In the relativity theory, every object is a four-dimensional structure traveling along a world-line in the four dimensional world of space-time. We can chart or graph the position in time of anything (a particle or a person) that exists in time. This is called a "world-line."

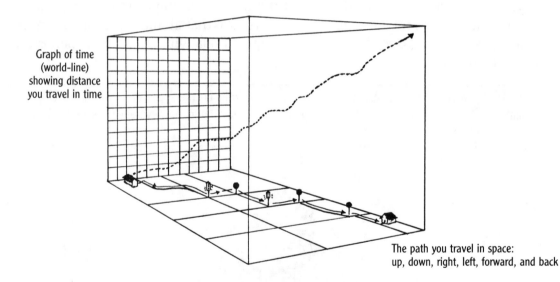

Graph of time (world-line) showing distance you travel in time

The path you travel in space: up, down, right, left, forward, and back

World-line: a journey from your house to a friend's house shown in both space and time

The Twin Paradox Gravity and speed affect time. According to this idea, if you could travel at or near the speed of light, your personal time would be much slower compared to someone who was not moving. When people imagined this possibility they came up with the **twin paradox** or clock paradox that Einstein first suggested in 1905. A paradox is an apparent contradiction, something that should be impossible, yet it seems to be happening. In the twin paradox there are two twins; let's call them Maria and Mark. Maria leaves on an expedition out into space traveling at or near the speed of light. Mark stays at home on Earth. After awhile,

Maria turns around and heads home at the same speed. When the two meet again, they are in for a big surprise.

Each twin's clock and body has recorded the normal passage of time for that person only. The other twin is living in a completely different time frame. By traveling near the speed of light, Maria has slowed down her clock, calendar, and life rate compared to Mark's. According to the Lorentz-FitzGerald contraction formula, at 0.9999995 the speed of light, Maria's clock would be running at 1/1,000 the rate it would have if she were on Earth. The closer you approach the speed of light, the greater the effect on time. Each twin has the impression that he/she is at rest and the other person is moving. In addition, the other person's time seems to be going extraordinarily slowly; 1,000 times slower than normal. Imagine what their voices would sound like when they called each other on the phone. If they checked each other's heartbeats that used to occur once every second, they would have to wait 17 minutes between each one. They would have to wait 4 days in between hourly beeps on their watches.

Now for the surprise after the journey. Maria was in two space-times separated by an acceleration, and Mark was only in one space-time. As far as Maria is concerned, everything in her world was going along at a normal rate. She was gone for 2 weeks, so naturally she will be 2 weeks older when she returns. Since everything in Maria's world was actually happening at 1/1,000 the speed that things were happening to Mark on Earth, Maria will have aged far less compared to her brother. After 2 weeks, Maria will return to Earth 2 weeks older but her brother will be 38 years older!

You can see where the twin paradox leads your imagination. A "normal" voyage to α Centauri would take anywhere from 57,500 to 115,000 years in Earth time depending on your speed. But if the spacecraft traveled at or near the speed of light, the journey would take about 4 years.

> There once was a young lady named Bright
> who traveled much faster than light,
> She started one day
> in the relative way,
> and returned the previous night.

Warped Space-Time   According to relativity physics, an object moves on the straightest possible path along a line following the contours of a surface (geodesics), unless something acts on it. This includes anything that moves in time, including vibrations of light or sound. The strong gravitational field around the Sun should slow down the frequency of light near the Sun, shifting it very slightly toward the red.

Such a slowing down or shift would be due to the light following the contours of the warping or curve of space-time. Einstein predicted that the light traveling from stars near the Sun would follow a curve. He also said that you could detect such a curving by measuring the positions of stars close to the rim of the Sun during a total solar eclipse. In 1919 **Sir Arthur Stanley Eddington (1882–1944)**, the English astronomer, set out for Africa with a group of scientists to observe a total eclipse of the Sun and to look for the predicted deflection of light. Their observations convinced them that such bending did occur. In this next project you can visualize the warping of space-time with a model representing the "fabric of the universe."

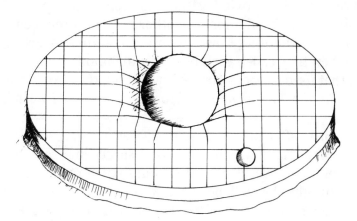

★ ★ ★ ★ ★ **Project 62: Making a Model of Warped Space-Time** ★ ★ ★ ★ ★

MATERIALS

large square piece of rubber cut from a tire tube
white paint
straight edge
large metal ball or an orange
ruler
small paintbrush
marble
embroidery hoop
several books

PROCEDURE

1. Cut out a square piece of rubber from a tire tube.
2. Draw a grid on the piece of rubber using the ruler. Paint the lines white.
3. Stretch the piece of rubber onto the frame of the embroidery hoop.
4. Set some books under the edges of the embroidery hoop.
5. Place the heavy ball in the center of the painted grid.
6. Roll the marble across the piece of rubber to the other side.

OBSERVATIONS

Notice what happens to the lines of the grid as you place the heavy ball in the center. What kind of path does the marble follow as it rolls across the contours of the grid?

Space doesn't actually warp. What changes or bends are our perceptions of the coordinates used to measure space. Your measuring devices for both time and space are always accurate for *you* wherever *you* are. But when you and I are not in the same space-time frame and you look at my measuring devices, you will see them as warped compared to yours.

READING MORE

Apfel, Necia H. *It's All Relative: Einstein's Theory of Relativity.* New York: Lothrup, Lee and Shepard Books, 1981.

Calder, Nigel. *Einstein's Universe.* New York: Penguin Books, 1980.

(*photo courtesy of Observatoire de Haute Provence*)

Section 2   STARS

In the second chapter, you looked at stars from the point of view of their names, what they look like, and where they live. This is as much information as you usually have about people when you first meet them. Later, as you get to know them better, you begin to learn about how they live. In this section, you are going to meet the stars again and see what they tell you about their lives, how they are born, go through infancy, mature, grow old, and eventually die. Most of what we know about the stars we have learned from their light.

Why Do Stars Twinkle?   The light from the stars is relatively constant, but the Earth's atmosphere distorts it, so the whole night sky shimmers. The colors of stars like Arcturus and Sirius seem to pulsate, changing into the colors of the rainbow. To the ancients, the stars were flickering fires from the torches or campfires of the gods.

One theory about the stars is that they really are fires. These fires send their light out into space, which gradually passes through the air in the atmosphere surrounding us on Earth. This air is often in movement, with warm currents rising up to meet cold currents coming down. Layers of air also sweep across the sky filled with tiny particles of dust. When you look at the light coming from a star, what you are seeing is what the light looks like after it has managed to pass through all of the different movements and layers of the atmosphere. The result is that the starlight itself does quite a bit of moving and bouncing around in the process and arrives twinkling instead of in a steady stream of light.

Stars twinkle less the higher they are above the horizon. On the horizon, stars twinkle a lot more. Their light travels through more air, which has the potential to move more. The turbulent air acts like a series of prisms and lenses, refracting the light in small, changing ways until it reaches your eyes. The effect is much like the view you have through the waves of heat rising from a hot pavement.

The Moon and planets do not usually twinkle. The sunlight reflected off the surface of the Moon and the planets comes from a surface that appears larger to us than that of a star. The twinkling and jumping of light is spread out and becomes less noticeable. The result is a clear and steady light.

Olbers' Paradox   If the stars are like Suns and everywhere you look there are billions and billions of stars, why isn't the night sky filled with light? This mystery had puzzled scientists for over 100 years when Heinrich Wilhelm Olbers, who discovered the first asteroid, began working on it in 1823. People soon called this puzzle Olbers' paradox. Like Einstein's twin paradox, Olbers' paradox made sense but it didn't. The answer that seems to explain the situation the best so far has to do with distant galaxies red-shifting to a point in space where their light hasn't reached us yet. This has a dimming effect on the total amount of light reaching the Earth.

Spectral Class   In 1872 Henry Draper (1837–1882) took the first photograph of the spectra of stars. In the 1880s at Harvard College Observatory, astronomer **Edward C. Pickering** (1846–1919) began classifying the spectra of stars. **Annie Jump Cannon** (1863–1941) completed the task with a group of dedicated young women assistants. Together they invented a system of **spectral classes** based on the number and appearance of spectral lines. The classes started with A for the spectra with strong hydrogen lines, then B, C, up to O. When Cannon published the *Henry Draper Catalog* from 1918 to 1924, it contained spectral information on 225,320 stars. This catalog became the basis for all modern astronomical spectroscopy.

Annie Jump Cannon

Spectral Class	Temperature (K)	Color	Stars
O	40,000°	Very blue	Alnitak (ζ Orionis)
B	18,000°	Bluish-white	Spica (α Virginis)
A	10,000°	White	Sirius (α Canis Majoris)
F	7,000°	Yellowish-white	Procyon (α Canis Minoris)
G	5,500°	Yellow	The Sun
K	4,000°	Orange	Arcturus (α Boötis)
M	3,000°	Red	Antares (α Scorpii)

The Birth, Life, and Death of a Star: Stellar Evolution What a star will go through in its life and how long it will live depends on its mass and how much hydrogen and helium it contains. The more massive stars will have shorter lives. Most basic main-sequence stars go through the following stages:

1. Birth
2. Childhood
3. Adolescence
4. Maturity
5. Middle age
6. Old age
7. Death

Birth (Protostar) The assumed starting point for the life of a star is a vast cloud of swirling stardust in space called a **nebula**. (See section 3 in this chapter for more about nebulae.) Nebulae are the nurseries for billions of stars. Right now stars are being born in the Orion Nebula and the Lagoon Nebula.

A nebula contains mainly hydrogen with traces of helium and other natural elements. The temperature in the nebula is just a few degrees above absolute 0. Slight motions within the nebula gather some of the matter together. Particles of dust and gas fall toward this center of condensation. As more matter keeps falling inward, it creates gravitational forces that further pack the matter together until it takes on an enormous mass of billions of tons. This mass is a **protostar,** the "embryo" of a star. Heat and pressure build up as more and more matter is attracted to the protostar. At first, the protostar is too cold to send out any visible light. It might send out radio waves. Then it begins to shine dimly in the dust of the nebula. A star is born.

Childhood (Contraction)   The process of condensing continues within the newborn star. Its own gravitational pull shrinks the star, which changes its potential energy into heat.

Adolescence (Pre-main Sequence)   The heat in the star moves by convection first, then by radiation. (See chapter 6, section 1, for more on convection and radiation.) The star's radiation changes from radio to infrared, so the star is now an **infrared star.** The star contracts from a radius 100 times the radius of the Sun to a radius about 1½ times the radius of the Sun.

The temperature at the star's core rises to about 28 million degrees absolute. The temperature is high enough to start the thermonuclear transformation of hydrogen as well as deuterium, lithium, beryllium, and boron into helium and carbon into nitrogen. This is **nuclear fusion,** and it is how stars "burn." The nuclear energy in a star comes from its mass, according to Einstein's formula $E = mc^2$.

Maturity (Main Sequence)   You can now see the star shining. Gravitational contraction has stopped and now the proton-proton chain of thermonuclear reactions provides the star's energy. In this reaction, four protons fuse into a helium nucleus, releasing energy. The star's temperature is about 10 million degrees. Stars spend most of their lives as mature stars. The Sun is a mature star.

Middle Age (Red Giant)   To produce energy, stars either use hydrogen for fuel or else they go back to their childhood habit of depending on gravity. During middle age, some stars rely on gravity to produce energy when their supply of hydrogen runs out. This increased pressure at the core makes it get hotter. The carbon-nitrogen cycle thermonuclear reaction begins when three hydrogen atoms yield one helium atom. The combination of gravity acting on the helium core and thermonuclear reactions on the hydrogen-burning surface causes the outer layers of the star to swell up to several times their original diameter, forming an outer shell.

Since the shell is so far from the core, which is the source of heat, the temperature of the shell drops. The star becomes cooler and glows as a **red giant** or a **red supergiant**, depending on the mass of the star. Aldebaran, Betelgeuse, and Antares are red giants.

Old Age (Variables)   While the star is expanding and its helium core is contracting, the temperature at the core continues to rise. When the core's temperature reaches a certain level, its helium fuses into carbon. The star again begins to rely on gravity for its energy and starts contracting. The gases of the star compress so tightly that the star begins to resemble a solid. As this process continues, the star will start to become unstable and will pulsate. Those few stars that establish a temporary, stable, pulsating (oscillating) system are the Cepheid variables and RR Lyrae–type giant stars.

Death

White Dwarf and Black Dwarf   The fate of a star depends on its mass. If the mass of the star is less than 1.4 times the mass of the Sun, the star will become a **white** or a **black dwarf**. Most stars become white dwarfs. When the star is out of fuel, it shrinks to 1/100 its original diameter. It is now about the size of a planet. At this size, since brightness depends on the size of the star's surface and temperature, whatever brightness the star may have is lost to sight. The star is white hot. Because of its color and size, we call it a **white dwarf. W. S. Adams** in 1915 determined that Sirius B, the star orbiting Sirius that Friedrich Bessell studied in 1844 and that **Alvin Clark** had detected with his telescope in 1862, was a previously unknown type of star. It was a white dwarf, the first one to be discovered. Procyon in Canis Minor also has a white dwarf companion.

The helium at the core of a white dwarf has already changed to carbon in an earlier stage. The star has run out of energy sources: no hydrogen and no gravity. The negatively charged particles are not able to supply any energy. Energy provided by the positively charged nuclei produces heat and light for awhile. When they can no longer be an energy source no light comes from the star. It is then a **black dwarf.** You can't see it. The only way you will know that the star is there is by noticing its gravitational pull on other stars.

Some white dwarfs are actually yellow. We call them white dwarfs because the first one discovered (Sirius B) was white. Rigel (in Orion) also has a nice white dwarf companion that you can see with a 6-inch telescope.

Nova   If the mass of the star is slightly more than 1.4 times the mass of the Sun, its internal pressure drops and the star can no longer support its own weight. The star will explode so it can shed a part of its mass and become a **nova.** It may have to go through this process several times.

The word *nova* in Latin means "new." To Brahe and Kepler this was a good word to describe their situation when they looked up at a sky they knew very well and found a star that wasn't there the night before! Actually, the star had been there, only they couldn't see it. The star had generated more energy than its surface could radiate into space. To get rid of the excess energy, the star "let off steam" and cast off its thin outer shell with an explosion. Such an explosion is also necessary for some stars to lose excess mass before entering the white dwarf stage. What Brahe and Kepler saw was the moment of explosion. Star explosions are extremely powerful. Most novae only have to explode like this once. Then they calm down into the condition they were in before. Some explode again. After most of the star has been blown away, what is left is the very hot, dense core of a **white dwarf.**

The Crab Nebula

Supernova   If the mass of the star is far more than 1.4 times the mass of the Sun, it will explode violently and shed most of its mass as a **supernova.** A supernova, as you might guess from the name, is the most powerful of all stellar explosions. Supernovae can reach an absolute magnitude as high as -20, radiating as much energy in 1 year as the Sun does in a billion.

Supernovae are as rare as they are mighty. People have recorded only three in our galaxy. The first appeared in 1054. The Chinese and Japanese reported it, naming it the "guest star." On July 4, 1054, Chinese records describe the supernova this way: "It was visible by day, like Venus; pointed rays shot out from it on all sides; the color was reddish white. Altogether it was visible for 23 days." The native North Americans in Zuni, New Mexico, recorded what we believe to be an image of this event. Arab astronomers noted it. So far, we have found no contemporary European record of this supernova. The supernova of 1054 today is the Crab Nebula.

The second supernova appeared in 1572 in the constellation Cassiopeia. This was the bright "new star" Tycho Brahe saw. It was possible to see this supernova for two years. Tycho Brahe described his encounter with the supernova of 1572 like this:

> One evening, when, as usual, I was contemplating the heavenly dome whose face was so familiar to me, I saw with inexpressible astonishment . . . a radiant star of extraordinary magnitude. Struck with surprise, I could hardly believe my eyes. . . . Its brightness was greater than that of Sirius, and Jupiter. It could only be compared with that of Venus. People gifted with good eyesight could see this star in daylight, even at noon.

The third and last supernova seen in our galaxy appeared in 1604 in the constellation Ophiuchus. Kepler studied this one.

A supernova is the death cry of a very massive star that has run out of its main sources of fuel. It expands to 100 million times its size. Being too massive to collapse smoothly into the white dwarf stage, its pent-up energy bursts forth in an explosion that sends most of the star out into space. What is left is a highly dense core with a mass greater than the Sun compressed into an area the size of an asteroid. The supernova explosion results in the loss of 50% of the supernova's mass. What remains is either a **neutron star** or **black hole.**

Neutron Star   As the star continues to lose energy into space, it burns slower. After a while this type of star will lose all its energy (like the white dwarf) and will move through space (like a black dwarf) with no light and only a gravitational field around it to let you know it is there. A neutron star can be a compact ball of subatomic particles (neutrons) left as a core of a supernova explosion. Having no charge, these particles don't repel each other and can be tightly packed together. A neutron star four times as big as the Sun can shrink to 6 miles (10 km) in diameter. They can rotate 30 times a second on their axis. A rotating neutron star that pulses in the radio spectrum is a **pulsar.** (See section 3 of this chapter for more about pulsars.)

Black Hole   Depending on how far a particle is from the center of a gravitational field, the least speed (velocity) it can have at that place for it to be able to move away is called the **velocity of escape.** You would use the velocity of escape to figure out how much thrust a rocket or spacecraft would need to leave the surface of a planet by escaping its gravitational field.

In a star that has a gravitational field, there is a point where the velocity of escape is the speed of light. Since no known material particle can go this fast, this point forms a barrier, trapping all matter (including light) from escaping. This barrier point is the **Schwartzchild radius,** named after **Karl Schwartzchild (1873–1916),** who described it a few years after Einstein introduced general relativity. Already in 1796, **Pierre Simon, Marquis de Laplace (1749–1827)** had thought about what it would be like if there was an object with such a strong gravitational field that it would take more than the speed of light in order to escape. In such a place, since light couldn't escape, it would be bent back into itself and head back toward the object instead of away from it. From a distance, you would not see the object. Its body would be hidden. For this reason, Laplace called such objects **corps obscurs** (hidden bodies). **John A. Wheeler,** a physicist at Princeton, came up with the same conclusion years later and named these objects "black holes."

Another name that people suggested for a black hole was **collapsar.**

In the words of one astronomer, a black hole is matter that dug a hole, jumped in, and pulled the hole in afterward. A black hole is no longer a star.

The size of the Schwartzchild radius is proportional to the mass of the star. For a star the mass of the Sun, the black hole would have a radius of about 1.86 miles (3 km) or a diameter of 3.73 miles (6 km), which is one-third the size of a solar-mass neutron star.

Are there any black holes? If there are and you can't see them how would you find them? What is left behind that can tell you that they are there is the star's gravitational field. This field will have an effect on other stars nearby. The stars nearest to each other are those in a binary system. If one of the stars is invisible, has a mass too high to be a white dwarf or a neutron star, and is a collapsed object of extremely small size, it could be a black hole. Matter falling into the region of the Schwartzchild radius will be traveling at an incredible speed and therefore will be generating very high temperatures (up to 100 million°K or more). Such hot matter emits radiation in the form of X rays, which you can detect with X-ray telescopes on Earth or from satellites in space.

In the inner part of the accretion disk, the matter attracted or gas blown by solar wind is revolving around the black hole so fast that internal friction heats it up to the temperature where it emits X rays. This may be what is happening to the Cygnus binary system. Cygnus X-1 is an invisible X-ray star with a mass nearing 10 times that of the Sun. If it were a small, collapsed object, this star could be a black hole. If it is, the strong X-ray activity could be due to gas heated by spiraling into the black hole.

In this next project you can get an idea of what happens to the material in a star next to a black hole by making a model of a black hole.

Table

Embroidery hoop

Black handkerchief
with salt or sugar granules

Star

Black Hole

Vacuum cleaner hose

★ ★ ★ ★ ★ ★ ★ **Project 63: Making a Model of a Black Hole** ★ ★ ★ ★ ★ ★ ★

MATERIALS

embroidery hoop (or wooden frame) table
black handkerchief or part of a sheet vacuum cleaner
salt or sugar

PROCEDURE

1. Stretch the handkerchief tightly over an embroidery hoop or a wood frame.

2. Sprinkle about one teaspoon of salt or sugar (the *star*) onto the handkerchief.

3. Rest part of the hoop on the edge of a table. Hold the vacuum cleaner hose (*the black hole*) in one hand under the hoop a few inches away from the salt or sugar. Turn on the vacuum cleaner. Make a small space between the vacuum cleaner hose and the handkerchief with your finger and thumb so that the star begins to vibrate and move toward the black hole.

OBSERVATIONS

Notice how the black hole concentrates the escaping portions of the orbiting star's atmosphere. Notice the trail left as these particles are drawn into the black hole. This is also what happens in periodic novas in binary systems. Hydrogen or helium is pulled away from the red giant companion and falls onto the small dense star and "ignites."

The Hertzsprung-Russell Diagram   In the early 1900s, two astronomers, each working alone, drew up a chart on which they could plot the life history of a star. In 1911 the Danish astronomer **Ejnar Hertzsprung (1873–1967)** compared colors and luminosity, and in 1913 the American astronomer **Henry Norris Russell (1877–1957)** compared absolute magnitude and spectral classes. Independently, they came up with the chart's design. Therefore, we call the chart by both of their names, the Hertzsprung-Russell, or the **H-R diagram**.

In the H-R diagram you indicate each star with a dot. The star's luminosity and spectral class determines where the dot will appear on the chart. Dots of neighboring stars show up at various places on the diagram. These places have nothing to do with where the stars are in the sky. What they show are stages in the life cycle of a star. Whatever stars are in this particular stage of their life will show up on the H-R diagram in the section for that stage. In this next project you can plot a number of stars in the H-R diagram yourself to see how it works.

Absolute Temperature (°K)

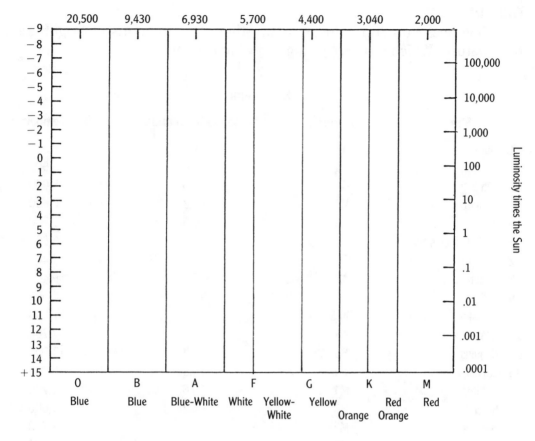

Spectral type

★ ★ ★ ★ ★ ★ ★ Project 64: Plotting the Life Cycles of Stars ★ ★ ★ ★ ★ ★ ★
(H-R Diagram)

MATERIALS
graph   pencil
table of stars   access to photocopier
colored pencils

PROCEDURE
1. Photocopy the graph above.
2. Lightly shade in the colors mentioned in the graph with colored pencils.

3. Plot each star from the table onto the graph by making a dot and writing the name of the star next to it.

OBSERVATIONS

How does our Sun compare with other stars in terms of brightness and temperature? Which stars are young and which are old?

H-R Diagram

Star	Spectrum	Absolute Magnitude	Surface Temperature
1. Sirius	A1	1.4	9,500
2. Procyon	F5	2.8	6,500
3. Sun	G2	5.0	5,000
4. Barnard's Star	M5	13.2	2,600
5. Vega	A0	0.5	9,700
6. Van Maanen's Star	F0	14.2	5,800
7. Canopus	F0	−4.6	6,400
8. Deneb	A2	−7.1	9,400
9. Pollux	K0	1.0	4,100
10. Mintaka	O9.5	−5.1	21,000
11. Altair	A5	2.4	7,700
12. Regulus	B8	−0.7	13,000
13. Luyten 745-6	F0	14.3	5,900
14. Antares	M1	−3.0	2,700
15. Rigel	B8	−6.2	11,000
16. Betelgeuse	M2	−5.6	2,700
17. Aldebaran	K5	−0.5	3,500
18. Capella	G0	−0.5	5,000
19. Arcturus	K1	−0.0	3,900
20. Spica	B1.5	−2.2	19,500
21. Acrux	B1	−2.7	19,000
22. Fomalhaut	A3	2.1	8,900
23. Rigel Kentaurus	G0	−0.5	5,800
24. Wolf 424 A	M6	14.4	2,500
25. Alnitak	O9.5	−5.9	23,000

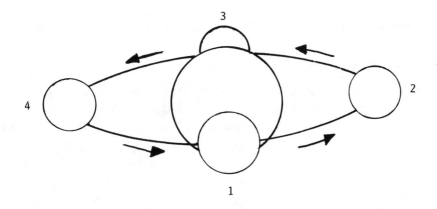

A binary star system with one star orbiting around another

Binaries   In 1650 **John Baptist Riccioli** (1598–1671) accidentally discovered that the star Mizar in the handle of the Big Dipper was part of a **two-star system,** where one star revolves around another like a planet around the Sun. Up until then people assumed two stars near each other only looked that way from our viewpoint on the Earth. They were most likely one far behind the other, the farther one therefore appearing dimmer. William Herschel thought such stars were good examples to measure for the parallax between the two. He published three catalogs listing more than 800 "double stars." He was amazed to find out that most of these were actually two stars revolving around each other. Herschel's son, John, continued his father's search for multiple stars from his observatory in South Africa. His search located 1,202 double and multiple stars, mostly in the Southern Hemisphere. Another famous father and son team, **Friedrich Georg Wilhelm Von Struve** (1793–1864) and **Otto Wilhelm Von Struve** (1819–1905), working at their observatory near Leningrad, cataloged 3,110 double stars from the Northern Hemisphere.

It's likely that at least one star in 20 among the brighter stars is a **visual binary star,** the name given to two-star systems. This is how the path of a star around another in a binary star system looks. The star with the greater mass becomes the focus of an ellipse which the star with the smaller mass travels.

Sometimes when the traveling star is behind the stationary one, you can't see it from the Earth. The larger star eclipses it. In a lesser way, the traveling star can partially block the stationary one. The change from eclipsing to being visible also changes how bright the stars appear to us.

Variable Stars   Over 18,000 stars have brightnesses and spectral characteristics that change over time. They do this either by expanding and contracting regularly or exploding part of their mass into space. Observers of these pulsating and exploding variable stars have used information from these stars and made important discoveries about the nature of stars in general. There are several groups of variable stars:

The Pulsating Stars: Cepheids I, Cepheids II, RR-Lyraevariables, long-period variables

The Exploding Stars: Novae and Supernovae.

Cepheid Variables   These get their name from the star δ Cephei. The other Cepheid variables come from different constellations. Polaris, for example, is a Cepheid variable. These stars have a moment of maximum light and a moment of minimum light. The time between two maximum or two minimum moments is called the **period**. Cepheid variables have periods of from 1 to 50 days. In 1784 a 19-year-old deaf English astronomer, **John Goodricke (1764–1786)**, discovered that a particular Cepheid varies from magnitude 4.4 to 3.7 with a period of 5.4 days.

In 1912 **Henrietta Swan Leavitt (1868–1921)**, while working at the Harvard College Observatory, discovered a remarkable relationship between the periods of Cepheid variables and their absolute magnitudes. When she plotted the periods of the Cepheids in the Small Magellenic Clouds of the Southern Hemisphere with their magnitudes, she found that when the periods of the Cepheids increase, their apparent magnitudes also increase. Those with the same periods have the same absolute magnitude.

Henrietta Swan Leavitt

Since we know how to find distance by using the inverse square law, we can find the distance to a star or to any groups of stars the star happens to be in. Suppose you find that a certain Cepheid has a period of 10 days. Then you would find the apparent magnitude of the star. You would calculate the absolute magnitude. Take the apparent magnitude and subtract it from the absolute magnitude. This gives you the loss in light intensity. You can then convert this information into the distance of the star.

In this way you can actually determine the **period** (the time between the two brightest or two dimmest dates) and **luminosity** (amount of light) of a Cepheid variable from your observations.

READING MORE
Branley, Franklyn M. *Black Holes, White Dwarfs and Superstars.* New York: Thomas Y. Crowell, 1976.
Degani, Meir H. *Astronomy Made Simple.* New York: Doubleday, 1976.
Kaufmann, William J., III. *Black Holes and Warped Spacetime.* San Francisco: W. H. Freeman, 1979.

Two galaxies, M81 and M82 (*photo courtesy of Observatoire de Haute Provence*)

Section 3   THE GALAXY

Galaxies are vast collections of billions of stars, gas, and dust held together by gravity. They act as separate "island universes" or independent systems of stars.

The Milky Way Galaxy contains our entire solar system, which is only a very tiny part of the "island universe." Other nonstellar members of our Galaxy include comets, meteoroids, nebulae, quasars, pulsars, and cosmic rays.

Comets   In 1950 astronomer **Fred Whipple** described comets as "dirty snowballs." Most people believe comets to be a mixture of ice and dust frozen out of the solar mix of gas (hydrogen, oxygen, and nitrogen becoming frozen methane, ammonia, and water)—the same material that we theorize makes up Uranus and Neptune. Comets remain frozen while their orbit keeps them in the outer solar system past the trans-Saturnian planets. The Chinese called comets and novae guest stars.

Comet comes from the Greek word κομητης (*kometes*) = long haired, from κομη (*kome*) = hair, which is *coma* in Latin.

Composition

Head   The *nucleus* is the bright center of a comet made mostly of ice—bright because it reflects sunlight. It is about ½ to 6 miles (1–10 km) in diameter.

The *coma* is made of gas and dust and reflects sunlight. Gas glows from absorbing radiation and ultraviolet rays from the Sun. The coma often has an enormous size, sometimes extending 62,140 miles (100,000 km) or more. Every time a comet passes the Sun and forms a coma, it loses part of its material. The coma shrinks as it forms the tail. After passing close by the Sun nearly a thousand times, the coma uses itself up.

Tails   Tails develop only when a comet approaches the Sun, if at all. The tails face away from the Sun. Chinese comet observers noticed this first. The tail is made from material ejected from the nucleus and pushed away by solar radiation and solar wind. Most comets have two tails. One is nearly straight and is made of ionized particles. The other is curved and made mostly of dust. As a comet approaches the Sun, its tails get longer. Ion tails can be as long as 190 million miles (300 million kilometers).

In 1744, when he was 14, **Charles Messier** (1730–1817) observed a brilliant comet. From that day on, comets became the focus of his whole life. He drew up a catalog of objects that at first may seem to be comets but were really star clusters and nebulae. His list was an effort to help him find more comets. Today, astronomers still use the **Messier Catalog** for this and other purposes. There is a copy of Messier's Catalog in Sky Files. Messier saw Comet Halley within a month after it had been first seen in its 1758 apparition.

Comet Abe

Origin   Most astronomers think that comets come from a nonvisible cloud of orbiting comets and meteors surrounding the solar system at about 150,000 AU from the Sun. This idea came from **Ernst Opik** in 1932, and in 1952 the Dutch astronomer **Jan Oort** refined it. Gravity from stars passing within a few light-years of the Sun and in between the **Oort Cloud** forces millions of comets out of the cloud. Since bodies in space affect each other's orbits at times, this interaction of gravity fields can cause a change in direction and speed. This produces an object that visits the inner solar system. Some comets head out beyond the solar system. Others change their orbits but remain within the cloud. Still other comets stop their motion and, lacking the momentum of their own orbit, fall toward the Sun in a new, slow orbit through the solar system. The planets (especially Jupiter) and the Sun exert pulls and deflections on the comets that further shape their orbits. These orbits are so large that you can only see a comet for the short time when it travels near the Sun. The rest of its orbit is beyond the range of our visibility. The time between when you can see the comet again would be so long that you might think you were seeing a new comet instead of the return of an old one.

In the next project you can make a model of a comet.

331

★ ★ ★ ★ ★ ★ ★ ★ **Project 65: Making a Model of a Comet*** ★ ★ ★ ★ ★ ★ ★ ★

MATERIALS

cotton balls   glue
crepe paper (two colors)   paint (two colors)
tape

PROCEDURE

1. Using glue to stick the cotton balls together, make a ball the size of a softball (4 in. or 10 cm in diameter).

2. Paint the nucleus and coma two different colors. The nucleus is a tiny dot compared to the coma.

3. Cut each color of crepe paper into long strips (about 25 feet [8 m]).

4. Tape or glue one end of each of the crepe paper strips to the cotton balls.

5. Tape the entire comet to the wall with one tail nearly straight and one at a slight angle. Both tails should spread out at the ends.

OBSERVATIONS

Your comet is a scale model: 1 inch = 75,000 miles (1 cm = 50,000 km). How does the head of the comet compare in size to the tail? On which side of your comet would the Sun be?

The first person to discover a comet that you could only see through a telescope was the American astronomer **Maria Mitchell** (1818–1889). In 1848 she won a medal from the King of Denmark for her discovery and the honor of having the comet named after her. Inscribed on the medal in Latin were the words "Not in vain do we watch the setting and rising of the stars." **Caroline Herschel** (1750–1848) was the first woman to discover a comet, in 1786. Over the years, she discovered seven more. The most recent comet discoveries by a woman are being made by **Carolyn Shoemaker,** who has discovered over 13 comets so far.

---

*This project is adapted from a project developed by Dennis Schatz of the Pacific Science Center. Used with permission.

Maria Mitchell

Caroline Herschel

"Shooting Stars"   Have you ever been outside at night looking at the stars when suddenly a thin line of light darts across the sky then disappears as quickly as it came? It's a delightful surprise to see these "shooting" or "falling" stars. What you're seeing is a **meteor**, not a star. We have found out what meteors are by finding them when they fall to the ground. On the ground we call them **meteorites**. Before they appear in our atmosphere as streaks of light, they travel through space as meteoroids.

Meteor comes from the Greek word μετα (*meta*) = beyond and ἀειρω (*aeiro*) = raise, or any thing raised beyond the atmosphere.
The study of watery meteors (rain, hail, snow, etc.) = **meteorology.**

Meteoroids   A meteoroid is a rocky scrap of rubble, smaller than an asteroid, moving through space in orbit around the Sun. It can weigh as little as a grain of sand or as much as several tons. In 1866 G. V. Schiaparelli and **Hubert Anderson Newton (1830–1896)** discovered that the Perseid meteor shower occurred whenever the Earth crossed the orbit of Comet 1862 III (now known as Swift-Tuttle). Checking other meteor showers and comet paths, people came to the conclusion that meteoroids must be small particles of rubble scattered from the wreckage of comets and asteroids. Meteoroids travel in their own orbits.

Meteors   The Earth regularly journeys through areas thick with orbiting meteoroids. Meteoroids that don't pass through the Earth's atmosphere skim across it, burning up in the friction. They light up their paths like sparks from a firework before they disappear. You can see this as a streak of light that lasts for a few seconds. These brief sparks of light are meteors. They collide and burn up in Earth's upper atmosphere so regularly that people have named and dated their "showers." The names of the showers are the constellations from which the showers seem to be coming. The best time to observe meteors is 6:00 A.M., but there is too much sunlight then; 4:00 A.M. is the second best time but the least practical for most of us. Any time after midnight is fine since the side of the Earth we are on after midnight is moving away from the meteoroids. Since it takes the meteoroids longer to catch up with us, they take longer to burn up and we can see them for a longer time.

Meteor Showers Chart

Name of Showers (Constellation from Which Showers Appear to Come)	Number of Days Shower Occurs	Day of Peak Activity	Related Comet	Meteors per Hour
Quadrantids* (Quadrant)	4	January 3	No Known Parent Comet	28–80
Lyrids (Lyra)	4	April 21	Thatcher 18 GY I	7–15
Eta Aquarids (Aquarius)	8	May 4	Halley	7–35
Delta-Aquarids (Aquarius)	3	July 30	No Known Parent Comet	27
Perseids (Perseus)	25	August 11	Swift-Tuttle	50–75
Draconids (Draco)	1	October 9	Giacobini-Zinner	10
Orionids (Orion)	14	October 20	Halley	21
Taurids (Taurus)	10	October 31	Encke	?
Andromedids (Andromeda)	2	November 14	Biela	10
Leonids (Leo)	7	November 16	Temple-Tuttle	21
Geminids (Gemini)	14	December 13	3200 Phaeton Asteroid	60

*This meteor shower occurs in what was once the old constellation Quadrans Muralis (the Mural Quadrant formed by LeLande in 1795). This constellation is no longer recognized. It is now between the right foot of Hercules, the left hand of Boötes, and the constellation Draco.

Seeing a meteor shower is an exciting event that most of us "just happen" to see. In the next project you can plan ahead so you can observe and record one or many meteor showers.

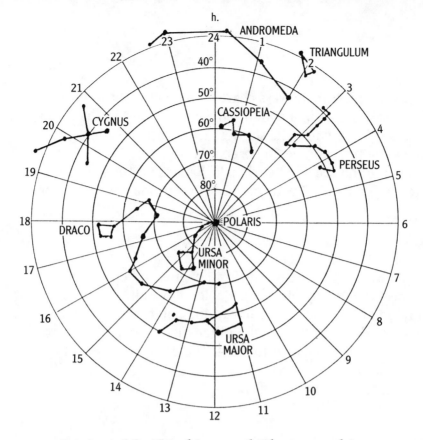

★ ★ ★ ★ ★ ★ ★ ★ **Project 66: Tracking and Photographing** ★ ★ ★ ★ ★ ★ ★ ★
a Meteor Shower

PART 1
MATERIALS

meteor showers chart
watch
flashlight covered with paper bag
pencil and paper

clipboard (use the one from
    Project 55)
warm clothes
chair

PART 2
MATERIALS

star chart (from Sky Files)
colored pencils

access to a photocopier

PART 3
MATERIALS

red felt-tip pen or colored pencil
camera (use fast lens f/2.8 or better)
tripod

film: Tri-X (ASA 400) or 2475
    Recording Film (ASA 1,000) or
    Kodak VR1000 or Fuji ASA 1600/
    3200 or Kodak T-Max 3200

PART 1
PROCEDURE
1. Check the meteor showers chart for a good night to observe.
2. Dress warmly; sit in a comfortable chair facing in the general direction of the constellation from which the showers will appear to come.
3. Check the time you begin observing.
4. Whenever you see a meteor, make a mark on the paper.
5. After an hour, count your marks to determine how many meteors you saw.

PART 2
PROCEDURE
1. Photocopy the star chart.
2. Locate where the first meteor trail begins and ends.
3. Connect the two points using a colored pencil.
4. Draw an arrowhead on the line at the point where it ends.
5. Draw similar lines for all the other meteor tails. The arrowheads should show the direction the meteor is moving. The point at which all the trails seem to begin is the *radiant*.
6. Mark the radiant with a red *R*.

PART 3
PROCEDURE
1. Set your camera up on the tripod on a night when you know a particular meteor shower is expected and the sky is dark.
2. Aim the camera about 50° above the horizon and 45° from the radiant.
3. Expose the film for 10 to 20 minutes at a setting one stop smaller than wide open.
4. Develop and print the film.
5. Draw arrowheads on the meteor trails to indicate the direction they are moving.
6. Mark the radiant as in Part 2, using a red felt-tip pen.

OBSERVATIONS
Can you tell from which constellation the shower is coming? How many meteors did you see per hour?

Barringer Meteorite Crater, Arizona, U.S.A. (*photo courtesy of NASA*)

Meteorites   The Earth's atmosphere prevents most meteoroids from reaching our planet's surface. Those that actually survive their passage through the Earth's atmosphere and fall to the ground are meteorites. The large one that fell in Arizona about 15,000 to 40,000 years ago left a crater 4,150 feet (1,265 m) across and 560 feet (170 m) deep. You can also see spectacular cratering on Mercury and the Moon.

Not all meteorites make craters. Most don't. Instead they become part of the mixture of sand and soil on Earth's mantle adding about four million tons of matter to the Earth each year. The largest meteorite ever found is in Nambia, Africa. It weighs about 60 tons and is about 4.2 cubic feet (.1189 cu m) in volume. Some meteorites are heavy since they are about 85% to 95% iron and the rest mainly nickel. Most meteorites, however, have more silicate and stone and only 10% to 15% iron and nickel.

About 100 tons of meteorite dust falls into Earth's atmosphere each day. There are enough flakes of iron and nickel in even the tiniest meteorite for you to be able to pick them up by brushing a magnet across the ground. Of the particles you collect, about 20% will be meteorite particles.

The Radio Sky

Quasars   In 1960 two radio astronomers, **Allan Sandage** and **Thomas Matthews**, were hoping to see what they had only been able to detect as radio source 3C 48 (which means that in the 3rd Cambridge Catalogue of Radio Sources, this is the 48th object in the list). So far the only objects people had found in both the visible and the radio sky had been the Sun, Jupiter, and objects the size of a galaxy.

Sandage and Matthews aimed the 200-inch Polamar telescope in the direction of 3C 48. What they found on the photographic plates from the telescope was a pale, bluish "star." Optical and radio astronomers working together found other photographic images of faint, blue starlike objects that gave off radio signals. These objects were clearly not stars. They were almost like stars so optical astronomers began calling them "quasi-stellar objects." Radioastronomers preferred the name "quasi-stellar radio sources." In 1964 **Hong-Yee Chiu** of Columbia University invented the word *quasar* for *quasi-star,* which is the name people use today.

Quasi comes from the Latin word *quasi* = as if.

Quasars show considerable red shift in their spectra. Today, astronomers estimate that 25% of all radio sources in the sky are quasars. We have found over 1,500 of them, which we have named, photographed, and studied. We still wonder exactly what they are, where this energy comes from, and how far away they are. Could quasars come from supernovae? From collisions? From our galaxy or other galaxies? From black holes? These are a few of the ideas astronomers are looking into, including the possibility that quasars follow physical laws that we haven't discovered yet. As British-born astrophysicist **Geoffrey Burbridge** once said, "We're egomaniacs to say that we know all there is to know about physics."

Quasar 3C 273

Horrid quasar, Near or far, This truth to you I must confess:
My heart for you is full of hate.
O superstar, Imploded gas, You glowing speck upon a plate,
Of Einstein's world you've made a mess!
　　　　　—written by Jesse Greenstein on blackboards
　　　　　at the California Institute of Technology

Pulsars In the summer of 1967, **Jocelyn Bell Burnell**, a graduate student from Northern Ireland studying at Cambridge University, was studying surveys of radio sources in the constellation Vulpecula. The weekly surveys appeared on 400 feet (122 m) of paper charts. Burnell's charts kept showing that her radio telescopes were picking up regular pulses of stray radio interference. The pulses came every night at a regular rate of about $1/30$ of a second every 1.33728 seconds. Radio astronomers pinpointed the source as coming from a fixed point in space well beyond the solar system that rose and set with the stars. Whatever was causing the signals had an accuracy equaling some of the best clocks on Earth. Could they be signals from intelligent beings on another planet? For a few weeks, radio astronomers even called the pulsating source LGM (*l*ittle *g*reen *m*en). After more sources turned up, it became clear that these sources weren't sending messages. Their new name became **pulsars** (*pulsa*ting *r*adio *s*ources).

A **pulsar** doesn't really pulse. It is only the impression you have of its radiation when you see it from the Earth. By calling it a pulsar, you are describing the object by what you see, by what *appears* to be happening rather than what may actually be happening. This is similar to describing the stars as part of a moving celestial sphere and the Sun as rising and setting.

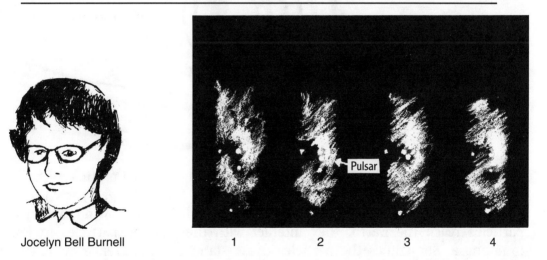

Jocelyn Bell Burnell   1   2   3   4

What are pulsars? One theory states that pulsars are rotating neutron stars, formed in supernovae explosions. This theory came about in the 1930s from **Walter Baade** (1893–1960) and **Fritz Zwicky** (1898–1974), the codiscoverers of supernovae. The British astronomer Thomas Gold (who worked with Fred Hoyle on the steady state theory) further developed the ideas of Baade and Zwicky. The pulsar found in the heart of the Crab Nebula, the remains of a supernova, helped prove the neutron star theory. The force of a supernova explosion would cause the core of the dying star to cave in, driving the charged particles into the nucleus to combine with the other charged particles. The result would be a tiny, densely packed clump of neutrons: a neutron star that spun very fast, throwing off charged particles that leaked from the star's surface. These particles would eventually send out beams of radiation from the magnetic poles of the star. When one of the poles faces the Earth, we detect the radiation as a radio pulse just as we see the steady light on top of a police car as a flashing light.

Radio astronomers have found over 150 pulsars.

Cosmic Rays   You cannot see the charged particles we call **cosmic rays**, which come from the cosmos. They are usually harmless. But once every several years, charged particles from the Sun during a solar flare arrive on Earth in such large concentrations as to cause considerable damage to the structure of living cells. On the Earth our atmosphere protects us and the magnetic field surrounding the Earth deflects and absorbs lethal particles.

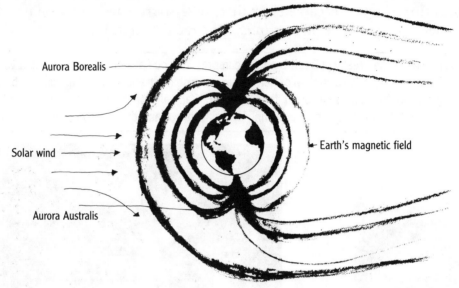

The Solar Wind   The Sun is constantly emitting charged particles. The Sun's corona which stretches far out into space carries these charged particles to the Earth and possibly as far as Pluto in what we call the **solar wind**. When these particles reach the Earth, they interact with the charged particles in Earth's ionosphere. Sometimes the particles cause static or interference on television, radio, and telephone services. At other times they are changed into light energy and glow about 60 miles (km) above the horizon as pale rose or green bands known as auroras. Auroras occur most frequently near the magnetic north and south poles of the Earth and we call them the **Aurora Borealis** (Northern Lights), or the **Aurora Australis** (Southern Lights). The effects of the solar wind are particularly strong during sunspot activity and about 20–30 hours after intense solar flares.

Aurora is the Latin Word for "dawn." **Borealis** is the Latin word for "north," and **australis** is the Latin word for "south."

In this next project you can notice the effects of charged particles.

★ ★ ★ ★ ★ ★ ★ ★ Project 67: Observing Charged Particles ★ ★ ★ ★ ★ ★ ★ ★ ★

MATERIALS
    television or radio
    fluorescent lamp

PROCEDURE
1. Notice what happens to your television or radio during sunspot activity or solar flares.

2. Look for auroras in the early evening especially from September through October and March through April. If you live between 50°N latitude and the North Pole or between 50°S latitude and the South Pole, you should be able to see auroras almost 240 nights of the year.

3. Watch what goes on inside a fluorescent lamp when you turn it on.

OBSERVATIONS
The inside of a fluorescent lightbulb is coated with light-emitting substances. These substances are also used to make numbers on watches glow in the dark. The tube is filled with mercury vapor. When electricity goes through the mercury vapor, the vapor produces ultra violet light, which is invisible. Just as in the case with the Sun's charged particles striking the Earth's ionosphere, when the charged particles of ultra violet light strike the fluorescent substances in the lightbulb, energy is released in streams of visible light.

Nebulae   In space, like on Earth, there are clouds. The clouds of cosmic gas and dust among the stars are **nebulae**, and they come in four forms: **emission**, **reflection**, **dark**, and **planetary**.

Emission   The **Orion Nebula** is an example of this kind of nebula where the ultraviolet light from the stars in it excites the hydrogen and oxygen present, causing the nebula to "light up."

Reflection   The wispy clouds around the **Pleiades** are an example of a reflection nebula. The cloud itself is not emitting light, but it is reflecting light from the stars in it.

Dark   The **Horsehead Nebula** in Orion is a wonderful example of a dark nebula that, containing no light, can be seen in front of an illuminated nebula behind it. (See section 2 of this chapter for more information about nebulae.)

Planetary   The Ring Nebula looks like a doughnut-shaped circle in the sky. It contains glowing layers of gases that expand in a planet-shaped disk around certain very hot stars.

Nebulae provide some of the most beautiful astronomical photographs of any objects in space. The Orion Nebula could easily be the most photographed celestial object.

341

Clusters   Clusters are groups of many stars gathered in spheres around our Galaxy. Clusters may appear tightly packed as in a globular cluster, or loosely arranged as in an open or double cluster.

Galaxies   In the mid-1800s we found out that the Andromeda "nebula" was really a galaxy of stars like our own Milky Way Galaxy. In 1845 the Third Earl of Rosse (1800–1867), using the 72-inch mirror of his gigantic telescope, discovered the spiral structure of some of the objects that were previously thought to be nebulae. We gradually came to realize that these spiral nebulae were galaxies. The Milky Way was not the whole universe after all, but one of many galaxies. This meant that the universe was much larger than anyone had imagined. In the Southern Hemisphere, you can see the two Magellenic Clouds—160,000 light-years away—outside the Milky Way.

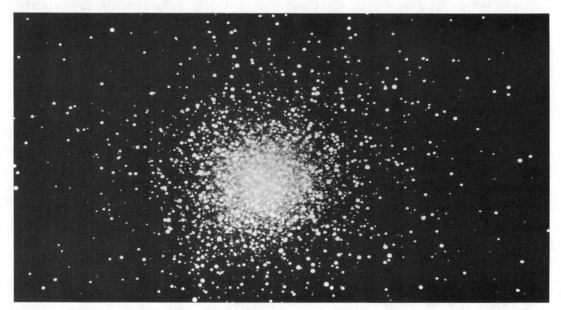

Globular Cluster

★ ★ ★ ★ ★ ★ ★ Project 68: Viewing Galaxies, Nebulae, and ★ ★ ★ ★ ★ ★ ★ Clusters with a Telescope

MATERIALS

binoculars or telescope
LIST OF OBJECTS:
M2 Globular Cluster in Aquarius
M4 Globular Cluster in Scorpius
M13 Globular Cluster in Hercules
M20 Trifid Nebula in Sagittarius
M27 Dumbell Nebula, Planetary
    Nebula in Vulpecula

M31 Andromeda Galaxy in
    Andromeda
M33 Spiral Galaxy in Triangulum
M42 Orion Nebula, Emission Nebula
    in Orion
M51 Whirlpool Galaxy in Canes
    Venatici

M57 Ring Nebula, Planetary Nebula in Lyra

M81 Spiral Galaxy in Ursa Major

M101 Pinwheel Galaxy in Coma Berenices

M104 Sombrero Galaxy in Virgo

NGC 104 47 Tucana, Globular Cluster in Tucana

NGC 869, 884 Double Cluster in Perseus

NGC 7000 North American Nebula, Emission Nebula in Cygnus

NGC 2070 Tarantula Nebula in Dorado

NGC 5128 Elliptical Galaxy in Centaurus

NGC 5139 Omega Centauri, Globular Cluster in Centaurus

The Pleiades, Open Cluster in Taurus

The Hyades, Open Cluster in Taurus

Veil Nebula, Supernova Remnant in Cygnus

Magellenic Clouds, Galaxies in Tucana, Mensa, and Dorado

PROCEDURE

1. Use a low-power eyepiece and locate the objects listed. Sometimes it is easier to find things by looking a little to one side of the object rather than directly at it.

2. Make a log of your observations, recording name of object, right ascension, declination, power of eyepiece, time, and date.

3. Make a careful sketch of one example of a cluster and one nebula or galaxy.

OBSERVATIONS

Try to observe at least one example of each of the following kinds of objects:

1. Open star cluster
2. Globular star cluster
3. Galactic nebula
4. Planetary nebula
5. Galaxy

Check the Messier Catalog in Skyfiles and see how many objects you can find.

The shape of the spiral arms of a galaxy is similar to many of the spirals that occur elsewhere in nature. You can see these spirals everywhere: the heads of daisies and sunflowers, elephant tusks and the horns of wild sheep, whirlpools, the webs of certain spiders, the canals in the human ear. Descartes, who invented coordinate geometry, discovered that in these spirals, the arms are spaced farther and farther apart as they wind outward. The width of the spaces increases in a regular order. If you measure the widths, you will find that the order follows a progression in which the measurement of the third width is equal to the first and second widths multiplied together. The measurement of the fourth is equal to the second and third widths multiplied together, and so on. We call this process of growing larger by multiplication a **geometric progression**. This relationship has given the spirals in nature researched by Descartes the name **logarithmic spirals**.

An **arithmetic** spiral would be one whose spaces in between the spiral arms are equal. An example would be a phonograph record.

The logarithmic spiral is the geometric expression of organic growth and movement. It appears in the microscopic world in the trail left by subatomic particles. On Earth it appears in winds, water, plants, and animals (like the chambered nautilus). In the sky it appears in the solar system, wind storms on planets, and the shape of galaxies.

In this next project you can draw a logarithmic spiral and create the shape of galaxies, daisies, and all kinds of spiraled things.

★ ★ ★ ★ ★ ★ ★ Project 69: Drawing the Shape of the Galaxy ★ ★ ★ ★ ★ ★ ★ (Logarithmic Spirals)

MATERIALS

tracing paper
white paper
straight edge
drawing compass

colored pencils
polar graph paper (photocopy
   from Sky Files)
access to a photocopier

PROCEDURE

1. Photocopy the polar graph paper from Sky Files and place it under a sheet of tracing paper. Draw a 4-inch (10 cm) diameter circle in the center of the page using the compass and the polar graph paper as your guide.

2. Divide the circle into 12 equal sections, 30° each.

3. Draw lines radiating from the center to all 12 points. Number each of the lines. Remove the polar graph paper from underneath. Replace it with a blank sheet of white paper.

4. Draw a line from point 12 to the radius at point 1 so that it meets the radius at 90° (perpendicular—a right angle).

5. Draw a perpendicular line to radius 2 from the point on radius 1 where the

first line you drew formed a right angle.

6. Continue drawing lines from each radius until you reach the center.

7. Draw lines the same way starting from points 3, 6, and 9.

8. Extend lines as shown on drawing to points 2, 5, 8, and 11.

9. Color each spiral with a lighter shade on the outside getting darker as it approaches the center.

10. Color the dark spaces blue on the outside of the spirals, with a lighter shade as you approach the spirals.

OBSERVATION

Compare your drawing with photographs of galaxies and other living things.

READING MORE

Berendzen, Richard, Richard Hart, and Daniel Seeley. *Man Discovers the Galaxies.* New York: Science History Publications, 1976.

Branley, Franklyn M. *Mysteries of the Universe.* New York: E. P. Dutton, 1984.

The Editors of World Book. *The Heavens.* Chicago: The World Book Press, 1985.

The launch of *Voyager 1,* 1977 (*photo courtesy of Jet Propulsion Laboratory*)

Section 4 GETTING THERE
Life Elsewhere

> Open wide the door for us, so that we may look out into the immeasurable starry universe; show us that other worlds like ours occupy the ethereal realms.
> —Giordano Bruno (1548–1600)
> (Medieval philosopher burned at the stake for this and other comments)

"It is not improbable, I must point out, that there are inhabitants not only on the Moon but on Jupiter too. . . . But as soon as somebody demonstrates the art of flying, settlers from our species of men will not be lacking. . . . Given ships or sails adapted to the breezes of heaven, there will be those who will not shrink from even that vast expanse." —Kepler

---

Does life, intelligent or otherwise, exist anywhere else in the universe? Life on Earth includes all the varieties of the kingdoms of nature that thrive under Earth's atmosphere and in its changing seasons. Life *as we know it* may or may not be present on other planets. There may also be a life-form unique to a certain planet and its particular conditions. What are the conditions required for what we call life?

1. A cell, the basic unit of living things
2. DNA (deoxyribonucleic acid) and RNA (ribonucleic acid), two carbon-containing molecules that control the process of heredity
3. Chemicals necessary for the synthesis of amino acids (the building blocks of life)
4. Water
5. An energy source

What do living things do that qualifies them as being alive?

1. Take in food
2. Make use of what they eat to grow
3. Break down part of what they eat to produce energy
4. Eliminate waste materials
5. Reproduce
6. React to changes around them

What conditions must a planet meet in order to support life?

1. The central star (Sun) should not be more than about 1½ solar masses.
   a. It must last long enough for life to evolve (at least several eras of geologic time.)
   b. It must not kill evolving life with too much ultraviolet radiation.
2. The central star should have at least 0.3 solar masses to be warm enough to create a large enough orbital area in which a planet could have liquid water.
3. The planet must orbit at the right distance from the star so that liquid water will neither evaporate nor permanently freeze.
4. The planet's orbit must be near enough to circular to keep it that proper distance and to prevent too drastic seasonal changes.
5. The planet's gravity must be strong enough to hold an atmosphere.

Some astronomers figure that there is the possibility that 0.001% of the stars may have a planet that has life on it. The nearest civilized planet won't be as close as 15 to 250 light-years away. Other astronomers figure that as few as one star in 100 million million may have a planet that supports life. The nearest of these planets would be about 10 million light-years away.

Is there an intelligent life-form anywhere else in the universe? There are receivers listening in on our nearest stars. In 1974 a giant radio telescope in Arecibo sent a coded message out into space toward the globular cluster M13 in the Milky Way. Various other programs such as the *Search* for *Extra*terrestrial *Intelligence* (SETI) continue to attract attention and support from around the world.

We have sent two other "letters of hello" into space. One is a 6 × 9 inch (15 × 23 cm) gold plaque on the outside of *Pioneer 10* with a drawing of a man and a woman and a map showing where Earth is in the solar system. The other "letter" is a gold record and a collection of slides on the outside of *Voyager II* containing sights and sounds from all over the world as well as messages of greeting and friendship in many languages.

What about intelligent life visiting us? The possibility of visitors from outer space arriving in spacecraft and flying saucers has captured headlines and our imagination for years. Many people report that they have seen or photographed alien spacecraft. Since what they have seen has not been identified as ordinary planes or rockets, people call these craft **unidentified flying objects** (UFOs). Others describe meeting with **aliens.**

Flying saucer is a term that a newspaper reporter invented to describe the object Kenneth Arnold saw above the Rocky Mountains in 1947. In January 1878, a Texas farmer saw a fast-moving object in the sky "looking like a large saucer."

Alien comes from the Latin word *alienus* = foreign or an outsider.

Alien can also mean someone or something that is to be excluded or even disliked. Can you think of a kinder word for people who come from another country or another planet?

Suppose you were to meet an astronaut from another planet. Do you think it would look like a human? Would it be friendly? Writers and moviemakers over the years have had fun coming up with answers to this question. Two thousand years ago, the Greek philosopher **Lucian of Samos** wrote the *True History* in which he describes a giant waterspout suddenly flinging a sailing ship from the Earth. The crew and the ship arrived on the Moon safely after an 8-day journey. There they discovered a race of alien beings. In some of our modern stories, creatures from space have come to our planet to warn us about our own safety if we continue to build and use nuclear weapons. Sometimes the aliens are warlike and seek to conquer the Earth. Friendly or not, the aliens in our literature and films seem to have a much further advanced technology that makes it possible for them to travel through space and time to reach us. They may even be able to change their shape and language to match ours. Some of the aliens are living beings. Others are robots.

Robot comes from the Czech word *robota* = forced hard work.

In his play *R.U.R.,* the Czechoslovakian writer **Karel Capek** (1890–1938) made up the word *robot* to describe an artificial being that was made of organic molecules and looked like a human. We use the word ***android,*** which comes from the Greek word ἀνδρος (*andros*) = man, to describe such a creature and use the word *robot* or *automaton* to mean a nonliving mechanical device shaped like a human being and usually made out of metal. The Greek god Hephaestus (Vulcan) created the first mechanical man. Its name was Talus and he was made all of bronze.

Flight

The dream of generations since ancient times has been to leave our planet to explore others. The Greek myth of Icarus and Daedalus tells the story of a father and his son who escaped imprisonment by applying wings to their arms with molten wax.

Steam Motors

People have been hard at work to develop the technology to make flight possible. One of the first heat engines converted steam pressure into jet reaction. Its inventor was **Hero**, a Greek mathematician and physicist working in Alexandria sometime between the first century B.C. and the third century A.D. Hero named his invention the **aeolipile** after Aeolus, god of the winds. The *Viking* rockets of the 1960s and X-15 rocket aircraft use similar steam–jet reaction methods for their flight control. As effective as the aeolipile was, no one took it seriously enough to put it to use for anything.

The Aeolipile

Leonardo da Vinci experimented with a number of flying machines. One was the first helicopter.

Helicopter comes from the Greek words ἑλικος (*helikos*) = spiral and πτερον (*pteron*) = wing.

Hot-Air Balloons The first people to move freely through the air did so in 1783 in a balloon designed by two paper makers, **Joseph Montgolfier (1740–1810)** and his brother **Jacques Etienne (1745–1799)**. This 5-mile (8 km) flight across Paris lasted 25 minutes. By 1859, balloonists were able to travel as far as 804 miles (1,294 km). The Montgolfier brothers called their balloon an **aereostatic machine**.

People still go up in hot air balloons. How do you think they steer and come to a landing?

Airplanes Two brothers, **Wilbur (1867–1912)** and **Orville Wright (1871–1948)** built and flew more than 1,000 gliders before they decided to put a motor on one. The Wright brothers were bicycle makers in Dayton, Ohio. Their first successful "Flyer 1" flight took place at Kill Devil Hill in North Carolina, at 10 o'clock in the morning on December 17, 1903. This is the birthday of the age of the airplane.

> **Airplane** or aeroplane comes from the Greek words ἀερο (*aero*) = air and πλανος (*planos*) = to wander.

In their open cockpits, the first fliers experienced the air on their faces, the sights and sounds of their engines in front of them, and the Earth below them. Some of them put their experience into words that burst into poetry:

> With an aeroplane you do a man's work and experience a man's cares. You are in touch with the wind, the stars, the night, with the sand and the sea. You outwit the forces of Nature. You await the dawn as a gardener awaits spring. You await the next stop like a Promised Land, and in the stars you look for truth.
> —Antoine de Saint-Exupery (1900–1944), *Terre Des Hommes*

Whatever moves through the air must do so with the least amount of wind resistance. Airplane wings are curved on the top. When a plane is flying, the air on top moves faster than the air underneath and has less pressure. The slower air underneath has more push and helps to lift the plane and hold it up.

The engine of an airplane drives a wooden or metal blade that churns up the air and drives or propels the airplane forward. This blade, the **propeller**, can have two, three, or more blades. The blades each have a slight twist in them that helps the propeller scoop out the air in front of it and push it behind.

Rockets into Space In the 1200s the Chinese and Japanese used rockets made of bamboo sticks packed with gunpowder both as fireworks and short-range weapons ("arrows of flying fire"). British versions of these caused the "rocket's red glare" that Francis Scott Key saw over Fort McHenry in 1814 and described in "The Star Spangled Banner."

In 1634 Kepler's *Somnium* (*The Dream*) was published posthumously. It tells of a journey to the Moon complete with the first descriptions of the Earth's gravity above the atmosphere. A few years later, **Francis Godwin** (1562–1633) told of a trip to the Moon in which he described weightlessness in space for the first time. In the 1800s the Russian scientist **Konstantin Eduardovick Tsiolkovsky** (1857–1935) was the first one to write about how rockets could be used to carry people into space rather than kill them in a war. Tsiolkovsky had scarlet fever when he was 10, which made him totally deaf. He went on to pursue his scientific research and became a high-school physics and math teacher. His favorite subject, however, was space travel, and he wrote several books on the subject, including a novel, *Outside the Earth*. Many of Tsiolkovsky's ideas about space travel have come true, including space suits, taking showers in space capsules, artificial satellites, space medicine, and solar energy.

Jules Verne (1828–1905) wrote his first space novel, *From the Earth to the Moon*, in 1865 and joined the growing ranks of writers imagining trips to our satellite. Once in space, Verne's travelers observed that "the constellations shone with a soft lustre; they did not twinkle, for there was no atmosphere to produce scintillation. These stars were soft eyes, looking out into the dark night, amidst the silence of absolute space." When the space travelers returned safely to Earth in their metal projectile, they landed in the Pacific Ocean, 3 miles from the spot where a century later *Apollo 13* was to splash down. Verne was quite clear in his writing that people needed to keep a healthy attitude toward the technology that made all of this possible and not get carried away with it. People are far more important.

In 1901 the British writer **H. G. Wells** (1866–1946) sent people to the Moon in his book *The First Men in the Moon.* His later work *The War of the Worlds* presented a terrifying picture of Martian monsters attacking the Earth. When Orson Welles (no relation to H. G.) broadcast this book as a play on the radio, it caused a panic, sending many people fleeing from their homes.

Two years after the publication of *The First Men in the Moon,* the first real men went up in the sky on a real flying machine. The writings of Jules Verne inspired **Robert Hutchings Goddard** (1882–1945). He was 14 when he decided to dedicate his life to making the dream of space flight a reality. Goddard's efforts to use robots to help balloons go higher won him the title "father of American rocketry." Goddard's contributions include the following:

1. Designs for both solid and liquid-fuel rockets

2. Plans for rockets to investigate the upper atmosphere (described in his 1919 pamphlet "A Method of Reaching Extreme Altitudes")

3. The first liquid-fuel rocket in history, which he built and launched on March 16, 1926. The rocket took 2.5 seconds to reach 41 feet (12½ m) and traveled 184 feet (56 m) down range at the top speed of 60 miles (97 km) per hour

4. 11-foot (3 m) rockets able to travel over 500 miles (805 km) per hour

5. First rocket with gyroscopic control system

6. First multistage rockets

7. First rocket with variable thrust engine

8. The suggestion that a rocket could carry people to the Moon

Robert Goddard with his first liquid-fuel rocket, which he launched on March 16, 1926
(*photo courtesy of NASA*)

People recognized Goddard's work only after his death in 1945. NASA named its **Goddard Space Flight Center** in his honor.

In 1927 a group of amateur rocket engineers in Germany had formed the **Society for Space Travel** (*Verein für Raumschiffsfart* or VFR). During World War II, the German military called the top members of the society to work on a special research project on the island of Usedom, off the coast of the Baltic Sea, near a small town called Peenemunde. Among the Space Travel Society members to work at the secret Peenemunde site were **Wernher von Braun** and **Hermann Oberth** from Romania.

Oberth was only one of three pioneers who lived to see the dawning of the space age. Like Tsiolkovsky and Goddard, Oberth was a teacher. Von Braun and Oberth joined many other rocket engineers. Together, they built, experimented, refined, and developed rocket techniques to the point where they were able to successfully launch 46-foot (14 m) long, 12-ton (10,886 kg) liquid-fuel rockets 60 miles (97 km) high with a range of 500 miles (805 km) at speeds of 360 miles (579 km) an hour. The most advanced of these rockets, the **V2**, became the ancestor of the modern rocket.

> "Do you realize what we accomplished today? Today the space ship was born!"
> —General Walter Dornberger to Dr. Wernher von Braun, October 3, 1942

After the war, the Peenemunde rocket engineers split up. Some of them went to the Soviet Union, others to the United States, where they continued to work in much the same kind of research facilities that they had enjoyed in Germany. Their efforts produced the rocket technology that has made Soviet and American space flight possible.

Newton's Laws of Motion

1. Every object continues to stay at rest or remain in motion in a straight line and at the same speed unless acted upon by an outside force.

2. The acceleration of an object is directly proportional to, and in the same direction as, the outside force acting on it and inversely proportional to the mass of the object.

3. For every action or force, there is an equal and opposite reaction or force.

In this next project you can experience these laws at work.

★ ★ ★ ★ ★ ★ **Project 70: Demonstrating the Laws of Motion*** ★ ★ ★ ★ ★ ★

MATERIALS

skateboard or pair of roller skates
two heavy objects (bricks, rocks, etc.)

*This project is adapted from *Science Experiments for the Space Age* by Sam Rosenfeld. Irvington, NJ: Harvey House, 1972.

PROCEDURE

1. Go outside and stand on the skateboard or put on the roller skates.
2. Hold the two heavy objects, one in each hand.
3. Stand still, point the skateboard or both roller skates forward, and throw one heavy object.
4. While you are moving backward, throw the other heavy object.
5. Try again, but throw each object farther, then try throwing both objects at the same time.

OBSERVATIONS

Why did you move backward? When you threw the second heavy object, did you move faster? What happened when you threw the objects farther and at the same time? The increase in your speed is like what happens to a rocket that has two or more stages. The first stage lifts the rocket from the launch pad at a certain speed. Then the first stage falls off and the next stage is ignited. This stage makes the moving rocket go faster (as when you threw the second heavy object). If more stages kept being ignited, they would move the rocket even faster.

In the 14th century, the Italian **Muratori** made up the word *rocchetta,* which comes from the Italian word *rocca* = a staff for holding the flax or wool from which thread is made by spinning.

How does a rocket work?

A **rocket** is a jet-propelled object that carries its engine and fuel along with it and whose functioning does not depend on the presence of an atmosphere.

Payload could be passengers or objects, limited by the amount of space required by fuel. An oxidizer is necessary for fuel to burn, especially if a rocket will be traveling beyond Earth's atmosphere where there is no oxygen. LOX (short for liquid oxygen) is a typical oxidizer. Also required is **liquid fuel**—ethyl alcohol, such as gasoline, kerosene, and liquid hydrogen—or **solid fuel**, such as potassium nitrate, sulfur, and charcoal packed tightly.

The **combustion chamber** is where oxidizer and liquid fuel mix and are ignited, burning rapidly, generating huge volumes of hot gases. The pressure in the chamber builds up. Vents above the chamber allow the gases to escape outward through the engine's nozzle. The mass of gas released and its exceptionally high speed of escape thrusts the rocket forward in the opposite direction of the outrushing gases.

Thrust is the force that propels a rocket; **propellant** is the substance or substances used to provide thrust for a rocket. The **vent** or opening is where the last gases are expelled, causing a forward thrust.

In this next project you can see how a rocket works.

Payload

Oxidizer

Thrust

Liquid fuel

Combustion chamber

Vent

Liquid-Fuel Rocket

Solid fuel

Thrust

Combustion chamber

Vent

Solid-Fuel Rocket

Bent paper clip

★ ★ ★ ★ ★ ★ **Project 71: Demonstrating How a Rocket Works** ★ ★ ★ ★ ★ ★

MATERIALS

long balloon
string or fishing line
two paper clips
cellophane tape

drinking straw or small, light piece of
   metal tubing
rubber band
barrel from a ballpoint pen or a
   mechanical pencil

PROCEDURE

1. Place the end of a long balloon over a small section of a drinking straw using the rubber band to keep them together.

2. Run a long length of string across the room. Attach both ends to the wall or to chairs.

3. Bend two paper clips into the shape shown in the illustration. Tape them onto the inflated balloon so they face the opposite way (just as in the illustration).

4. Hook the balloon onto one end of the string, and let go. Measure how far the balloon went and how long it took to get there.

5. Replace the straw with the plastic barrel from the outside of a ballpoint pen or a mechanical pencil with the pointed tip on the outside of the balloon. Reinflate the balloon, hook it onto one end of the string, and let go. Measure how far the balloon went and how long it took to get there.

OBSERVATIONS

Was there any difference in speed or distance between the straw and the pen tip? Why?

Solid-Fuel Rocket

1. You cannot control combustion and flight.
2. Once ignited, you cannot stop it.
3. You can build it and leave it ready to fire for years.
4. The amount of thrust that the fuel produces is pretty low.

Liquid-Fuel Rocket

1. Combustion and flight can be controlled.
2. You can start and stop it whenever you want.
3. You must store it empty and fuel it when you need it.
4. The fuel can produce much more power.

An **airscrew** (propeller) accelerates relatively large masses of air with a small increase in velocity. The blades push backward against the air as they turn.

Gas-filled balloon

Thrust

Airscrew propeller

Thrust

Gas turbine

Thrust

Rocket

Thrust

A **gas turbine** accelerates the gas masses (air and combustion) with a relatively large increase in velocity. It uses air to burn its fuel and can only work in the atmosphere.

A **rocket** accelerates masses at rest (propelled or combustion products) to a very high exit velocity. With its self-contained oxygen supply, the rocket is useful anywhere.

Living in Space   Traveling in space is a remarkable experience. No weight. No noise. It also presents problems. Our bodies and our form of life require certain conditions that do not exist in space. You have to be inventive if you want to reproduce these conditions in space, especially if you want to live there.

U.S. astronaut Bruce McCandless using his jetpack to move in weightless space, February 7, 1984 (*photo courtesy of NASA*)

The history of space travel has meant preparing both people and machines to be capable of such a journey. The history of rocketry lists the events in the development of a rocket capable of leaving the Earth's atmosphere. Wings, fins, and propellers make use of the air in our atmosphere to move airplanes and jets once outside the atmosphere. Where there is no air, these devices no longer work. To enter this airless environment, you must develop enough speed to escape the pull of Earth's gravity. To do this, you need to travel 25,000 miles (40,233 km) per hour. This is the escape velocity. See the information chart on the planets in Sky Files for the planets' escape velocity.

In order to develop the amount of energy necessary to move at speeds this fast, you need a powerful rocket with large amounts of fuel. At least 75% of a rocket's weight would have to be fuel. All of this hardware adds to the weight of the package you are trying to launch into space. To keep the weight of the rocket down and the quantity of the fuel up, the fuel tanks on the *Atlas* rocket are so thin-walled, they cannot even stand up under their own weight. The *Saturn 5* rocket that carried the *Apollo* astronauts to the Moon weighed 3,000 tons at lift-off.

When it lifted off, the rocket's five engines burned off 4,400,000 pounds of LOX and kerosene-type fuel in 2½ minutes, developing 7½ million pounds of thrust.

The Vehicle Assembly Building at Cape Canaveral is the world's largest building.

Gravity   As a creature of the Earth, you are used to walking with your feet on the ground and drinking from glasses whose liquid content stays at the bottom until we pour it out. On Earth, "what goes up, must come down," or as my friend used to say, "whatever is down, must have been up." In space, there is no up or down. This condition of no weight causes medical problems. You get motion sickness. Your red blood cell count drops for about a month, and you produce less blood. Your pulse rate drops, and your bones discard calcium. You also lose nitrogen and phosphorus. Space travel presents a real challenge to doctors, nurses, and medical research to understand and treat these conditions. The challenge to the engineers and architects is to re-create the forces of gravity within their space villages. To create an Earthlike gravity, the arm of a space station would have to spin 3½ times a minute.

At such a rate, you also get another Earthlike condition, the Coriolis effect. (See chapter 4, section 4.) This is the source of dizziness and motion sickness, when a person is rotating rapidly. Because we are small, compared to the Earth, the effects are larger. A space station that is bigger than a person but smaller than the Earth will have to deal with the Coriolis effect, or else water or objects traveling in the air will have sharp curves in their paths.

For a variety of reasons, the most comfortable rotation rate for a space station has been set at 1 rpm. At this rate to achieve normal gravity (1.8), you would have to be a mile from the center. A popular design is the **torus design**, which looks like a huge bicycle tire, 1 mile (1.6 km) in diameter and 400 feet (122 m) wide.

The term ***space station*** comes from the science fiction novel *Between Two Planets* by **Curd Lasswitz** (1848–1910), published in 1897.

Gravity would be different at different places within the space station. There would be less at the center and more at the ends. This could have some curious effects on life within your own home. If you lived in a two-story space station home, gravity would be about 0.5% weaker in the second story. If you weighed 100 pounds, you would lose half a pound just by walking upstairs. Imagine the change in your weight if you lived near the center of the space station and visited a friend who lived at one of the ends!

In this next project you can make your own model of a spinning space station.

Cardboard

Button

String

Paper clip

Spool

Paper cup

Rubber band

Can

Paper clip

★ ★ ★ ★ ★ ★ ★ ★ ★ **Project 72: Demonstrating a Rotating** ★ ★ ★ ★ ★ ★ ★ ★ ★ ★
Space Station*

MATERIALS

thick piece of cardboard, 20 × 1 inch
   (50 × 2½ cm)
strong tape
two paper drinking cups
modeling clay
scissors
long rubber band

two paper clips
button
nail
spool of thread
string
water
empty tin or cardboard can

PROCEDURE

1. Poke a hole with the nail into the center of the lid of the can.
2. Put the button on top of the spool and the spool on top of the lid of the can.
3. Straighten out a paper clip. Bend one end into a hook and use it to hold one end of the rubber band inside the can. Push the other end of the paper clip through the hole in the can and up through the spool and the button. Bend about 1 inch (2½ cm) of the paper clip so that it doesn't slip through the button.
4. Use the nail to poke two small holes in the sides of the can opposite each

*Part of this project is adapted from *Holt Life Science.* New York: Holt, Rinehart and Winston, 1982.

other about 1 inch (2½ cm) from the open end of the can.

5. Straighten out the other paper clip and push it through one of the holes in the side of the can. Pull the rubber band down in front of the hole; push the paper clip through the opening in the rubber band and through the hole on the other side of the can. Bend both ends of the paper clip so that it doesn't slip through the can. The can is now the *power station.*

6. Put a small hole in the exact center of the long piece of cardboard and a hole ½ inch (12 mm) from each of the ends. The piece of cardboard is now the *arm.*

7. Push the paper clip wire from the top of the power station through the hole in the center of the arm. Rebend the paper clip (if necessary) and tape it securely to the arm. Wind the arm up and test it to see that it rotates freely and that the paper clip is secure.

8. Trim down the two drinking cups using the scissors so that the cups are each about 2½ inches (6 cm) tall. Punch two holes opposite each other in the sides of each drinking cup near their tops. The drinking cups are now the *cylinders.*

9. Tie a piece of string to one of the holes in one of the cylinders. Thread the string through the other hole in the opposite side. Repeat for the other cylinder.

10. Wind the arm up about 50 turns while holding your finger over the center to keep it from moving. Hold the power station from underneath and extend it away from you. Slowly remove your finger from the arm. It should turn. Hold the power station sideways so that the arm turns vertically. This is the orbiting position for a space station or space colony.

11. Wind up the arm again. Put a modeling-clay person in each cylinder. Let the arm speed up slowly in the orbiting position. As the cylinders swivel up level with the arm, the people remain on their feet. If the cylinder was a space station, you could stand up and walk around.

12. Try the same experiment with water. Fill the cylinders about half full of water. Have the arm speed up at steady rate in the orbiting position. The water stays at the bottom of the cylinders. If the cylinder was a space station and there was a bathtub inside, you could take a bath.

OBSERVATIONS

Your project shows you how people imagine that it will be possible to re-create certain Earth conditions, such as gravity, in space. How would you equip a space station or space colony to provide all the materials humans need to live normal life?

1. How would you provide for food?
2. How would you provide for water?
3. How would you recycle oxygen and carbon dioxide?
4. What would you do with human waste?
5. Draw a plan for a space station or a space colony. Include places for work, recreation, sleeping, food production, and any other areas you feel would be needed.

As one science writer described it, the space colony will be small, like a medieval village. You could walk around it in an hour or so. Settlers there will raise families which will parent the first space children, children who know no other home. Perhaps one day, the colony may declare itself to be a new nation, independent of Earth, or even the Sun, as they set their course through space as citizens of the galaxy.

Soviet cosmonaut Yuri Gagarin,
the first person in space

When I looked toward the horizon I saw an unusual distortion, very distinctly. The Earth was ringed by a light blue halo, which gradually darkened, turned turquoise, dark blue violet, then coal black.

Trembling with excitement, I watched a world so new and unknown to me, trying to see and remember everything. Astonishingly bright cold stars could be seen through the windows. They were still far away—oh, how far away—but in orbit they seemed closer than the Earth. But the point was not the distance (my distance from the Earth was but a drop in the ocean compared to the light-years separating us from the stars) but the principle. Man had overcome the force of Earth's gravity and gone out into space.

—Yuri Gagarin (1934–1968), the first person to look at Earth from outer space

READING MORE
Feldman, Anthony. *Space.* New York: Facts on File, 1980.
Harrison, Harry, and Malcolm Edwards. *Spacecraft in Fact and Fiction.* New York: Exeter Books, 1979.
Osman, Tony. *Space History.* New York: St. Martin's Press, 1983.

(photo courtesy of NASA)

SKY FILES

HELPFUL NUMBERS FOR MEASURING

LENGTH

1 inch = 25.4 millimeters	1 centimeter = 0.3937 inches
1 inch = 2.54 centimeters	1 meter = 1.0936 yards
1 foot = 0.3048 meters	1 meter = 3.3 feet
1 yard = 0.9144 meters	1 kilometer = 0.6214 miles
1 mile = 1.6093 kilometers	

1 Astronomical Unit (AU) = 92,960,116 miles (149,597,870 km)
1 parsec = 2062265 AU
        3.262 light years
speed of light = 186,291 miles per second (299,792.458 km per second)
1 light year = 5.88 trillion miles (9.46 trillion km)
1 year = 365.242199 days
1 Å = 1 ten-billionth of a meter

FORCE UNITS

1 ounce = 28 grams
1 pound = 16 ounces
1 ton = 2,240 pounds

MASS UNITS

1 kilogram = 2.2046 pounds
1 gram = 0.0353 ounce

TEMPERATURE

Celsius (centigrade) = Fahrenheit° $- 32 \times {}^5/_9$
Fahrenheit = Celsius° $\times {}^9/_5 + 32$
Kelvin = Fahrenheit° $+ 459° \times {}^5/_9$
Kelvin = Celsius° $+ 273$

AT ONE ATMOSPHERE OF PRESSURE

Freezing Point (water)	Boiling Point (water)
273 K	373 K
32° F	212° F
0° C	100° C

THE CIRCLE

one circle = 360°

$1° = 60$ minutes of an arc = $60'$

$1' = 60$ seconds of an arc = $60''$

$\pi = 3\ 1/7$ or $22/7$ or 3.14159

circumference = $\pi \times$ diameter or $C = \pi d$

THE GREEK ALPHABET

Αα	alpha
Ββ	beta
Γγ	gamma
Δδ	delta
Εε	epsilon
Ζζ	dzeta
Ηη	eta
Θθ	theta
Ιι	iota
Κκ	kappa
Λλ	lambda
Μμ	mu
Νν	nu
Ξξ	ksi
Οο	omicron
Ππ	pi
Ρρ	rho
Σσ	sigma
Ττ	tau
Υυ	upsilon
Φφ	phi
Χχ	chi
Ψψ	psi
Ωω	omega

MATERIALS FOR THE PROJECTS AND WHERE TO FIND THEM

You can find most of the materials required for the projects at discount stores, drug stores, hardware stores, flea markets, Goodwill, or Salvation Army stores. There also are a number of science supply stores that provide items such as diffraction grating, magnets, etc. If there isn't one near your home, check with Edmund Scientific Company, 101 East Gloucester Pike, Barrington, New Jersey, 08007.

bag of lime *(Project 8)* hardware store

bolt with wing nut and washer *(Project 26)* hardware store

cable release *(Project 47)* photography store or department

cellophane strips *(Project 17)* plastic wrap for food

clear glass globe *(Project 22)* light fixture department

dark glass *(Project 18)* art supply store

diffraction grating *(Project 50)* Edmund Scientific Co.

grease pencil/china marker *(projects throughout book)* art or office supply store

fine powder (lycopodium) *(Project 36)* drug store

glycerine *(Project 36)* drug store

lead weights *(Project 40)* fishing sinker from sporting goods department

lodestone *(Project 30)* nature store, science section of large toy store, or Edmund Scientific Co.

magnet *(Project 30)* nature store, science section of large toy store, or Edmund Scientific Co.

metal eyelet *(Projects 11, 12, 15)* sewing department

metal ring *(Project 28)* a key ring or a paper clip

observing lens *(Project 46)* eye loupe from hardware store

rubber cut from a tire tube *(Project 62)* gas station or tire store

rubber or plastic tubing *(Project 33)* sporting goods department

sheet of plastic *(Projects 2, 15, 21, 60)* report covers (the thicker the better) from stationery departments

suspension wire *(Project 40)* hardware store

thermometers *(Projects 33, 49, 58)* long, without a back, from housewares department

white pencil *(Project 27)* art or stationery department or office supply store

GREEK GODS AND GODDESSES
(Planets, Moons, and Constellations)

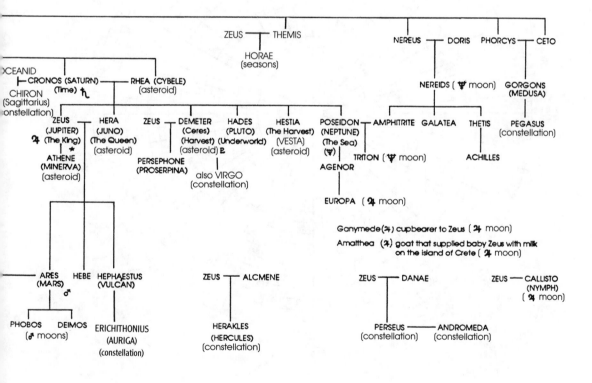

ZEUS —— THEMIS

HORAE
(seasons)

NEREUS —— DORIS   PHORCYS —— CETO

NEREIDS (♆ moon)   GORGONS
(MEDUSA)

OCEANID
├─CRONOS (SATURN) ——— RHEA (CYBELE)
CHIRON   (Time) ♄   (asteroid)
(Sagittarius)
constellation)

ZEUS   HERA   ZEUS —— DEMETER   HADES   HESTIA   POSEIDON —— AMPHITRITE   GALATEA   THETIS   PEGASUS
(JUPITER)   (JUNO)   (Ceres)   (PLUTO)   (The Harvest)   (NEPTUNE)   (constellation)
♃ (The King)   (The Queen)   (Harvest) (Underworld)   (VESTA)   (The Sea)
        ✷   (asteroid)   (asteroid) ♇   (asteroid)   (♆)   TRITON (♆ moon)   ACHILLES
ATHENE   PERSEPHONE   AGENOR
(MINERVA)   (PROSERPINA)   also VIRGO
(asteroid)   (constellation)   EUROPA (♃ moon)

Ganymede(♃) cupbearer to Zeus (♃ moon)

Amalthea (♃) goat that supplied baby Zeus with milk
        on the island of Crete (♃ moon)

ARES   HEBE   HEPHAESTUS   ZEUS —— ALCMENE   ZEUS —— DANAE   ZEUS —— CALLISTO
(MARS)   (VULCAN)   (NYMPH)
♂   (♃ moon)

PHOBOS   DEIMOS   ERICHITHONIUS   HERAKLES   PERSEUS ——— ANDROMEDA
(♂ moons)   (AURIGA)   (HERCULES)   (constellation)   (constellation)
                    (constellation)   (constellation)

POLAR GRAPH PAPER

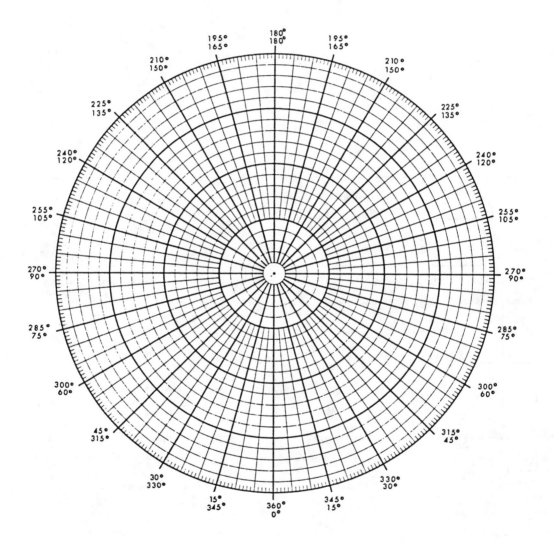

COMPUTER PROGRAM FOR PROJECT 28

```
                        10 SCREEN 2: SCREEN 0:CLS:DIM H(1000), Y(1000), J(1000)
20 I=1:M=50+(80/11)
30 INPUT "calibration for which latitude?",A%
40 INPUT "radius for equatorial circle?",B%      (This can be in inches or centimeters.)
50 INPUT "step differential?",C%           (This is the number of degrees between coordinates.
60 FOR D=0 TO 90 STEP C%                        10 is usually enough.)
70 F=B%*COS(A%/M)
80 G=SIN(A%/M)+SIN(D/M)
90 H(I)=F/G
100 Z=B%*COS(D/M)
110 J(I)=Z/G
120 I=I+1:NEXT D
140 R(1)=B%*TAN(33.75/M)
150 R(2)=B%
160 R(3)=B%*TAN(56.25/M)
170 I=I-1:J(I)=0
190 X=-B%*TAN(A%/57.27273):V=1
200 FOR W=10 TO 180 STEP 10
210 Y(V)=-B%*1/TAN(W/M)*1/COS(A%/M)
220 V=V+1:NEXT W:V=V-1
230 INPUT "printer? (Y/N)",K$
240 IF K$="Y" THEN GOTO 340 :ELSE
250 CLS:LOCATE 1,16:PRINT"ASTROLABE CO-ORDS"
260 PRINT:PRINT"For Lat.",A%," Circle Size",B%
270 PRINT"Tropic of Cancer    ",R(1)
280 PRINT"Equator             ",R(2)
290 PRINT"Tropic of Capricorn",R(3)
300 PRINT:PRINT"      X-plot                        Radius":PRINT
310 L=L+1:IF L=I+1 THEN GOTO 430
320 PRINT SPC(5) H(L) SPC(20) J(L)
330 GOTO 310
340 CLS:LOCATE 1,16:LPRINT"ASTROLABE CO-ORDS"
350 LPRINT:LPRINT"For Lat.",A%," Circle Size",B%
360 LPRINT"Tropic of Cancer    ",R(1)
370 LPRINT"Equator             ",R(2)
380 LPRINT"Tropic of Capricorn",R(3)
390 LPRINT:LPRINT"      X-plot                        Radius":PRINT
400 L=L+1:IF L=I+1 THEN GOTO 430
410 LPRINT SPC(5) H(L) SPC(20) J(L)
420 GOTO 310
430 INPUT "More?",T$
440 IF T$="Y" THEN GOTO 450:ELSE GOTO 600
450 IF K$="Y" THEN GOTO 530 :ELSE
460 PRINT"              Arc co-ords"
470 PRINT:PRINT"The Y co-ord remains constant at ";X
480 PRINT"the X co-ord varies as follows:"
490 FOR T=10 TO 170 STEP 10
500 PRINT,Y(S):S=S+1
510 NEXT T
520 PRINT"Use each X co-ord as a positive and a negative":PRINT"value to determi
ne the co-ord for both sets of arcs.":GOTO 600
530 LPRINT"              Arc co-ords"
540 LPRINT:PRINT"The Y co-ord remains constant at ";X
550 LPRINT"the X co-ord varies as follows:":PRINT
560 LFOR T=10 TO 170 STEP 10
570 LPRINT,Y(S):S=S+1
580 NEXT T
590 LPRINT"Use each X co-ord as a positive and a negative":LPRINT"value to deter
mine the co-ord for both sets of arcs.":END

600 for F-1 To 9000: NEXT F: END
```

371

TOTAL SOLAR ECLIPSES FROM 1992 THROUGH 2030

DATE	HOW LONG IT LASTS (minutes: seconds)	WHERE YOU CAN SEE IT (Path of center of eclipse)
1992 June 30	5:20	South Atlantic
1994 November 3	4:23	Bolivia, Brazil, South Atlantic
1995 October 24	2:10	India, S.E. Asia, Indonesia
1997 March 9	2:50	Siberia, Arctic
1998 February 26	4:08	Central America
1999 August 11	2:23	Central Europe, Middle East, India
2001 June 21	4:54	Southern Africa
2002 December 4	2:06	South Africa, Australia
2003 November 23	2:00	Antarctica
2005 April 8	0:42	South Pacific
2006 March 29	4:06	Africa, Turkey, E.U.N. (Former U.S.S.R.)
2008 August 1	2:24	Arctic, Siberia, China
2009 July 22	6:36	India, China, South Pacific
2010 July 11	5:18	South Pacific
2012 November 13	4:00	Northern Australia, South Pacific
2013 November 3	1:42	Atlantic, Central Africa
2015 March 20	4:06	North Atlantic, Arctic
2016 March 9	4:30	Indonesia, Pacific
2017 August 21	2:42	U.S.A., Pacific, Atlantic
2019 July 2	4:30	South America, South Pacific
2020 December 14	2:12	South America, South Pacific, South Atlantic
2021 December 4	1:54	Antarctica
2023 April 20	1:18	Indian Ocean, Indonesia
2024 April 8	4:30	South Pacific, Mexico, Eastern U.S.A.
2026 August 12	2:18	Arctic, Greenland, North Atlantic, Spain
2027 August 2	6:24	North Africa, Arabia, Indian Ocean
2028 July 22	5:06	Indian Ocean, Australia, New Zealand
2030 November 25	3:42	South Africa, Indian Ocean, Australia

CONSTELLATION CHART

North Celestial Pole

South Celestial Pole

THE CONSTELLATIONS CATALOG

CONSTELLATIONS (Stars — Greek Letters)	RA (α) hours/min./sec. (Epoch 2000)	DEC. (δ)* degrees/min./sec.	CULMINATION AT 9:00† (Approximate)
1. ANDROMEDA [And] (Andromedae)			November 23
(α) Alpheratz	0 08 23.7	+29° 05′ 26″	
(β) Mirach	1 09 43.8	+35° 37′ 14″	
(γ) Almach	2 03 53.9	+42° 19′ 47″	
2. ANTLIA [Ant] (Antilae)			April 10
(α)	10 27 09.1	−31° 04′ 04″	
3. APUS [Aps] (Apodis)			July 5
(α)	14 47 51.6	−79° 02′ 41″	
4. AQUARIUS [Aqr] (Aquaril)			October 9
(α) Sadalmelik	22 05 46.8	− 0° 19′ 11″	
(β) Sadalsuud	21 31 33.3	− 5° 34′ 16″	
5. AQUILA [Aql] (Aguilae)			August 30
(α) Altair	19 50 46.8	+ 8° 52′ 06″	
6. ARA [Ara] (Arae)			July 25
(α)	17 31 50.3	−49° 52′ 34″	
7. ARIES [Ari] (Arietis)			December 14
(α) Hamal	2 07 10.3	+23° 27′ 45″	
8. AURIGA [Aur] (Aurigae)			February 4
(α) Capella	5 16 41.3	+45° 59′ 53″	
9. BOÖTES [Boo] (Boötis)			June 16
(α) Arcturus	14 15 39.6	+19° 10′ 57″	
10. CAELUM [Cae] (Caeli)			January 15
(α)	4 40 33.6	−41° 51′ 50″	

APPARENT VISUAL MAGNITUDE (V) −1 = brightest +6 = dimmest	COLOR OF STARS	MEANINGS OF NAMES AND OTHER NOTES
		The daughter of King Cepheus and Queen Cassiopeia of Ethiopia, chained to a rock exposed to the sea monster Cetus as a punishment because Cassiopeia boasted that her daughter was more beautiful than the Nereids
2.06	Blue-white	The Horse's Navel
2.06	Orange-red	The Loins
2.18	White	The Earth-Kid
		Antlia Pneumatica, the air pump created by Lacaille
4.25	Red	
		The bird of paradise, created by Keyser and de Houtman
3.83	Orange-red	
		The water carrier sky-god pouring the waters of eternal life from the highest heaven upon the Earth
2.96	Yellow	The lucky star of the king
	Yellow	The luckiest of the lucky stars
		The eagle, a shape Zeus once appeared in to carry off Ganymede
0.77	Yellow-white	The flying eagle or vulture
		The altar
2.95	Blue	
		The ram that carried Phyrixus and his sister Helle on its back to Colchis so they could escape the wrath of their stepmother Ino. When the ram was sacrificed, its fleece turned to gold and became the object of the Argonaut's quest.
2.00	Yellow-orange	The full grown lamb
		The charioteer, Erichthonius, son of Hephaestus. Athene taught him how to harness horses to chariots. He became a king of ancient Athens.
0.08	Yellow	The little she-goat
		The ploughman steering the plough (Ursa Major) or the herdsman or bear-driver
−0.04	Yellow-orange	The bear guard
		Sculptorium, the burning or engraving tool created by Lacaille
4.45	Yellow	

CONSTELLATIONS (Stars — Greek Letters)	RA (α)* hours/min./sec.	DEC. (δ) degrees/min./sec.	CULMINATION AT 9:00† (Approximate)
11. CAMELOPARDALIS [Cam] (Camelopardalis)			February 6
(α)	4 54 03.0	+66° 20′ 34″	
12. CANCER [Cnc] (Cancri)			March 16
(α) Acubens	8 58 29.2	+11° 51′ 28″	
13. CANES VENATICI [CVn] (Canum Venaticorum)			May 22
(α) Cor Caroli	12 56 01.6	+38° 19′ 06″	
14. CANIS MAJOR [CMa] (Canis Majoris)			February 16
(α) Sirius	6 45 08.9	−16° 42′ 58″	
(β) Mirzam	6 22 41.9	−17° 57′ 22″	
15. CANIS MINOR [CMi] (Canis Minoris)			February 28
(α) Procyon	7 39 18.1	+ 5° 13′ 30″	
16. CAPRICORNUS [Cap] (Capricorni)			September 22
(α) Algedi	20 18 03.1	−12° 32′ 42″	
17. CARINA [Car] (Carinae)			March 17
(α) Canopus	6 23 57.1	−52° 41′ 44″	
(β) Miaplacidius	9 13 12.2	−69° 43′ 02″	
(ϵ) Avior	8 22 30.8	−59° 30′ 34″	
(ι) Turais (Aspidoske)	9 17 05.4	−59° 16′ 31″	
18. CASSIOPEIA [Cas] (Cassiopeiae)			November 23
(α) Schedar	0 40 30.4	+56° 32′ 15″	
(β) Caph	0 09 10.6	+59° 08′ 59″	
(γ) Cih	0 56 42.4	+60° 43′ 00″	
(δ) Ruchbah	1 25 48.9	+60° 14′ 07″	
(ϵ) Segin	1 54 23.6	+63° 40′ 13″	

APPARENT VISUAL MAGNITUDE (V) −1 = brightest +6 = dimmest	COLOR OF STARS	MEANINGS OF NAMES AND OTHER NOTES
		The giraffe or camel that brought Rebecca to Isaac, created by Petrus Plancius
4.29	Blue	
		The crab that Herakles crushed for pinching his toes during the hero's contest with the Hydra in the marsh of Lerna
4.25	Blue-white	The claw
		The hunting dogs Asterion and Charra, hounds of Boötes, created by Hevelius
2.90	White	The heart of King Charles I, first mentioned in 1725 by British Catholic royalist, Edward Sherburne
		The greater dog of Orion
−1.46	Blue	The dog star, the scorching one or Isis
1.98	Blue-white	The announcer or proclaimer, the brightest star in the sky
		The lesser dog of Orion
0.38	Yellow-white	Before the dog, i.e., the bright star that rises before Sirius
		The horned sea goat. It could be Pan who, in his panic at the approach of the monster, Typhon, jumped into the Nile and turned himself into half a fish.
3.57	Yellow	The kid
		The keel from the ship Argo Navis (Puppis & Vela form the other parts) built by Argos for Jason and his 50 Argonauts to find the golden fleece
−0.72	Yellow-white	A city in ancient Egypt named after the chief pilot of the fleet of Menelaus that destroyed Troy in 1184 B.C.
1.68	Blue-white	The 2nd brightest star in the sky
1.86	Orange-red	The stern ornament of an ancient ship
2.25	Pale yellow	
		The Queen of Ethiopia, seated in her chair and forced to rotate around the North Pole as punishment for bragging about her daughter's beauty; "the lady of the chair."
2.23	Orange-yellow	The breast
2.27	Yellow-white	The stained hand
2.47	Blue-white	In Cassiopeia's girdle
2.68	White	The knee of "the lady of the chair"
3.38	Blue-white	Near the foot

CONSTELLATIONS (Stars — Greek Letters)	RA (α)* hours/min./sec.	DEC. (δ) degrees/min./sec.	CULMINATION AT 9:00† (Approximate)
19. CENTAURUS [Cen] (Centauri)			May 14
(α) Rigil Kentaurus	14 39 36.7	−60° 50′ 02″	
(β) Agena, Hadar	14 03 49.4	−60° 22′ 22″	
(γ) Muhlitain	12 41 30.9	−48° 57′ 34″	
(θ) Menkent	14 06 40.9	−36° 22′ 12″	
20. CEPHEUS [Cep] (Cephei)			November 13
(α) Alderamin	21 18 34.6	+62° 35′ 08″	
(μ) The Garnet Star			
21. CETUS [Cet] (Ceti)			November 29
(α) Menkar	3 02 16.7	+ 4° 05′ 23″	
(β) Diphda	0 43 35.3	−17° 59′ 12″	
(o) Mira	2 19 20.6	− 2° 58′ 39″	
22. CHAMAELEON [Cha] (Chamaeleonis)			April 15
(α)	8 8 31.7	−76° 55′ 10″	
23. CIRCINUS [Cir] (Circini)			June 14
(α)	14 42 28.0	−64° 58′ 43″	
24. COLUMBA [Col] (Columbae)			February 1
(α) Phact	5 39 38.9	−34° 04′ 27″	
25. COMA BERENICES [Com] (Comae Berenices)			May 17
(α) Diadem	13 09 59.2	+17° 31′ 45″	
26. CORONA AUSTRALIS [CrA] (Coronae Australis)			August 14
(α)	19 09 28.2	−37° 54′ 16″	
27. CORONA BOREALIS [CrB] (Coronae Borealis)			July 3
(α) Alphecca (Gemma)	15 34 41.2	+26° 42′ 53″	
28. CORVUS [Crv] (Corvi)			May 12
(α) Alchiba	12 08 24.7	−24° 43′ 44″	
(γ) Gienah	12 15 48.3	−17° 32′ 31″	

APPARENT VISUAL MAGNITUDE (V) −1 = brightest +6 = dimmest	COLOR OF STARS	MEANINGS OF NAMES AND OTHER NOTES
		The stern centaur
0.00	White-yellow	The centaur's foot
0.61	Blue	The centaur's knee
2.17	Blue-white	Right fore foot
2.06	Orange-red	The bright star in the centaur's belly
		The King of Ethiopia, husband of Cassiopeia and one of the Argonauts
2.44	White	The right forearm
	Red	Named by William Herschel. It is the reddest naked-eye star.
		The sea beast descended from Pontus. Cetus was sent to devour Andromeda but was turned to stone at the sight of the Medusa's head which Perseus was holding
2.53	Orange-red	The nostril
2.04	Yellow-orange	The southern branch of the sea monster's tail
(3.04) variable	Red	Wonderful
		The Chamaelion, created by Keyser & de Houtman
4.07	Yellow	
		The pair of geometrical compasses named by Lacaille
3.19	White	
		The dove of Noah with a branch in its beak, created by the Dutch theologian and geographer Petrus Plancius
2.64	Blue	The ring dove
		Berenice's hair, Berenice, queen of Egypt, cut off her amber hair as a sacrifice to Aphrodite to ensure her husband Ptolemy a safe return from a dangerous voyage. Created by Mercator.
4.32	Yellow-white	
		The southern crown or wreath, named by Hipparchos
4.11	Blue-white	
		The northern crown or wreath of Ariadne, daughter of King Minos
2.23	White	The broken or fractured one
		The crow, or raven, messenger to Phoebus Apollo
4.02	Yellow-white	
2.59	Blue	Left wing of the raven

CONSTELLATIONS (Stars — Greek Letters)	RA (α)* hours/min./sec.	DEC. (δ) degrees/min./sec.	CULMINATION AT 9:00† (Approximate)
29. CRATER [Crt] (Crateris)			April 26
(α) Alkes	10 59 46.4	$-18°$ 17′ 56″	
30. CRUX [Cru] (Crucis)			May 12
(α) Acrux	12 26 35.9	$-63°$ 05′ 56″	
(β) Becrux	12 47 43.2	$-59°$ 41′ 19″	
31. CYGNUS [Cyg] (Cygni)			September 13
(α) Deneb	20 41 25.8	$+45°$ 16′ 49″	
(β) Albireo	19 30 43.1	$+27°$ 57′ 35″	
(γ) Sadir	20 22 13.5	$+40°$ 15′ 24″	
32. DELPHINUS [Del] (Delphini)			September 14
(α) Sualocin	20 39 38.1	$+15°$ 54′ 43″	
33. DORADO [Dor] (Doradus)			January 31
(α)	4 33 59.8	$-55°$ 02′ 42″	
34. DRACO [Dra] (Draconis)			July 8
(α) Thuban	14 04 23.2	$+64°$ 22′ 33″	
(β) Rastaban	17 30 25.8	$+52°$ 18′ 05″	
(γ) Eltanin	17 56 36.2	$+51°$ 29′ 20″	
(δ) Grumium	17 53 31.5	$+56°$ 52′ 21″	
(ϵ) Kuma	17 32 10.3	$+55°$ 11′ 03″	
35. EQUULEUS [Equ] (Equulei)			September 22
(α) Kitalpha	21 15 49.3	$+$ 5° 14′ 52″	
36. ERIDANUS [Eri] (Eridoni)			December 25
(α) Achernar	1 37 42.9	$-57°$ 14′ 12″	
(β) Cursa	5 07 50.9	$-$ 5° 05′ 11″	
37. FORNAX [For] (Fornacis)			December 17
(α)	3 12 04.2	$-28°$ 59′ 13″	
38. GEMINI [Gem] (Geminorum)			February 19
(α) Castor	7 34 35.9	$+31°$ 53′ 18″	
(β) Pollux	7 45 18.9	$+28°$ 01′ 34″	

APPARENT VISUAL MAGNITUDE (V) −1 = brightest +6 = dimmest	COLOR OF STARS	MEANINGS OF NAMES AND OTHER NOTES
		The cup of Apollo
4.08	Orange-red	
		The Southern Cross, created during Counter-Reformation times by Spanish and Portuguese navigators from stars at the hind feet of Centaurus in 1679
1.41	Blue	a(lpha) Crucis = acrux
		The swan, and the Northern Cross
1.25	White	The hen's tail
3.08	Yellow & blue	The hen's beak
2.20	Yellow-white	The hen's breast
		The dolphin
3.77	Blue-white	Named after Nicolaus Venator by spelling his first name backward. Venator was Piazzi's assistant at the Palerno Observatory.
		The goldfish (or swordfish) created by Keyser & de Houtman
3.27	Blue-white	
		The dragon that Athene snatched from the giants and whirled up to the sky. It became the monster that Herakles killed and whose teeth he sowed for a crop of armed men.
3.65	Pale yellow	The serpent or dragon
2.79	Yellow	The serpent's head
2.23	Orange-yellow	The dragon's head
3.75	Orange-yellow	The under jaw
4.88	White	
		The foal, named by Hipparchos
3.92	Yellow-white	The part or section of the horse
		The river, the longest constellation. It flowed into the Euxine Sea, where the Argonauts found the golden fleece.
0.46	Blue-white	The end of the river
2.79	White	The foremost chair of Orion
		Fornax Chemica, the chemical furnace formed by Lacaille
3.87	White	
		The twins (the Dioscuri) sons of Leda
1.58	White	The mortal brother; the horseman, son of Tyndarus
1.14	Yellow-orange	The immortal brother; the boxer, son of Zeus

CONSTELLATIONS (Stars — Greek Letters)	RA (α)* hours/min./sec.	DEC. (δ) degrees/min./sec.	CULMINATION AT 9:00† (Approximate)
39. GRUS [Gru] (Gruis)			October 12
(α) Alnair	22 08 13.8	− 46° 57′ 40″	
40. HERCULES [Her] (Herculis)			July 28
(α) Rasalgethi	17 14 38.8	+ 14° 23′ 25″	
41. HOROLOGIUM [Hor] (Horologii)			December 25
(α)	4 14 00.0	− 42° 17′ 40″	
42. HYDRA [Hya] (Hydrae)			April 29
(α) Alphard	9 27 35.2	− 8° 39′ 31″	
43. HYDRUS [Hyi] (Hydri)			December 10
(α)	1 58 46.2	− 61° 34′ 12″	
44. INDUS [Ind] (Indi)			September 26
(α)	20 37 33.9	− 47° 17′ 29″	
45. LACERTA [Lac] (Lacertae)			October 12
(α)	22 31 17.3	+ 50° 16′ 57″	
46. LEO [Leo] (Leonis)			April 15
(α) Regulus	10 08 22.2	+ 11° 58′ 02″	
(β) Denebola	11 49 03.5	+ 14° 34′ 19″	
(γ) Algieba	10 19 58.3	+ 19° 50′ 30″	
47. LEO MINOR [LMi] (Leonis Minoris)			April 9
(β) Praecipua	10 27 52.9	+ 36° 42′ 26″	
48. LEPUS [Lep] (Lipi)			January 28
(α) Arneb	5 32 43.7	− 17° 49′ 20″	
49. LIBRA [Lib] (Librae)			June 23
(α) Zubenelgenubi	14 50 52.6	− 16° 02′ 30″	
(β) Zubeneschemali	15 17 00.3	− 9° 22′ 58″	
50. LUPUS [Lup] (Lipi)			June 23
(α)	14 41 55.7	− 47° 23′ 17″	

APPARENT VISUAL MAGNITUDE (V) −1 = brightest +6 = dimmest	COLOR OF STARS	MEANINGS OF NAMES AND OTHER NOTES
		The crane (symbol of the star observer in Egypt) created by Keyser & de Houtman in 1595–1597
1.74	White	The bright one
		Herakles
3.19	Orange-red	Head of the kneeler
3.86	Orange-red	A pendulum clock created by Lecaille
1.98	Yellow-orange	The sea serpent (female) preventing the crow (Corvus) from drinking from the cup
		The solitary (star) of the serpent
2.86	White	The water monster (male) created by Keyser & de Houtman in 1595–1597
3.11	Orange-red	The American Indian, created by Pieter Dirksz Keyser & Frederick de Houtman in 1595–1597
3.77	White	The lizard formed by Hevelius
		The Nemean lion, which came from the Moon. Herakles carried it back to the heavens after he slayed it.
1.35	Blue-white	The prince, named by Copernicus
2.14	White	The lion's tail
2.28	Orange-yellow	The forehead
		The lesser lion, formed by Hevelius in 1690
4.21	Yellow	Chief
		The hare, placed in the heavens to be close to its hunter, Orion
2.58	Yellow-white	The hare
		The balance or scales
2.75	White	The southern claw
2.61	Blue-white	The northern claw
		The wolf, named by Hipparchos
2.30	Blue	

CONSTELLATIONS (Stars — Greek Letters)	RA (α)* hours/min./sec.	DEC. (δ) degrees/min./sec.	CULMINATION AT 9:00† (Approximate)
51. LYNX [Lyn] (Lyncis)	9 21 03.2	+34° 23′ 33″	March 5
52. LYRA [Lyr] (Lyrae)			August 18
(α) Vega	18 36 56.2	+38° 47′ 01″	
53. MENSA [Men] (Mensae)			January 28
(α)	6 10 14.6	−74° 45′ 11″	
54. MICROSCOPIUM [Mic] (Microscopii)			September 18
(α)	20 49 57.8	−33° 46′ 47″	
55. MONOCEROS [Mon] (Monocerotis)			February 19
(α)	7 41 14.8	− 9° 33′ 04″	
56. MUSCA [Mus] (Muscae)			May 14
(α)	12 37 11.0	−69° 08′ 07″	
57. NORMA [Nor] (Normae)			July 3
(γ)	16 17 00.7	−50° 04′ 05″	
58. OCTANS [Oct] (Octanis)			Circumpolar
(α)	21 04 42.7	−77° 01′ 25″	
(δ)	21 08 44.9	−88° 57′ 24″	
59. OPHIUCHUS [Oph] (Ophiuchi)			July 26
(α) Rasalhague	17 34 55.9	+12° 33′ 36″	
(η) Sabik	17 10 22.5	−15° 43′ 30″	
60. ORION [Ori] (Orionis)			January 27
(α) Betelgeuse	5 55 10.2	+ 7° 24′ 26″	
(β) Rigel	5 14 32.2	− 8° 12′ 06″	
(γ) Bellatrix	5 25 07.8	+ 6° 20′ 59″	
(δ) Mintaka	5 32 00.3	− 0° 17′ 05″	
(ε) Alnilam	5 36 12.7	− 1° 12′ 07″	
(ζ) Alnitak	5 40 45.5	− 1° 56′ 34″	
(κ) Saiph	5 47 45.3	− 9° 40′ 11″	
(λ) Heka (Meissa)	5 35 08.2	+ 9° 56′ 02″	

APPARENT VISUAL MAGNITUDE (V) −1 = brightest +6 = dimmest	COLOR OF STARS	MEANINGS OF NAMES AND OTHER NOTES
		The tiger, created by Hevelius
3.13	Orange	
		The harp or lyre invented by Hermes and given to his half-brother, Apollo, who in turn passed it on to his son, Orpheus, the musician of the Argonauts
0.03	Blue-white	The falling eagle or vulture
		The table, formed by Lacaille and named after Table Mountain, which lies behind Cape Town, South Africa, where Lacaille worked
5.09	White-yellow	
		The microscope, formed by Lacaille
4.90	White-yellow	
		The unicorn, created by Petrus Plancius
3.93	Yellow-orange	
		The southern fly, or bee, created by Keyser & de Houtman
2.69	Blue	
		The level, formed by Lacaille (originally, Norma & Regula, the architect's level and square)
4.99	Yellow	
		Octans Halecianus, the octant or reflecting quadrant formed by Lacaille in 1752
5.15	White	The star closest to the south celestial pole
5.47	Blue-white	
		The medicinal serpent holder Aesculapius, the ship's surgeon of the Argo
2.08	White (sapphire)	The head of the serpent collector or charmer
2.43	Blue-white	The driver
		Orion the giant, mighty hunter and warrior. He was the lover of the huntress-goddess Diana. Orion died from the sting of Scorpius, the scorpion, as punishment for bragging.
0.50	Orange-red	The armpit of the white-belted sheep
0.12	Blue-white	Orion's left foot
1.64	Blue-white	The female warrior, the Amazon Star
2.23	Blue	The belt
1.70	Blue	The string of pearls
1.77	Blue	The girdle
2.06	Blue-white	The sword of the powerful one
3.39	Yellow-white	The circle of hairs

CONSTELLATIONS (Stars — Greek Letters)	RA (α)* hours/min./sec.	DEC. (δ) degrees/min./sec.	CULMINATION AT 9:00† (Approximate)
61. PAVO [Pab] (Pavonis)			August 29
(α) Peacock	20 25 38.7	− 56° 44′ 06″	
62. PEGASUS [Peg] (Pegasi)			October 16
(α) Markab	23 04 45.5	+ 15° 12′ 19″	
(β) Scheat	23 03 46.3	+ 28° 04′ 58″	
(γ) Algenib	0 13 14.1	+ 15° 11′ 01″	
63. PERSEUS [Per] (Persei)			December 22
(α) Mirfak (Algenib)	3 24 19.3	+ 49° 51′ 40″	
(β) Algol	3 08 10.1	+ 40° 57′ 21″	
64. PHOENIX [Phe] (Phoenicis)			November 18
(α) Ankaa	0 26 17.0	− 42° 18′ 2″	
65. PICTOR [Pic]			January 30
(α)	6 48 11.4	− 61° 56′ 29″	
66. PISCES [Psc] (Piscium)			November 11
(α) Alrescha	2 02 02.7	+ 2° 45′ 49″	
67. PISCIS AUSTRINUS [PsA] (Piscis Austrini)			October 9
(α) Fomalhaut	22 57 38.9	− 29° 37′ 20″	
68. PUPPIS [Pup] (Puppis)			February 22
(ζ) Lyn	8 03 35.0	− 40° 00′ 12″	
(χ) Naos	7 49 17.6	− 24° 51′ 35″	
69. PYXIS [Pyx] (Pyxidis)			March 21
(α)	8 43 35.5	− 33° 11′ 11″	
70. RETICULUM [Ret] (Reticuli)			January 3
(α)	4 14 25.5	− 62° 28′ 26″	

APPARENT VISUAL MAGNITUDE (V) −1 = brightest +6 = dimmest	COLOR OF STARS	MEANINGS OF NAMES AND OTHER NOTES
		The peacock. Hera changed Argos, the builder of the ship Argo, into a peacock when the gods placed the Argo in the sky. Created by Keyser & de Houtman
1.94	Blue	
		The winged horse. Poseidon commanded that Pegasus spring forth from the sea where blood from the severed head of Medusa had dropped.
2.49	Blue-white	Riding, or anything that carries a person
2.42	Red	The leg
2.83	Blue-white	The side
		The champion, rescued Andromeda by showing the severed head of Medusa to the sea monster Cetus who immediately turned to stone
1.80	Yellow-white	The elbow or the side
2.12	Blue	The demon's head
		The phoenix created by Keyser & de Houtman
2.39	Orange-red	Equuleus Pictoris, the painter's easel, created by Lacaille
3.27	White	The fishes, possibly Aphrodite and her son Eros, who plunged into the Euphraetes to protect themselves from the monster Typhon
		The rope or cord
3.79	White	The southern fish, drinking the flow from Aquarius
		The month of the southern fish
1.16	Blue-white	The stern of the ship Argo created by Lacaille in 1752
2.25	Yellow	
3.34	Yellow	Pyxis Nautica, the mariner's compass, created by Lacaille
3.68	Blue	The net or rhombus in honor of the reticule or micrometer used to measure the position of stars created by Lacaille
3.35	White-yellow	The arrow, shot by either Zeus or Herakles toward the Eagle or the Swan

CONSTELLATIONS (Stars — Greek Letters)	RA (α)* hours/min./sec.	DEC. (δ) degrees/min./sec.	CULMINATION AT 9:00† (Approximate)
71. SAGITTA [Sge] (Sagittae)			August 30
(α) Sham	19 40 05.6	+18° 00′ 50″	
72. SAGITTARIUS [Sgr] (Sagittarii)			August 21
(α) Rukbat	19 23 53.0	−40° 36′ 58″	
(σ) Nunki	18 55 15.7	−26° 17′ 48″	
73. SCORPIUS [Sco] (Scorpii)			July 18
(α) Antares	16 29 24.3	−26° 25′ 55″	
(β) Graffias (Acrab)	16 05 26.1	−19° 48′ 19″	
(δ) Dschubba	16 00 19.9	−22° 37′ 18″	
(λ) Shaula	17 33 36.4	−37° 06′ 14″	
74. SCULPTOR [Scl] (Sculptoris)			November 10
(α)	0 58 36.3	−29° 21′ 27″	
75. SCUTUM [Sct] (Scuti)			August 15
(α)	18 35 12.2	−8° 14′ 39″	
76. SERPENS [Ser] (Serpentis)			July 21
(α) Unukalhai	15 44 16.0	+ 6° 25′ 32″	
77. SEXTANS [Sex] (Sextantis)			April 8
(α)	10 07 56.2	− 0° 22′ 18″	
78. TAURUS [Tau] (Tauri)			January 14
(α) Aldebaran	4 35 55.2	+16° 30′ 33″	
(β) Elnath	5 26 17.5	+28° 36′ 27″	
79. TELESCOPIUM [Tel] (Telescopii)			August 24
(α)	18 26 58.2	−45° 58′ 06″	
80. TRIANGULUM [Tri] (Trianguli)			December 7
(α) Metallah	1 53 04.8	+29° 34′ 44″	

APPARENT VISUAL MAGNITUDE (V) −1 = brightest +6 = dimmest	COLOR OF STARS	MEANINGS OF NAMES AND OTHER NOTES
4.37	Yellow-white	The arrow
		The archer, the centaur Chiron, wise teacher of Aesculapius, Jason, Achilles, and Hercules, shown with bow drawn and arrow aimed at the heart of the Scorpion
3.97	Blue-white	The archer's knee
2.02	Blue	The sea
		The scorpion, slayer of Orion
0.96	Red	The rival of Mars
2.64	Blue	The crab
2.32	Blue	The forehead or front of the scorpion
1.63	Blue	The sting
		The sculptor, the sculptor's studio or tools, created by Lacaille in 1751–1752. The south galactic pole lies in this constellation.
4.31	Blue	
		Scutum Scobiescianum, the shield of John Scobiesci III, the Polish king who aided Hevelius when his observatory in Danzig burned to the ground.
3.85	Yellow-orange	
		The serpent
2.65	Yellow-orange	The serpent's neck
		Sextans Uraniae, or sextant, named by Hevelius in honor of the instrument that he used to measure the stars at Danzig from 1658–1679
4.49	White	
		The bull into which Zeus changed himself to carry away Europa
0.85	Yellow-orange	The follower (of the Pleiades)
1.65	Blue-white	The one butting with horns
		Tubus Astronomicus, or the telescope, created by Lacaille
3.51	Blue	
		The triangle, created by Keyser & de Houtman
3.41	Yellow-white	

CONSTELLATIONS (Stars — Greek Letters)	RA (α)* hours/min./sec.	DEC. (δ) degrees/min./sec.	CULMINATION AT 9:00† (Approximate)
81. TRIANGULUM AUSTRALE [TrA] (Trianguli Australis)			July 7
(α) Atria	16 48 39.8	−69° 01′ 39″	
82. TUCANA [Tuc] (Tucanae)			November 1
(α)	22 18 30.1	−60° 15′ 35″	
83. URSA MAJOR [UMa] (Ursae Majoris)			April 25
(α) Dubhe	11 03 43.6	+61° 45′ 03″	
(β) Merak	11 01 50.4	+56° 22′ 56″	
(γ) Phecda	11 53 49.7	+53° 41′ 41″	
(δ) Mergrez	12 15 25.5	+57° 01′ 57″	
(ε) Alioth	12 54 01.7	+55° 57′ 35″	
(η) Alkaid	13 47 32.3	+49° 18′ 48″	
(ζ) Mizar	13 23 55.5	+54° 55′ 31″	
(80) Alcor	13 25 13.4	+54° 59′ 17″	
84. URSA MINOR [UM] (Ursae Minoris)			June 27
(α) Polaris	2 31 50.4	+89° 15′ 51″	
(β) Kochab	14 50 42.2	+74° 09′ 19″	
(γ) Pherkad	15 20 43.6	+71° 50′ 02″	
85. VELA [Vel] (Velorum)			March 30
(λ) Alsuhail	9 07 59.7	−43° 25′ 57″	
86. VIRGO [Vir] (Virginis)			May 26
(α) Spica	13 25 11.5	−11° 09′ 41″	
(γ) Porrima	12 41 39.5	− 1° 26′ 57″	
(ε) Vindemiatrix	13 02 10.5	+10° 57′ 33″	
87. VOLANS [Vol] (Volantis)			March 4
(α)	9 02 26.9	−66° 23′ 46″	
88. VULPECULA [Vul] (Vulpeculae)			September 8
(α)	19 28 42.2	+24° 39′ 54″	

*For each **hour** earlier than 9 P.M., add 15 days.
 For each **hour** later than 9 P.M., subtract 15 days.

†For each **week** earlier than dates given, add 28 minutes to 9 P.M.
 For each **week** later than dates given, subtract 28 minutes from 9 P.M.

APPARENT VISUAL MAGNITUDE (V) −1 = brightest +6 = dimmest	COLOR OF STARS	MEANINGS OF NAMES AND OTHER NOTES
		The southern triangle
1.92	Orange	Entryway into the main room
		The toucan, created by Keyser & de Houtman
2.86	Orange-red	
		The greater bear, who was once the beautiful Callisto until jealous Hera turned her into a bear. People also know this constellation as "the Wain" (the Wagon) or "the Plough."
1.79	Yellow-orange	The back of the greater bear
2.37	White	The loins of the greater bear
2.44	White	The thigh of the greater bear
3.31	White	The root of the tail of the greater bear
1.77	White	The extremely bright one
1.86	Blue-white	The leader or governor of the daughters of the bier
2.27	White	The veil, trousers, or waist cloth
4.01	White	The abandoned or friendless one
		The lesser bear
2.02	Yellow	The polestar since 300 A.D.
2.08	Orange-yellow	The North Star—named during the period when it was the brightest star near the pole, from about 1500 B.C. to 300 A.D.
		The sail, from the ship Argo
2.21	Orange-red	
		The young woman, perhaps Persephone, daughter of Demeter or Demeter herself
0.98	Blue-white	The ear of wheat
2.75	White	The goddess of prophecy
2.83	Yellow	The female grape gatherer
		Piscis Volans, the flying fish, created by Keyser & de Houtman
4.00	White	
		Vulpecula cum Ansere, the little fox with a goose, created by Hevelius
4.44	Orange-red	

THE CONSTELLATIONS WITHOUT CONNECTING LINES

THE BRIGHTEST STARS

STAR	APPARENT MAGNITUDE (V)
1. Sirius (α Canis Majoris)	−1.46
2. Canopus (α Carinae)	−0.72
3. Arcturus (α Bootis)	−0.04
4. Rigel Kentaurus (α Centauri)	0.00
5. Vega (α Lyrae)	0.03
6. Capella (α Aurigae)	0.08
7. Rigel (β Orionis)	0.12
8. Procyon (α Canis Minoris)	0.38
9. Achernar (α Eridani)	0.46
10. Betelgeuse (α Orionis)	0.50
11. Hadar (α Centauri)	0.61
12. Altair (α Aquilae)	0.77
13. Aldebaran (α Tauri)	0.85
14. Antares (α Scorpii)	0.96
15. Spica (α Virginis)	0.98
16. Pollux (β Geminorum)	1.14
17. Fomalhaut (α Piscis Austrini)	1.16
18. Deneb (α Cygni)	1.25
19. Becrux (β Crucis)	1.25
20. Regulus (α Leonis)	1.35

THE NEAREST STARS

NAME	DISTANCE
1. The Sun	93,000,000 miles (150,000,000 km)
2. α Centauri A	4.3 Light-years
3. α Centauri B	4.3
4. α Centauri C	4.3
5. Barnard's Star (Ophiuchus)	5.9
6. Wolf 359 (Leo)	7.6
7. Lalande 21185 (Ursa Major)	8.1
8. Sirius A (Canis Major)	8.6
9. Sirius B	8.6
10. Luyten 726-8A (Cetus)	8.9
11. Luyten 726-8B (UV Ceti)	8.9
12. Ross 154	9.4
13. Ross 248	10.3
14. ε Eridani	10.7
15. Luyten 789-6	10.8
16. Ross 128	10.8
17. 61 Cygni A	11.2
18. 61 Cygni B	11.2
19. ε Indi	11.2
20. Procyon A	11.4
21. Procyon B	11.4

THE MESSIER CATALOG OF NEBULAE AND STAR CLUSTERS

Messier number	NGC or (IC) (1980)	Right ascension	Declination (1980)	Apparent visual magnitude	Description
1	1952	5h 33.3m	+22°01'	8.4	Crab Nebula in Taurus; remains of SN 1054
2	7089	21h 32.4m	−0°54'	6.4	Globular cluster in Aquarius
3	5272	13h 41.2m	+28°29'	6.3	Globular cluster in Canes Venatici
4	6121	16h 22.4m	−26°28'	6.5	Globular cluster in Scorpius
5	5904	15h 17.5m	+2°10'	6.1	Globular cluster in Scorpius
6	6405	17h 38.8m	−32°11'	5.5	Open cluster in Scorpius
7	6475	17h 52.7m	−34°48'	3.3	Open cluster in Scorpius
8	6523	18h 02.4m	−24°23'	5.1	Lagoon Nebula in Sagittarius
9	6333	17h 18.1m	−18°30'	8.0	Globular cluster in Ophiuchus
10	6254	16h 56.1m	−4°05'	6.7	Globular cluster in Ophiuchus
11	6705	18h 50.0m	−6°18'	6.8	Open cluster in Scutum Sobieskii
12	6218	16h 46.3m	−1°55'	6.6	Globular cluster in Ophiuchus
13	6205	16h 41.0m	+36°30'	5.9	Globular cluster in Hercules
14	6402	17h 36.6m	−3°14'	8.0	Globular cluster in Ophiuchus
15	7078	21h 28.9m	+12°05'	6.4	Globular cluster in Pegasus
16	6611	18h 17.8m	−13°47'	6.6	Open cluster with nebulosity in Serpens
17	6618	18h 19.6m	−16°11'	7.5	Swan or Omega Nebula in Sagittarius
18	6613	18h 18.7m	−17°08'	7.2	Open cluster in Sagittarius
19	6273	17h 01.4m	−26°14'	6.9	Globular cluster in Ophiuchus
20	6514	18h 01.2m	−23°02'	8.5	Trifid Nebula in Sagittarius
21	6531	18h 03.4m	−22°30'	6.5	Open cluster in Sagittarius
22	6656	18h 35.2m	−23°56'	5.6	Globular cluster in Sagittarius
23	6494	17h 55.8m	−19°00'	5.9	Open cluster in Sagittarius
24	6603	18h 17.3m	−18°26'	4.6	Open cluster in Sagittarius
25	(4725)	18h 30.5m	−19°16'	6.2	Open cluster in Sagittarius
26	6694	18h 44.1m	−9°25'	9.3	Open cluster in Scutum Sobieskii
27	6853	19h 58.8m	+22°40'	8.2	"Dumbbell" planetary nebula in Vulpecula
28	6626	18h 23.2m	−24°52'	7.6	Globular cluster in Sagittarius
29	6913	20h 23.3m	+38°27'	8.0	Open cluster in Cygnus
30	7099	21h 39.2m	−23°16'	7.7	Globular cluster in Capricornus
31	224	0h 41.6m	+41°10'	3.5	Andromeda Galaxy
32	221	0h 41.6m	+40°46'	8.2	Elliptical galaxy; companion to M31
33	598	1h 32.7m	+30°33'	5.8	Spiral galaxy in Triangulum
34	1039	2h 40.7m	+42°43'	5.8	Open cluster in Perseus
35	2168	6h 07.5m	+24°21'	5.6	Open cluster in Gemini
36	1960	5h 35.0m	+34°05'	6.5	Open cluster in Auriga
37	2099	5h 51.1m	+32°33'	6.2	Open cluster in Auriga
38	1912	5h 27.3m	+35°48'	7.0	Open cluster in Auriga
39	7092	21h 31.5m	+48°21'	5.3	Open cluster in Cygnus
40		12h 21m	+59°		Close double star in Ursa Major
41	2287	6h 46.2m	−20°43'	5.0	Loose open cluster in Canis Major
42	1976	5h 34.4m	−5°24'	4	Orion Nebula
43	1982	5h 34.6m	−5°18'	9	Northeast portion of Orion Nebula
44	2632	8h 39m	+20°04'	3.9	Praesepe; open cluster in Cancer
45		3h 46.3m	+24°03'	1.6	The Pleiades; open cluster in Taurus
46	2437	7h 40.9m	−14°46'	6.6	Open cluster in Puppis
47	2422	7h 35.7m	−14°26'	5	Loose group of stars in Puppis
48	2548	8h 12.8m	−5°44'	6	"Cluster of very small stars"; identifiable
49	4472	12h 28.8m	+8°06'	8.5	Elliptical galaxy in Virgo
50	2323	7h 02.m	−8°19'	6.3	Loose open cluster in Monoceros
51	5194	13h 29.1m	+47°18'	8.4	Whirlpool spiral galaxy in Canes Venatici
52	7654	23h 23.3m	+61°30'	8.2	Loose open cluster in Cassiopeia
53	5024	13h 12.0m	+18°16'	7.8	Globular cluster in Coma Berenices
54	6715	18h 53.8m	−30°30'	7.8	Globular cluster in Sagittarius
55	6809	19h 38.7m	−30°59'	6.2	Globular cluster in Sagittarius

THE MESSIER CATALOG OF NEBULAE AND STAR CLUSTERS

Messier number	NGC or (IC) (1980)	Right ascension	Declination (1980)	Apparent visual magnitude	Description
56	6779	19h 15.8m	+30°08′	8.7	Globular cluster in Lyra
57	6720	18h 52.8m	+33°00′	9.0	Ring Nebula; planetary nebula in Lyra
58	4579	12h 36.7m	+11°55′	9.9	Spiral galaxy in Virgo
59	4621	12h 41.0m	+11°46′	10.0	Spiral galaxy in Virgo
60	4649	12h 42.6m	+11°40′	9.0	Elliptical galaxy in Virgo
61	4303	12h 20.8m	+4°35′	9.6	Spiral galaxy in Virgo
62	6266	16h 59.9m	−30°05′	6.6	Globular cluster in Scorpius
63	5055	13h 14.8m	+42°07′	8.9	Spiral galaxy in Canes Venatici
64	4826	12h 55.7m	+21°39′	8.5	Spiral galaxy in Coma Berenices
65	3623	11h 17.9m	+13°12′	9.4	Spiral galaxy in Leo
66	3627	11h 19.2m	+13°06′	9.0	Spiral galaxy in Leo; companion to M65
67	2682	8h 50.0m	+11°53′	6.1	Open cluster in Cancer
68	4590	12h 38.4m	−26°39′	8.2	Globular cluster in Hydra
69	6637	18h 30.1m	−32°23′	8.0	Globular cluster in Sagittarius
70	6681	18h 42.0m	−32°18′	8.1	Globular cluster in Sagittarius
71	6838	19h 52.8m	+18°44′	7.6	Globular cluster in Sagitta
72	6981	20h 52.3m	−12°38′	9.3	Globular cluster in Aquarius
73	6994	20h 57.8m	−12°43′	9.1	Open cluster in Aquarius
74	628	1h 35.6m	−15°41′	9.3	Spiral galaxy in Pisces
75	6864	20h 04.9m	−21°59′	8.6	Globular cluster in Sagittarius
76	650	1h 41.0m	+51°28′	11.4	Planetary nebula in Perseus
77	1068	2h 41.6m	−0°04′	8.9	Spiral galaxy in Cetus
78	2068	5h 45.7m	0°03′	8.3	Small emission nebula in Orion
79	1904	5h 23.3m	−24°32′	7.5	Globular cluster in Lepus
80	6093	16h 15.8m	−22°56′	7.5	Globular cluster in Scorpio
81	3031	9h 54.2m	+69°09′	7.0	Spiral galaxy in Ursa Major
82	3034	9h 54.4m	+69°47′	8.4	Irregular galaxy in Ursa Major
83	5236	13h 35.4m	−29°31′	7.6	Spiral galaxy in Hydra
84	4374	12h 24.1m	+13°00′	9.4	Elliptical galaxy in Virgo
85	4382	12h 24.3m	+18°18′	9.3	Elliptical galaxy in Coma Berenices
86	4406	12h 25.1m	+13°03′	9.2	Elliptical galaxy in Virgo
87	4486	12h 29.7m	+12°30′	8.7	Elliptical galaxy in Virgo
88	4501	12h 30.9m	+14°32′	9.5	Spiral galaxy in Coma Berenices
89	4552	12h 34.6m	+12°40′	10.3	Elliptical galaxy in Virgo
90	4569	12h 35.8m	+13°46′	9.6	Spiral galaxy in Virgo
91	Omitted				
92	6341	17h 16.5m	+43°10′	6.4	Globular cluster in Hercules
93	2447	7h 43.7m	−23°49′	6.5	Open cluster in Puppis
94	4736	12h 50.0m	+41°14′	8.3	Spiral galaxy in Canes Venatici
95	3351	10h 42.9m	+11°49′	9.8	Barred spiral galaxy in Leo
96	3368	10h 45.7m	+11°56′	9.3	Spiral galaxy in Leo
97	3587	11h 13.7m	+55°07′	11.1	Owl Nebula; planetary nebula in Ursa Major
98	4192	12h 12.7m	+15°01′	10.2	Spiral galaxy in Coma Berenices
99	4254	12h 17.8m	+14°32′	9.9	Spiral galaxy in Coma Berenices
100	4321	12h 21.9m	+15°56′	9.4	Spiral galaxy in Coma Berenices
101	5457	14h 02.5m	+54°27′	7.9	Spiral galaxy in Ursa Major
102	5866(?)	15h 05.9m	+55°50′	10.5	Spiral galaxy (identification as M102 in doubt)
103	581	1h 31.9m	+60°35′	6.9	Open cluster in Cassiopeia
104†	4594	12h 39.0m	−11°31′	8.3	Spiral galaxy in Virgo
105†	3379	10h 46.8m	+12°51′	9.7	Elliptical galaxy in Leo
106†	4258	12h 18.0m	+47°25′	8.4	Spiral galaxy in Canes Venatici
107†	6171	16h 31.4m	−13°01′	9.2	Globular cluster in Ophiuchus
108†	3556	11h 10.5m	+55°47′	10.5	Spiral galaxy in Ursa Major
109†	3992	11h 56.6m	+53°29′	10.0	Spiral galaxy in Ursa Major
110†	205	0h 39.2m	+41°35′	9.4	Elliptical galaxy (companion to M31)

†Later additions made to catalog

COMPARING THE SIZES OF THE PLANETS

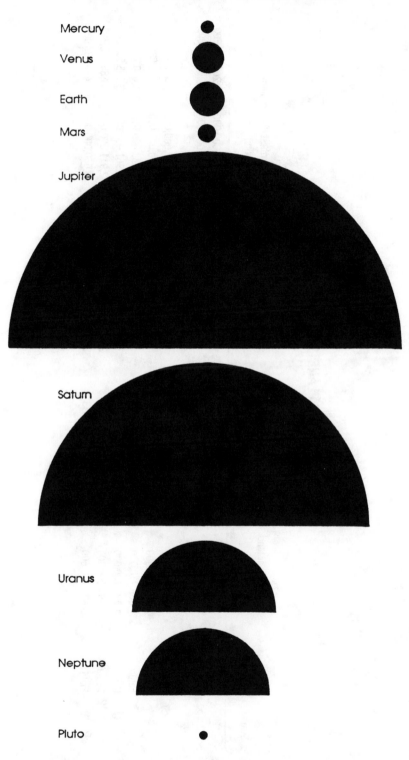

The diameter of the Sun = 9½ times the diameter of Jupiter.

THE PLANETS

Symbol	Planet	Average distance from the Sun (mi)	(km)	AU	Closest distance from the Earth (mi)	(km)	Farthest distance from the Earth (mi)	(km)
☿	Mercury	35,984,000	57,910,000	0.387	57,000,000	91,730,100	129,000,000	207,599,700
♀	Venus	67,236,000	108,200,000	0.7233	26,000,000	41,841,800	160,000,000	257,488,000
⊕	Earth	92,960,116	149,597,870	1.0000				
♂	Mars	141,640,000	227,940,000	1.5237	35,000,000	56,325,500	247,000,000	397,497,100
♃	Jupiter	483,640,000	778,320,000	5.2028	367,000,000	590,613,100	600,000,000	965,580,000
♄	Saturn	886,710,000	1,427,000,000	9.5388	741,000,000	1,192,491,300	1,032,000,000	1,660,797,600
♂, ♅	Uranus	1,783,100,000	2,869,600,000	19.1819	1,605,100,000	2,583,087,400	1,961,000,000	3,155,837,300
♆	Neptune	2,794,100,000	4,496,600,000	30.0578	2,675,100,000	4,305,038,400	2,911,000,000	4,684,672,300
♇, ♀	Pluto	3,674,708,800	5,913,708,900	39.53	2,672,000,000	4,300,049,600	4,660,000,000	7,499,338,000

Planet	Mass (Earth = 1)	Diameter (mi)	Diameter (km)	Average density (g/cm³)	Surface gravity (Earth = 1)	Escape velocity (mi/sec)	Escape velocity (km/sec)	Number of known moons	Period of orbit	Inclination of planet's orbit to the ecliptic	Eccentricity of the planet's shape (circle = 0)	Sidereal rotation period	Tilt of the planet
Mercury	0.554	3,013	4,850	5.4	0.377	2.58	(4.3)	0	88 days	7°	0.206	59 days	28°
Venus	0.815	7,543	12,140	5.2	0.905	6.24	(10.4)	0	225 days	3.39°	0.007	244 days	177°
Earth	1.000	7,926	12,756	5.5	1.000	6.72	(11.2)	1	365.26 days	0°	0.017	23h 56m 04s	23°27'
Mars	0.107	4,219	6,790	3.9	0.379	3.18	(5.3)	2	1.88 years	1.85°	0.093	24h 37m 22.6s	23°59'
Jupiter	317.89	88,736	142,800	1.3	2.54	36.12	(60.2)	16	11.86 years	1.30°	0.048	9h50m to 9h55m	3°05'
Saturn	95.26	74,978	120,660	0.7	1.07	19.38	(32.3)	20	29.45 years	2.48°	0.056	10h14m to 10h38m	26°44'
Uranus	14.6	31,940	51,400	1.7	0.86	13.5	(22.5)	15	84.07 years	0.80°	0.046	12h to 24h	97°55'
Neptune	17.2	30,778	49,530	1.6	1.14	14.34	(23.9)	8	164.81 years	1.76°	0.010	16h 3m	28° 8'
Pluto	0.0026	1,400	2,253	0.8	0.03	?		1	248.5 years	17.12°	0.246	6 days 9h 17m	60°?

GLOSSARY

Aberration of starlight The apparent change in the position of a star due to the Earth's motion.

Absolute magnitude The magnitude a star would have if it were at a distance of 10 parsecs (32.6 light-years) from the observer.

Absorbtion lines Dark lines in the spectrum of light from a star.

Albedo The percentage of light an object (such as a planet) reflects compared to the total amount of light it receives.

Altitude The distance in degrees of the angle between the horizon and an object.

Aphelion The point in the orbit of a planet or a comet where it is farthest from the Sun.

Apogee The point in the orbit of the Moon or a planet where it is farthest from the Earth.

Apparent magnitude The measurement of the brightness of a star or other object in the sky as you see it from the Earth.

Asteroid (planetoid, minor planet) A small body in orbit around the Sun.

Astronomical unit (AU) The average distance between the Earth and the Sun. 92,960,116 miles (149,597,870 km).

Azimuth The angle in degrees measured along the horizon starting from the north point and moving eastward to the vertical circle that passes through the star.

Binary star (double star) Two stars revolving around each other.

Black hole A star that has collapsed under its own gravity with the result that not even light can escape.

Celestial equator The projection of the Earth's equator onto the sky, creating a great circle around the middle of the celestial sphere that is 90° from each of the poles of the celestial sphere.

Celestial sphere The imaginary sphere out in space that surrounds the Earth and serves as a screen on which we see all of the objects in the sky.

Cepheid variable A star that pulsates, changing its brightness in a regular rhythm. Based on the star δ in the constellation Cepheus.

Chromatic aberration (color defect) The blurring resulting from the difference in focal points for light passing through a lens.

Circumpolar stars The constellations that are around one of the poles of the celestial sphere.

Comet A swarm of ice and solid particles that orbits the Sun.

Conjunction The apparent lineup of two or more planets or the Sun and one or more planet.

Constellation The groups of stars that form 1 of 88 patterns that are named for animals, heroes, and gods.

Cosmogony The study of the origin and evolution of the material in the universe.

Cosmology The study of the organization and structure of the universe and its evolution.

Culmination The position of a star when it is on the meridian.

Declination The distance of an object north or south of the celestial equator measured in degrees. It is like latitude in maps of the Earth.

Density The amount of matter contained in a given volume, measured in grams per cubic centimeter.

Doppler effect The apparent change in the wavelength of sound, radio waves, or light due to the motion of the object toward or away from the observer.

Eclipse The blocking of light from the Sun by the Moon (solar) or the Moon by the Earth (lunar).

Ecliptic The apparent path of the Sun on the celestial sphere or the plane of the Earth's orbit projected onto the sky.

Ellipse The shape of all planetary orbits, more of an oval than a circle.

Elongation The apparent angle between the Sun and a planet.

Equinox One of the two points where the ecliptic and the celestial equator cross. When the Sun is at one of these points, the length of day and night are equal.

Galaxy A vast island of stars, dust, and gas forming one system.

Geocentric system The system that describes the Earth as the center of the universe.

Globular cluster A collection of tens of thousands of stars forming a sphere that gathers around a galaxy.

Heliacal rising When a star or planet rises before sunrise.

Heliocentric system The system that describes the Sun as the center of the solar system.

Hertzsprung-Russell (H-R) diagram A chart that shows the life cycle of the stars by graphing them according to their luminosity and temperature.

Inclination (of an orbit) The angle between the plane of the orbit of a planet and another plane, such as the celestial equator or the ecliptic.

Inferior planets Those planets between the Earth and the Sun. They include Mercury and Venus.

Latitude The horizontal lines on a map showing the distance north or south of the equator on the Earth.

Light-year The distance that light travels in one year, about 5.88 trillion miles (9.46 trillion kilometers).

Local group The cluster of about 20 galaxies to which the Milky Way belongs.

Longitude The vertical lines on a map showing the distance east and west around the Earth from a north-south line running through Greenwich, England.

Main sequence The diagonal band on the H-R diagram that contains most of the stars.

Mass The amount of matter contained in an object and its resistance to motion.

Meridian An imaginary line on the celestial sphere running north and south through the observer's zenith and nadir. On Earth maps, a meridian is a vertical line running from pole to pole and crossing the equator at right angles.

Meteor The bright streak of light that occurs when a particle from outside the Earth's atmosphere enters the atmosphere and the friction causes it to burn up.

Meteorite The part of a meteoroid that makes it through the Earth's atmosphere and lands on the ground.

Meteoroid An interplanetary chunk of rock smaller than an asteroid.

Milky Way The speckled band of faint stars that forms the edge of our galaxy.

Nadir The point on the celestial sphere directly below the observer.

Nebula A cloud of gas or dust in space.

Neutron star A dense, highly contracted star composed mainly of neutrons.

Node The point where one orbit crosses another.

Nova A dying star that suddenly brightens and then fades again as it throws off a shell of hot gases.

Nutation The small variations in the movement of the Earth's poles.

Occultation When the Moon or another planet passes in front of a star or another planet, temporarily hiding it.

Opposition When a planet is directly opposite the Sun or another planet as seen from the Earth.

Orbit The path of one body revolving around another.

Parallax (stellar) The apparent shift of a star against the background of more distant stars due to the motion of the Earth around the Sun.

Parsec The distance of an object having a stellar parallax of one second of an arc. 1 parsec = 3.26 light-years.

Perigee The point in the orbit of the Moon or a planet when it is nearest the Earth.

Perihelion The point in the orbit of a planet or celestial object when it is nearest the Sun.

Planet A celestial object that orbits a star and shines by reflecting light. There are nine known planets orbiting around the Sun in the solar system.

Precession The slow wobble of the Earth's axis that sweeps out a circle in 26,000 years. This brings about a change in the position of the celestial poles and the celestial equator.

Precession of the equinoxes The gradual falling back of the equinox points along the zodiac due to the precession of the Earth.

Proper motion The motion of a star across the background of the rest of the stars as seen from the Sun.

Pulsar An object that sends out rapid "pulses" of radio waves and sometimes light at regular intervals. It is possibly a very dense star, like a neutron star, spinning rapidly.

Quasar A "quasi-star" or "quasi-stellar object" that looks like a star but generates incredible amounts of energy. They are the most luminous objects known in the universe and shine from enormous distances.

Radio astronomy The branch of astronomy that studies objects that emit radio waves.

Red giant The stage in the life of a star when it expands to a huge size and cools to a red color.

Refraction The bending of a ray of light when it passes from one substance to another one with a different density.

Relativity The theory that all motion depends on the observer's frame of reference and is therefore relative and not absolute.

Revolution The motion of one object around another. An orbit is the path a planet makes as it revolves around the Sun.

Right ascension (RA) The distance of an object east or west along the celestial equator measured in degrees or hours. It is like longitude in maps of the Earth.

Rotation The motion of an object turning on its own axis. The spin of the Earth is a rotation, which takes 24 hours.

Saros The eclipse cycle with intervals of 18 years, 11 days, between two lunar or two solar eclipses of the same series.

Sidereal time Time that is reckoned according to a planet's position compared to the stars instead of the Sun.

Solar system The system that includes all the objects which revolve around the Sun. The solar system contains the Sun, the planets and their moons, comets, asteroids, meteoroids, etc.

Solstice One of the two points on the ecliptic when the Sun is farthest north or south of the celestial equator.

Spectroscope An instrument that separates light from a star into its color wavelengths (spectrum) so that you can measure and analyze it.

Star A large sphere of intensely hot gas under great pressure that shines by the light of its own energy.

Superior planets Those planets beyond the Earth heading away from the Sun. They include Mars, Jupiter, Saturn, Uranus, Neptune, and Pluto.

Synodic period The time between two of the same alignments of planets (e.g., from conjunction to conjunction, full moon to full moon, etc.).

Terminator The line that separates the dark half of the Moon or a planet from the half that is lit.

Transit The passing of Mercury or Venus across the disk of the Sun as seen from the Earth. A transit is also the passing of a star across the meridian.

Universal Time (UT) The time at the 0° meridian passing through Greenwich, England. Used as a world standard.

Variable star A star whose brightness changes either regularly or irregularly.

White dwarf The stage in the life of a star near death when the star has collapsed into a very dense, very hot mass with a small diameter and burning with a white light.

X-ray stars Stars that send out radiation between the frequencies of ultraviolet radiation and gamma rays. These are the frequencies of X rays that are not visible.

Zenith The point on the celestial sphere directly overhead.

Zodiac The band of 12 constellations centered on the ecliptic 18° wide through which the Sun, Moon, and planets move as seen from the Earth.

INDEX

55; mapping, 253; names for, 247–48; path of, 5; phases, 28, 30, 249–51; in the zodiac, 58
Moore, Sir Patrick, 70
Moulton, Forrest, 147
Müller, Johannes, 150
Muratori, 354

nadir, 96
nanometer, 231
neap tides, 258
nebulae, 317–18, 341–43
Nebular Hypothesis, 146
Neptune, 267, 276, 298–300, 302–3, 330; composition, 299–300; moons, 300
Nereid, 300
neutron stars, 321–22, 339
Newton, Hubert Anderson, 333
Newtonian telescope, 213
Newton, Sir Isaac, 123, 198, 201–2, 211, 213, 225–26, 228, 258, 298
Niepie, Joseph, 216
night, 26, 31
NightStar, 105
nocturnal, 36–38
nodal line, 261
node, 261
nova, 319–20
nuclear fusion, 241, 318
nuclear winter, 153–54
nutation, 193

Oberth, Hermann, 352
objective, 206–9, 214–15
oceanography, 150
Oersted, Hans Christian, 226
Olbers, Heinrich Wilhelm Mattias, 285, 316
Olbers' Paradox, 316
Olympus Mons, 281
Oort Cloud, 331
Oort, Jan, 331
Opik, Ernst, 331
optic nerve (the eye), 203
orbits, 195–97, 252, 295; of comets, 331; of Mercury,

267; of Nereid, 300; of Pluto, 302–3
Oscillating Universe, 146, 148–49
outer core (earth's), 158, 160
outer planets, 147, 276. See also Jupiter; Mars; Neptune; Pluto; Saturn; Uranus
ovoid regions, 298

Pangaea, 162–63
parabola, 197
parallax, 307–8
parsec, 309
Pellegrini, Antonio Snyder, 161
penumbra, 242
Penzias, Arno A., 145
phases: of Mercury, 267; of the Moon, 28, 30, 249–51; of Venus, 272
Phobos, 283, 302
photocathode, 220
photocell, 220
photoelectric effect, 220–21
photographing stars and planets, 218–20
photography, 216–18
photosphere, 241–42, 244
Piazzi, Guiseppi, 201, 285
Picard, Jean, 123
Pickering, Edward C., 316
Pickering, W. H., 300
Pioneer I, 170
Pioneer II, 286, 292
Pioneer III, 170
Pioneer 10, 347
pixels, 221–22
planesphere, 60, 62
Planetesimal Theory, 147
planets, 5, 8, 219. See also individual planets
plate tectonics, 161
Plato, 85, 87
Platonic solids, 85–87, 195, 200
Plutarch, 245
Pluto, 267, 271, 276, 300–305; composition, 303; moon, 303, 305; names for, 301–2; orbit, 302

polestar, 2–3, 11, 58, 95
Pope, Alexander, 198
populations, 149
Potter, Robert, 151–52
precession of the equinoxes, 62, 100, 261
Prime focus telescope, 213
prisms, 215, 225–26
prominences (solar), 246
propellant, 354
propeller, 350
protostar, 318
Ptolemy, Claudius, 90–91, 93, 98, 109–10, 112, 125, 178–80, 194–95, 252
Ptolemy II Euergetes, 43
pulsars, 321, 339–40
pupil (of the eye), 203
Pythagoras, 84, 179, 195, 272
Pythagorean Brotherhood, 84–85

quadrant, 115–16, 123, 194
quasars, 337–38

radar astronomy, 234–35
radiant, 336
radio astronomy, 112, 231–32, 235, 337–38, 340
radio interferometry, 232
radio telescopes, 232–33, 339
radio waves, 168, 232, 234, 252
rain, 173–74
Ramsay, William, 241
Reber, Grote, 232
red giants, 318–19, 324
red-shift, 310, 338
reflecting telescopes, 211–13
refracting telescopes, 209–10, 215
refraction, 203–204
Reginald, King, 46
Regnier, Gemma Frisius, 112
relativity, 311–12, 321
resolving power, 206–8
resources, 151–52
retina (the eye), 203
retrograde motion, 180–82
revolution, 193
rhumb line, 129–30

About the Author

Richard Moeschl is the president of NightStar Products, Inc., a company that produces and distributes astronomy education products, and is the director of Star Resources, an astronomy information service. He has taught science, art, and ancient history, specializing in astronomy at the 6–8 grade level, and is the author of *Teaching Astronomy with NightStar* and *Learning with NightStar*. Richard Moeschl has his own half-hour radio show weekly on local public radio titled "The Milky Way Starlight Theater" and appears daily on local public television on a two-minute show called "Starwatch." He has two sons and lives in Ashland, Oregon.

ZIGGURAT BOOKS
FROM CHICAGO REVIEW PRESS

Ziggurat A temple of the ancient Assyrians and Babylonians, having the form of a terraced pyramid of successively receding stories. Assyrian *ziqquratu*, summit, mountain top, from *zaqaru*, to be high.

—*American Heritage Dictionary of the English Language*

Ziggurat Books are project books for talented young people of middle and high school age, ten or eleven and up. Many are science or technology oriented; others involve literature or the fine and applied arts. All emphasize a hands-on, experimental approach to adult disciplines such as physics, astronomy, the graphic arts, architecture, and creative writing.

Ziggurat Books give students a taste of a wide variety of adult professions. They provide innovative, challenging material for science and art fairs, class and individual school projects. Most important, they enable young people to explore their talents as they experience the effort and the excitement of creative work.

Art of Construction:
Projects and Principles for
Beginning Engineers and Architects
by Mario Salvadori
ISBN 1-55652-080-8
144 pages, paper, $9.95

Faraday's Chemical History
of a Candle:
Twenty-Two Experiments
and Six Classic Lectures
by Michael Faraday
ISBN 1-55652-035-2
136 pages, paper, $9.95

The Art of the Handmade Book:
Designing, Decorating, and
Binding One-of-a-Kind Books
by Flora Fennimore
ISBN 1-55652-146-4
144 pages, paper, $11.95

Real Toads in Imaginary Gardens:
Suggestions and Starting Points for
Young Creative Writers
by Stephen Phillip Policoff
and Jeffrey Skinner
ISBN 1-55652-137-5
192 pages, paper, $11.95

Seeing for Yourself:
Techniques and Projects
for Beginning Photographers
by Roger Gleason
ISBN 1-55652-159-6
200 pages, paper, $14.95

The Spark in the Stone:
Skills and Projects from
the Native American Tradition
by Peter Goodchild
ISBN 1-55652-102-2
132 pages, paper, $11.95

These books are available through your local bookstore or directly from **Independent Publishers Group, 814 North Franklin Street, Chicago, IL 60610 1-800-888-4741**. Visa and MasterCard accepted.